Federico Fellini:

An Annotated International Bibliography

by
Barbara Anne Price
and
Theodore Price

The Scarecrow Press, Inc.
Metuchen, N.J. & London
1978

Z 8291.6
P74

Library of Congress Cataloging in Publication Data

Price, Barbara Anne, 1945-
　Federico Fellini : an annotated international
bibliography.

　Includes index.
　1.　Fellini, Federico--Bibliography.　I.　Price,
Theodore, 1924-　　joint author.
Z8291.6.P74　　[PN1998.A3]　　016.79143'0233'0924
ISBN 0-8108-1104-9　　　　　　　　　　　77-26310

To

the loving memory of Sammy Marcus

CONTENTS

v

FOREWORD

We are a husband and wife team, very much in love, with this project and with each other; and our fondest hope is that Federico and Giulietta, whom we also love, will always remain together and live happily ever after.

The husband of our team has been working for some time now on a 600-page book on Fellini's films, Fellini: The Artist as Conjuror and Clown, which, it would be nice to think, some future bibliographer might annotate as "the longest and most detailed work on Fellini's films in any language, using multi-language primary and secondary sources." In the course of working on this study, the husband found that there were no adequate bibliographic data on Fellini and his films, so the wife began to compile them for him. It then occurred to us that a full Fellini bibliography would be of value to many others, and so we decided to write one. The wife did most of the hard-core detective work, hunting down and tabulating the material, as well as preparing meals for the husband, as Giulietta does for Federico.

We are not library-science trained bibliographers, nor are we language specialists. We ask your indulgence in matters of any missing important items, in sins of style, or in errors of translation. If you notice any--especially any items we've missed--please write our publisher, bringing them to our attention, and we'll correct things the next time around. Although we've picked up a few items since, we've used a cut-off date of February 28, 1977.

In our annotations, our guiding principle has been, besides giving descriptive and informative data, to note "insights" about the films. In this way, we have tried to make even a bibliography interesting to read, in its own right, aside from its information value. We hope, for instance, even if you never get to hunting down the original material, that you might get the same thrill we got on learning how Fellini decided on the finale of $8\frac{1}{2}$. He had shot and was expecting to use the "railway car" ending. Then he just went on to shoot what was to be merely a coming-attractions trailer for the film, where he had all the characters of the film come down the passerella-like spaceship-tower stairs. But suddenly he was so wondrously and magically moved that he decided to use this for what is now the definitive ending of the film (see 220).

In our annotations we have normally avoided expressing our

own judgments, except for an occasional "indispensable" about what we feel are exceptionally important items. Especially in the "rotten" reviews of, say, <u>Dolce vita</u> and $8\frac{1}{2}$, we've let the writers speak for themselves. In this way, the husband is, after a fashion, bringing to fruition an early project of his--to subsidize a memorial statue to those critics who gave scathing notices to the poems of Baudelaire when the poems first appeared (Baudelaire lived and died thinking himself a failure and got his one book of poems printed only because he had a friend, Poulet Malassis, in the publishing business), so that people could remember men like Louis Goudall, whose one claim to fame was that he wrote a malicious and contemptible review of <u>Les Fleurs du Mal</u>.

The husband of our team is a college teacher, who has earlier specialized in George Eliot, of whose cultural tradition (hard to believe but true) Fellini is a direct descendant, and who also has priests scurrying through all her works. The husband teaches film courses, so he has had the opportunity to watch Fellini's films over and over again.

We'd like to thank our publisher for his encouragement, and all his associates, who have been marvelously congenial and very helpful. We've had kind access to the resources of the splendid cinema collection of Rutgers University's Alexander Library--a grand library, where the computerization helps, not hinders.

Our work could not possibly have been done without the help of Montclair State College's Sprague Library Interlibrary Loan staff, Norman Stock and Alkmene Reimer, who performed above and beyond the call of duty. Thanks too to Miklos Sebek for translating the Hungarian articles and to the public relations department of Universal Pictures for providing so quickly the cast and credits of <u>Casanova</u>.

Nor to be forgotten is our acknowledgment of the special efforts of those administrative officers and curriculum committee colleagues of our college who arranged for the cancellation of the husband's scheduled 1977 Winter Session course, <u>Masterpieces of the Horror Film: a Psychoanalytical Approach,</u> without which we would have been unable to complete this book. To each of them: many thanks.

Barbara Anne Price
Theodore Price

Montclair State College
Upper Montclair, New Jersey
April 1, 1977

PART I

PRIMARY SOURCES

A. SCREENPLAYS

(in Italian and in translation)

Luci del varietà

ITALIAN
> We have been unable to locate any Italian edition.

ENGLISH

1 Early Screenplays: Variety Lights, The White Sheik. Trans.
Judith Green. New York: Grossman Publishers, 1971. 198 p.
This is the only version of the Luci del varietà screenplay
in any language that we have been able to locate. Eighteen
photos. Cast and credits.

Lo sceicco bianco

ITALIAN

2 Il primo Fellini: Lo sceicco bianco, I vitelloni, La strada, Il
bidone. Introduzione di Renzo Renzi. Bologna: Cappelli, 1969.
326 p.
Introduced by Renzo Renzi, "Fellini che va, Fellini che
viene," contains valuable excerpts from conversations with Fellini about Fellini's theories of creativity. Fellini: "I am an
unnaturally cruel father of my films once they're finished. I
don't want to see them again. I don't want to talk about them.
Even a new film of mine pleases me only while I'm planning
and making it. Even if it isn't released, it doesn't matter
much to me. A film is like some malady that's been expelled
from my body. They're tumors, growths, diseased limbs."
Renzi: "What if I wrote that the early Fellini isn't the films
contained in this volume, but is all the films you've made so
far as well as the one you're making now?" Fellini: "Very
good. I'd agree." In small type are reproduced those parts
of each screenplay that were either not shot or were cut out.
Over 100 clear, moderately large, black-and-white photos.
Twenty-four photos from Sceicco bianco. Cast and credits.

ENGLISH

Early Screenplays: Variety Lights, The White Sheik. Trans.

Judith Green. New York: Grossman, 1971. 198 p.
   Does not contain scenes that either were not filmed or that
were cut, which are contained in Renzi's Italian edition, Il
primo Fellini.

GERMAN

3 [Le notti di Cabiria, Le tentazioni del Dottor Antonio, Toby
   Dammit, Satyricon, Lo sceicco bianco, I vitelloni, La strada,
   Il bidone, I clowns, Block-notes di un regista.] Zürich:
   Diogenes-Verlag.

SPANISH

4 El Jeque Blanco, I vitelloni, La strada, Il bidone. Trans.
   Esther Benitez. Madrid: Alianza Editorial, 1972. 543 p.

PORTUGUESE

5 O Sheik Branco. Trans. Joel Silveira. Rio de Janeiro: Civilização Brasileira, 1970. 153 p.

                              I vitelloni

ITALIAN

   Il primo Fellini: Lo sceicco bianco, I vitelloni, La strada, Il
   bidone. Introduzione di Renzo Renzi. Bologna: Cappelli, 1969.
   326 p.
      See 2. Twenty-three photos. Cast and credits.

6 Quattro film: I vitelloni, La dolce vita, 8½, Giulietta degli
   spiriti. Preceduti dalla Autobiografia di uno spettatore, di
   Italo Calvino. Torino: G. Einaudi, 1974. 493 p.
      Reviewed: See 539.

ENGLISH

7 Three Screenplays: I vitelloni, Il bidone, The temptations of
   Doctor Antonio. Trans. Judith Green. New York: Orion Press,
   1970. 288 p.
      Does not contain scenes that either were not filmed or that
   were cut, which are contained in Renzi's Italian edition, Il
   primo Fellini. 15 photos. Cast and credits. Reviewed: See
   567 and 568.

FRENCH

8 "I vitelloni," Cinéma, n. 5, December, 1952, 15-31, 99-100.
      The story of the film.

GERMAN

9 [Le notti di Cabiria, Le tentazioni del Dottor Antonio, Toby
Dammit, Satyricon, Lo sceicco bianco, I vitelloni, La strada,
Il bidone, I clowns, Block-notes di un Regista.] Zürich:
Diogenes-Verlag.

SPANISH

10 El Jequé Blanco, I vitelloni, La strada, Il bidone. Madrid:
Alianza Editorial, 1972.

PORTUGUESE

11 Os Boas-Vidas. Trans. Joel Silveira. Rio de Janeiro: Civilização Brasileira, 1971. 179 p.

CZECH

12 5 Scénářů. Trans. Adolf Felix, Jaroslav Pokorny and Zdeněk
Frýbort. Praha: Odeon, 1966. 506 p.
Includes Cabiria, Dolce vita, $8\frac{1}{2}$, La strada and Vitelloni.

Un'agenzia matrimoniale

None located.

La strada

ITALIAN

13 La strada. Bianco e nero, n. 9-10, September-October, 1954.

14 La strada. Roma: Bianco e Nero, 1955. 178 p.

Il primo Fellini: Lo sceicco bianco, I vitelloni, La strada, Il
bidone. Introduzione di Renzo Renzi. Bologna: Cappelli, 1969.
326 p.
See 2. Twenty-four photos. Cast and credits. Contains
scenes not shot or cut.

ENGLISH

15 La strada. ed. Robert Steele. New York: Ballantine Books,
1970.
Listed as having been published, but we have not been able
to confirm this. If not, we do not believe that there is an
English edition of the screenplay.

16 La strada, $8\frac{1}{2}$, Le notti di Cabiria, Toby Dammit, La dolce
vita. New York: Simon and Schuster.

Supposedly in preparation, but we have not been able to confirm.

FRENCH

17 La strada: un film de Federico Fellini. eds. R. Bastide, J.
Caputo, and C. Markera.   Paris: Editions du Seuil, 1955.
116 p.

18 La strada. L'Avant-Scène du Cinema, n. 102, April, 1970.
The screenplay, with the usual superb and loving Avant-
Scène care, noting scenes that were not shot or cut, how vari-
ously released versions differ, and with a panoply of helpful
notes.

GERMAN

19 La strada.   Introduction by M. Schlappnera.   Zürich, 1960.

[Le notti di Cabiria, Le tentazioni del Dottor Antonio, Toby
Dammit, Satyricon, Lo sceicco bianco, I vitelloni, La strada,
Il bidone, I clowns, Block-notes di un Regista.] Zürich:
Diogenes-Verlag.
See 3.

SPANISH

El Jeque Blanco, I vitelloni, La strada, Il bidone.   Madrid:
Alianza Editorial, 1972.
See 4.

PORTUGUESE

20 A Estrada.   Trans. Joel Silveira.   Rio de Janeiro: Civilização
Brasileira, 1970.   134 p.

CZECH

5 Scénařů.   Trans. Adolf Felix, Jaroslav Pokorny and Zdeněk
Frýbort.   Praha: Odeon, 1966.   506 p.
Includes Cabiria, Dolce vita, 8½, La strada, I vitelloni.
See 12.

RUSSIAN

21 Scenarii ital'yanskogo kina. [Scenarios of the Italian cinema.]
Moscow: Iskusstvo, 1958.   575 p.
Contains La strada.   We do not know whether this is the
complete screenplay.

Il bidone

ITALIAN

Il primo Fellini: Lo sceicco bianco, I vitelloni, La strada, Il
bidone. Introduzione di Renzo Renzi. Bologna: Cappelli, 1969.
326 p.
    See 2. Nineteen photos. Cast and credits.

ENGLISH

Three screenplays: I vitelloni, Il bidone, The temptations of
Doctor Antonio. Trans. Judith Green. New York: Orion, 1970.
288 p.
    Does not contain scenes that either were not filmed or that
were cut, which are contained in Renzi's Italian edition, Il
primo Fellini. See 7. Reviewed: See 567 and 568.

FRENCH

22 Il bidone. Trans. Dominique Delouche. Paris: Flammarion,
    1956. 288 p.

GERMAN

[Le notti di Cabiria, Le tentazioni del Dottor Antonio, Toby
Dammit, Satyricon, Lo sceicco bianco, I vitelloni, La strada,
Il bidone, I clowns, Block-notes di un Regista.] Zürich:
Diogenes-Verlag.
    See 3.

SPANISH

El Jeque Blanco, I vitelloni, La strada, Il bidone. Madrid:
Alianza Editorial, 1972.
    See 4.

PORTUGUESE

23 Il bidone. Rio de Janeiro: Editôra Civilização Brasileira.

Le notti di Cabiria

ITALIAN

24 Le notti di Cabiria. ed. Lino del Fra. Bologna: Cappelli,
    1957, 239 p.

25 Le notti di Cabiria. ed. Lino del Fra. Bologna: Cappelli,
    1965, 239 p.
    Contains scenes not shown or cut. By Del Fra: "Dopo
La strada," "Masce Cabiria," "L'inchiesta," "Dal trattamento

alla sceneggiature," "La Regia," "La musica," "Copia campi-
tone," "Testimonianze," "Undici produttori"; Giulietta Masina,
"Io e Cabiria"; Tullio Pinelli, "Realtà favolosa"; Pier Paolo
Pasolini, "Nota su Le notti"; Del Fra, "Utile umiltà." One
hundred and eleven small but reasonably clear photos. Cast
and credits.

ENGLISH

La strada, 8½, Le notti di Cabiria, Toby Dammit, La dolce
vita. New York: Simon and Schuster.
    Supposedly in preparation, but we have not been able to
confirm. See 16.

GERMAN

26 Texte moderner Filme. ed. Lino del Fra. Frankfurt am Main:
    Suhrkamp Verlag (seria "Spectaculum"), 1961. 447 p.

    [Le notti di Cabiria, Le tentazioni del Dottor Antonio, Toby
    Dammit, Satyricon, Lo sceicco bianco, I vitelloni, La strada,
    Il bidone, I clowns, Block-Notes di un Regista.] Zürich:
    Diogenes-Verlag.
    See 3.

PORTUGUESE

27 Le notti di Cabiria. Rio de Janeiro: Editôra Civilização
    Brasileiro.

                              La dolce vita

ITALIAN

28 La dolce vita. ed. Tullio Kezich. Bologna: Cappelli, 1959.
    279 p.
        The complete screenplay, including the "Dolores" and other
    episodes that do not appear in the final film; but there are no
    indications as to what actually appears only in the final film.
    There is a 127-page introduction, "Bloc-notes," on every as-
    pect of the film. Contains 129 photos and a very full cast and
    credits.

29 La·dolce vita. ed. Tullio Kezich. Rocca San Casciano: Cap-
    pelli, 1961. 272 p.

30   Reviewed: "Italian Hours," Times Literary Supplement,
    March 3, 1961, 140.
            Compares the scripts of L'Avventura and Dolce vita.
    Antonioni's script has few changes between it and the fin-
    ished film; Fellini's, many. "The difference is significant,
    and basic: Signor Antonioni is the intellectual, the theorist,

and Signor Fellini the instinctive, the intuitive creator, who works best when most free to invent and improvise." Says that after L'Avventura, Dolce vita cannot but seem a minor work. But Fellini is a real artist. "He has his own world and with his two regular collaborators, Tullio Pinelli and Ennio Flaiano (who seem to represent respectively the devout, mystical side and the skeptical, ironic side of his nature) he is the master of it."

Quattro film: I vitelloni, La dolce vita, $8\frac{1}{2}$, Giulietta degli spiriti. Preceduti dalla Autobiografia di uno spettatore, di Italo Calvino. Torino: G. Einaudi, 1974. 493 p.
See 6. Reviewed: See 539.

ENGLISH

31 La dolce vita. Trans. Oscar DeLiso and Bernard Shir-Cliff. New York: Ballantine Books, 1961. 274 p.
The screenplay as derived from the final film. This is not a translation of the Kezich Italian edition. Has many small photos and a reprinted review of the film by Hollis Alpert (see 747).

32 Films and Filming, 7 (January, 1961), 14, 44.
Script extract.

La strada, $8\frac{1}{2}$, Le notti di Cabiria, Toby Dammit, La dolce vita. New York: Simon and Schuster.
Supposedly in preparation, but we have not been able to confirm. See 16.

GERMAN

33 Das süsse Leben. Zürich: Diogenes-Verlag, 1974. 206 p.

SPANISH

34 La dolce vita. Trans. Concepción Díaz-Plaja. Introduction by A. García Seguí. Barcelona: Aymá, 1963. 171 p.

PORTUGUESE

35 A Doce Vida. Trans. Nemésio Sales. Rio de Janeiro: Civilização Brasileira, 1970. 382 p.

CZECH

5 Scénářů. Trans. Adolf Felix, Jaroslav Pokorny and Zdeněk Frýbort. Praha: Odeon, 1966. 506 p.
Includes Cabiria, Dolce vita, $8\frac{1}{2}$, La strada, and Vitelloni. See 12.

RUSSIAN

Scenarii ital'yanskogo kina.   Moscow: Iskusstvo, 1967.
    See 21.

HUNGARIAN

36 Az Edes Elet.   Budapest: Gondolat, 1970.

Le tentazioni del dottor Antonio

ITALIAN

37 Boccaccio '70. ed. Carlo Di Carlo and Gaio Fratini.   Bologna:
    Cappelli, 1962.   226 p.   Reprinted in Otto e mezzo.   ed. Camil-
    la Cederna. Bologna: Cappelli, 1965.   190 p.   (Includes the
    introductory material.)   See 40.
        There is an introduction, "Solo uno scherzo." Fellini has
    called Dr. Antonio "just a joke." But this isn't so.   It goes
    back to the blistering criticism, especially by La civiltà catto-
    lica, against the alleged immorality of Dolce vita.   Fellini really
    took this to heart and was only buoyed up by other priests and
    Jesuits who came to the film's defense.   Dr. Antonio is his re-
    action to the attacks on Dolce vita.   He gives Dr. Antonio the
    name of a minister of the extreme right.   The story is supposed
    to have been written in two weeks.   Fellini calls Dr. Antonio
    "this pinwheel-firecracker," who has "the aspect of a clown."
    The edition also contains an outline of the "story" of the film.

ENGLISH

    Three Screenplays: I vitelloni, Il bidone, The temptations of
    Doctor Antonio.   Trans. Judith Green.   New York: Orion, 1970.
    288 p.
        Contains all of the screenplay contained in the Italian edi-
    tion, but not the introduction or the "story" given there.
    See 7.   Reviewed: See 567 and 568.

GERMAN

    [Le notti di Cabiria, Le tentazioni del dottor Antonio, Toby Dam-
    mit, Satyricon, Lo sceicco bianco, I vitelloni, La strada, Il bi-
    done, I clowns, Block-notes di un regista.] Zürich: Diogenes-
    Verlag.
    See 3.

PORTUGUESE

38 [Toby Dammit, Le tentazioni del dottor Antonio.] Rio de Janei-
    ro: Editôra Civilização Brasileira.

Otto e mezzo

ITALIAN

39 Otto e mezzo. ed. Camilla Cederna. Bologna: Cappelli, 1963.
    155 p.
        The shooting script, including many scenes that were not
    shot or cut, but there is no indication in the text to identify them.
    There is a long introduction by Cederna (85 pages), "La bella
    confusione," on the making of the film. Fellini's comment on
    the film: "It is, in short, a beautiful confusion, wherein I feel
    myself alive. " There are one hundred and fifteen very clear
    photos and a brief, incomplete cast and credits.

40 Otto e mezzo. ed. Camilla Cederna. Bologna: Cappelli, 1965.
    190 p.
        Same as 39, but this edition includes Le tentazioni del dottor
    Antonio. See 37.

    Quattro film: I vitelloni, La dolce vita, $8\frac{1}{2}$, Giulietta degli spi-
    riti. Preceduti dalla Autobiografia di uno spettatore, di Italo
    Calvino. Torino:. G. Einaudi, 1974. 493 p.
        See 6. Reviewed: See 539.

ENGLISH

41 $8\frac{1}{2}$. ed. Robert Steele. New York: Ballantine Books, 1970.
        This was supposed to have been published, but we do not
    believe it ever was.

    La strada, $8\frac{1}{2}$, Le notti di Cabiria, Toby Dammit, La dolce vi-
    ta. New York: Simon and Schuster.
        Supposedly in preparation, but we have not been able to con-
    firm. See 16.

FRENCH

42 Huit et demi. Histoire d'un film racontée par Camilla Cederna.
    Trans. H. de Mariassy and C. de Lignac. Paris: R. Julliard,
    1963. 218 p.

43 Huit et demi. L'Avant-Scène, n. 63, 1966.
        We have not been able to examine this: but, judging from
    the other Avant-Scène editions, this can be assumed (1) to be
    the complete screenplay as derived from the actual film, (2) to
    include scenes not shot or cut, with full identification, and (3)
    to be superbly edited in general. Includes excerpts from inter-
    views with Fellini and samples of the critical response to the
    film, as well as stills and prints.

GERMAN

44 Acht und halb. Trans. Annemarie Czaschke. Afterword by

Hans Stempel and Martin Ripkens. Hamburg: Schröder, 1963.
117 p.
   Translated from the Cederna Italian edition, 39.   For the
Afterword, see 1058.

45 8½. Trans. Eva Rechel-Mertens, Toni Kienlechner, Francois
Bondy, and others. Zürich: Diogenes-Verlag, 1974. 176 p.

SPANISH

46 Ocho y medio. Trans. Manuel Vázquez. Barcelona: S. Bar-
ral, 1964. 208 p.

PORTUGUESE

47 8½. Rio de Janeiro: Editôra Civilização Brasileira.

CZECH

48 8½. Světovà Literatûra (Praha), n. 6 (November-December,
1963).

   5 Scénářů. Trans. Adolf Felix, Jaroslav Pokorny and Zdeněk
Frýbort. Praha: Odeon, 1966. 506 p.
   See 12.

                    Giulietta degli spiriti

ITALIAN

49 Giulietta degli spiriti.   ed. Tullio Kezich. Bologna: Cappelli,
1965. 177 p.
   The shooting script only. There is no Italian edition of the
final film, which differs most markedly from the shooting script,
which is remarkably illuminating for an understanding of the film.
(For English and German screenplays derived from the actual
film see 52 and 58.) This edition contains Kezich's 57-page
"L'intervista lunga" (see 253), which also contains "Vent'anni
dopo." There are 97 stills, almost all black-and-white, and
cast and credits. Kezich's introductory interview has an eight-
page section, "Il mondo magio," that is not in the English editions. Asked about the influence of Jung on his work, especially
after 8½, Fellini answers: "I admire and envy Jung's unshakable
honesty, in which he has never wavered. He's been a scientist
and seer who has managed to penetrate the two areas of science
and magic, each through the other. And yet he is neither loved
nor appreciated as he ought to be."

   Quattro film: I vitelloni, La dolce vita, 8½, Giulietta degli spi-
riti. Preceduti dalla Autobiografia di uno spettatore, di Italo
Calvino. Torino: G. Einaudi, 1974. 493 p.
   See 6. Reviewed: See 539.

ENGLISH

50 Juliet of the Spirits.   ed. Tullio Kezich.   Trans. Howard Green-
    field. New York: Orion Press, 1965.   181 p.
         Translation of the Kezich Italian edition (49).   Does not con-
    tain the transcription of the actual film contained in the English
    Ballantine edition (52). Has fifteen excellent black-and-white
    stills.

51   Reviewed: Choice, 3 (January, 1967) 1031.

52 Juliet of the Spirits.   ed. Tullio Kezich.   Trans. Howard Green-
    field.   Transcription of final screenplay by John Cohen.   Trans.
    Cecilia Perrault.   New York: Ballantine Books, 1966.   318 p.
         Besides transcription of the final screenplay, contains the
    original screenplay on which the film was based.   Original
    screenplay contains much material that does not appear in the
    final version and that is indispensable for a complete under-
    standing of the film.   This screenplay, says Fellini, tries to
    convey "the feeling of the film" and was valuable to him as a
    "series of provisional notes from which to begin the preparation
    and organization of the film itself."   Kezich's "Long Interview"
    of Fellini (see 253).   Also an introduction by Kezich, "Twenty
    Years After": Everytime Fellini moves on the set, "cameras
    snap, television cameras roll, tape recorders take down his
    every word.   This is the tribute he pays to success."   The
    "twenty years" are the two decades that have passed since Open
    City. Contains fifty-two poorly printed stills.

53   Reviewed: Book Review Digest, April, 1967.

54   Choice, 10 (March, 1973) 38.

55   Library Journal, 90 (December, 1965), 5412.

56   Publishers Weekly, 189 (January 10, 1966)   95.

57   Young, Vernon.   Hudson Review, 19 (Summer,
                    1966), 296.   Reprinted in On Film, p. 284-292.
                    (see 690).
                         "The screenplay of that tawdry film takes up
                         two-thirds of the book.   Publication was jus-
                         tified by the first third, 'The Long Inter-
                         view.'"

GERMAN

58 Julia und die Geister.   Hamburg: M. von Schröder, 1966.   193
    p.
         Transcription of the German version of the film, as recorded
    by Max D. Willutzki, in a loving presentation, carefully descri-
    bing what is taking place on the screen and not just the dialogue.

59 Julia und die Geister.   Trans.   Francois Bondy, Margaret Car-
    rous, Toni Kienlechner, Eva Rechel-Mertens, and others.   Zür-
    ich: Diogenes-Verlag, 1974.   186 p.
    We believe that this is a translation of the Kezich Italian ed-
    ition.   With sixty-six photos.

PORTUGUESE

60 Giulietta degli spiriti.   Rio de Janeiro: Editôra Civilização Bra-
    sileira.

Toby Dammit

ITALIAN

61 Tre passi nel delirio.   ed. Liliana Betti, Ornella Volta, Bernar-
    dino Zapponi.   Bologna: Cappelli, 1968.   227 p.
    Besides the screenplays of all three films there is an intro-
    ductory essay by Ornella Volta, "Come e nato Tre passi nel de-
    lirio"; one by Liliana Betti, "Alla ricerca di Toby Dammit"; and
    an Italian translation of the Edgar Allan Poe story, "Never Bet
    the Devil Your Head," on which Fellini's film is based: "Non
    scommettete la testa col diavolo." There are twenty-nine clear
    black and white photos.   One of these is a drawing by Fellini of
    Poe with Fellini's note, "Important.   Make Terence up like Poe
    (but without the mustache)." Another shows a newspaper clipping
    that Fellini had of an auto flying off into the air across a wrecked
    bridge.

ENGLISH

    La strada, $8\frac{1}{2}$, Le notti di Cabiria, Toby Dammit, La dolce vi-
    ta.   New York: Simon and Schuster.
    Supposedly in preparation, but we have not been able to con-
    firm.   See 16.

GERMAN

    [Le notti di Cabiria, Le tentazioni del dottor Antonio, Toby Dam-
    mit, Satyricon, Lo sceicco bianco, I vitelloni, La strada, Il bi-
    done, I clowns, Block-notes di un Regista.] Zürich: Diogenes-
    Verlag.
    See 3.

PORTUGUESE

    Toby Dammit, Le tentazioni del dottor Antonio.   Rio de Janeiro:
    Editôra Civilização.
    See 38.

Director's Notebook

ITALIAN

62 Fellini TV. Block-notes di un regista, I clowns. ed. Renzo
    Renzi. Bologna: Cappelli, 1972. 215 p.
        Contains the screenplays of Director's Notebook (Block-notes
    di un regista) and Clowns. There is an introduction by the edi-
    tor, "Dal nostro inviato in Memoryland" (see 73); a letter by
    Fellini to the producer explaining the film, "Le rovine di Mas-
    torna"; and "Come non detto" by Fellini about his experiences
    in making films for TV. There are twenty-five photos, mostly
    black-and-white, and a stunning color still of Fellini, in black
    hat and coat, carrying a bag and a cello case.

GERMAN

    [Le notti di Cabiria, Le tentazioni del dottor Antonio, Toby Dam-
    mit, Satyricon, Lo sceicco bianco, I vitelloni, La strada, Il bi-
    done, I clowns, Block-notes di un Regista.] Zürich: Diogenes-
    Verlag.
    See 9.

Satyricon

ITALIAN

63 Fellini Satyricon. ed. Dario Zanelli. Bologna: Cappelli, 1969.
    303 p.
        Contains a long foreword by the editor, "Dal planeta Roma,"
    that includes various valuable items of information about the film
    as well as portions of interviews with Fellini; Bernadino Zapponi,
    "Lo strano viaggio"; Betsy Langman, "Il mio amore con Fellini";
    a Preface by Fellini and the "Treatment," i. e. , a detailed out-
    line of the story; the screenplay, i. e. , the "shooting script,"
    with notations of modifications during the shooting, the editing,
    and the sound recording; Luca Canali, "Friderico Profante";
    transcription of the Latin dialogue; the cast and credits; and 104
    photos, in good reproductions, some in color.

ENGLISH

64 Fellini's Satyricon. ed. Dario Zanelli. Trans. Eugene Walter
    and John Matthews. New York: Ballantine Books, 1970. 280 p.
        Contains only about half of Zanelli's "From the Planet Rome"
    (the Introduction to the Italian edition) and lacks the Langman and
    Canali essays and the Latin dialogues. Has the photos and the
    cast and credits. Fellini's preface, the "treatment," and the
    screenplay, including variants, are complete. (For Langman see
    1244).

65   Reviewed: Best Sellers, 30 (October 1, 1970), 265.

66   Bookworld, 4 (March 8, 1970), 8.

67   Library Journal, 95 (July, 1970), 2510.
                  Brief, descriptive listing of the Ballantine
                  1970 English edition of the screenplay. Re-
                  commends it for libraries with comprehensive
                  performing arts collections.

68   Publishers Weekly, 196 (December 29, 1969), 70.
                  "Ballantine has shown us the Italian version
                  of the film book, of which they are doing the
                  English translation, and the photos are out
                  of sight."

GERMAN

[Le notti di Cabiria, Le tentazioni del dottor Antonio, Toby Dammit, Satyricon, Lo sceicco bianco, I vitelloni, La strada, Il bidone, I clowns, Block-notes di un Regista.] Zürich: Diogenes-
Verlag.
See 9.

PORTUGUESE

69 Satyricon.   Rio de Janeiro: Editôra Civilização Brasileira.

HUNGARIAN

70 Szatirikon. Budapest: Gondolat, 1970.

                              I clowns

ITALIAN

71 I clowns. ed. Renzo Renzi. Bologna: Cappelli, 1970. 406 p.
        The screenplay and a wealth of ancillary material. Indispen-
    sable. See 432.

72   Reviewed: Ciment, Michel. Positif, n. 131, October, 1971,
            78-79.

73 Fellini TV: Block-notes di un regista, I clowns. ed. Renzo
    Renzi. Bologna: Cappelli, 1972. 213 p.
        Contains the screenplays of Clowns and Director's Notebook.
    The former is a reprint from I clowns (71). There is an intro-
    duction by the editor, "Dal nostro inviato in Memoryland," with
    extensive quotes from Fellini, books on Rome, and on art, as
    well as material on the TV aspect of the two films. There are
    also notes on Keaton in connection with the films. There is the

long essay by Fellini, "Un viaggio nell'ombra," which appeared
originally in I clowns and which is translated in Fellini on Fellini (see 112) under the title, "Why Clowns?" There is also the
short essay by Fellini, "Come non detto," on Fellini's experiences in making the two films for TV. There are thirty photos
from Clowns, almost all in black-and-white.

GERMAN

[Le notti di Cabiria, Le tentazioni del dottor Antonio, Toby Dammit, Satyricon, Lo sceicco bianco, I vitelloni, La strada, Il bidone, I clowns, Block-notes di un regista.] Zürich: Diogenes-
Verlag.
  See 9.

Roma

ITALIAN

74 Roma. ed. Bernardino Zapponi. Bologna: Cappelli, 1972.
    374 p.
       The official screenplay, edited by Fellini's co-scenarist on
    the film. Contains (1) the pre-shooting script and (2) the script
    derived from the film as shot and edited. Four episodes that
    Fellini and Zapponi wrote are not given in their entirety in (1).
    Several scenes were eventually cut from (2), but these are not
    noted. (The Avant-Scène French edition notes them. See 75).
    Contains a long (pp. 9-73) introductory essay by Zapponi, "Roma
    & Fellini"; an essay by Luca Canali, "Una Trilogia Su Roma";
    and one by Gerald Morin, "L'Autopsia di un Eterno Spettacolo."
    Thirty-one photos, seven in color, a caricature of Zapponi by
    Fellini, and reproductions of two drawings from Marc' Aurelio
    that were used to reconstruct the boardinghouse in the film.

FRENCH

75 Fellini Roma. L'Avant-Scène, n. 129, October, 1972, 3-72.
       A work of scholarship and love, to which all students of
    Fellini are indebted. A careful transcription of the scenario of
    the film as shown in Italy and France, noting what scenes may
    have been cut though the versions differ. Twenty-two black-and-
    white photos with informative captions. Cast and credits. A
    "bio-filmography" of Fellini. Selections from eleven reviews of
    the film. Includes a clear reproduction of the official advertise-
    ment for Roma, featuring the three-breasted young woman (pat-
    terned after Romulus and Remus's suckling wolf), with the head-
    line, "Rome is a splendid place to await the end of the world."
    Contains an ample extract from two conversations Fellini had
    with his co-scenario writer, Zapponi: Fellini gives some of his
    feelings about what Rome means to him. Among other things,
    Rome is "a mother with too many chickens, so she can't concern

herself with any one in particular. She doesn't ask anything of
you, she doesn't expect anything of you. She receives you when
you come, she lets you go when you depart, like the lawcourt
in Kafka. In this there's wisdom--very ancient, almost African,
prehistoric. " Rome is a "horizontal" city, part water, part
earth, spread out, an ideal "launching pad" for "fantastic flights".
Intellectuals, artists, whoever keep rubbing up against the two
different dimensions of realism and fantasy, find in Rome just
the right kind of liberating drive for the mental flights plus the
comfort of having "an umbilical cord that binds them firmly to
the concrete. "

76 Roma. Trans. Marie-Hélène Ciosil. Paris: Solar, 1972.
    220 p.
    Translated from the Italian.

GERMAN

77 Roma. Trans. Toni Kienlechner. Zürich: Diogenes-Verlag,
    1972. 224 p.
    Translated from the Italian, with fifty photos. See 74.

SPANISH

78 Roma. Barcelona: Ayma.
    In preparation 1976.

CZECH

79 Rím. Trans. E. Hepnerova. Film a Doba, 19 (January, 1973),
    20-25.
    Five-page extract only.

BULGARIAN

80 Rim. Kinoizkustvo, 28 (June and July, 1973).

                              Amarcord

ITALIAN

81 Il Film Amarcord. ed. Gianfranco Angelucci and Liliana Betti.
    Bologna: Cappelli, 1974. 330 p.
    The screenplay, derived from the final film, splendidly edi-
    ted by Betti. There is an introductory, documented overview of
    Fellini's films through Amarcord, "Fellini $15\frac{1}{2}$ e la poetica dell'
    onirico," by Gianfranco Angelucci; Fellini's long, highly illumi-
    nating, autobiographical essay, "Il mio paese," (the latter is re-
    printed from La Mia Rimini (see 115 and 123); a conversation
    between Fellini and Enzo Siciliano, "In teatro persino il mare,"
    on Fellini's film aesthetic (see 293); an interview with Fellini by

Valerio Riva, "Il fascismo dentro di noi," (see 292); and a "letter" to Renzo Renzi on the film, "Un dramma anche qui," by the editor, Liliana Betti. There are seventy-seven photos, four in color, and a definitive listing of cast and credits.

FRENCH

82 Amarcord: découpage du film. Trans. Michèle Natacha Nahon. Introduction. G. Lo Duca. Paris: Seghers, 1974. 204 p.
Translated from the Italian.

GERMAN

83 Amarcord. Trans. Margaret Carroux, Eva Rechel-Mertens, Inez De Florio-Hansen and others. Zürich: Diogenes-Verlag, 1974. 318 p.
Translated from the Italian, with sixty-two photos.

CZECH

84 Amarcord. Film a Doba, 20 (March, 1974), 144-151.
A seven-page extract.

Casanova

GERMAN

85 Casanova. Trans. Inez De Florio-Hansen. Zürich: Diogenes-Verlag.
In preparation.

B. OTHER PUBLISHED SCREENPLAYS
ON WHICH FELLINI COLLABORATED

Screenplays of Unrealized Films

86 Moraldo in città. Cinema (Rome) (new series), n. 139 (Aug. 10, 1954); n. 142 (Oct, 1954); n. 144 (Nov. 10, 1954); n. 145 (Nov. 25, 1954); n. 146-147 (Dec. 10-25, 1954).
The story only, of Moraldo, the vitellone of Vitelloni, who leaves at the end of the film for the big city.

87 Il viaggio di G. Mastorna.
Neither story nor screenplay has ever been published. Fellini is said to have worked on this project in collaboration with the novelist Dino Buzzatti. Shooting was supposed to have started in December, 1966, envisioning four months of shooting in Rome, Milan, Naples, Amsterdam, New York, and Calcutta. But all this kept being put off and then abandoned when Fellini became gravely ill. Fellini has described the project: "The story is about a town that helps G. Mastorna, a capricious cellist, recover a certain mysterious object that he has lost." For Fellini's cinematic "notes" on the film, see Director's Notebook in Fellini TV, 62.

Screenplays on which Fellini Collaborated
See H, Filmography, for the extent of Fellini's contribution to these screenplays.

ITALIAN

88 Roma, città aperta, in Roberto Rossellini, La trilogia della guerra, edited and with an introduction by Stefano Roncoroni. Bologna: Cappelli, 1972. 316 p.
Derived, by Roncoroni, directly from various copies of the film. The shooting scripts no longer exist. In his introduction Roncoroni describes his efforts in collating various copies of the film, parts of which are no longer clear, in arriving at a text. There are 34 photos from the film, not stills.

ENGLISH

89 Open City, in Rossellini: The War Trilogy. Trans. Judith

Green. New York: Grossman, 1973. 467 p.
Some of Roncoroni's introduction has been omitted.

FRENCH

90 Rome ville ouverte. L'Avant-Scène du Cinéma 71 (June, 1967).

SPANISH

91 [The War Trilogy] In preparation (1976). Madrid: Alianza Editorial.

ITALIAN

92 Paisà (Quinto Episodio), in La trilogia della guerra (see 88), 201-218.
This is the monastery episode. There are six photos from the film. There is also a photo of a skinny Fellini, with a "tattoo" on his chest. (It doesn't look real.) The "tattoo" reads, "The Daredevil" ("Il temerario").

ENGLISH

93 Paisa (Fifth Episode), in Rossellini: The War Trilogy (see 89), 287-316.

ITALIAN

Il miracolo.
We have found no Italian edition.

FRENCH

94 Le miracle (excerpt only, of the story). La Revue du Cinéma, June 14, 1948.

ITALIAN

95 Francesco, giullare di Dio. Inquadrature, Sept. , 1959.

C. OTHER FICTIONAL CREATIONS BY FELLINI

Amarcord

ITALIAN

96 Fellini, Federico, and Tonino Guerra. Amarcord. Milano: Riz-
    zoli, 1973. 156 p.
      The story of Amarcord in novel form, by Fellini and his co-
    writer and scenarist. Contains material not in the film. The
    "Titta" of the film is here named Bobo. Exceptionally illumin-
    ating for an understanding of the film and a fine story in its own
    right. The epigraph is in the form of a poem (in Romagnole
    dialect and in Italian), "Io mi ricordo": "I know, I know, I
    know, that a man of fifty always has clean hands, and I wash
    mine two or three times a day. But sometimes I see that my
    hands are dirty. Then I remember when I was a boy. "

ENGLISH

97 Fellini, Federico, and Tonino Guerra. Amarcord: Portrait of
    a Town. Trans. Nina Rootes. New York: Berkley Windhover,
    1975. 142 p.
      Translated from the Italian.

98   Reviewed: Ackroyd, Peter. "Against the Grain," Specta-
        tor, 232 (June 22, 1974), 771-772.
            Had expected to dislike the book (novelizations
        of films have a bad record) but instead, liked it very much.
        The book is "a short but powerful exposition of time past,"
        proving once again that "the surfaces of life are far more
        profound than its supposed interiors. " Fellini and Guerra
        open "a space for a number of minor lives which would
        otherwise die of asphyxiation in more rotund prose. " Amar-
        cord "breathes fresh air. " Ackroyd is literary editor of the
        Spectator.

99   Nowell-Smith, Geoffrey. "Showman and Shaman,"
        Times Literary Supplement, October 31, 1975, 1311.
            Says that Amarcord: Portrait of a Town "hardly
        deserves the honorific title of novel. " It is "a mish-mash"
        and "a literary experiment" that gets "lost in the transla-
        tion" from a script to novel.

100   _Observer_, July 14, 1974, 33.

FRENCH

101   Fellini, Federico, and Tonino Guerra.   _Amarcord._   Trans.
Lucile Laks. Paris: Gallimard, 1974.   173 p.
Translated from the Italian.   See 96.

SPANISH

102   Fellini, Federico, and Tonino Guerra.   _Amarcord._   Barcelona:
Editorial Noguer, 1974.

La dolce vita

FRENCH

103   Lo Duca, Giuseppe.   _La douceur de vivre._   Paris: Julliard,
1960.   227 p.
     Lo Duca's interesting, illuminating novelized version of
Dolce vita.   Fellini personally told Lo Duca the story of the
film, from which Lo Duca wrote a one-page summary that in-
duced the film's French producer to participate in the production.   This novelization contains an episode, "La Fête sur
l'eau," shot but edited out of the final version of the film.
(It was to be placed between the sequences of Steiner playing
the organ and the false miracle.)   Lo Duca has an Introduction
where he calls _Dolce vita_ "the long ballad of a moulding civilization, a world condemned--by God or men, what difference
does it make?--a dance of spectres."   The opening scene,
Christ on the way to Rome carried by a helicopter, seems to
him to be the obvious key to the film.   "The death of faith, as
Nietzsche defined the death of God, shouts its terrible news
continuously through the film's seven episodes."   The monster
fish at the end is "a messenger with a final warning."

GERMAN

104   Fellini, Federico, and Giuseppe Lo Duca.   _Das süsse Leben._
Hamburg, 1961.   136 p.

105   Fellini, Federico, and Giuseppe Lo Duca.   _Das süsse Leben._
Trans. Joseph Marie.   1962.
German translation of 103.

SPANISH

106   Lo Duca, Giuseppe.   _La dulce vida._   Trans. M. Orta Manzanol.
Barcelona: Cedro, 1963.   254 p.
Spanish translation of 103.

TURKISH

107   Fellini, Federico, and Giuseppe Lo Duca.   Tatli Hayat.   Istan-
      bul, 1966.   152 p.
      Turkish translation of 103.

                    La dolce vita (short story version)

108   Fougeres, Roland.   "La Douceur de Vivre. "
         Fougeres retells the film in the form of a short story.   He
      includes the "Dolores" episode that does not appear in the film.
      In an autumn afternoon by the sea, Marcello looks at Paola and
      Dolores, "the two goals of life for a woman.   But Paola was
      the unattainable dream. " We have been unable to locate in
      which French magazine the story appeared.

                  La dolce vita (captioned-photo version)

109   Fellini, Federico, and Giuseppe Lo Duca.   La dolce vita.   Par-
      is: Pauvert, 1960.   170 p.
         Remarkably interesting.   One hundred and ninety stills or
      prints from the film with captions by Lo Duca that, along with
      the photos, capture the mood of the film.   Lo Duca sometimes
      "editorializes" by inserting epigraphs that prove illuminating:
      when we see Paola at the end, he quotes Peguy, "La petite
      fille espérance. " His epigraph for the whole story is Matthew
      24:30, "The Son of Man will come on the clouds of heaven... ,"
      which he places near the opening helicopter photo.   He has an
      introduction, "Il dolce Fellini. " Dolce vita, says Lo Duca, is
      "a testament and confession of faith. " It "seeks to 'dedrama-
      tise' (and not just to 'demystify') certain aspects of our world;
      it gets us used to looking the monsters in the face, one by one.
      For they are monsters. " The film suggests courage and opti-
      mism.   "This virile, courageous contact with the monsters is
      meant to achieve a feeling of release and serenity, something
      that all of Fellini's work has for its goal. "

110   Reviewed: Gillett, John.   Sight and Sound, 30 (Winter,
      1960-1961), 47.

D. ESSAYS, INTRODUCTIONS, AND OCCASIONAL WRITINGS

Essays: Book-length Collections

111 Fellini, Federico. Aufsätze und Notizen. Trans. Anna Keel
and Christian Strich. Zürich: Diogenes-Verlag, 1974. 230 p.
This is the German equivalent of Fellini on Fellini (see
112).

112 Fellini, Federico. Fellini on Fellini. Trans. Isabel Quigley.
New York: Delacorte Press, 1976. 180 p.
Indispensable source material. Though under 177 pages,
it is the largest collection in English in a single book of writings or interviews with Fellini, in his own words. Key articles are "Rimini my home town," "Sweet beginnings," "Letter
to a Jesuit priest," "Via Veneto: Dolce vita," "The bitter life
of money" and "Why clowns?"; but all the essays, interviews,
and miscellany are important and illuminating. Lovingly edited: "It was an exciting, instructive and enjoyable task." Fellini seems just to have given away not only the rights to his
writings but many manuscripts and documents that he'd been
accumulating on his desk. "Out of friendship, to demonstrate
his confidence in us, and half in order to get rid of us and
them." Fellini: "I'm not a collector. I don't preserve anything. I'd like to be new-born every day." Also contains an
ample filmography through Amarcord, credits and cast.

113   Reviewed: Booklist, 72 (June 15, 1976), 1441.
"... a rich digest of the experiences and ideas re-
flected in films."

114   Limbacher, James L. Library Journal, 101
(July, 1976), 1552.
"This anything-but-orthodox collection of writings pro-
vides a well-rounded view of Fellini."

115 La mia Rimini. ed. Renzo Renzi. Bologna: Cappelli, 1967.
244 p.
Indispensable source material on Fellini's home town, Rimini, as an artistic influence on his films. Contains 298 contemporary photos, many of which reflect directly and indirectly
on themes and scenes of his films. Includes Renzo Renzi's
"Gli antenati di Fellini," Fellini's "Il mio paese" (see 123),

Guido Nozzoli's "L'avventurosa estate de birri," Liliano Faenza's
"Venti secolie passa," and Piergiorgio Pasini's "Breve storia
dell' arte a Rimini." In discussing Satyricon Fellini has said,
"If you want to understand my Satyricon, you should read La
mia Rimini."

116 Paine, Wingate. [Photographs] Mirror of Venus. Francoise
     Sagan and Federico Fellini. New York: Random House, 1966.
         Supposedly sensual photographs of young women, in nude or
     otherwise provocative poses. Fellini wrote the captions to some,
     Sagan to others. Nothing very serious, and possibly a parody.
     Sample: "She might easily kill you. But then, calculated risks
     are not unattractive." There is also an edition of this book in
     German.

Essays in Books

117 Fellini, Federico. "Come non detto," Fellini TV (see 73),
     209-213.
         What he has learned from making films for television,
     Director's Notebook and Clowns.

118 Fellini, Federico. "Essay," Il Resto del Carlino, ed. Unknown.
     Bologna, n. d. Reprinted in Aufsätze und Notizen (see 111) and
     also in Fellini on Fellini, Miscellany II, n. 29 and 30 (see 112).
         At a film festival he's not troubled by the atmosphere of
     exhibitionism, frivolity, carnival. What does trouble him is
     the ideological bias that he thinks is so prevalent among the
     judges and critics. The festivals are "blackmailed" by these
     ideologies biased toward a culture based on "collective guilt,
     a sense of duty, commitment and social expiation." He is not
     against a political cinema. What he is against is the idea that
     the political content of a film should be considered the criterion
     whether the film is good or not.

119 Fellini, Federico. "I vitelloni," Questa Romagna: Storia, Cos-
     tumi E Tradizioni, ed. A. Emiliani. Bologna: Alfa, 1968.

120 Fellini, Federico. "Preface," Fellini's Satyricon (see 64), 43-
     46.
         English translation of 122.

121 Fellini, Federico. "Preface," The Classic Cinema: Essays in
     Criticism, ed. Stanley J. Solomon. New York: Harcourt,
     Brace, and Jovanovich, 1973, 321-323.
         This is an excerpt of 120.

122 Fellini, Federico. "Premessa," Fellini Satyricon, ed. Dario
     Zanelli, Bologna: Cappelli, 1969, 107-110.
         He read Petronius's work for the first time in high school
     "with the fun and greedy curiosity of the adolescent." He has

always remembered it with "special vividness," that turned it into a "continual and mysterious temptation." "We seem indeed to perceive disconcerting analogies between Roman society before the final advent of Christianity--cynical, unfeeling, corrupt, and unrestrained--and the society of today, which has become more and more unsure and confused. Then, as today, we are faced with a social world, on the surface in full splendor, but that clearly shows signs of a progressive deterioration; a society where politics have become the sordid, administrative routine of a vulgar prosperity and an end in itself; where business, with the brutality of its operations, the vulgarity of its goals, is manifest at every social level; a society where every religious, philosophic, ideologic, and social belief has collapsed, and for this vacuum has been substituted a sick, frenetic, and impotent eclecticism; and where what goes for knowledge disintegrates into a frivolous and insignificant knapsack of notions or in a dark and fanatic elitism."

123   Fellini, Federico.   "Rimini, My Hometown," ["Il mio paese,"] La mia Rimini, ed. Renzo Renzi (see 115). In English in Fellini on Fellini, Trans. Isabel Quigley (see 112), 1-46.
      One of the most important source materials among all data on Fellini outside of the films themselves. A beautiful, moving piece of memoir literature in its own right. Fellini tells of his serious illness when he was thinking of making Il viaggio di G. Mastorna; the Rimini of his childhood; and the Rimini he found so actually and symbolically changed when he visited it after he had become a famous director. Reads as a gloss to Amarcord, with the real Titta, Gradisca, Giudizio, vitelloni, and others later portrayed with so few changes in that film. Tells of one fellow who takes all the girls in town to bed with him and once left an idiot girl pregnant, whose baby everyone said was "the devil's child." The episode in Il miracolo came from this idea as well as the "deep uneasiness" that made Fellini make La strada. Tells of Fellini's feeling for cars, trains, and the sea, and the element of terror he always associated with religion. Ostia, near Rome, reminded Fellini of his old Rimini, and so he made Vitelloni there: "because it is an invented Rimini, more real than the real one." Especially valuable for Fellini's attitude to the new youth generation that Fellini found on his return to Rimini and which he found so strange and foreign to him: "While we were busy discussing the change from neo-realism to realism ... these youngsters were growing up in silence; then they suddenly turned up like an army from another planet, an unexpected, mysterious army that ignored us." For description of La mia Rimini see 115.

124   Fellini, Federico.   "Le rovine di Mastorna," Fellini TV (see 73), 35-37.
      Letter to the producer of Director's Notebook explaining the project and its relation to the film he never made, Il viaggio di G. Mastorna.

125 Fellini, Federico. "Why clowns?," Translation of "Un viaggio
     nell' ombra," I clowns (see 71) and in Fellini TV (see 73).
     Reprinted in English in Fellini on Fellini (see 112).
          Indispensable for illuminating Fellini's notion of the clown
     metaphor in his work, which for him looms as an "archetype."
     Clowns was originally made for TV, and Fellini tells how he
     made his first TV film, Director's Notebook, and how he liked
     the intimate, conversational aspect of TV in contrast to cinema.
     Clowns are the "ambassadors" of Fellini's calling. "The vio-
     lence and abnormal whims are an apparition from my childhood,
     a prophecy, the anticipation of my vocation 'the annunciation
     made to Federico'." To Fellini the circus isn't "just a show;
     it's a way of travelling through" his life. It represents for him
     "stepping into the limelight ... you must exhibit yourself." He
     throws round the circus and clowns an "aura of death," and
     this proves their "vitality" for him. Clowns stand for the "in-
     stinct," for whatever is "rebellious" in us and "stands up to the
     established order." The two types of clown: the "white clown"
     and the "Auguste." The white clown gives orders, the Auguste
     disobeys. The white clown is a bourgeois; the Auguste, a
     tramp. "The bourgeois family is a group of white clowns, in
     which the child is put into the position of the Auguste." Not
     just the circus, not just Fellini's home town, but the world is
     "full of clowns." Hitler and Freud are white clowns. Picasso,
     Einstein, Mussolini, Jung are Augustes. Fellini: "I'm an Au-
     guste. But a white clown too. Or perhaps I'm the ring-mas-
     ter, the lunatics' doctor, himself a lunatic." The article in-
     cludes several scenes not used in the final film.

                              Introductions

126 Fellini, Federico. "Foreword," The History of Comics, by
     J. Steranko. Reading, Pennsylvania: Super Graphics, 1970.
          Comics had a terrific influence on him and the children of
     his generation. One of his heroes was Flash Gordon, the color
     and verve of whose world Fellini seeks at times to find in his
     films. He likes the Marvel characters because they "know how
     to laugh at themselves." They search "masochistically within
     themselves to find a sort of maturity." He feels that "we can-
     not die from obstacles and paradoxes if we face them with
     laughter."

127 Fellini, Federico. "Pourquoi j'aime Toulouse-Lautrec," Henri
     de Toulouse-Lautrec, eds. Philippe Huisman and M. G. Dortu.
     Milan: Fratelli Fabbri, 1971. Reprinted in Gazette des Beaux-
     Arts, 87 (February, 1976).
          Fellini has always felt that Toulouse-Lautrec was his "broth-
     er" and "friend," partly for his cinematic style, partly for his
     attraction to the "insulted and injured." He detested high so-
     ciety and believed that the loveliest and purest flowers "grow
     in the wastelands." He thought "hypocrisy" and "pretense" the
     worst vices of all. He isn't dead but through his pictures
     lives in the hearts of us all.

128 Fellini, Federico. "Preface," The Art of Humorous Illustra-
    tions. New York: Watson Guptill, 1973. Reprinted in Fellini
    on Fellini (see 112), Miscellany II, n. 10 and Miscellany III,
    n. 11.
    Fellini's sketches are almost always functional--"signposts"
    to the scene designer, make-up man to fix and visually clarify
    some setting, custom, or "feeling" Fellini wants to use in a
    film. He never makes drawings of scenes that he's already
    shot. That would be "as pointless as a dressmaker basting
    seams in a dress already finished."

129 Fellini, Federico. "Tribute to Dreyer," Jesus, by Carl Drey-
    er. New York: Dial Press, 1972.
    He knows only a few of Dreyer's films, but by these he
    has been "enthralled and bewitched." Dreyer's films are "pre-
    cise," "pristine," "rigorous," "chaste," "austere." They seem
    to come to Fellini "from a distant, mythical land, and their
    creator a kind of artist-saint."

                          Essays in Magazines

130 Fellini, Federico. "L'altra notte al Colosseo," Il Dramma,
    44 (November, 1968), 11-12.

131 Fellini, Federico. "Amarcord." Trans., E. Zimmerman.
    Filmrutan, 17 (1974), n. 2, 71-72.

132 Fellini, Federico. "Answer to an Open Letter of Massimo
    Mida," Il Contemporaneo, n. 17, 1955.

133 Fellini, Federico. "The Bitter Life of Money," Films and Fil-
    ming, 7 (January, 1961), 13, 38. Reprinted in Film-makers
    on Film-making, ed. Harry M. Geduld. Bloomington, Indiana:
    Indiana University Press, 1967, 191-194. Also in Fellini on
    Fellini (see 112), 87-91. In German in Aufsätze und Notizen
    (see 111).
    He feels confident that the success of Dolce vita will not
    affect him, that he will be able to resist its "lure." It's only
    after he's made a film that producers come to him (usually to
    make a sequel to a successful film that he has no interest in
    making.) His trouble with producers: he had to try fifteen be-
    fore he found one who'd make La strada. Even after La strada
    and Cabiria, he had trouble finding a producer for Dolce vita.
    Fellini is not one for sequels. Dolce vita is not a sequel to
    Vitelloni: There is no connection between Moraldo and Marcel-
    lo: "The only connection is the autobiographical vein that is in
    all my work." He looks on his production company office as
    a workshop: "I want to surround myself with saltimbancs, story
    tellers, and jesters, as in a medieval court."

134 Fellini, Federico. "End of the Sweet Parade: Via Veneto,"
    Esquire, 59 (January, 1963), 98-108+.

Indispensable as background to <u>Dolce vita</u> and many of Fellini's other films. Says he has never been a "regular" of Via Veneto, always feeling a little uneasy there. The feeling harks back to pre-war days "when, a very young man, I came to Rome from the provinces to seek my fortune. The Rome I met most in those days was the slightly squalid distraction of furnished rooms and unsavory boarding houses near the station, a distraction haunted by poverty--provincials, prostitutes, tricksters." Toward the Via Veneto he's always had an "inferiority complex." The Via Veneto of <u>Dolce vita</u> is not the real-life Via Veneto (though later it tended to model itself after Fellini's film). Fellini's Via Veneto is an imaginative fiction, "an allegorical fresco built into a non-existent dimension." Just so of <u>Vitelloni</u>: "I never took part in the seaside cafe life described in the film, and only viewed the lazy heroes of the beach and deck chair from afar. I invented them wholesale, including their name." After World War II Rome changed, "becoming the focus of a world eager to re-create a new jazz age, to roar its way toward the third world war, hoping for a miracle, resigned to the Martians if they should come." While developing the idea of <u>Dolce vita</u> he meets one evening a young homosexual who tells him that the Apocalypse is on its way and within a very few years the world will be caught up in a new flood. "Although ludicrous, his speech was not devoid of sincerely religious feeling."

135 Fellini, Federico. "Fellini's Formula," <u>Esquire</u>, 74 (August, 1970), 62+.
    Indispensable. Data that provide insight upon insight into Fellini's personality and his films, written with flair, charm, and brilliance. The world of the clowns is one that seems "inexorably destined for extinction, and, therefore, all the more melancholy and mysterious." He makes some films because he is "seduced" by his own curiosity. He is "congenitally" incapable of being an objective witness; everything that surrounds him is always "private and individual." In America, Western civilization is going through its most extreme moments: "It is there that the contradictions, the shadow zones ... the mortal dangers of today are exploding into flames." He is always "ashamed" to talk about his past work or what he is hoping to do. He thinks of his puppet theatre when he was a child; he looks back and feels that he has always approached his fantasy world as a "solitary artisan, another Geppetto whose Pinocchios also have a life of their own." He was never on the soccer field with the other boys; he was home, alone, with his theatre toys. His scripts have always ("I repeat always") been turned down by producers. No one wanted to distribute <u>Vitelloni</u>: "We went about like beggars, trying to get someone to show it." He closes with a remarkably interesting commentary on the hippies he saw while in the United States, a new race, a new breed. Their most "startling" rejection: "the sense of sexual possession." Watching them at a visit to the Electric Circus (a psy-

chedelic night club) he finds everything "burning," the old myths "melting away" and finds there "something sacrificial," a new way of being a man, and in which "salvation is perhaps still possible."

136   Fellini, Federico. "Fellini Roma," Cinéma (Paris), 168 (July-August, 1972), 66-71.

137   Fellini, Federico. "Fellini Talks About the Face of Anouk Aimée," Vogue, 150 (October 1, 1967), 160.
      "Face is always the first clue one has to understanding a person." In a film, if you want to express a certain feeling, you have to use faces. Even the face of a bit player has to be chosen carefully. "It's like a writer choosing one adjective after another." Fellini talks about creating a "new myth, a new type of woman," an intelligent, adult woman. We have to create a free woman, otherwise there can't be a free man. He says that Jung says that women represent "the other side of the moon, man's obscure side, man's mystery, the side of himself that man himself does not know." Then he adds, "I am the regressive type of man. I am the type the new generation has to kill."

138   Fellini, Federico. "Letter to a Jesuit Priest," Der Filmberater (Zürich), n. 15, September, 1957. Reprinted in Fellini on Fellini (see 112).
      Where Fellini, in response to a request by the priest, gives the "spiritual concept" of the world of his films. Fellini's preference is "for those who suffer most." His spiritual world is to do good to those who know only the evil of the world, "to make them catch a glimpse of hope." He wishes to find in everyone, "even the worst intentioned, a core of goodness and love." The spiritual need of the suffering being is for a God of love-and-grace, and Fellini's films are meant to provide a glimpse of such a God. After all that has happened to Cabiria (Fellini's latest sufferer), she still believes in love and in life. She still "carries in her heart a touch of grace."

139   Fellini, Federico. "Letter to a Marxist Critic," Il Contemporaneo, n. 15, April 9, 1955. Reprinted in Fellini on Fellini (see 112).
      Written to a critic who had quoted hostile criticism of La strada. So Fellini quotes from various encomiums about the film written in French by Marxist French critics. He cites Louis Aragon as stating that The Gold Rush, Potemkin, and La strada are the best films he has ever seen. Fellini says that when he has Zampanò learn the importance of his need for Gelsomina, this is not irrelevant to socialism. If we do not solve the problems of man to man ("our trouble, as modern man, is loneliness"), we may find ourselves tomorrow "facing a society externally well organized, outwardly perfect and faultless, but in which private relationships ... are empty, indifferent,

isolated, impenetrable. " He quotes Engels as agreeing with
this notion.

140 Fellini, Federico. "Marcello at Home: Is He?," Vogue, 152
     (November 15, 1968), 134-135.
         A very light bit of fluff. Fellini is shooting some scenes
     of Marcello at Marcello's new house in Rome for Director's
     Notebook. "A film crew ... is like a plague of locusts."
     They drink Marcello's liquor, scatter his wardrobe about the
     garden. Marcello has "the same nonchalance, detachment, and
     docility" that make him an "intelligently responsive actor."

141 Fellini, Federico. "My Dolce Vita," Oui, March, 1973, 35-36,
     108-110.

142 Fellini, Federico. "My Experience as a Director," Interna-
     tional Film Annual, 3 (1959), 29.

143 Fellini, Federico. "My Sweet Life," Films and Filming, 5
     (April, 1959), 7.

144 Fellini, Federico. "$9\frac{1}{2}$: A Self-Portrait of the Movie Director
     as an Artist," Show, May, 1964, 86, 105.
         One of the most revealing and illuminating of Fellini's per-
     sonal statements. Many points are the repeating or reshaping
     of points he has made before or after, thereby confirming their
     truth and importance. Others are singular. He says that he
     used to be timid, thought he could never be a director, that
     he'd be "paralyzed" by the fascination of all those beautiful ac-
     tresses. He refers to himself as a mixture of "pirate," "pri-
     vate eye," "despot," "clown," "seducer" and "executioner"
     since these are what every director must be. He refers to di-
     recting as his "destiny--the dragon I would have to do battle
     with. " Some of his favorite books: Kafka, Don Quixote, Gul-
     liver's Travels, Dostoyevsky, Oblomov, Orlando Furioso. For
     Giulietta he once wanted to do the story of a witch, another
     time, the story of a nun who was half witch and half saint.
     "I wanted to try to tell a story of contact with the supernatural
     world, expressing it through a human creature who might, with-
     in the dimensions of our own world, live a troubling, fascina-
     ting, marvelous adventure with unknown horizons, which not
     everyone can see or even glimpse. " And this is the sort of
     story he plans for Giulietta.

145 Fellini, Federico. "Notes on Censorship," La Tribuna del Ci-
     nema, n. 2, (August, 1958). Reprinted in Fellini on Fellini
     (see 112). Also in Aufsätze und Notizen (see 111).
         Just what the title says, a series of "notes" about censor-
     ship, none too illuminating. Besides censorship in general,
     there's Italian censorship in particular, which reflects a special
     Italian attitude: "a lack of self-criticism, a belief in the pri-
     vilege of being Italian, and in the quality of the blue sky above
     us. "

146 Fellini, Federico. "Ogni margine è bruciato," Cinema (ter-
     zaserie), n. 139.

147 Fellini, Federico. "Reply to Renato Barneschi," Oggi Illustra-
     to, February 12, 1972. Reprinted in Fellini on Fellini (see
     112); the title there is "Whom do you most admire?"
         Exceptionally illuminating of Fellini's attitudes and energies
     in making his films. Fellini tells whom he most admires, no-
     ting that his choices are determined by stages in life: cycle
     of childhood, youth, maturity. His grandmother, "someone who
     really ruled." An old clown, who represented for Fellini "all
     the irrational aspects of man, the instinctive part of him."
     An old film extra, one of the old extras that Fellini loves to
     find over and over again in his films and who represents "the
     archetypal figure" in his work. Picasso, a "tutelary deity ...
     protective, nourishing, vital ... the archetype of creativity."
     Jung, "prophet-scientist," "a meeting place between science and
     magic ... reason and fantasy." Moravia, "cool, lucid ...
     comforting and reassuring." Borges, whose writing is "like a
     dream ... incongruous, absurd, contradictory, arcane, repeti-
     tive." Fellini leaves some people off his list not because he
     doesn't admire them but because he admires them "constantly,
     lastingly." For example? "My lifelong companion, Giulietta
     Masina."

148 Fellini, Federico. "Sînt un mincinos idar sînt sincer," Ci-
     nema (Bucharest), 11 (March, 1973), 15.
         Autobiographical notes.

149 Fellini, Federico. "Thoughts on the Conception of Roma."
     Unpublished publicity release (to potential reviewers) distributed
     by United Artists, September, 1972. 7 p.
         These "thoughts," as Fellini prepared for production. "This
     most elusive city, full of paradox (so easily loved, hated,
     mourned)." He wants to talk about its life, its most intimate
     moments, "its secret melancholy, secret joy," in a portrait
     that will become increasingly obscure and complex the deeper
     one probes. Before arriving in Rome in 1938, he had dreamed
     about and desired her for years. "A true Mediterranean moth-
     er: this is what Rome seemed to me ... untidy, affectionate
     and severe, like all mothers. And pregnant with familiarities
     which only mothers permit." Exceptionally illuminating through-
     out.

150 Fellini, Federico. "Via Veneto: dolce vita," L'Europeo, n.
     27, 1962. Reprinted in English in Fellini on Fellini (see 112),
     and in German in Aufsätze und Notizen (see 111).

151 Fellini, Federico. "What Fellini Thinks Mastroianni Thinks
     About Women," Vogue, 142 (August 15, 1963), 50, 133, 135.
         Absolutely indispensable. Writing in the form of a mono-
     logue by Mastroianni, Fellini freely details the kinds of women

to whom he is attracted. Some samples: "A careless, dis-
orderly, lighthearted, deliciously useless woman, one that would
never call you to account." "The perfect housekeeper, who
surrounds you with quiet and order." "Bitter-sweet young girl,
one you can severely and painstakingly shape to your own desires." "The icy, ascetic, abstract woman, who projects you
into the world of the future, where sex is left behind." The
"'edible woman,' whose flesh grows back at every bite." And
the opposite: "a woman who devours and swallows you ... the
'praying mantis' type." And perhaps what tempts him most:
"to join two of the extremely contrasting facets of a woman:
the virgin and the prostitute." When "Marcello" asks "Federico" how he feels about all this, Federico answers: "I say that
you're quite right."

E. DRAWINGS AND PHOTOGRAPHS

Books

152 Buono, Oreste del, and Liliana Betti. Federcord: disegni per Amarcord di Federico Fellini. Milan: Milano Libri, 1974. 79 p.
Fellini's miscellaneous drawings for Amarcord. Over 60 drawings, in color and black-and-white. Contains "Vita (Presunta, Provvisoria, Precaria) con Federico Fellini: Case chiuse--Casanova, Mar. , 1971-Mar. , 1974," by Oreste del Buono, and commentaries, and interviews with Fellini on Amarcord, by Betti. Indispensable source material.

153 Fellini's Filme, ed. Christian Strich. Zürich: Diogenes-Verlag, 1976. 343 p.
Four hundred photographs, many in startling color, from all of Fellini's films from Luci del varietà through Casanova, in this large-format, handsome edition. The photos are displayed, film by film, in chronological order, with an ample synopsis of the story of each film, and an excellent listing of cast and credits for each. With a foreword by Georges Simenon: "In my eyes Fellini is cinema. Not the commercial cinema, nor the cinema of the avantgarde. And not the cinema of every technique or method; not drama, comedy, or the grotesque. Rather, the cinema of a man who with every bit of means at his disposal, sometimes in a completely unexpected way, shares with us all the humanity as well as the nightmares that boil up within him. "

154 Fellini's Zeichnungen, ed. Christian Strich. Zürich: Diogenes-Verlag, 1976. 131 p.
Eight hundred of Fellini's sketches for characters, scenery, costumes, as well as just doodlings and graffiti. All are dated and identified. Some go as far back as Sceicco bianco, but most are from 1968 on. Many are in color and large format in this beautifully printed book. This by no means includes all the published drawings extant (see below); but such a work has been long awaiting, and, among other things, it will prove a gold mine for projective-technique psychology and psychoanalytic specialists. With a foreword by Rolan Topor.

Miscellaneous

155 Barker, "A Set of Caricatures" (see 1186).
(1) A bloated, laurel-wreathed figure.

156 Entretiens avec Federico Fellini (see 378).
(1) A striking, white-on-black self-portrait; (2) Flaiano and
Pinelli; (3) Nino Rota at music stand; (4) birdlike nuns and a
midget nun; (5) balding man with dark glasses and a cigarillo;
(6) big-nosed man with magnifying glass; (7) Fellini, Flaiano,
and Pinelli as monks.

157 Fellini, ed. Bogemski' (see 379).
(1) Cabiria with umbrella, by tree and billboard; (2) Fellini,
Flaiano, and Pinelli as monks; (3) man with glasses and cigarillo; (4) nunlike figure; (5) caterpillar and striped Cabiria; (6)
Cabiria and Mathilde; (7) Nino Rota at music stand.

158 Fellini, I Clowns (see 432).
(1) Opera curator, in color; (2) white clown, in color; (3)
white clown, in color: Ingmar Bergman? (4) clown, inspired
by Fortunello; (5) drawings of Fellini's friends: Liliana Betti,
Danilo Donati, Tristan Rémy, Bernadino Zapponi, Nino Rota,
and Ornella Volta, in color.

159 _____, La dolce vita (see 28).
(1) Panther woman, model for Kit Kat Club chorus girl
costumes; (2) model for the clown Polidor as an animal trainer.

160 _____, La mia Rimini (see 123).
(1) a peasant woman, (2) a very beautiful bathing beauty,
(3) three mustachioed men, (4) the Rimini Grand Hotel--all in
color.

161 _____, Le notti di Cabiria (see 25).
(1) First drawing of Cabiria, against a tree; (2) the original
Mathilde, Cabiria's enemy; (3) a "pappa" during the inquiry,
with a little cross on his cravate; (4) a prostitute in the rail-
road station neighborhood.

162 _____, Il primo Fellini (see 2).
(1) The white sheik; (2) Wanda, at Fregene, before the
sheik; (3) Cabiria, Mathilde, and the fire-eater; (4) the vitelloni
by the sea in winter; (5) Gelsomina (from the rear) with trumpet; (6) Zampanò's motorcycle; (7) sketches for Bidone; (8) a
vitellone at the pool table.

163 _____, Roma (see 74).
(1) Caricature of Bernadino Zapponi.

164 _____, Toby Dammit (see 61).
(1) Toby in car, with priest and interpreter; (2) the little
devil-girl.

165 Hamblin, "Which Face Is Fellini?" (see 273).
(1) White clown, (2) stationmaster, (3) inhabitants of the
town in Clowns.

166 Herman, "Federico Fellini" (see 515).
(1) Cabiria and Mathilde.

167 Kornatowska, Federico Fellini (see 384).
(1) Gelsomina at her drum, (2) Cabiria on duty.

168 Salachas, Federico Fellini (see 395).
(1) Black-and-white reproduction of watercolor, fellow in
rowboat serenading a mermaid, done around the time of Fellini's first meeting with Rossellini; (2) Cabiria and Mathilde;
(3) Gelsomina in overcoat; (4) Fellini, Flaiano, and Pinelli as
monks.

169 Schwartzman, "Fellini's Unlovable Casanova" (see 1640).
Full-page drawing in color of Casanova (in profile), showing comparison with photo of Donald Sutherland as made up for
the film.

170 Walter, "Federico Fellini: Wizard of Film" (see 574).
(1) Cabiria; (2) Gelsomina; (3) Giulietta and Sandra Milo for
Giulietta.

F. INTERVIEWS

1. On Television or Film

TV

171 "A Channel 13 Special on the Unorthodox Cinematic Vision of the Italian Film Director." Early in 1970.
Centered on Satyricon which opened in New York City March, 1970. Includes an interview by Vincent Canby. See 258.

172 "A Conversation with Federico Fellini," WNBC-TV Open Mind Series. Summer, 1966.
A filmed interview with Fellini at the Saffa Palatine Studios in Rome. The interviewer was Irving R. Levine. For annotation, see 208.

173 Reviewed: Gould, Jack. "Fellini Talks of Film Art on Open Mind," New York Times, October 31, 1965, Section II, 13.
Fellini is "absorbing," but the static nature of the TV interview is in a visual rut.

174 Entretiens avec Federico Fellini. Texte extract des émissions télévisées La Double Vue. Co-production de la Radiodiffusion télévision belge, 1962. See 378.

175 An Hour and a Half with the Author of $8\frac{1}{2}$. Rome television. Directed by Sergio Zavoli. 1963.

176 An Interview with Giulietta Masina over Italian television, re-broadcast over Channel 47, New York City, in 1974.
At the time of the release of Amarcord. (We have not been able to trace this interview down more firmly.) She says that she is very attached to the characters in La strada, Cabiria, and Amarcord. They are complex, whole characters. She recognizes their reality. The presence and beauty of life.

Film

177 Ciao Federico! --The Making of Satyricon. Directed by Gideon Bachmann. 16mm, color, 55 minutes.

Indispensable. Brilliant documentary by a very knowledge-
able and sensitive fan of Fellini's. Filmed during the shooting
of Satyricon, the film shows the maestro actualizing himself as
he directs. Documents all the on-the-set written accounts of
how Fellini, the man and the director, operates. Includes a
serious interview with Fellini. Bachmann shot a total of 16
hours of film and 20 hours of sound before editing. In the film
Bachmann tried "to show how Fellini works, who he is, and
why he makes the kind of film he makes." Fellini intrigues
Bachmann as "an absurd remnant of another time transplanted
into our century--a circus director in the industrial age, a min-
strel in a factory, an artist who has managed to remain totally
himself in a medium that is completely collective."
  The entire issue of Cinemages (1973) is devoted to Fellini
and in particular to Ciao Federico. Contains the full script,
cast and credits, and a lecture given by Bachmann on Fellini
at Harvard.

178   Reviewed: Educational Film Library Association, 1972,
       7906.

179   Greenspun, Roger. "Film: Portraits of 2 Ar-
       tists," New York Times, November 27, 1971, 23.
         Ciao Federico gives us a few "glimpses" of what takes
       place on location for Satyricon. Claims that the intention
       of Ciao Federico is to show us how Fellini works, but it is
       best at showing us what Fellini "works through." Ciao
       Federico "...gives you something of the man if nothing of
       the master."

180   Landers Film Reviews, 18 (April, 1974), 216.

181   Limbacher, James L. Sightlines, 6 (March/April,
       1973), 17.

182   Mallett, Richard. Punch, May 5, 1971, 614.
         "No one would pretend that this is a serious worked-
       out documentary," but it is enjoyable.

183   Observer (London), May 2, 1971, 28.
         Fellini emerges as "a terrible ham, but not without a
       foul-mouthed charm."

184   Sightlines, 5 (May/June, 1972), 5.

185   Taylor, John Russell. Times (London), April
       30, 1971, 10.
         Doesn't like the "jokesy musical comments" or the
       "speeded-up motion." It does give us some "character in-
       sights." Gives Bachmann credit for leaving in the "moans"
       and "grumbles" from Fellini whenever Bachmann "hoves"
       into Fellini's view.

186   Fellini--The Director As Creator.   English version adapted by
       Harold Mantell.   16mm, black and white, 29 minutes.
       Follows Fellini behind and in front of the camera during
       the shooting of Giulietta.

187   Reviewed: Media and Methods, 8 (November, 1971), 46.

188   Reilly, A.   Filmmakers, 8 (March, 1975), 57.
       Finds it "somewhat disappointing" but "still worth see-
       ing him [Fellini] at work on one of his great films. "

189   School Library Journal, 97 (April, 1972), 60.

2.   In Print

                                     General

190   Alexandresco, M.   "Eminenta sa are covîntol," Cinema (Buch-
       arest), 11 (February, 1973), 10-11.

191   Amfitheatrof, Erik.   Time, 104 (October 7, 1974), 7+.
       In his Rome office.   Absolutely indispensable for under-
       standing Fellini's serious attitudes as of 1974.   He says he is
       not pessimistic, but his ideas give that impression.   Dolce vita
       caught a "sense of anxiety" that ran through the euphoria of the
       late '50s and early '60s and hinted that the future might be "in-
       decipherable. "   That's why so many people began to go for a
       carnival-like hedonism at the end of World War II.   Things have
       grown worse in the '70s, a "deeper mistrust" we all have for
       each other.   "People are losing faith in the future. "   There is
       left a feeling of "impotence and fear. "   That's why he so ad-
       mires Kubrick's Clockwork Orange.   It is a "chilling documen-
       tary on what could be, and perhaps already is. "   He fears that
       the feminist movement has made men feel less secure: "Another
       reason for men to mistrust the future. "

192   "Anxiety Modified by Poise; Add 'Auteur' Idea for Noise," Var-
       iety (66th Anniversary Edition), January 5, 1972.   Reprinted in
       Fellini.   ed. James R. Silke.   Washington, D. C. :   The Ameri-
       can Film Institute, 1970.   (See 220.)
       Starts out discussing the "crisis" in the cinema i. e. that
       of changing taste.   Wishes that we could have smaller movie
       houses;   seating 200-400, so that there could be a restoration
       of "the aristocracy of film going. "   But then he goes into a
       not-so-tongue-in-cheek diatribe against producers, who, he says,
       really don't serve any function.   The producer is an authoritari-
       an figure who risks nothing, presumes to know public taste,
       and "always wants to change the end of the film. "   He inveighs
       against their "spurious judgments, betrayals, and clumsy inter-
       ference. "   He repeats that eleven producers refused to back him for
       Dolce vita, but were standing in line suggesting sequels: Dolce
       vita '70, The Daughter of Gelsomina, The Sons of the Vitelloni.

193 Bachmann, Gideon. Sight and Sound, 33 (Spring, 1964), 82-87.
     Serious, complex, illuminating remarks that Bachmann has
     condensed from long interviews with Fellini. Fellini fears that
     his life as director, like that of most directors, will be short.
     He is troubled by bad reviews, not for his feelings of films
     already made but which may inhibit future films. He gets "de-
     pressed and unhappy. " Such a critic is his "most mortal ene-
     my. " Just as the critic in 8½ kills Guido's spontaneity. "Each
     time Guido is about to come to life, this man tells him that it
     isn't worth being born. " Pictures are like friendly talks be-
     tween men. He wants people to find it pleasant "to listen to
     one man tell his story. " He doesn't "understand" people who
     say they don't understand his film. "You watch the story of a
     man who tells you about his work, his mistress, his troubles,
     his relationship to God. " What is there to "understand. "?
     It's just "listening and feeling whether the problems of this man
     are your own problems. That's all. " (Some of this material
     appears also in 194.)

194 _____. "Disturber of the Peace," Mademoiselle, 60 (Nov-
     ember, 1964), 152+.
     Quite indispensable. Fellini's views in depth on his phil-
     osophy, religion, women, his films in general, and Cabiria,
     Dolce vita and 8½ in particular. (A good part of the interview ap-
     pears also in 193, but not all.) Fellini says that he tries to show
     in his films "a world without love, people full of egotism who
     exploit others, a selfish world. " But he always inserts "a
     small being that wants to give love and lives for love. " In
     Dolce vita everyone does "nothing but talk of love, and Mar-
     cello does nothing but run after women, seeking love, but he
     is afraid, he cannot give any. " He says that Dolce vita in this
     sense "may be a Christian film. " He doesn't, however, feel
     that it is a film of "desperation" because he "tried to make it
     full of sympathy and pity for the whole world. " If Dolce vita
     resembles "the trial of a society," it is a trial "conducted by
     accomplices. " He feels that all "salvation" is individual, and
     possible on that level. "The final design of the story of hu-
     manity is harmony, felicity, and the junction with something
     we have lost. " Tragedy is "the tragedy of being human," but
     sometimes "in moments of peace, of grace, of inspiration" a
     mysterious thing happens that permits us to leave our tensions
     and fears, and "we make a leap, we set ourselves free from
     the world. " He thinks our age is particularly difficult because
     we are conditioned to judge life "according to a moral sense
     that will no longer be acceptable to a future tommorrow. "
     Does he believe in God? "Yes, of course. " He feels that in
     life and in art we must at least leave open the possibility that
     God exists ... "this faith, this confidence. "

195 _____. "Un entretien Federico Fellini," Cinéma '65, (1965),
     71-89.
     While Fellini was making Giulietta. (The article contains
     several stills from the film with remarkably illuminating cap-

tions that précis the story.) But Fellini, in reply to Bachmann's probing and to-the point questions, talks about various
aspects of his filmmaking. Especially interesting, his remarks
about two films he never made. Moraldo in città: He'd wanted
to make it after he finished Vitelloni. He was interested in the
Moraldo character: "I wanted to know what would happen to
him. Later on, this question that occupied me so, the life of
a boy from a small town who leaves for the big city, found its
answer in my own life, so I no longer felt the need to make the
film. " After Cabiria, "I got excited by the idea of a woman,
scorned and accused by everyone, who would find in herself the
power and faith to go on living in spite of her suffering and disillusionment and who through her ingenuousness would save another derelict. " The film was to be called Voyage with Anita.
There would be a businessman, a married man, dried-up and
weary, who would go off on a trip with a prostitute. "Through
meeting her he would come to realize that his life, as prominent as it was, was a failure, and he'd think back on the real,
human values of his youth. " But here too, says Fellini some
greater problems in his life intervened and took him away from
this film. Later, "I resolved them with Dolce vita. "

196   _____. "Federico Fellini: An Interview," Film: Book I.
ed. Robert Hughes, New York: Grove Press, 1959. Also in
Film: A Montage of Theories. ed. Richard Dyer MacCann.
New York: Dutton, 1966, 97-105. In Italian in Film 1961.
Milano: Feltrinelli, 1961, 63-72.
       Transcript of a radio program. Fascinating, revealing,
informative. All his films to date "are concerned with people
looking for themselves. " The loneliness of empty piazza streets
seems to Fellini the best atmosphere in which to see such people. His first impression of Rome, he says, was when he left
Rimini at sixteen. He had no job, no idea of what he wanted
to do. "The image of the town at night, empty and lonely, has
remained in my soul from those days. " He describes clearly and
precisely, why he feels he is still a neo-realist filmmaker. He
looks at "inside" as well as "outside" reality, spiritual reality
as well as social. Neorealism is "parking yourself in front of
reality without any preconceived ideas. " It is simply "telling
the story of people. " The theme of all his films is the problem
people have, "the desperate anguish to be with ... another person. " He does all his own cutting--it's emotional with him,
seeing the picture "begin to breathe ... like seeing your child
grow up. " He never reshoots. A good film has to have mis-
takes in it, "like life, like people. " He describes movingly how
he feels when he sees his first "answer print" before the on-the-
set sounds have been removed. "I would like to retain these
memories. . Once they put the clean, new track on it, it's like
a father seeing his little girl wear lipstick for the first time. "
But when asked if he feels that he has remained faithful in all
his films to what he was trying to say when he started them,
he answers, "Yes, I do. "

197 _____. "How I Make Films: An Interview with Federico
Fellini," U.S. Camera World Annual, (1967), 139-141, 202-205.

198 Corradini, A. "Fellini contre Fellini," Cine Revue, 54 (April
18, 1974), 7-11.

199 _____. "Les trois amours de Federico Fellini: le telephone, sa femme et ... lui même!" Cinéma Revue, 55 (February 6, 1975), 35-37.

200 "Crusi e neo-realismo," Bianco e Nero, n. 7 (July, 1958), 3-
4.

201 De Villallonga, Jose Luis, ed. "Fellini on Fellini," Vogue, 160
(August 15, 1972), 94-99.
    Purportedly, direct quotations from a four-hour interview
in Rome, offering details of Fellini's early life that dovetail
(suspiciously too perfectly) with episodes of the films. Nothing
in the interview is contradicted by other evidence (though Fellini
sounds rewritten), and if the data are genuine, this article is
of eminent value as source material. Fellini would like to have
known his father better and to have "loved him better." The
story of the "real" Saraghina is told in considerable detail,
where the eight-year-old Fellini sees her as beautiful and falls
in love with her. In the same way, again in considerable detail, is related the story of Fellini's first contact with the circus, as shown in the opening sequence of Clowns. Of Musso-
lini: "People in Italy really loved him. Why deny it? The
proof is that they hanged him by his feet from a butcher's hook.
The way one hangs a lover who has monstrously betrayed you."

202 "Director's Direction--Spontaneous Method of Moviemaking Is
Italian Master's Basic Approach," New York Times, June 23,
1963, Section II, 7.
    When he was "a kid in Rimini" he used to go to the movies
as much as he could. His heroes were Tom Mix, George
O'Brien, "Wally Beery." In 8½ he tells the story of one man.
He thinks it useless to try and tell the story "of everybody."
All his films have been about inner problems of men: "real
men, with real problems--wives, women, work, Church, doubts,
loneliness, self-confidence." But he never presents "solutions."
He wants the people who see his films to try to find their own
solutions. He makes his movies in the same way he talks to
people: to clarify something in his life. His greatest joy is
when he gets letters from someone who has come away from
one of his films feeling that the film was about him and his
problems.

203 "Federico Fellini Vallomásai," Filmélet (Budapest), (1968),
211-213. ["Federico Fellini's Confessions of his Childhood and
the Beginnings of his Career."]
    When he was a child, as a joke, he smeared red ink on

his face, lay down at the foot of a staircase and pretended that
he had committed suicide. On the advantages of coming from
a small town: "I believe it's good for an artist to come from
a small town. His cultural formation is shaped in fantasy, that
is to say, under pressure, because of the quiet and boredom
forced upon his being locked in, so to speak. Afterwards this
develops in a mystical way, and this is the greatest wealth that
an artist can wish for. " He took Rossellini's charge that Dolce
vita was the work of a "provincial" artist as in fact a compli-
ment, but he felt that the breaking off of such a warm friendship was a "sad thing. " He tells in detail how he met Rossellini and how Rossellini asked him to help in the making of
Roma, città aperta. If there were still circuses, he might have
become a circus director because circus is really art: "precision and improvisation combined. "

204   "Fellini Satirical," Radio Times, April 25, 1974.
          An interview with Fellini in Rome on the occasion of the
      BBC's World Cinema showing a selection of his films.

205   Goressio, Sandra. "Fellini on Films: The Magic Art," Show
      Business Illustrated, 1 (October, 1961).

206   Gow, G. "The Quest for Realism: Discussion," Films and
      Filming, 4 (December, 1957), 13.

207   Gruen, John. Close-up. New York: Viking, 1963.
          Contains an interview with Fellini.

208   Levine, Irving R. "I Was Born for the Cinema: A Conversa-
      tion with Federico Fellini," Film Comment, 4 (Fall, 1966), 77-
      84.
          Transcription of a TV interview (See 171). Almost a sys-
      tematic summary of what Fellini has said at other times. How
      he got into making films and his view of his work as a "voca-
      tion. " (He calls himself "a ballad-singer of life. ") How he
      became "excited by" the atmosphere of show business. La
      strada and $8\frac{1}{2}$ are his "sentimental preferences," especially
      La strada "for what it reminds me of, for the season of my
      life in which I made it. " He's always had complete freedom
      in making his films, never had to cut out any frames. He's
      not been influenced by other filmmakers, but he's always liked
      Chaplin. "Naturally, first of all.... Chaplin is something like
      Santa Claus, like the mother. " And he learned from Rossellini,
      that cinematography "could be used as easily as one uses the
      pen in order to write. " He likes Wild Strawberries and The
      Silence, the only films of Bergman that he's seen, but they
      were enough to make him love Bergman "as a brother, a milk
      brother. " He likes Kurosawa, and Hitchcock's Birds. He tells
      why he thinks Italian films after World War II became so im-
      portant (the freedom from fascism and being able to see their
      country with "a virginal outlook--with new eyes. ") What he has

tried to do in Dolce vita, $8\frac{1}{2}$, Giulietta: "to trace the process
of individual liberation," to see where "certain illnesses started, where the psychological cancers were formed." He wanted
to render the educational conditioning "harmless so that the er-
ror may not be repeated." He can't make films in a foreign
land because he wouldn't know the "objects, even the neck-ties
that this society puts on." The only politics he's interested in
is the conditioning of individual freedom. He loves actors, like
a father and a marionette boss. He gives his aesthetic of color
vs. black-and-white. He tells his interviewer that he must
never trust what Federico Fellini has said at interviews.

209 Mazzocchi, G. "How I Create," Atlas, 9 (March, 1965), 182.
     Fellini tells why he doesn't talk about films he's working
     on, then talks (a little) about Giulietta. Tells about the birth
     of the ideas for $8\frac{1}{2}$ and Cabiria. Tells how he sets about work
     with his script-writers, and set designer. His method for
     choosing faces and actors and how he uses actors after he's
     chosen them. Agenzia matrimoniale was a "joke" he played on
     Zavattini: "I pretended ... to photograph reality--but instead
     I invented everything." Dr. Antonio was also a joke. (He had
     a grudge against the Jesuit magazine La civiltà cattolica and
     thought that censorship would be a good theme.) He comments
     on the relationship between cinema and literature and on why
     he doesn't go to movies often ("In the last few years I've seen
     ten films at most.") On his reputation for improvising: "My
     improvisations are not those of a dilettante: when I begin the
     act of shooting, the film already has its nucleus, a precise
     emotion to which I obstinately remain faithful, and which I never
     betray."

210 New York Times, October 1, 1974, 34.

211 "Noi e il telefono," Le Firme de Selezionando (Turin), Decem-
     ber, 1972.
     His friends say that Fellini is a fanatic at using the tele-
     phone. He doesn't think that he uses the phone more than
     others in his type of business, but he does feel a little magic
     about a phone. Communication is more intense: "Terror is
     terror in its present form; nothing is more chilling than a
     threat or a damning criticism pronounced on the telephone."

212 N [yklová], M. Film a Doba, 18 (October, 1972), 514.

213 Pepper, R. G. "Rebirth in Italy: Three Great Movie Direc-
     tors," Newsweek, 58 (July 10, 1961), 66-68.
     These three directors (Fellini, Antonioni, and Visconti) have
     taken a hard look at the world and have declared it a "moral
     shipwreck." Quotes Fellini: "In Italy, we are a confused lump
     of people of all kinds, all mixed up, and our boat is sinking.
     It's happening in other countries, too. There is this tragic
     fascination of witnessing a boat going down, taking an entire

epoch with it. " Fellini was working on Dr. Antonio at the time
of the interview. Fellini is optimistic about the future: "There
will be, I imagine, a new sense of mind and body--old senses
will be refound. "

214 Planète, n. 19 (November-December, 1964).

215 Playboy, 13 (February, 1966), 55.
        One of the most important presentations, in Fellini's own
     words, seriously and in depth, of Fellini's beliefs about the
     burden of the past, marriage, women, Catholicism, sex,
     working with actors in his films, his wife Giulietta, his
     casting from photos, his so-called improvising, other mod-
     ern directors, neo-realism, not-making a film in America,
     and death. Includes precise statements by Fellini of his
     purpose in $8\frac{1}{2}$, Giulietta, and Dr. Antonio. An example
     of the quality, sincerity, and vividness of Fellini's re-
     marks (he was asked whether $8\frac{1}{2}$ was his own "spiritual
     autobiography"): "It was. I wrote a story dealing with
     myself and my deepest secrets--or at least an idealistic
     approximation of me. Then I found a man who could be-
     come inhabited with all that had been inside me and I
     made him the incarnation of an imaginary person closely
     resembling me. A mysterious air arose on the set. I
     found myself ordering myself around like a disembodied
     spirit in limbo."

216 Ross, Lillian: "Profiles: Ten and a Half," New Yorker, 41
     (October 30, 1965), 63+.
        A New Yorker Profile--not really an article, almost a mo-
     nograph. Written in the form of a scenario, Fellini speaking
     for himself, written at the time Fellini was editing Giulietta.
     We get profiles of Fellini physically (he has swollen ankles
     and wears a wedding ring) and of Fellini and Giulietta at
     home. Fellini has a watch, given to him by one of his
     producers, like Guido in $8\frac{1}{2}$. His feelings for Giulietta,
     more important to him than his mother--the most impor-
     tant thing for him in his life. In Giulietta he wants to
     help Italian women become free from the type of condition-
     ing produced by middle-class marriage. He wants them
     to understand "that they are alone, and that is not a bad
     thing. To be alone is to be all of yourself." He wants
     his films to be less like stories, more like poems.
     "With metre and cadence." He thinks the young are so
     different today, "more free." Young men "do not have
     the guilt, the fear of women." But they are "without
     mystery." His mother is chagrined that he made Dolce
     vita. She'd rather he'd been a lawyer. Fellini thinks
     that it is necessary to become free from "the power of
     the mother." He says that he never made a lot of mon-
     ey from his films. Lots of details of Fellini's early

life. Says that the only times he goes to a church is to shoot
a scene for a film.

217   Samuels, Charles T. "Fellini on Fellini," Atlantic, 229 (April,
      1972) 84-88+. Reprinted in Encountering Directors. New York:
      Putnam, 1972, 117-141.
         Indispensable. Samuels knows Fellini's films well, is in-
      telligent, and is like a bulldog in not letting Fellini evade a di-
      rect question. Insight upon insight is revealed. Fellini says
      that a film's success with the public doesn't concern him. It's
      just a "prostitute" then. The two sides of the theatre are the
      ideal and the disillusioning, the faces of a single truth. "Both
      represent man." His constant movie parades show the "facade"
      of life, "people displaying themselves." Ascyltus is "an animal
      that cannot be restrained." While Wanda follows the White
      Sheik, her dream hero, Ivan follows his own "mythology ...
      the Pope, decorum, respectability, bersagliere, the nation, the
      king." Fellini feels that people who keep complaining about
      there being "freaks" in Fellini's movies wouldn't do so if he
      could put a mirror before them where they could recognize
      themselves. Vitelloni is "a story of men who haven't grown
      up." The hero of Bidone is "desperate with the knowledge he
      will end badly." Dolce vita is not intended to mean the "easy
      life" but the "sweetness of life." Paola and Claudia are myths
      produced by a Catholic upbringing: a wish for "purity, some-
      thing morally complete and angelic." He liked the Cabiria
      character because she had a "nocturnal vagabond spirit so typ-
      ical of Rome." In Sceicco bianco she is a "night spirit in love
      with flame." In Cabiria, a "woman in love with love." The
      monster in Dolce vita is an "expression of absurdity, irration-
      ality." He admits that 8½ was an attempt to make friends with
      himself, "fearlessly and without hope." The critic stifles Gui-
      do. He has to kill his type of mentality. Otherwise he can't
      give vent to his "world of games and marvels." Claudia is
      Guido's "childish desire for protection, his romanticism." She
      mocks him because "she is only an abstraction." Toby Dammit
      is "perhaps" his "most representative" film. The devil is
      Toby's "own immaturity--hence, a child." He feels that his
      own Satyricon is faithful to the "darkness" that surrounds Pet-
      ronius, to all that is "incomplete", "mutilated", and "seduc-
      tive." He used Victoria Chaplin in Clowns by way of "paying
      homage to her father." Asked how he feels about being sur-
      rounded so by friends, he replies, that he has very few friends:
      "I am always alone." He has remarked that he wishes to be
      "free." Samuels notes that Guido "is constantly asking to be
      freed." Fellini answers: "I am Guido."

218   "A Self-Portrait," Esquire, 57 (February, 1962), 92.
         Contains a line-caricature, presumably by Fellini, and his
      answers to eleven questions that Esquire asked various famous
      people. E. g., his Most Paradoxical Quality: "I must be sur-
      rounded by chaos in order to be able to work in an orderly

fashion. " Terrible Temptation: "I would like so much to be
able to always say the truth about myself without displeasure
to anybody. " Secret Satisfaction: "An audience of unknown
people who are smiling or whose eyes are glistening right at
those points of your film where you had imagined you would
cause them to smile or to be stirred. "

219   Siciliano, Enzo.   "The Birth of a Film," Il Mondo, September
      13, 1973.   Reprinted in German in Aufsätze und Notizen.   Zür-
      ich: Diogenes-Verlag, 1974.   Also in English in Fellini on Fel-
      lini.   New York: Delacorte Press, 1976.
            A key interview, full of contradictory but illuminating pro-
      nouncements by Fellini, about his very personal attitude towards
      his films.   (Some statements probably contradict what he has
      said elsewhere, and what are known facts: "In my films there
      is nothing in the form of anecdotes. ")   He tells of first getting
      the idea for a film.   What fascinates him here is its "purity. "
      Then, the "seamier" side: signing the contract and knowing
      that the film is going to make money for him.   Next, writing
      the screenplay, which has a literary "rhythm" different from
      film rhythm.   Here the film resists, you have to pull it along
      "by the hair. "   Now the happiest phase, casting the film, "when
      all possibilities ... are open to it. "   Now the production sched-
      ule, which takes from Fellini his "wish to change and dream.
      Indifferent workmen are busy with the things I have imagined.
      Everything is losing its allusiveness. "   For the editing, Fellini,
      unlike when he makes the film, likes to be alone.   And then
      the final cutting, when he wants to "avoid" the film, not wishing
      to look it "in the face. "   Each phase alters the Platonic idea
      he once had of the film.   Each time, he sees it is different,
      sometimes "unworthy. "   Once the film is out, he's through with
      it.   He's never seen a film of his again in a public theatre.

220   Silke, James R.   Federico Fellini, Washington D. C. :   The
      American Film Institute, 1970.
            American Film Institute transcript of the question period
      after a screening of Satyricon, January 12, 1970, in Beverly
      Hills, California.   Giulietta Masina, Anthony Quinn, and Sam
      Fuller are on the podium with Fellini.   Exceptionally valuable
      (1) because this is a transcript, (2) the questions were especially
      knowledgeable by people who were familiar with Fellini's earlier
      statements and who let him respond to and clarify certain im-
      portant points, and (3) Fellini was answering in English.   He
      comments, liberally and illuminatingly, on using both seasoned
      and amateur actors, the structure of Satyricon and its relation
      to his other films, his shooting methods, and the music in La
      strada and Satyricon.   The three most interesting sections are
      on his rarely (now) looking at rushes (he prefers to "go on like
      a blind man," following the idea he has of the film and "to de-
      lude" himself that he is going in the right direction); his not
      really improvising, going on the set without a script etc.
      ("That is stupid gossip.   ... Making a movie is a mathematical

operation. It is like sending a missile to the moon. "); and
most interesting of all, how he came to shoot and use the great
finale of $8\frac{1}{2}$ when he had already shot a different (the train) ending. He shot it rudimentarily simply as a proposed trailer to
the film. But "when the music, the band started to play and
all the people came down, I was very moved ... and I felt this
was the right ending for my picture." So he got everybody back
and shot the finale as we know it.

221 La stampa, March, 1973.

222 "Su La dolce vita la parola a Fellini," Bianco e Nero, 21 (February, 1960).
      Indispensable. Discussion held at the Centro Sperimentale
di Cinematografia in Rome on the occasion of the showing of
Dolce vita. The full script of the interview. A long extract
in English is in Budgen's Fellini (see 371). The film, says
Fellini, derives from Moraldo in città. In Dolce vita he was
remaking the story "of a provincial who comes to the city with
a certain stock of dreams, of fantasies and hopes, and who
then yields in the dramatic encounter with a different reality.
... Only Moraldo remained, Moraldo, no longer as he was when
he arrived in Rome, but twenty years later, already a little
hardened, already on the edge of shipwreck. " Also included
are comments by Mastroianni.

223 "Sweet Beginnings," Segnocolo (Bologna), August, 1961. In
English in Atlas, February, 1962. Reprinted in German in
Aufsätze und Notizen. Zürich: Diogenes-Verlag, 1974. And
reprinted in English in Fellini on Fellini. New York: Delacorte Press, 1976, 41-46.
      How Fellini worked in his Funny Face Shop, met Rossellini
and helped get Open City started, how important Paisà was for
him. This, he said, was his first real contact with the cinema
and from which he learned that filmmaking was his true metier,
"in view of my laziness, my ignorance, my curiosity about life,
my inquisitiveness, my desire to see everything. " Seeing things
"with love" was his true profession, this "communion ... between you and a face, between you and an object. " This could
fill his life and help him find a meaning.

224 Tabori, Paul. "Federico Fellini," The Club Interview, (c.
1974), 36-38.
      In his office at Cinecittà, just returning from London for
the Amarcord opening, planning Casanova. Don Juan and Casanova are both Catholics. Sex and women represent for them
"liberation from the oppression of the Churches. " He casti-
gates Casanova, pretending to be a poet, warrior, and businessman. To Fellini he is "the incarnation of all that is shabby,
pretentious, and insincere. " The common component of all his
films is "the intention to destroy myths. " In Sceicco bianco he
wanted to destroy the image of romantic, sentimental love; in

Vitelloni, to destroy the myth of those who seek "fulfillment, happiness, success in the big cities"; in Amarcord, "to put finish to the myth of nostalgia, of returning to the past, of sunny childhood seen as the only dimension of purity." But while he does this, he probably becomes involved in the same myths he is trying to fight, "in nostalgia, in love." When a picture is finished, it is finished. He never sees his films a second time. If you don't escape from it, very very fast, you are menaced "with being eaten by what you have done." He finds Clockwork Orange a "mirror of terrifying power" for older people (like himself) to reflect upon. What the Church robbed him of: "The joy of mystery ... the joy of life ... the joy of body." The Church left "the obligation of feeling always guilty."

225 Walter, Eugene. "The Wizardry of Fellini," Films and Filming, 12 (June, 1966), 19-26.
        An expanded, more authoritative and more useful version of his Atlantic article (see 574). Bits of information: In $8\frac{1}{2}$ it is Caterina Boratto's face on the statue of the Virgin in little Guido's school. Anita Ekberg originally waded into the Trevi fountain and was photographed by a paparazzo. Fellini then put the scene into Dolce vita, with her coming out of the water, an "Aphrodite rising from the waves." He has interesting and illuminating stories about Gherardi at work. The Fellinis at home, entertaining, playing charades and feeding their many cats. When shooting $8\frac{1}{2}$ Fellini stuck a piece of brown paper near the viewer of the camera on which he had written, "Remember that this is a comic film." First-hand quote from Fellini: "Cinema is an old whore, like circus and variety, who knows how to give many kinds of pleasure. Oh, they've been trying to wash her face and make her respectable, but it can't be done.... Once a whore always a whore."

226 Warhol, A. and P. Hackett. Inter/View, 35 (August, 1973), 6-7.

227 "What Directors Are Saying," Action, September/October, 1969, 32.

228 "What Directors Are Saying," Action, May/June, 1970, 30.

In Print by Film

I vitelloni

229 "Fellini: A Personal Statement," Film, 11 (January/February, 1957), 8.

La strada

230 Bluestone, George. Film Culture, 3 (October, 1957), 3-4, 21.
With Fellini in Rome. Fellini is angry that Cinema Nuova
has called him for La strada "a traitor to neo-realism." Says
a good book on his work is Geneviève Agel's. (See 366). Says
that Italian neo-realism was a beginning, not an end. Criticizes
Zavattini's notion that a filmmaker must not try to influence reality by telling a story, that his job is just to record what passes in front of the camera. "No film was ever made that way.
Not even by Zavattini." Fellini's films so far have been mostly
autobiographical: "They've been based on childhood experiences
that made a profound impression on me." Of La strada: "Even
Zampanò needs someone to love." Of Vitelloni: "adolescents
who cannot see anything more in life than satisfying their animal
desires, sleeping, eating, fornicating. I was trying to say
there is something more. ...Life must have a meaning beyond
the animal." Interview contains some very interesting stories
of the response by Zampanò-like husbands to La strada. (They
returned to their wives.)

"Fellini: A Personal Statement," Film, 11 (January/February,
1957), 8. Same as 229.

Le notti di Cabiria

231 "La Table Ronde," Radio talk. Université Radiophonique, Paris,
May, 1960. Printed in German in Aufsätze und Notizen. Zür-
ich: Diogenes-Verlag, 1974. Reprinted in English in Fellini on
Fellini. New York: Delacorte Press, 1976, Miscellany III, n. 2.
Why do his films have no "final scene," no "conclusion"?
Because he wants to leave the audience with a responsibility.
Each of us "must decide what Cabiria's end must be." If we've
been troubled by what happens in the film, then it's our moral
responsibility to start treating the Cabirias of the world more
kindly. "Anyone may be Cabiria."

232 Thirard, Paul-Louis. "Les nuits blanches de Fellini," Positif,
n. 28 (April, 1958).

La dolce vita

233 "Fellini Films a Private World," Times (London), December
13, 1960, 15.
Fellini talks about how he first conceives of a film. Fellini
first thought of Dolce vita as a "vast fresco." Fellini says that
Dolce vita is, "in a sense a study of a particular type of Italian
life, but not in anger--rather, in pity. It is a picture of a
world in which people are bored and aimless, and how can you
attack them savagely for that? You can only feel sorry for them."

234 Lane, John Francis. "Fellini Tells Why," Films and Filming,
     6 (June, 1960), 30.

235 Monod, Martine. Les Lettres Françaises, April 21, 1960.
     A collection of Fellini's remarks.

236 Peri, Enzo. Film Quarterly, 15 (Fall, 1961), 30-33.
     Took place when Fellini was shooting Dr. Antonio. Com-
     ments are mostly on neo-realism, Dolce vita, and interrelation-
     ship between his various films. "The horrid Fascist lie made
     us believe for twenty years that we were the most beautiful and
     perfect people in the world. " After Mussolini's overthrow and
     the war's end, they did look freely around and saw themselves
     with wonder and astonishment, with "virgin eyes. " This is
     "why Rossellini could move the entire world. " It's as though
     the first man went to the moon and brought back pictures--
     everyone would be interested. But after a while we wouldn't
     be satisfied with just photos and reports. "We would want to
     send a poet there, the artist who would give us a new vision
     of that new reality. " In Dolce vita, Marcello is like someone
     confessing to a friend "his confession, his contradiction, and
     his deceptions. " In this sense, he's really like Zampanò.
     Marcello is just "more cultured, and more guilty because he is
     more intelligent. "

237 Walter, E. "Dinner with Fellini," Transatlantic Review, 17
     (Autumn, 1964), 47-50. Reprinted in Behind the Scenes: The-
     ater and Film Interviews, Joseph F. McCrindle, ed. New York:
     Holt, Rinehart and Winston, 1971.
     Not really a formal interview but bits of conversation be-
     tween Walter and Fellini (after 8½ and before Satyricon) at a
     twenty-five guest dinner party at Fellini's beach house at Fre-
     gene. A little of the atmosphere of the Steiner party in Dolce
     vita, Walter's questions are a little like those of the interviewer
     in 8½. Fellini and his wife feed thirty-odd cats, mostly aban-
     doned by summer visitors. Giulietta herself stirs the big pot
     of spaghetti sauce. After dinner the Steiner-like collection of
     guests plays charades. (There is a pantomime of the corona-
     tion of Pope Joan with Lina Wertmueller in the title role, and
     Fellini a member of the college of Cardinals.) Fellini charac-
     terizes cinema as a whore: "an old whore, like circus and
     vaudeville, who knows how to give many kinds of pleasure.
     They've been trying to wash her face and make her respectable,
     but it can't be done.... Once a whore, always a whore. "
     "Fiction imposes order and invents a manner to contain life,
     but cinema just picks up her muddy skirts and chooses a path
     through chaos. She just wants to give pleasure. "

Otto e mezzo

238 Bachmann, Gideon. Film Journal, n. 21 (April, 1963), 116-
     118.

239 Cinema (Beverly Hills), August/September, 1963, 19-22.

240 Fallaci, Oriana. The Egotists: Sixteen Surprising Interviews. Chicago: Henry Regnery, 1968.
    Contains some of Fellini's most important comments on $8\frac{1}{2}$. Fellini likens Guido to the hero of the Commedia "of that other great director." Guido is a man "lost in a dense, dark wood." Says that what happens to Guido happened to himself. He'd work with Flaiano, Pinelli, Rondi, without any conviction. The conclusion to the film is, "We must never strain ourselves trying to understand, but try to feel with abandon." He says that St. Augustine said the same thing: "Love, and do what you want." Fellini's most illuminating comment on the film comes when Miss Fallaci remarks how "sad" the movie was, "all those old people, all those priests, that atmosphere of decay and death." Fellini replies, "Then you didn't understand it much; it isn't a sad movie."

241 Gruen, John. "Fellini's Game with Actors," New York Herald Tribune, June 23, 1963.
    Illuminating remarks not only by Fellini but by Mastroianni. Fellini got the idea for $8\frac{1}{2}$ when he went for a rest cure at a time in his life when things were at a low ebb. "I was in limbo, taking stock of myself. I needed to reconcile my fears." He asked himself the "usual" questions: "Who am I? What am I doing? Where am I going?" Mastroianni says that he was right for the part of Guido because Fellini saw in him some of his own "laziness, much of his weakness and indecision."

242 Livi, Grazia. Epoca (Milan), February 11, 1962. Reprinted in German in Aufsätze und Notizen. Zürich: Diogenes-Verlag, 1974. Reprinted in English in Fellini on Fellini. New York: Delacorte Press, 1976, Miscellany III, n. 17-18.
    As a man, Fellini's interested in everything; but as a film-maker he is interested only in the concrete elements of life, not in ideological abstractions. What hinders his imagination is a particular person or memory that has moved him. Also, Fellini cares about liberating the individual from constricting conventions that sometimes make a man "worse than he really is." To love life, says Fellini, "be what you are ... discover yourself."

243 Moravia, Alberto. "Federico Fellini: Director as Protagonist," Atlas, 5 (April, 1963), 246-248.
    Exceptionally important article by someone whose work Fellini admires greatly and who is a member of Fellini's personal and intellectual milieu. Says this film deals with "the fundamental drama of our age"--the leitmotif of the impotence or collapse of creative powers due to lack of vitality. The film delineates "the mysteries of artistic creation." Says that Guido recalls Leopold Bloom and that Fellini must "obviously" have read Ulysses. There are particular echoes of Joyce's Circe

episode in the harem sequence. But though the film reminds
Moravia of Joyce, Pirandello, and works of modern art, Fellini
"with his baroque and riotous imagination" makes all these elements his own. "They are not derivations, but analogies."
But the best parts in the film, he feels, come from Fellini's
own recollections. The first half of the film is better than the
second half, which occasionally "tends to drag" and is "perhaps
too explicit at the end." The characterization of the film's intellectual, the critic, is a "complete success" after the (to him)
poorly drawn one of Steiner in Dolce vita. Introduction to this
translation contains a quotation from Guido Aristarco about $8\frac{1}{2}$,
which, he says, lacks genuine subject matter.

244   Rigamonti, Francesco. Amica (Milan), September 30, 1962.
      Reprinted in German in Aufsätze und Notizen. Zürich: Dio-
      genes-Verlag, 1974. Also reprinted in English in Fellini on
      Fellini. New York: Delacorte Press, 1976, Miscellany II, n.
      17.
          When he casts for a film, what is important is not so much
      a particular actor as a particular face. "What matters is the
      face." A new face may "completely revolutionize the film."
      He falls in love with his actors, "like a puppetmaster who falls
      in love with his puppets."

245   Solmi, Angelo. "Fellini Reveals the Backstage Story of the Most
      Eagerly-awaited Film of the Year," Oggi, n. 7, 1963.

246   "Two Chaps Come to Town: Federico Fellini, the Famous and
      Controversial Italian Director and Marcello Mastroianni, the
      Star," Vogue, 142 (August 15, 1963).
          They are in town for the New York premiere of $8\frac{1}{2}$. Quotes
      Mastroianni: "With Fellini you are an accomplice, it's una fug-
      ga; with him you live a great adventure. He lets you be your
      horrible self." Quotes Fellini about the harem fantasy: "Ev-
      ery man needs a harem, has a dream one; it exists."

247   "With $8\frac{1}{2}$ in Moscow," Panorama (Milan), October, 1963. Re-
      printed in German in Aufsätze und Notizen. Zürich: Diogenes-
      Verlag, 1974. Reprinted in English in Fellini on Fellini. New
      York: Delacorte Press, 1976.
          Fellini at the Moscow Film Festival, where $8\frac{1}{2}$ is competing
      for the festival prize. At first it seems that $8\frac{1}{2}$ will not get
      the prize because Moscow prizes must go only to films dedicated
      to peace and friendship between peoples. A compromise: it
      gets the prize because it bears witness to the work of an artist
      in search of truth. Fellini tells of a Russian friend of his who
      likes the film personally but as a Communist feels the film is
      dangerous, ahead of its time. As Fellini watches the film be-
      fore the large audience, he becomes uneasy, suddenly realizing
      that "this was a personal story--my memories of childhood, my
      present troubles, my relationship with producers."

Giulietta degli spiriti

248 Davis, Melton S. "First the Pasta, Then the Play," New York
      Times Magazine, January 2, 1966, 10.
          Giulietta Masina talks about herself, Fellini's guidance of
      her career, and their life together. Quotes Miss Masina: "I'd
      rather cook for Federico for the rest of my life than get into
      a picture he felt I was not ready for."

249 "Fellini--Reveals--and Conceals--Fellini," New York Times,
      October 31, 1965, Section II, 13.
          This is a transcription of a major portion of the "Open
      Mind" interview. (See 208 for annotation of this interview.)

250 "Giulietta of the Spirits," New York Herald Tribune, October
      31, 1965, 50.
          Excerpts from the long Kezich interview (see 253).

251 Gruen, John. "Fellini's $9\frac{1}{2}$," New York Herald Tribune, Aug-
      ust 1, 1965, 33.
          With Fellini after the film has been shot but before the
      soundtrack has been finished. What Fellini is trying to do in
      Giulietta is "to fix in time--our time--some of the signposts
      that lead us into states of fear--of inner collapse." At the
      lunch table someone whispers that all the defects of Fellini's
      own marriage are in the film. Fellini says that the film is the
      "least biographical" of his movies. But as with any of his other
      performers, he wants Giulietta to play herself. Fellini says
      that usually he really only appears to be improvising. He de-
      scribes his method as "attentive passivity." He "allows for
      things to happen."

252 Kast, Pierre. "Giulietta and Federico," Cahiers du Cinéma,
      n. 164, March, 1965. Reprinted in Cahiers du Cinema (Eng-
      lish), n. 5, (1966), 24. Also reprinted in Interviews with Film
      Directors, by A. Sarris. New York: Bobbs, 1967, 141-154.
          Fellini has not yet finished shooting the film. It concerns
      "once again" the emancipation from a particular education, psy-
      chology, set of myths. It is a "try for freedom," this time
      made by a woman, as in $8\frac{1}{2}$ it was made by a man. It is the
      story of the struggle by a woman against "certain monsters in
      herself," the psychic components in her that have been "de-
      formed by educational taboos, moral conventions, false ideals."
      But they won't be told in literary or psychoanalytical terms but
      rather "in terms of fable." At bottom, he says, he is "always
      making the same film." Each time he is "telling the story of
      characters in quest of themselves." The woman's slow pro-
      gress towards her freedom: "I do not see why a woman must
      wait for everything to come from a man." The interview con-
      tains a discussion of the difficulties of making a film in color.
      All sorts of variables may damage what the director had in
      mind. It's as if "one adjective appears instead of another."

253 Kezich, Tullio. "The Long Interview," Federico Fellini. Ju-
     liet of the Spirits. Trans. Howard Greenfield. New York:
     Ballantine Books, 1966.
       Contains a wealth of data on Fellini's feelings about almost
     all his previous films, his childhood, his method of directing,
     his feelings toward his wife, and his attitude toward some of
     his favorite films by others. He was "moved to tears" by City
     Lights; he found The Informer "unforgettable"; he thinks Mon-
     sieur Verdoux Chaplin's best picture, perhaps the most beauti-
     ful film he has ever seen. Kezich notes the importance of the
     marriage-theme in Fellini's films and goes on to compare the
     marriage situation in Giulietta with that of La strada: "Giorgio,
     who puts a black mask over his eyes and plugs in his ears in
     order to sleep, who neither sees nor hears--isn't he a modern
     Zampanò in the guise of public relations man? And isn't Giul-
     ietta a middle-class Gelsomina, a child surrounded by adults
     who don't understand a person of good sense who shows us ways
     unlearned through knowledge?" Fellini says that at the end of
     Giulietta Giulietta, now left alone, is discovering her individual-
     ity. What she has dreaded most, for Giorgio to leave her, is
     revealed as a gift of providence. She no longer need depend
     on his paternal figure; yet she, "like everyone and everything
     in the film, both good and bad hallucinations, have enriched
     her life and have helped the process of her liberation. "

254 Lyon, Ninette. "Second Fame: Good Food," Vogue, 147 (Jan-
     uary 1, 1966), 152-154.
       Lunch with Fellini and Giulietta at the time that Fellini was
     working on the soundtrack. Interviewer asks Fellini if food
     played a part in his career. He tells her that his first article
     had been about cooking. When she starts writing this down, he
     confesses that he was joking. Listed are Fellini's recipes for
     Sangria and Giulietta's for Salsa Verde and Spaghetti all' Ama-
     triciana.

                              Satyricon

255 Alpert, Hollis. "Fellini at Work," Saturday Review, 52 (July
     12, 1969), 14. Reprinted in Film 69/70. S. Kanfer and J.
     Morgenstern, eds. New York: Simon and Schuster, 1970, 14-
     17.
       With Fellini at lunch during the shooting of the film. Per-
     haps the clearest, most precise statements by Fellini of what
     he intended in the film. The film is in another moral "dimen-
     sion," a story in which there is the "absence of Christ. " The
     pagan Romans were a race with no conception whatever of
     Christian morality or dogma. For them, any debauchery was
     "worth trying. " Encolpius and Ascyltus are two students from
     the provinces, beatniks, not dissimilar to those of our day.
     They go from one adventure to another with no remorse what-
     ever with the innocence and vitality of two young animals. They

are ignorant of, or detached from, the society in which they find themselves--again like some of our own young. The film is an allegory, satiric of our present-day world.

256 Bachmann, Gideon. "Federico Fellini," Cinemages, 1973. Entire issue is devoted to Fellini.

257 Burke, Tom. "Fellini Finds 'An Unknown Planet for Me to Populate!'" New York Times, February 8, 1970, Section II, 15.
     Fellini in New York City to promote the opening. Perhaps the single most important commentary by Fellini on Satyricon and one of the most illuminating interviews on Fellini's feelings and ideas at this period. Fellini speaks here in English. Fellini says that "only the old" are puzzled by the film. The young people in France and Italy, where the film was very successful, simply accept it intuitively. "They understand." To antiquity Christianity was a new myth, which produced wonder for them. Today it is the same. "We are finished with the Christian myth, and await a new one." The hermaphrodite episode shows the constant recurring "need for a miracle. And we keep on having that need, though miracles and religions disappoint us." This is the significance of the "miracle" episodes in Cabiria and Dolce vita as well. The article is full of good quotes: "All art is autobiographical; the pearl is the oyster's autobiography."

258 Canby, Vincent. "Fellini: A Channel 13 Special on the Unorthodox Cinematic Vision of the Italian Film Director," Image (Channel 13/WNDT Program Guide), 7 (May, 1970), 4-7.
     Includes only a portion of the interview (by Vincent Canby) presented on the air. What "fascinated" Fellini about Petronius's attitude: it was "detached and at the same involved." Petronius's point of view: "to judge and to feel guilty at the same time." Fellini's ambition was to make a picture in which "there was no sign of Christ--Christ has not yet come." On the set, is Fellini like a general? "I can be everything. I can be the father, the son, the policeman, the clown." He never shoots too much film now. He shoots "knowing very well what I'm after." He cuts as he shoots. Canby asks, why Fellini's emphasis on "grotesque" people? Fellini: "Personally, I don't feel they are grotesque." Canby asks Fellini why he has great affection for bizarre characters. Fellini answers: "But I think we live in a bizarre world."

259 Cancogni, Manlio. La Fiera Letteraria, August, 1968.
     Part of this interview is reprinted in 1215, p. 60.

260 Cinema (Beverly Hills), 5 (Fall, 1969), 2-11.
     Declining Rome was quite similar to our world today: "the same fury of enjoying life, the same violence, the same lack of moral principles and ideologies, the same despair and the

same self-complacency. " The "most correct definition" of the
film would be "science fiction" in the sense that "it is like a
journey into the unknown--a planet like Mercury or Mars, but
in this case a pagan planet. Unknown to the spectator." Satyricon is an "old project" of his. He's wanted to do it for a
long time. He's not really concerned with analogies between
Satyricon-Rome and our own day, but the analogies exist: "the
decadence of a society, a society in decay," and we refuse to
accept the "new message which we cannot understand, just as
the pagans refused to accept the Christian way of life." But
he is not making his film because our society bears these same
symptoms. To show vice or a corrupt world would be to him
"vulgar." He goes on carefully to characterize Encolpius and
Ascyltus as "two students who are half bourgeois provincials,
half beatniks, such as we can see in our times on the Spanish
steps in Rome, or in Paris, Amsterdam, and London." No
source is given for the interview, just individual quotations from
Fellini. Extremely valuable.

261   Cinema (Beverly Hills), 5 (Fall, 1969), 12-13.
      "Since I am both a Christian and a Catholic, it will be in-
evitable that certain moral aspects crop up in Satyricon. "
"These 2000 years of Christianity--a Christianity which has
made of us stuttering babes crying for our mammas, our
Church, our Pope, our political leaders--can't help but influence
me in some way in the picture I will paint of the pagan world
that was. So, perhaps I won't be entirely successful in giving
an unbiased look at this world--a look which neither condemns
nor judges, but merely contemplates. But as far as I am able,
this is my intention. " He says he refuses to be "typed. "
That's why he tries to escape the images presented of him to
the extent of "even repudiating myself. "

262   L'Express, September 15, 1969. Reprinted in German Aufsätze
      und Notizen. Zürich: Diogenes-Verlag, 1974. Reprinted in
      English in Fellini on Fellini. New York: Delacorte Press,
      1976, Miscellany III, n. 5, 16.
      Doesn't like the idea of "commitment" either for people or
films. It reminds him of the time when people were committed
to fascism. He is "suspicious" of Marxist terminology of a
"committed" cinema. Then too he feels happy at the fact that
old concepts and conventions are being wrecked. He sees such
desolation not "as a sign of the death of civilization but on the
contrary, as a sign of its life. " Feels that we "must start
from scratch, make a clean sweep of everything. " Says that
the young know that "a new world is beginning," and its "dawn"
moves him.

263   Films and Filming, 16 (November, 1969), 26-31.

264   Lane, John Francis.   "Fellini Talks about His Interpretation of
      Satyricon, " Times (London), September 8, 1969, 11.

Lane saw the "rough cut" version of the film, then talked with
Fellini afterwards. Says that there is a "special kind of magic"
in seeing a film in this condition. Fellini's sound tracks should
be made public as one conserves early sketches of paintings or
drafts of novels. The Satyricon sound track, like that of La
dolce vita, is a babel of languages, with Fellini's voice every
now and then giving instructions in English or Italian. Talks
about the morality of the film and says that people will be "dis-
appointed" when they see what a "chaste" film it is. Quotes
Fellini: "I didn't want sex to seem like something gluttonous
and forbidden ... I tried to look at it with an objective eye,
without inner prejudices about sin." Says perhaps Fellini was
too "objective."

265 Lui, August, 1969.
The interviewer tells Fellini that Moravia has referred to
his personality as that of an erotomaniac, a masochist, a myth-
omaniac, a buffoon, a mystificateur, and a blunderer. Fellini
repeats the list. "Nothing else? ...Sadistic? I don't know.
I don't think so."

266 Moravia, Alberto. "Fellini," Vogue, 155 (March 1, 1970), 168-
171+. Also in Fellini's Satyricon. Dario Zanelli ed. New
York: Ballantine Books, 1970.
Indispensable. The interview where Fellini speaks of his
films as a "documentary of a dream" and how he was trying to
get into his film and across to his audience the sense of an unknown and "alien" era. (It is from this interview that so many
commentaries on Satyricon are cribbed.) Moravia presents his
own cogent interpretation of the film. Fellini is seeing antiquity with the eyes of a Christian of the year 1000. Fellini's
idea is that of an early Christian to whom antiquity represented
"temptation, danger, challenge, exactly because that was still
alive and so close to him." To which Fellini replies, "I started
out by wanting to look at pagan Rome with eyes unclouded by
myths and by 2000 years of ideologies; to hear you compare me
to an early Christian gives me a funny feeling."

267 Pearson, Kenneth. "Fellini Faces: The Depravity of Rome,"
Sunday Times, December 8, 1968, 55.
Much of this is description of what the interviewer saw when
he met Fellini on the soundstage in Cinecittà. Fellini mentions
that the Church created "problems" for him. In Satyricon Fellini wants to show us pagan life before the Christian ethic.
Fellini also says that "only serious people can laugh. It is
people who seem to be serious who are the real clowns."

268 Salachas, G. Telecine, n. 156 (c. 1969).
Fellini: "What I was trying to do was to look at this world
like some stranger from afar. I was really making a science-
fiction movie: I was off in quest of some unknown dimension:
like an astronaut, or, like a diver plunging to the bottom of the
sea."

269 Shivas, Mark. "Fellini's Back, and Mae West's Got Him,"
     New York Times, October 13, 1968, Section II, 21.
     Fellini talks about the difficulty in getting enough money to
     make a movie the way he'd like to make it. Fellini originally
     had hoped to have people like Mae West and Danny Kaye in
     Satyricon. Quotes Fellini: "United Artists has given us enough
     money to shoot the credits of this picture. They will be very
     beautiful credits. The rest of the screen will be blank. We
     lock the doors and the audience must imagine its own film. It
     is very creative for them."

270 "Tie Tale," Times (London), September 15, 1969, 8.
     Fellini in England looking over a group of "strange-types"
     for his new film Satyricon.

271 Tornabuoni, Lietta. "Fellini's Next Film A Pagan Dolce: What
     He Says About It--and Himself," Atlas, 16 (November, 1968), 62-64.
     A strange interview, at an early stage in the production of
     the film. Fellini seems truculent, drunk, or putting the inter-
     viewer on. One has to judge for oneself. Says he is making
     this film because it differs so radically from all his others and
     only such a film can pull him out of his inertia: "Only in this
     way can I recapture the joy of feeling that my creative powers
     are not yet spent." Says that he wanted Toby Dammit to be a
     "parody" of the Fellini style, that he is fed-up with his way of
     making films, with all his banalities. "I can't stand myself any-
     more." Says that he has taken mescaline and gives an account
     of his scientific experiment with LSD. His definition of his Sat-
     yricon: "A barbaric, opulent fable, a horror story." Article
     also contains suggestive first-hand comments from co-author of
     the screenplay, Zapponi, who said that the film would be a sa-
     tire on the corruptness of society during the first century A. D.
     and so the theme would be very reminiscent of Dolce vita.

I clowns

272 "Entretien avec Federico Fellini sur son Les clowns," Cahiers
     du Cinéma, n. 229, 1971, 52.

273 Hamblin, D. J. "Which Face Is Fellini?" Life, 71 (July 30,
     1971), 58-61.
     Indispensable. Fellini in top form, commenting on the na-
     ture of the film. The circus is "half magic and half slaughter-
     house, the presence of laughter and the imminence of death."
     "The white clown is the symbol of authority. He is your moth-
     er, or your teacher, or the nun who was always right. The
     auguste is yourself, doing all the things you'd like to do." Why
     his pre-occupation with "freaks"? "Because we are all freaks."
     Although he is often a white clown when he directs, he allies
     himself firmly with the auguste: "The auguste is the one who
     wins. ... He bungles his way to victory." The article contains
     color photos of Fellini's drawings, Fellini on the set, and a
     stunning reproduction of the famous photo of Fellini with half

his face painted like a clown's: "Half of my face is that of a clown, but the other half is more so. "

Roma

274 Curtiss, Thomas Quinn. New York Times, February 17, 1971, 30.
"Rome is like a very old man. It has seen everything and it remembers everything. It is wise, but like sagacious ancients, a bit eccentric, a bit foolish. It understands resignation and compromise. Paganism and Christianity, deadly opposed forces, have lived here together for 2000 years. " The interview took place before the film was shot. Fellini at the time postulated an opening sketch in which "a young Roman nobleman, disgusted with vulgarity of modern life, dreams nostalgically of the Church's might and power in the past. "

275 Krims, M. "Fellini's Rome," Holiday, 55 (January, 1974), 36-37+.
An interview with Fellini as he starts work on Amarcord, but Fellini's comments are how he feels about Rome. "You have chosen the wrong man to tell you about Rome. In my films, I built Rome from my imagination, as I saw it when I was a boy in Rimini. When my films were finished, Rome was taken down to make room for the next film. Now when I look at the Colosseum, the Forum, St. Peter's, the other Roman monuments, I am surprised to find them still standing. "

276 Levy-Klein, S. and D. Taranto. "Entretien avec Federico Fellini sur Roma," Positif, 140 (July-August, 1972), 8-11.

277 New York Times, May 1, 1972, 40.

278 Volta, O. "Impressions of the First Cutting of Roma by Fellini," Positif, 135 (February, 1972), 68-71.

279 Williamson, Bruce. Playboy, October, 1972.
An interview with Fellini after the Italian opening of Roma, which proves to be a big hit. Fellini says, "The real Roma still escapes me. It is elusive, like a woman you have possessed and loved, then you meet her later and she has become elusive, a stranger ... you wonder if you ever possessed her at all. " He expresses a degree of disenchantment with the young: "There is a generation gap. It's impossible to talk to them.... Sex is no longer a problem for them, yet they are not really liberated sexually, they are simply under the power of other, equally strong taboos. "

Amarcord

280 Arbasino, A. Trans. R. Alleman. Vogue, 164 (October, 1974), 220+.

Fellini says that his recollection of childhood is not entirely nostalgic. He remembers a stagnant mood, indolent, annoying, of life wasted, with little hope and "certain myths" like the ones found in American films of the '30s. But these were "his" years, and he does not renounce them or put them aside. They are part of him.

281   "En attendant une version Française pour Montreal: Fellini dit Amarcord," Cinéma Quebec, 4 (December, 1974), 43-44.

282   Carroll, Kathleen. "Fragments, Fantasies, and Federico Fellini," Sunday News, October 13, 1974.
Personal interview for the New York opening. Fellini wanted the film to convey a sense of events that somehow seem more romantic when changed by passing of time and viewed from a distance. Fellini originally wanted to call the film Il Borgo, a community enclosed by walls and mountains. Fellini thought that this title expressed the isolation and suffocating effect of Fascism that was an important theme of the film. When Fellini mentions his age to her (fifty-four), she feels that he is very aware of his age and suspects that he is apprehensive of growing older.

283   Cinemasud, n. 56 (April, 1973), 50.

284   Gussow, M. "Fellini: 'The Picture Will Direct Me'," New York Times, October 1, 1974, 34.
Fellini answers those who accuse him of improvising on the movie set. Fellini always has a script. He just wants to be free to change his mind if the film doesn't seem to convey his intentions.

285   Lane, John Francis. "Fellini Looks Back Again--But Maybe Forwards Too," Films and Filming, 19 (September, 1973), 30-31.
On the set, early part of shooting. It is not a straight question-and-answer interview, but Lane provides bits-and-pieces of information not available elsewhere: Fellini drew a sketch for a Rome paper where Amarcord was sort of a Noah's Ark. Lane asks Fellini if he thinks there is any hope of survival; Fellini says he doesn't think so. Fellini gets angry when it is suggested that he is always showing ugly or monstrous people. Fellini: "How many people are beautiful? Go to a press show and look at all the critics who are going to write that I only like ugly people. Go to any party in London or New York; the beautiful people are always in a minority. "

286   Lavrencic, J. "Pogovor s Federicom Fellinijem (Amarcord)," Ekran, n. 115/116 (1974), 280-284.

287   Mont-Servan, J.-P. "Federico Fellini: 'Chacun de mes films se rapporte à une saison de ma vie'," Ecran, 18 (September-October, 1973), 4-8.

288 Noli, Jean. "Fellini: 'Je ne suis qu'un oeil ... '," <u>Paris-
Match</u>, February 9, 1974, 3-4, 21.
     In Rome, two months after the Italian opening of the film,
which is a big hit. Extended and important remarks on the
film by Fellini. In <u>Amarcord</u> "I've been hunting down myths
without rage, without judging, without bitterness. " He would
have preferred the title of <u>Il Borgo</u>. (His producers didn't
think that would be commercial enough.) The film is really the
story of a "Borgo" in the medieval sense of that term: a walled
town, where the walls protect the inhabitants but also preclude
"any chance of escape. " These walls constitute "a suffocating
kind of protection, a prison that could be compared to excessive
mother-love or the stern love by the Church. " He is "morti-
fied" when he hears <u>Amarcord</u> called an autobiographical work.
The story of the film is not the story of his life. He just uses
"some of my memories, some of my dreams of long ago, some
of my disillusionments--in a new context. " But he does have a
base of solidarity with the people in the film: they've been part
of his life, "the companions of my confusions, my bad deeds,
my hypocrisy. "

289 "Past and Present," <u>Continental Film Review</u>, 21 (c. 1973), n.
10.
     Quotes Fellini: "I simply wanted to create a portrait of a
little northern Italian town ... a town with its fantasy, its cyni-
cism, its superstitions, its confusions, its fêtes, and the passing
of seasons. "

290 Pieri, F. and A. Tassone. <u>Revue du Cinéma/Image et Son</u>, n.
284 (May, 1974), 59-67.
     Collection of various remarks by Fellini in Italian publica-
tions and translated into French. Perhaps the longest, sustained
explication by Fellini himself of <u>Amarcord</u> available in one place.
It's the story not of Rimini but any Italian provincial town
brought up under the shadow of the Church and "the boot of fascism. " It's the story of "indolent provincial life, impenetrably
coiled up, with its idle, shabby joys, its somewhat silly aspira-
tions and desires: watching, fascinated, the mythical oceanliner
Rex, as it passes, out-to-sea, inaccessible, useless; American
movies with their false and not very stimulating idols; and the
April 21 parade. " Just as <u>Satyricon</u> liberated him from the
high school and the ancient <u>Romans; Roma</u>, from "the baggage
of nightmare about the brazen capital"; and <u>Clowns</u>, from the
circus; so does now <u>Amarcord</u> liberate him from "the bugbears
of Romagna, of childhood sensuality, of the fascists of the time,
and of his bungling upbringing in those years. " He equates fascism with adolescence, which is in all of us. "We can't fight
fascism without identifying it with a part of ourselves--ignorant,
petty, and full of whims. " He speaks of adolescence and fascism, where someone is always doing the thinking for us: our
mother, our father, the mayor, the Duce, the Madonna, or the
Bishop. But it is more complex than this because "there is

nostalgia too. " For such a world? Yes: "Because it's all
been a part of our life. And the regret is as inevitable as the
rejection. " What the film is hopefully meant to do is "to
change, assimilate, and transform the past. "

291 Positif, n. 158 (April, 1974), 2-9.

292 Riva, Valerio. "Il fascismo dentro di noi," Il Film Amarcord.
eds. G. Angelucci and Liliana Betti. Bologna: Cappelli, 1974,
(see 81), 101-107. Reprinted in French in Positif, n. 158,
April, 1975, 10-14, trans. by P. L. Thirard. Also in Kinoizkustvo (Bulgaria), 29 (July, 1974), 76-77. (We believe that this
interview appeared originally in L'Espresso, October 7, 1973.)
     Fellini: 'What I am saying is that even today what really
interests me is the emotional and psychological manifestation of
being fascist.... A sort of block, of halt in the period of adolescence. I believe that this block, this repression of a person's natural development, must surely result in compensatory
tangles. " He discusses the so-called autobiographical aspects
of the film and how he came to choose the title.

293 Shales, Tom. "Everything Is Possible in His Films," Sunday
Star-Ledger (Newark, N. J.), October 13, 1974, Section IV.
     In New York for the opening. Fellini's off-the-cuff defini-
tion of the film's title: "I remember, but I remain--the moments come to me; it is not that I go to them. It is a judgment and a tenderness. " The fascist parade in the film is not
supposed to be comic. "No, they are grotesque. The fascists
are so stupid that they appear naive. " How does he feel about
Americans? "For people of my generation, 'Americans' are
still the Americans that for the first time I met in the movies,
are still Gary Cooper. " As in another interview about this
time, he mentions that he is fifty-four years old.

294 ____. "Fellini's Stormy World: Viewing Life Through a
Haze," Washington Post, October 6, 1974, Section E, 1.
     A more complete version of 293. Americans for Fellini
are still those that he met in American films when he was
twelve, so he has a lot of affection for them. "For me, when
I was a student, they were myths. So you say, 'What do you
think of Americans?' I think about Fred Astaire and I say, 'I
like him' or Alice Faye--do you remember Alice Faye?--or
Joan Blondell. " He had always hoped to direct these old stars
of his youth: "I say to myself in a very crazy way: 'I want
Mae West, Gary Cooper,' and I try to change the stories so
they can appear. " Asked why he does not like to explain his
films or to comment about things in general: "I don't want to
define things ... I don't want to understand the world. Why
the world has to be understood by me? I refuse to make clear
ideas about life. "

295 Siciliano, Enzo. "In teatro persino il mare," Il Film Amarcord.

eds. G. Angelucci and Liliana Betti. Bologna: Cappelli, 1974
(See 81), 89-97.
A conversation with Fellini after he has finished shooting
and editing the film but while he is still involved in adding the
soundtrack. Not so much on Amarcord itself. (Fellini doesn't
want to talk about it: "A film can't be described in words. ")
Rather it is about Fellini's film aesthetic. "In Amarcord I
built the sea. And nothing is more real than this sea on the
screen. It is the sea that I wanted and that the real sea could
never have given me. "

296 Szymanska, H. (Trans.) "Uplynniam do dna wszystkie zapasy,"
Kino (Poland), 9 (December, 1974), 50-51.

297 Werba, H. "Fellini Now Lensing Amarcord; Raps Stiff Terms
of Italo Unions' New Pact," Variety, March 7, 1973, 32+.

Casanova

298 Arbasino, A. Trans. , R. Alleman. Vogue, 164 (October,
1974), 220+.
Fellini says that he's read Casanova's Memoirs twice, finds
them "enormously repetitive and dry--like a telephone book. "
Reading them is for him like being in a vast, dust-filled space,
and this will be the key to the film. Casanova is "a spiteful
old man who wants to recall his past but doesn't really recall
anything. "

299 Davis, Melton. "Federico Fellini's Far Out Casanova," New
York Times, August 31, 1975, Section II, 1.
During the shooting of the film. It is from this interview
that many later quotations are taken. Fellini says that Casanova is "imprisoned, trapped in a design that escapes him. "
He is not happy with the Memoirs, says they read "like the
telephone directory. " Fellini says that he's always discussed
"Casanovism"; this just one more "conversation" with his films'
viewers. Casanova is an "eternal type": infantile, astute,
egotistical, narcissistic. He chose Sutherland because his
image is completely "alien" to what people have of the conventional Italian lover-type; and in the film Fellini wants to turn
the traditional model "upside down. "

300 Polk, Peggy. "After Amarcord, Fellini Looks to Casanova,"
Virginian-Pilot (Norfolk), August 3, 1975.
Fellini calls Casanova "infantile, a marionette" who em-
bodies the worst flaws of the perpetually adolescent Italian male.
He foreshadows "that coarse, elementary satisfaction with self
that is typified by Fascism. " Fellini thinks of the 18th century as "the most worn-out, exhausted and bloodless of all. "
This and the hero gave him a feeling of irrelevance and disgust and the idea for the film. It was this "nausea" and "re-

vulsion" that suggested the way to make the film, "its only possible point of view." This is the reference point for telling
about Casanova and his "non-existent life." What he wants to
make is a "film of non life." Fellini sees the Casanova of the
Memoirs as "a man who never was."

301 Simenon, Georges. "Fellini interviewé par Simenon sur son
     Casanova," L'Express, n. 1337 (February 21-27, 1977), 61-67.
        A lovely discussion, on both sides, that illuminates Casa-
     nova as much by its general tone as by specific bits of infor-
     mation. Fellini: "Casanova at the end, having become a mari-
     onette himself, mechanically contemplates, without hope, his
     feminine universe.... He is symbolic too of the artist, im-
     prisoned in the neurotic condition of creative make-believe."
     The film is a watershed, not only in his career but in his very
     life. It marks the crossing of a line, "the sliding down toward
     the last slope of my life. I am fifty-seven years old; I'm al-
     most sixty. Unconsciously perhaps, I've put into this film all
     my anxieties, the fear that I feel incapable of confronting.
     This film, perhaps, has been nourished by this fear." He says
     to Simenon, 'We've been telling each other only of our failures.
     All the Simenon novels are a history of a failure. And Fellini's
     films? Are they any different? ...Yet I believe that what art
     is, is the possibility of transforming defeat into victory, depres-
     sion into joy. This is the miracle of art."

302 Tassone, Aldo. Positif, May, 1976, 4-12.

303 _____. Positif, June, 1976, 34-43.

304 Volta, Ornella. "Fellini," Positif, May, 1976, 3.

G. DISCOGRAPHY

305 McGillivray, David. "Filmography," Focus on Film, 11 (Autumn, 1972) 9.

Includes the titles and release-dates of all films for which Rota wrote the music, from Treno Popolare (1933) through Roma (1972).

306 Rosenthal, Stuart. "Nino Rota," Focus on Film, 11 (Autumn, 1972), 9.

1. Original Soundtrack Albums

307 La Dolce Vita. RCA Victor International, FOC/FSO-1, 1961.

Side 1

1. 3:55
   La dolce vita
   Titoli di testa
   Canzonetta

2. 5:40
   Cadillac
   Arriverderci Roma
   Caracalla's

3. 2:45
   Via Veneto
   Notturno

4. 3:45
   Patricia
   Canzonetta
   Entrata dei gladiatori
   Valzer (Parlami di me)

5. 4:25
   Lola (Yes Sir, That's My
   Baby)
   Valzer (Parlami di me)
   Stormy Weather

Side 2

1. 1:22
   Via Veneto e i nobili

2. 5:40
   Blues
   La dolce vita dei no-
   bili

3. 1:30
   Notturno e mattutino

4. 3:03
   La dolce vita
   La bella melanconica

5. 6:15
   La dolce vita nella villa di
   Fregene
   Can Can
   Jingle Bells
   Blues
   La dolce vita
   Why wait

6. 3:00
   La dolce vita
   Finale

308 Le tentazioni del dottor Antonio.   In Boccaccio '70, RCA Victor,
     International, FOC/FSO-5, 1962.

309 8½.   RCA Victor International, FOC/FSO-6, 1963.

Side 1

     La passerella di Otto e Mezzo (2:20)
     Cimitero/Gigolette/Cadillac/Carlotta's Galop (5:32)
     E poi (Walzer) (3:00)
     L'illusionista (2:15)
     Concertino alle terme (1:54)
     Nell'ufficio produzione di Otto e Mezzo (2:54)
     Ricordo d'infanzia/Discesa ai fanghi (3:45)

Side 2

     Guido e Luisa--Nostalgic Swing (3:10)
     Carlotta's Galop (2:29)
     L'Harem (4:28)
     Rivolta nell'Harem/La ballerina pensionata
     (Cą c'est Paris)/La conferenza stampa del regista (6:13)
     La passerella di addio (5:11)

310 Giulietta degli spiriti.   Mainstream Records, 56062.

Side 1

     Amore per tutti (1:57)
     Faccette Scintillanti (1:32)
     Rugiada sui ranocchi (1:40)
     Il vascello di Susi (2:00)
     Amore per tutti/La Ballerina del Circo Snap (5:00)
     Il teatrino delle suore (2:35)
     Valzerino del nonno (1:13)

Side 2

     Cupido ha sonno (3:30)
     La maestra d'amore (4:00)
     Ecco i diavoli (2:10)
     Il Charleston Il Giulietta (1:25)
     Il giardino delle fate (1:50)
     L'arcobaleno per Giulietta (1:20)

311 Satyricon.   United Artists Records, 5208, 1970.

Side 1

     Teatrino di Vernacchio
     Il giardino delle delizie
     Notturni nella Suburra

    La schiavetta innamorata
    La cena de Trimalcione
    Madejà--Perimadejà
    Mio amato Gitone
    La cena de Trimalcione
    Tema di Gitone

Side 2

    Il Trionfo del nuovo Cesare
    Encolpio e Ascito prigionieri
    Sulla nave di Lica
    Le nozze sul mare
    Il fuoco delle Vestali
    L'Oracolo salmodiante
    Mi ascolti Gitone?
    Storia della matrona de Efeso
    Encolpio ha perduto la sua spada
    Il Minotauro
    La danse des singes
    La nuova isola

312 I clowns. Columbia, S 30772.
       Titles of individual selections not specified.

313 Roma. United Artists Records, UA-LA052-F, 1973.

Side 1

    Aria di Roma
    Feast of the Snails
    Trasteverina
    Veronica
    Chitarra Romana
    Vitelloni's Bar
    Barafonda Theatre
    Rumba numero uno
    Vieni ce una strada nel
    Ma le gambe
    Mare blu cielo blu (Deep Purple)
    Ho un sassolino nella scarpa
    La piecinina (Penny Serenade)
    Seranata dell (somarello)
    Son fili d'oro
    La famiglia canterina
    La romanina
    Maramao perche sei morto
    Rosamunda

Side 2

    Trasteverina

Ecclesiastical Fashion Show
Roman Festival
La scoieta dei magnaccioni
Roma non far la stupida stasera
Comi bello far l'amore quanno è sera
Roma nostra mia, Roma mia
Arrivaderci Roma

314 Amarcord. RCA RED SEAL, ARL1-0907, 1974. (Released in
Europe by CAM)

Side 1

Amarcord (Amarcord) (2:02)
Winter Fireworks (La "fogaraccia") (2:11)
Feathers of Spring (Le "manine" di primavera) (3:07)
Sidewalk Parade (Amarcord Medley) (Lo "struscio") (3:54)
The Emir and his Odalisques (L'emiro e le sua odalische)
    (2:28)
Gary Cooper (Gary Cooper) (1:20)

Side 2

Gradisca and the Prince (La Gradisca e il principe) (2:25)
Siboney (Tri ricordi "siboney") (2:05)
Dancing in the Mist (Danzanelo nella nebbia) (1:48)
The Rex (Tutti vedere il Rex) (2:26)
How I Like Gradisca (Quanto mi piace la Gradisca) (3:08)
The Wedding (La Gradisca si spoza e se ne va) (2:17)

315 Casanova. CAM, SAG 9075, 1976.

Side 1

O Venezia, Venaga, Venusia (3:42)
L'uccello magico (2:07)
A pranzo dalla Marchesa Durfé (1:50)
The Great Mouna (2:00)
Canto della buranella (1:23)
L'uccello magico a Parigi (1:36)
L'intermezzo della "mantide religiosa" (3:40)

Side 2

Pin Penin (3:05)
L'uccello magico a Dresda (1:24)
Ricordo di Henriette (2:02)
L'uccello magico a Roma (1:50)
Il duca di Wurtenberg (4:26)
La poupée automate (1:47)

Reviews of Original Soundtrack Albums

316   Cook, P. (Review of Clowns album), Films in Review, 22 (June,
      1971), 361-363.

317   "La Dolce Vita Music by Fellini and Nino Rota." Le Guide du
      Concert, n. 278 (June 24, 1960), 840.

318   Soll, Bernard. (Review of Dolce vita album), American Record
      Guide, 28 (Oct., 1961), 160-161.
            Fellini's choice of Rota to write the music was "a stroke
      of genius." Rota "succeeds with almost uncanny skill in com-
      plementing the director's intentions so that one is not especially
      aware of the music while watching the film; it is only later, in
      the solitude of one's home while listening to the soundtrack re-
      cording, that the true musical beauty and invention is revealed."

319   Variety. (Review of Amarcord album), n. 1 (Feb. 12, 1972),
      278.

      2.   Selected Musical Items from Fellini's Films
           Other than from Original Soundtrack Albums

320   Nino Rota: musiche da film. CAM, SAG 9054, 1973.
            Only Fellini selection is from Dolce vita. Good represen-
      tation of Rota's non-Fellini film music. A selection each from
      Napoli milionaria, La montagna di cristallo, Sunset sunrise,
      Notti bianche, Guerra e pace, Giulietta e Romeo, Il Gattopardo,
      Rocco e i suoi fratelli, La bisbetica domata, Plein soleil, and
      Il padrino. With photos of Rota and an introduction by Mario
      Balvetti.

321   Rota: Tutti i film di Fellini. CAM, SAG 9053, 1975.
            Supervised by Rota with Fellini's collaboration, this album
      is just about part of the official canon. Beautifully and lovingly
      designed, with stunning color photos from the films, recent col-
      or photos of Fellini and Rota, and caricatures by Fellini, in
      color, of Rota, conducting and at the piano. Contains music
      from films heretofore, for the most part, unavailable: Sceicco
      bianco, Vitelloni, La strada, Il bidone, Cabiria, Dr. Antonio,
      and Toby Dammit. Included also are selections from most of
      Fellini's other films. With an introduction by Liliana Betti:
      "When you see Fellini and Rota side by side, they seem almost
      to be two characters out of some fairy tale, myth, incantation,
      or ritual."

322   La voix de son maître. Métropolitaine (Paris).
            Selections from La strada, by Frank Pourcel and his or-
      chestra.

H. FILMOGRAPHY

(Credits and Casts)

A. Where Fellini Is Not the Filmmaker

323 1939 Lo vedi come sei (Mario Mattoli). Gag writer.

324 1940 No me lo dire (Mario Mattoli). Gag writer.

325 Il pirato sono io (Mario Mattoli). Gag writer.

326 1941 Documento Z-3 (Alfredo Guarini). Collaborated on screen-play.

327 1942 Quarta pagina (Nicola Manzari and Domenico Gambino). Collaborated on story with Piero Tellini. Collabor-ated on screenplay with Edoardo Anton, Ugo Betti, Nicola Manzari, Spiro Manzari, Giuseppe Marotta, Gianni Puccini, Piero Tellini, and Cesare Zavattini.

328 Avanti c'è posto (Mario Bonnard). Collaborated on story and screenplay with Mario Bonnard, Aldo Fabrizi, and Piero Tellini.

329 Chi l'ha visto? (Goffredo Alessandrini). Collaborated on story and screenplay with Piero Tellini.

330 Campo de' Fiori (Mario Bonnard). Collaborated on screenplay with Mario Bonnard, Aldo Fabrizi, and Piero Tellini.

331 1943 Apparizione (Jean de Limur). Collaborated on screenplay with Giuseppe Amato and Jean de Limur.

332 L'ultima carrozzella (Mario Mattoli). Collaborated on story and screenplay with Aldo Fabrizi and Piero Tel-lini.

333 Tutta la città canta (Riccardo Freda). Collaborated on story.

334 1945 Roma città aperta (Roberto Rossellini). Assistant to the director. Collaborated on the screenplay with Sergio Amidei and Roberto Rossellini.

72

335 1946 Il delitto di Giovanni Episcopo (Alberto Lattuada). Collaborated on the screenplay with Suso Cecchi D'Amico,
Aldo Fabrizi, Alberto Lattuada, and Piero Tellini.

336   Paisà (Roberto Rossellini). Collaborated on the story
with Sergio Amidei, Victor Haines, Marcello Pagliero,
and Roberto Rossellini. Collaborated on the screenplay
with Roberto Rossellini (the monastery episode). Assistant director.

337 1947 Senza pietà (Alberto Lattuada). Assistant director. Collaborated on the story with Tullio Pinelli. Collaborated on the screenplay with Lattuada and Pinelli. Music was by Nino Rota. Cast included John Kitzmiller,
Carla del Poggio, and Giulietta Masina.

338 1948 Il miracolo, second episode of Amore (Roberto Rossellini). Assistant director. Wrote the story. Collaborated on the screenplay with Tullio Pinelli and Rossellini. Played the part of the blond stranger. Anna
Magnani starred.

339   In nome della legge (Pietro Germi). Collaborated on the
screenplay with Aldo Bizzarri, Germi, Giuseppe Mangione, Mario Monicelli, and Tullio Pinelli.

340 1949 Il mulino del Po (Alberto Lattuada). Collaborated on the
screenplay with Tullio Pinelli.

341 1950 Francesco, giullare di dio (Roberto Rossellini). Assistant director. Collaborated on the screenplay with
Rossellini.

342   Il cammino della speranza (Pietro Germi). Collaborated
on story with Germi and Tullio Pinelli. Collaborated
on screenplay with Pinelli.

343 1951 La città si difende (Pietro Germi). Collaborated on story
with Luigi Comencini and Tullio Pinelli. Collaborated on
screenplay with Germi, Giuseppe Mangione, and Pinelli.

          Luci del varietà (see Section B). Although co-directed
by Alberto Lattuada, this film is considered a full-
fledged member of the Fellini film canon.

344   Cameriera bella presenza offresi (Giorgio Pastina). Collaborated on screenplay with Tullio Pinelli. Cast included Aldo Fabrizi, Vittorio de Sica, Peppino de Filippo, Alberto Sordi, and Giulietta Masina.

345 1952 Il brigante di Tacca del Lupo (Pietro Germi). Collaborated on the story adaptation with Germi and Tullio
Pinelli. Collaborated on screenplay with Germi, Pinelli, and Fausto Tozzi. Cast included Amedeo Nazzari.

346   Europa '51 (Roberto Rossellini). Collaborated on screen-
       play with Sandro de Feo, Diego Fabbri, Mario Panun-
       zio, Ivo Perilli, and Rossellini. Cast included Ingrid
       Bergman, Alexander Knox, and Giulietta Masina.

347 1958 Fortunella (Eduardo de Felippo). Collaborated on story
       and screenplay with Ennio Flaiano and Tullio Pinelli.
       Music was by Nino Rota. Film starred Giulietta Ma-
       sina. Cast included Alberto Sordi, Paul Douglas,
       Franca Marzi, and Aldo Silvani.

       B. Where Fellini Is the Filmmaker

348 1950 Luci del varietà
            Co-directed with Alberto Lattuada. Story: Fellini.
Screenplay: Fellini, Ennio Flaiano, Lattuada, Tullio Pinelli.
Music: Felice Lattuada. Cinematography: Otello Martelli.
Sets: Aldo Buzzi. Editing: Mario Bonotti. Production: Ca-
pitolium Film together with the directors, the cast, and the
technicians of the film. Black-and-white. 93 minutes. Released in the United States on May 6, 1964.

Cast

Checcho Dalmonte	Peppino De Filippo
Liliana	Carla Del Poggio
Melina Amour	Giulietta Masina
Renzo (the singing-lawyer who throws the dinner party for the troupe)	Carlo Romano
Valeria (the tough-looking member of the troupe)	Gina Mascetti
Johnny, the black trumpet player	John Kitzmiller
Liliana's lover and new manager	Folco Lulli
Kali (member of the troupe who eats a light bulb)	Giulio Calì
Bruno (journalist who makes a play for Valeria at the party)	Silvio Bagolini
The top comic	Dante Maggio
The choreographer and designer	Franca Valeri

and
Nando Bruno, Alberto Bonucci, Vittorio Caprioli, Joe Falletta,
Vanya Orico, Checcho Durante, Fanny Marchiò, Marco Tulli.

349 1952 Lo sceicco bianco
            Screenplay by Fellini and Tullio Pinelli, with the col-
laboration of Ennio Flaiano, from a story by Michelangelo Antonioni, Fellini, and Pinelli. Music: Nino Rota, conducted
by Fernando Previtali. Cinematography: Arturo Gallea. Editing: Rolando Benedetti. Asst. Director: Stefano Ubezio.

Continuity: Moraldo Rossi. Sets: Raffaello Tolfo. Sound: Armando Grilli, Walfredo Traversari. Cameraman: Antonio Belviso. Make-up: Franco Titi. Photographer: Osvaldo Civirani. Production Director: Enzo Provenziale. Inspectors: Antonio Greco, Vincenzo Taito. Secretary: Renato Panetuzzi. Producer: Luigi Rovere. A. P. D. C. -O. F. I. film. Black-and-white. 86 minutes. Released in the United States on April 25, 1956.

Cast

Wanda Giardino Cavalli (the wife)	Brunella Bovo
Ivan Cavalli (the husband)	Leopoldo Trieste
Fernando Rivoli (the White Sheik)	Alberto Sordi
Cabiria (the good-natured prostitute)	Giulietta Masina
Felga (the good-looking harem model)	Lilia Landi
The old fumetti director	Ernesto Almirante
Marilena Velardi (the magazine editor)	Fanny Marchiò
Ivan's uncle	Ettore Margadonna
The White Sheik's wife	Gina Mascetti
The hotel porter	Enzo Maggio

and

Jole Silvani, Anna Primula, Nino Billi, Armando Libianchi, Ugo Attanasio, Elettra Zago, Giulio Moreschi, Piero Antonucci, Aroldino.

350 1953 I vitelloni
Story: Fellini, Ennio Flaiano, Tullio Pinelli. Screenplay: Fellini and Flaiano. Music: Nino Rota, conducted by Franco Ferrara. Photography: Otello Martelli, Luciano Trasati, Carlo Carlini. Editing: Rolando Benedetti. Sets: Mario Chiari. Cameramen: Roberto Girardi, Franco Villa. Production Manager: Luigi Giacosi. Production Inspector: Danilo Fallani. Production Secretary: Ugo Benvenuti. Produced by Lorenzo Pegoraro. An Italian-French Joint Production, PEG FILMS - CITE FILMS. Black-and-white. 104 minutes. Released in the United States on October 23, 1956.

Cast

Moraldo	Franco Interlenghi
Alberto	Alberto Soldi
Fausto	Franco Fabrizi
Leopoldo	Leopoldo Trieste
Riccardo	Riccardo Fellini
Sandra	Leonara Ruffo
Fausto's father	Jean Brochard
Michele (Fausto's shopkeeper boss)	Carlo Romano
Giulia (the shopkeeper's wife)	Lida Baarova
Alberto's sister	Claude Farère

Natale (the homosexual actor who tries to seduce Leopardo)	Achille Majeroni
The showgirl Fausto goes to bed with	Maja Nipora
Woman at the movies that Fausto tries to pick up	Arlette Sauvage
Sandra's father	Enrico Viarisio
Sandra's mother	Paola Borboni
Giudizio (the simpleton who prays to the stolen statue)	Silvio Bagolini
Leopoldo's "Chinese" date at the masked ball	Vira Silenti

and
Franco Gandolfi, Gondrano Trucchi, Guido Marturi, Milvia Chianelli.

351 1953 Un' agenzia matrimoniale (Episode in L'Amore in città.
The other episodes are "L'amore che si paga," directed by Carlo Lizzani; "Tentato suicidio," by Michelangelo Antonioni; "Paradisio per tre ore," by Dino Risi; "Storia di Caterina," by Francesco Maselli and Cesare Zavattini; and "Gli Italiani si voltano," by Alberto Lattuada.)

Story and screenplay: Fellini and Tullio Pinelli. Music: Mario Nascimbene. Cinematography: Gianni Di Venanzo. Editing: Eraldo Da Roma. Sets: Gianni Polidori. Produced by Cesare Zavattini, Renato Ghione, Marco Ferrere. Faro Film. Black-and-white. 20 minutes. Released in the United States on April 19, 1961.

Cast

Antonio Cifariello, Lidia Venturini, student actors, and others supposedly recreating their real-life roles. The student actors were from the Centro Sperimentale di Cinematografia.

352 1954 La strada
Story and screenplay: Fellini, Tullio Pinelli. Collaborator on screenplay: Ennio Flaiano. Dialogues: Fellini, Pinelli. Music: Nino Rota, conducted by Franco Ferrara. Cinematography: Otello Martelli. Cameraman: Roberto Girardi. Editing: Leo Catozzo. Asst. Editor: Lina Caterini. Art Direction: Mario Ravasco. Costumes: M. Marinari. Production Manager: L. Giacosi. Production Assistants: Danilo Fallani, Giorgio Morra, Angelo Cittadini. Asst. Director: Moraldo Rossi. Artistic Collaborator: Brunello Rondi. Assistant: Paolo Nuzzi. Continuity: Narciso Vicario. Sound: A. Calpini. Recording: R. Baggio. Sets: E. Cervell. Makeup: Eligio Trani. Still Photography: A. Piatti. Produced by

Carlo Ponti, Dino De Laurentiis. Black-and-white, 107 minutes. Released in the United States on July 16, 1956.

Cast

Gelsomina, the Clown	Giulietta Masina
Zampanò, the Strongman	Anthony Quinn
Il matto, the Mad Fool (the tightrope walker)	Richard Basehart
Colombaioni, the circus owner	Aldo Silvani
The widow at the wedding (who gives Zampanò her dead husband's suit)	Marcella Rovena
The young nun	Lidia Venturini

In the dubbed-in-English version Anthony Quinn and Richard
Basehart do the dubbing for their original roles.

353 1955 Il bidone
          Story and screenplay: Fellini, Ennio Flaiano, Tullio
Pinelli. Advisor: Brunello Rondi. Music: Nino Rota, con-
ducted by Franco Ferrara. Cinematography: Otello Martelli.
Cameraman: Roberto Girardi. Asst. Cameraman: Arturo
Zavattini. Editing: Mario Serandrei, Giuseppe Vari. Sets
and costumes: Dario Cecchi. Production Director: Giuseppe
Colizzi. Asst. Directors: Moraldo Rossi, Narciso Vicario.
Assistants to the Director: Dominique Delouche, Paolo Nuzzi.
Continuity: Nada Delle Piane. Make-up: Eligio Trani; Hair-
dresser: Fiamma Rocchetti. Still photography: G. B. Polet-
to. Interior Decoration: Massimiliano Capriccioli. Sound:
Giovanni Rossi. Production Inspector: Antonio Negri, Produc-
tion Secretary: Manolo Bolognini. Administrative Secretary:
Ezio Rodi. A joint Italian-French Production of Titanus-S. G. C.
Black-and-white, 92 minutes. Released in the United States
on November 19, 1964.

Cast

Augusto	Broderick Crawford
Roberto	Franco Fabrizi
Picasso	Richard Basehart
Iris, Picasso's wife	Giulietta Masina
Rinaldo (the big-time drug dealer who throws the New Year's Eve party)	Alberto de Amicis
Luciana, Rinaldo's girl	Xenia Valderi
Stella Fiorina (one of the women who get swindled at the beginning)	Maria Zanoli
Marisa (the girl at Rinaldo's party)	Irene Cefaro
Patrizia, Augusto's daughter	Lorella de Luca
Susanna (the crippled girl at the end)	Sue Ellen Blake
Vargas (one of the swindlers who stone Augusto at the end)	Giacomo Gabrielli

Bevilacqua (one of the men who get
  swindled at the housing project)   Ettore Bevilacqua

and

Mario Passante, Lucietta Muratori, Riccardo Garrone, Paul
Grenter, Emilio Manfredi, Sara Simoni.

354 1957 Le notti di Cabiria
             Story and screenplay: Fellini, Ennio Flaiano, Tullio
Pinelli. Additional dialogue: Pier Paolo Pasolini. Advisor:
Brunello Rondi. Music: Nino Rota, conducted by Franco Ferrara. Cinematography: Aldo Tonti. Editing: Leo Catozzo.
Sets and costumes: Piero Gherardi. Production Manager:
Luigi de Laurentiis. Assistant Directors: Moraldo Rossi, Dominique Delouche. Sound: Roy Mangano. Production Inspector: Emimmo Salvi. Production Secretary: Nando Bolognini.
Continuity: Narciso Vicario. Make-up: Eligio Trani. Produced by Dino De Laurentiis for Paramount. Black-and-white,
110 minutes. Released in the United States on October 28,
1957.

Cast

Cabiria   Giulietta Masina
Oscar D'Onofrio (the "accountant")   François Périer
The movie star   Amadeo Nazzari
The hypnotist   Aldo Silvani
Wanda (Cabiria's chubby girl friend)   Franca Marzi
Jessy (the movie star's blonde girl
  friend)   Dorian Gray
The friar   Polidor
The cripple in the "miracle" sequence   Mario Passante
Matilda (the tough prostitute who has a
  fight with Cabiria)   Pina Gualandri

and

Ennio Girolami, Christian Tassou.

355 1959 La dolce vita
             Story: Fellini, Tullio Pinelli, Ennio Flaiano. Screen-
play: Fellini, Flaiano, Pinelli, Brunello Rondi. Advisor: Rondi. Music: Nino Rota, conducted by Franco Ferrara, with the
participation of I. Campanino and Adriano Celentano. Cinematography: Otello Martelli. Cameraman: Arturo Zavattini.
Asst. Cameraman: Ennio Guarnieri. Editing: Leo Catozzo.
Sets and costumes: Piero Gherardi, assisted by Giorgio Giovannini, Lucia Mirisola, Vito Anzalone. Asst. Directors:
Giudarini Guidi, Paolo Nuzzi, Dominique Delouche. Production
Managers: Manlio Moretti, Nello Meniconi. Production Assistants: Giancarlo Romani, Gianfranco Mingozzi, Lilli Veenman.
Make-up: Otello Fava. Hairdresser: Renata Magnanti. Sound:

Agostino Moretti. Continuity: Isa Mari. Production Inspector: Alessandro von Norman. Production Secretaries: Mario Basile, Mario de Biase, Osvaldo de Micheli. Executive Producer: Franco Magli. Produced by Giuseppe Amato and Angelo Rizzoli. A joint production of Riama Film (Rome) and Pathé Consortium Cinema (Paris). Black-and-white, Totalscope, 173 minutes. Released in the United States on April 19, 1961.

Cast

1. Christ the Workingman, over Rome

Marcello Rubini, third-rate journalist	Marcello Mastroianni
Paparazzo, newspaper photographer	Walter Santesso

2. Chance Meeting with Maddalena at Night Club

1st photographer	Giulio Paradisi
2nd photographer	Enzo Cerusico
3rd photographer	Enzo Doria
Maddalena	Anouk Aimée
Angry gentleman (who makes Marcello "squat")	Cesare Miceli Picardi
1st female companion	Donatella Esparmer
2nd female companion	Maria Pia Serafini

3. Marcello, Maddalena, and the Prostitute

The prostitute	Adriana Moneta
2nd prostitute	Anna Maria Salerno
1st procurer	Oscar Ghiglia
2nd procurer	Gino Marturano

4. Emma's Attempted Suicide

Emma, Marcello's mistress	Yvonne Furneaux
Reporter at the hospital	Thomas Terres
Interne	Carlo Mariotti
Doctor	Leonardo Botta

5. Sylvia, the Hollywood Star, over Rome

Sylvia	Anita Ekberg
Edna, Sylvia's secretary	Harriet White
The producer, Totò Scalise	Carlo di Maggio
Radio announcer	Francesco Luzi

Asst. producer	Francesco Consalvo
Producer's secretary	Guglielmo Leoncini
Interpreter at the press con- ference	Sandy von Norman
Robert, Sylvia's fiancé	Lex Barker
Movie magazine publisher	Tiziano Cortini
Journalists at the press con- ference	Henry Thody, Dona- tella della Nora, Maité Mor- and, Donato Castellaneta, John Francis Lane, Concet- ta Ragusa, François Dieu- donné, Mario Mallamo, Na- dia Balabine, Umberto Fel- ici, Maurizio Guelfi
Rock 'n Roll singer	Adriano Celentano
Waiter at Caracalla's	Gondrano Trucchi
Effeminate male	Gio Staiano
Black dancer	Archie Savage
Frankie Stout	Alan Dijon
Butler at Maddalena's home	Paolo Labia
Maddalena's father	Giacomo Gabrielli

6. **Chance Meeting with Steiner
   in the Church**

Steiner, intellectual friend of Marcello's	Alain Cuny
The priest	Gianfranco Mingozzi

7. **Tragedy of the False "Miracle"
   at Terni**

Television director	Alfredo Rizzo
A priest at the "miracle"	Alex Messoyedoff
Mother of the lying children	Rina Franchetti
Uncle of the lying children	Aurelio Nardi
Woman who befriends Emma	Marianna Leibl
The lying children	Giovanna and Massi- mo

8. **The Evening at the Steiner
   Home**

Signora Steiner	Renée Longarini
Poetess	Iris Tree
Her friend (who quotes Shakespeare)	Desmond O'Grady
Woman writer	Leonida Repaci
Others at the party	Anna Salvatore, Le- tizia Spadini, Margherito Russo, Winie Vagliani

Paola, the innocent	Valeria Ciangottini
Angry man on the Via Veneto	Nello Meniconi
Gossipmonger on the Via Veneto	Massimo Busetti

9. Marcello's Father Visits Rome

Marcello's father	Annibale Ninchi
Manager of the Kit Kat night club	Vittorio Manfrino
The clown (with trumpet and balloons)	Polidor
Fanny, a chorus girl	Magali Noël
Lucy	Lilly Granado
Gloria	Gloria Jones

10. Marcello's Night Out with the Aristocrats

Sophisticated blonde on the Via Veneto (the "Eskimo")	Nico Otzak
Prince Mascalchi	Prince Vadim Wolkonsky
don Giulio Mascalchi	Giulio Questi
don Eugenio Mascalchi	Prince don Eugenio Ruspoli di Poggio Suasa
don Giovanni Mascalchi	Count Ivenda Dobrzensky
Sonia (the English woman who sleeps with Marcello)	Audrey MacDonald
Spanish nobleman	Juan Antequera
English medium	Rosemary Rennel Rodd
Maddalena's lover	Ferdinando Brofferio
The lady in the white coat	Donna Doris Pignatelli, Principessa di Monteroduni
Debutante of the year	Ida Galli
Tired boy with the dogs	Mario de Grenet
The horseman	Franco Rossellini
Massimilla	Maria Marigliano
Woman in sexual frenzy during seance	Loretta Ramaciotti
Laughing woman	Christina dei Conti Paolozzi
Sleeping duchess	Countess Elisabetta Cini
Tired woman	Maria Teresa Wolodimeroff
Man with the watch	Count Carlo Kechler
Boy in the mink coat	Count Brunoro Serego Aligheri
Woman with mirror	Nani Colombo

11. The Steiner Murders and Suicide

Police commissioner	Giulio Girola
Doctor	Giuseppe Addobbati
Asst. Police commissioner	Paolo Fadda
Police commissioner for the zone	Vando Tres
Journalist using telephone	Franco Giacobini
Steiner's maid	Giuliana Lo Jodice
Neighbor of Steiner's	Federika André
Policeman	Giancarlo Romani

12. The Orgy in the Villa at Fregene

Nadia	Nadia Gray
Nadia's lover	Mino Doro
1st transvestite	Antonio Jacono
2nd transvestite	Carlo Musto
The muscleman	Tito Buzzo
Spoleto Ballerina	Sondra Lee
Matinée idol	Jacques Sernas
Matinée idol's mistress	Leontine van Strein
Black dancer	Leo Coleman
Laura, the blonde actress-singer	Laura Betti
Daniela	Daniela Calvino
Girl eating the chicken	Christine Denise
Riccardo, owner of the villa	Riccardo Garrone
Mute boy	Decimo Cristiani
Boy who helps Nadia undress	Umberto Orsini
Girl sitting beside him	Sandra Tesi
Tall boy	Renato Mambor
Man with the brassiere on his head	Mario Conocchia
An admirer of Nadia	Enrico Glori
Girl confessor	Lucia Vasilico
Girl covered with feathers	Franca Pasutt

Alain Cuny was dubbed by Romolo Valli; Anouk Aimée, by Lilla Brignone; Yvonne Furneaux, by Gabriella Genta.

356 1962 Le tentazioni del dottor Antonio (Act II in Boccaccio '70--
a scherzo in four acts conceived by Cesare Zavattini.
The other acts are "La riffa," directed by Vittorio De
Sica; "Renzo e Luciana," by Mario Monicelli; and "Il
lavoro," by Luchino Visconti.)

Story and screenplay: Fellini, Ennio Flaiano, Tullio
Pinelli, in collaboration with Brunello Rondi and Goffredo Par-
ise. Music: Nino Rota. Cinematography: Otello Martelli.
Editing: Leo Catozzo. Sets: Piero Zuffi. Production Mana-
gers for Boccaccio '70: Lucio Orlandini, Alfredo Nelidoni.
Produced by Carlo Ponti, Ugo Tucci, Sante Chimirri, Antonio
Cervi. A joint production of Concordia Campagna Cinematogra-

fica-Cineriz (Rome) and Francinex-Gray Film (Paris). Technicolor, wide-screen, c. 70 minutes. Released in the United States on June 26, 1962.

Cast

Dr. Antonio Mazzuolo	Peppino de Felippo
Anita	Anita Ekberg
Commendatore La Pappa (the official that Dr. Antonio goes to see to try and ban the billboard)	Antonio Acqua
Antonio's sister	Donatella Della Nora
The little-girl Cupid	Eleanora Maggi

and
Lina Alberti, Monique Berger, Giacomo Furia, Alberto Sorrentino, Mario Passante, Silvio Bagolino, Dante Maggio.

357 1962 8½ (Otto e mezzo)
Story: Fellini, Ennio Flaiano. Screenplay: Fellini, Flaiano, Tullio Pinelli, Brunello Rondi. Music: Nino Rota. Cinematography: Gianni di Venanzo. Cameraman: Pasquale de Santis. Editing: Leo Catozzo. Asst. Editor: Adriano Olasio. Sets and costumes: Piero Gherardi. Make-up: Otello Fava. Asst. Director: Giudarino Guidi. Assistants to the Director: Giulio Paradisi, Francesco Alvigi. Continuity: Mirella Gamacchio. Sound: Mario Faraoni, Alberto Bartolomei. Sets and wardrobe assistants: Luciano Ricceri, Vito Anzalone, Orietta Nasali Rocca, Alba Rivaioli, Clara Poggi, Renata Magnanti, Eugenia Filippo. Production Manager: Nello Meniconi. Asst. Production Manager: Alessandro von Normann. Production assistants: Angelo Jacono, Albino Morandin, Mario Basili. Executive Producer: Clemente Fracassi. Produced by Angelo Rizzoli for Cineriz (Rome) and Francinex (Paris). Black-and-white, 135 minutes. Released in Italy, February, 1963. Released in France, May, 1963. Released in the United States on June 25, 1963.

Cast

The Stars

Guido Anselmi, the film director	Marcello Mastroianni
Carla, his mistress	Sandra Milo
Luisa, his wife	Anouk Aimée
Claudia (the actress and the girl in white)	Claudia Cardinale

At the Spa

Mario Mezzabotta, Guido's philandering friend	Mario Pisu

Gloria Morin, Mezzabotta's young mistress	Barbara Steele
Daumier (Fabrizio Carini), the critic-consultant	Jean Rougeul
Maurice, the magician	Ian Dallas
Maya, Maurice's mindreader	Mary Indovino
The unknown beautiful woman on the telephone	Caterina Boratto
The "snail-woman" French actress	Madeleine Lebeau
Her agent	Neil Robertson
American journalist	Eugene Walter
His wife (writes for ladies' magazines)	Gilda Dahlberg
Head clerk at the hotel	Prince Vadim Wolkonsky
Doctors at the Spa	Roberto Nicolosi, Luciana Sanseverino

Young Guido and his Parents

Guido as a boy (at school and in the finale)	Marco Gemini
Guido's mother	Giuditta Rissone
Guido's father	Annibale Ninchi

The Production Staff and the Camp Followers

Pace, the producer	Guido Alberti
His dumb-blonde girl friend	Annie Gorassini
Conocchia, the old assistant (who weeps for Guido)	Mario Conocchia
The production manager (who salutes Guido, in his underwear)	Cesarino Miceli Picardi
His two pretty "nieces"	Eva Gioia, Dina de Santis
The production secretary	Bruno Agostini
The production accountant	John Stacy

Luisa's Friends

Rossella	Rossella Falk
Luisa's sister	Elisabetta Catalano
Enrico, Luisa's admirer	Mark Herron
Luisa's other friends	Rossella Como, Francesco Ragamonti, Matilde Calnan

At the old Farmhouse

Guido as a child	Riccardo Guglielmi
His grandmother	Georgia Simmons

One of Guido's nurses	Maria Raimondi
The old peasant relative	Palma Mangini
The little girl who tells Guido to say	
Asa Nisi Masa	Roberta Valli

At the Parochial School

The school president	Maria Tedeschi

The Harem Sequence

Saraghina	Edra Gale
Guido's dark-haired nurse	Marisa Colomber
The airline hostess	Nadine Sanders
The "over-age" dancer, Jacqueline	
Bonbon	Yvonne Casadei
The sexy-blonde	Hedy Vessel
The black dancer	Hazel Rogers

The Clergy

The Cardinal	Tito Masini
The Monsignore	Comte Alfredo de Lafeld
The lay secretary	Frazier Rippy
The priest	Sebastiano de Leandro

At the Screen Tests

Claudia's agent	Mino Doro
Claudia's press agent	Mario Tarchetti
Actress playing Carla in the tests	Olimpia Cavalli
Actress playing Luisa in the tests	Sonia Gensner
Actress playing Saraghina in the tests	Grazia Frasnelli
Another actress playing Saraghina in the tests	Maria Antonietta Beluzzi
Cardinal in the tests	Comtesse Elisabetta Cini
One of the clowns in the parade-finale	Polidor

and
Giulio Paradisi, Valentina Lang, Annarosa Lattuada, Agnese
Bonfanti, Flaminia Torlonia, Anna Carimini, Maria Wertmüller,
Gideon Bachmann, Deena Boyer, John Francis Lane.

Fellini's entire 8½ production crew took part in the finale sequence.

358   1965   Giulietta degli spiriti
           Story: Fellini, Tullio Pinelli.   Screenplay: Fellini,

Ennio Flaiano, Pinelli, Brunello Rondi. Music: Nino Rota, conducted by Carlo Savino. Cinematography: Gianni di Venanzo. Cameraman: Pasquale de Santis. Editing: Ruggero Mastroianni. Sets and costumes: Piero Gherardi. Make-up: Otello Fava, Eligio Trani. Assistants to the Director: Francesco Aluigi, Liliana Betti, Rosalba Zavoli. Production Managers: Mario Basili, Alessandro von Normann. Production Supervisor: Walter Benelli. Continuity: Eschilo Tarquini. Set Architects: Luciano Riccieri, E. Benazzi Taglietti, Giantito Burchiellaro. Production Secretaries: Renato Fiè, Ennio Onorati. Sound: Mario Faraoni, Mario Morici. Interior Decoration: Vito Anzalone. Asst. Interior Decorator: Franco Cuppini. Costume Assistants: Bruna Parmesan, Alda Marussig. Hairdressers: Renata Magnanti, Marisa Fraticelli. Head Dressmakers: Clara Poggi, Alice Brugnaro. Production Executive: Clemente Fracassi. Produced by Angelo Rizzoli. A Federiz Film. Technicolor, 145 minutes. Released in the United States on November 3, 1965.

Cast

The Family

Giulietta, the wife	Giulietta Masina
Giorgio, the husband	Mario Pisu
The mother	Caterina Boratto
The pregnant sister, Adele	Luisa della Noce
The sister, the TV model	Sylva Koscina
The grandfather	Lou Gilbert
Giulietta as a child	Alba Cancellieri
The little nieces	Sabrina Gigli, Rossella di Sepio

Giulietta's Friends

Valentina (who takes Giulietta to Bhishma's)	Valentina Cortesa
Dolores (Dolly), the sculptress	Silvana Jachino
Elena	Elena Fondra

Giulietta's Maids

Teresina (the plump one with all the boy friends)	Milena Vucotich
Elisabetta (the slim, prim one)	Elisabetta Gray

Giorgio's Friends

José	José Luis de Villalonga
The one who "exercises" with Giorgio, taking giant-steps	Cesarino Miceli Picardi

Susy and Her Court

Susy, the beautiful neighbor	Sandra Milo
Iris, the apparition	Sandra Milo
Fanny, the circus rider with whom Grandfather elopes	Sandra Milo
Susy's grandmother	Irina Alexeiva
Susy's mother	Alessandra Mannoukine
The chauffeur	Gilberto Galvan
The oriental masseuse	Seyna Seyn
The maids	Yvonne Casadei, Hildegarde Golez, Dina de Santis
Russian teacher	Edoardo Torricella
Girl who keeps attempting suicide	Dany Paris
Momy, Susy's "fiance"	Raffaela Guida
Momy's son, the "Arabian Prince" who wishes to go to bed with Giulietta	Fred Williams
Others at Susy's	Wanani (Black woman), Robert Walders (bearded "corpse"), Carlo Pisacane (the monk who visits Susy), Alberto Cevenini (who has a sweaty body and opens the champagne), Jacques Herlin, Guido Alberti, Mino Doro, Jacqueline Gerard.

The Private Eye and His Crew

Lynx-Eyes	Alberto Plebani
The psychologist	Federico Valli
Other assistants	Remo Risaliti, Grillo Rufino

At Bhishma's

Bhishma	Waleska Gert
Bhishma's male assistant	Asoka Rubener
Bhishma's female assistant	Sujata
Bhishma's doctor	Walter Harrison
Bearded painter who "cuts off" Sujata's head	Gianni Bertoncini
Others	Elena Cumani, Bill Edwards

Friends and Enemies Participating

Lawyer in love with Giulietta	Mario Conocchia

Giulietta's doctor	Felice Fulchignoni
Doctor's wife	Lia Pistis
Headmaster, who fires grandfather from his teaching post	Friedrich von Lede-bur
Psychoanalyst	Anne Francine
Valentina's lover	Massimo Sarchielli
Dolores's male model	Nadir Moretti
Dolores's female model	Alba Rosa
The clairvoyant (who holds the pendulum over Giulietta's head and conducts the early seance)	Genius
Dancer on TV	Alicia Brandet
Other TV performer	Mary Arden
Woman with dark glasses at the garden party	Maria Tedeschi

359   1968   Toby Dammit (Episode in Tre passi nel delirio. Other two episodes are "William Wilson," directed by Louis Malle, and "Metzengerstein," by Roger Vadim.)

Story and screenplay: Fellini, Bernardino Zapponi, from the short story by Edgar Allan Poe "Never Bet Your Head on the Devil--A Tale With a Moral" ("Non scommettete la testa col diavolo"). Music: Nino Rota. Cinematography: Giuseppe Rotunno. Cameraman: Giuseppe Maccari. Editing: Ruggero Mastroianni. Assistant Editor: Adriana Olasio. Sets and costumes: Piero Tosi. Set Architect: Enzo del Prato. Assistant Director: Eschilo Tarquini. Continuity: Norma Giacchero. Production Manager: Tommaso Sagone. Special Effects: Joseph Nathanson. Produced by Alberto Grimaldi for P.E.A. (Rome), Les Films Marceau (Paris), Cocinor (Paris). Eastmancolor, Scope, c. 40 minutes. Released in the United States September, 1969.

Cast

Toby Dammit	Terence Stamp
The priest, Father Spagna	Salvo Randone
The actress	Antonia Pietrosi
The blind old actor	Polidor
Actor (with sombrero) who greets Toby at the Oscar gathering	Rick Boyd
Woman with the actor	Marisa Traversi
1st director	Fabrizio Angeli
2nd director	Ernesto Colli
TV commentator	Anna Tonietti
1st interviewer	Aleardo Ward
2nd interviewer	Paul Cooper
The little devil-girl	Marina Yaru

"Ruby" sung by Ray Charles.

360 1968 A Director's Notebook (Block-Notes di un regista)
Story and screenplay: Fellini, Bernardino Zapponi.
Music: Nino Rota, conducted by Rota. Cinematography: Pas-
quale de Santis. Editing: Ruggero Mastroianni. Assistant
Editor: Adriana Olasio. Assistant Directors: Maurizio Mein,
Liliana Betti. Production Manager: Lamberto Pippia. Conti-
nuity: Norma Giacchero. Series Unit Manager: Joseph Nash.
Dialogue Director: Christopher Cruise. English Dialogue:
Eugene Walter. Produced by Peter Goldfarb for National Broad-
casting Company Productions International. Eastmancolor,
Scope, 54 minutes. Released in the United States in 1969.

Cast

Fellini	Himself
Marcello Mastroianni	Himself
Giulietta Masina	Herself
Professor Genius	Himself
Script Girl	Marina Boratto
Sadistic woman at gladiator games	Caterina Boratto
Archeology professor	David Maumsell
Cesarino	Cesarino Miceli Pi-cardi
Long-nosed boy who whistles	Alvaro Vitali
His mother	Lina Alberti

361 1969 Satyricon
Story and screenplay: Fellini, Bernardino Zapponi,
freely adapted from the novel of Petronius Arbiter. Music:
Nino Rota; Ilhan Mimaroglu, Tod Dockstader, Andrew Rubin;
and folk music. Cinematography: Giuseppe Rotunno. Camera-
man: Giuseppe Maccari. Editing: Ruggero Mastroianni. Assistant Editor: Adriana Olasio. Sets and costumes: Danilo
Donati. Set assistants: Dante Ferretti, Carlo Agate. Costume
assistants: Franco Antonelli, Renzo Bronchi, Dafne Cirrocchi.
Decor sketches: Fellini. Set Architect: Luigi Scaccianoce.
Production Manager: Roberto Cocco. Assistant Director:
Maurizio Mein. Assistants to the Director: Liliana Betti, Lia
Consalvo. Director's bodyguard: Ettore Bevilacqua. Conti-
nuity: Norma Giacchero. Still photography: Mimmo Cattari-
nich. Production Inspectors: Lamberto Pippia, Gilberto Scar-
pellini, Fernando Rossi. Production Secretary: Michele Pesce.
Scene painters: Italo Tommasi, Sante Barelli, Carlo Rissone,
Paolo Mugnai. Make-up Chief: Rino Carboni; assistant: Pier-
ino Tosi. Chief Hairdresser: Luciano Vito. Special effects:
Adriano Pischiutta. Chief Electricians: Rodolfo Bramucci,
Alvaro Romagnoli. Chief Stagehands: Salvatore Mazzini, Domenico Mattei. Property Chief: Raffaele Vincenti. Script
Editor: Enzo Ocone. Translator and consultant for Latin
language: Luca Canali. Executive Producer: Enzo Proven-
zale. Produced by Alberto Grimaldi for P.E.A. (Rome) and
Les Productions Artistes Associés (Paris). Technicolor, Pana-

vision, 127-138 minutes.   Released in France in December,
1969, and in the United States in April, 1970.

Cast

Encolpio   Martin Potter
Ascylto   Hiram Keller
Gitone   Max Born
Eumolpo   Salvo Randone
Trimalchio   Mario Romagnoli
                                                     (Il moro)
Vernacchio (the actor)   Fanfulla
Actor playing Caesar in Vernacchio's
   troupe   Alvaro Vitali
Fortunata (Trimalchio's wife)   Magali Noël
Lica (Lichas)   Alain Cuny
Scintilla (Fortunata's lesbian friend)   Danika La Loggia
Abinna (Habbinas)   Giuseppe San Vitale
Trifena (Lica's wife)   Capucine
Young emperor (killed with spears)   Tanya Lopert
Young Oenothea   Donyale Luna
Old Oenothea   Maria Antonietta Bel-
                                                     izi
Patrician suicide   Joseph Wheeler
His wife   Lucia Bosè
Slave girl at the suicide-couple's
   villa   Hylette Adolphe
Robber (who kidnaps hermaphrodite)   Gordon Mitchell
Dwarf   Silvio Belusci
Magician   Pasquale Fasciano
Magician's assistant   Patricia Hartley
Nymphomaniac wife   Sibilla Sedat
Her husband   Lorenzo Piani
Their slave   Luigi Zerbinati
Ferryman (who kills Ascylto)   Gennaro Sabatino
Hermaphrodite   Pasquale Baldassare
Widow of Ephesus   Antonia Petrosi
Soldier at her husband's tomb   Wolfgang Hillinger
Quadraplegic pilgrim   Antonio Moro
Proconsul at Minotaur game   Marcello Bifolco
Minotaur   Luigi Montefiori
Ariadne   Elisa Mainardi
Ship captain   Carlo Giordana
Rich freedman   Genius
Owner of Garden of Delights   Elio Gigante
Notary   Vittorio Vittori
Trifena's attendant   Suleiman Ali Nash-
                                                     nush
Transvestite   Luigi Battaglia
Brothel girl   Tania Duckworth
Very fat prostitute   Maria de Sisti

362 1970 I clowns
Story and screenplay: Fellini, Bernardino Zapponi.
Music: Nino Rota, conducted by Carlo Savina. Cinematography:
Dario di Palma. Cameraman: Blasco Giurato. Editing: Rug-
gero Mastroianni. Assistant Editor: Adriana Olasio. Cos-
tumes: Danilo Donati. Make-up: Rino Carboni. Hairstyles:
Paolo Francheschi. Scenery: Renzo Gronchi. Sound: Alberto
Bartolomei. Production Manager: Lamberto Pippia. Assis-
tant Directors: Maurizio Mein, Liliana Betti. Special effects:
Adriano Pischiutta. Continuity: Norma Giacchero. Produced
by Elio Scardamaglia and Ugo Guerra. A co-production of
R. A. I. (Rome), O. R. T. (Paris), Bavaria Film (Munich), and
Compagnie Leone Cinematografica (Rome). Technicolor, 90
minutes. Released in the United States c. June, 1971.

Cast

The Italian Clowns   Billi, Scotti, Fanfulla, Rizzo, Pis-
                              toni, Furia, Sbarra, Carini, Terzo,
                              Vingelli, Fumagalli, Zerbinati,
                              Reder, Valentini, Merli, the Four
                              Colombaioni, the Martanas, Maggio,
                              Janigro, Maunsell, Peverello, Sor-
                              rentino, Valdemaro, Bevilacqua.

The French Clowns   Alex, Père Loriot, Maïss, Bario,
                              Ludo, Charlie Rivel, Nino.

The Fellini Camera-
Crew Clowns

The dumb script-girl   Maya Morin
The dark-haired woman   Lina Alberti
The long-nosed soundman   Alvaro Vitali
The cameraman   Gasperino
The director   Fellini

and
Liana Orfei, Rinaldo Orfei, Nando Orfei, Franco Migliorini
(the lion tamer), Anita Ekberg, Pierre Etaix, Annie Fratellini,
Victor Fratellini, Victoria Chaplin, Jean Baptiste, Tristan
Rémy.

363 1972 Roma
Story and screenplay: Fellini, Bernardino Zapponi.
Music: Nino Rota, conducted by Carlo Savina. Cinematography:
Giuseppe Rotunno. Cameraman: Giuseppe Maccari. Editing:
Ruggero Mastroianni. Assistant Editor: Adriana Olasio.
Scenery and costumes: Danilo Donati. Production Manager:
Lamberto Pippia. Assistant Production Manager: Maurizio
Mein. Assistants: Paolo Pietrangeli, Tonino Antonucci. Con-
tinuity: Norma Giacchero. Scenery assistants: Giorgio Gio-

vannini, Fernando Giovannoni. Interior Decoration: Andrea
Fantacci. Scenery and costume assistants: Romano Massaro,
Rita Giacchero. Special effects: Andriano Pischiutta. Make-
up: Rino Carboni. Hairdresser: Amalia Paoletti. Cashier:
Arcangelo Picchi. Production Inspectors: Alessandro Gori,
Fernandro Rossi, Alessandro Sarti. Interpreter: Marie-Claude
Francine Decroix. Still photography: G. B. Poletto. Assis-
tant Cameraman: Piero Servo. Assistants: Roberto Aristarco,
Michele Picciaredda. Sound: Renato Cadueri. Frescoes and
portraits: Rinaldo, Antonello, Giuliano, Geleng. Choreography:
Gino Land. Scenery painting: Italo Tomassi. Executive Producer: Danilo Marciani. Produced by Ture Vasile. A co-
production of Ultra Films-S. P. A. (Rome) and Les Productions
Artistes Associés (Paris). Technicolor, 128 minutes (Italy),
119 minutes (elsewhere). Released in France in May 1972, in
the United States in October, 1972.

Cast

Fellini as an adult	Himself
Fellini as an 18-year-old	Peter Gonzales
Fellini as a child	Stefano Majore
The Princess	Pia de Doses
Cardinal Ottaviani	Renato Giovannoli
Dolores (the young prostitute)	Fiora Florence
Underground guide	Marne Maitland
Script-girl	Britta Barnes
Opening dancer in "Bolero" act at	
vaudeville show	Libero Frissi
Tap dancer imitating Fred Astaire	Alvaro Vitali
Cameo appearances by	Anna Magnani
	Gore Vidal
	Alberto Sordi (cut
	outside of Italy)
	Marcello Mastroian-
	ni (cut outside
	of Italy)

and
Angela de Leo, Elisa Mainardi, Galliano Sbarra, Mario del
Vago, John Francis Lane, Alfredo Adami, Bireno, Paule Rout,
Paolo Natale, Marcelle Ginette Bron.

364   1973 Amarcord
        Story and screenplay: Fellini, Tonino Guerra. Music:
Nino Rota, conducted by Carlo Savina. Cinematography: Giu-
seppe Rotunno. Cameraman: Giuseppe Maccari. Editing:
Ruggero Mastroianni. Assistant Editor: Adriana Olasio.
Scenery and costumes: Danilo Donati. Collaborating on the
costumes: Mario Ambrosino; on the scenery: Antonello Ge-
leng. Set Architect: Giorgio Giovannini. Production Manager:
Lamberto Pippia. Production Inspectors: Alessandro Gori,

Gilberto Scarpellini. Assistant Director: Maurizio Mein. Assistants to the Director: Liliana Betti, Gerard Morin, Mario Garriba. Continuity: Norma Giacchero. Make-up Chief: Rino Carboni. Chief Hairdresser: Amalia Paoletti. Special effects: Adriano Pischiutta. Scenery Painter: Italo Tomassi. Cashiers: Enzo Consolini, Enzo Lucarini. Interior Decoration: Andrea Fantacci. Production Secretaries: Fernando Rossi, Giuseppe Bruno Bossio. Costume Assistants: Rita Giacchero, Aldo Giuliani. Technical: Jean Paul de la Motte. Sound: Oscar de Arcangelis. Assistant Cameramen: Massimo di Venanzo, Roberto Aristarco. Still photography: Pierluigi. Dubbing Director: Mario Maldesi. Produced by Franco Cristaldi. An Italian-French Co-production: F.C. Productions (Rome), P.E.-C.F. (Paris). Technicolor, Panavision, 127 minutes. Released in the United States in October, 1974.

Cast

The Kids

Titta	Bruno Zanin
Conte Poltavo	Gianfranco Marrocco
Naso (with the long nose)	Alvaro Vitali
Ovo	Bruno Scagnetti
Gigliozzi	Bruno Lenzi
Il ciccio (the fatty)	Fernando de Felice
Candela (who gets blamed for urinating during the math class)	Francesco Vona
Aldina Cordini (the girl Fatty likes)	Donatella Gambini
Oliva, Titta's brother	Stefano Proietti

The Adults

Titta's mother	Pupella Maggio
Titta's father	Armando Brancia
Titta's grandfather	Peppino Ianigro
Il pataca, Titta's younger uncle	Nando Orfei
The maid at Titta's	Carla Mora
Titta's mad uncle, Teo	Ciccio Ingrassia
Gradisca	Magali Noël
The lawyer (the narrator)	Luigi Rossi
The tobacco-shopkeeper	Maria Antonella Beluzzi
Volpina	Josiane Tanzilli
Biscein (the lying peanut-vendor)	Gennaro Ombra
Don Balosa (the priest)	Gianfilippo Carcano
Giudizio	Aristide Caporale
The Fascist leader	Ferrucio Brembilla
Count Lovignano	Antonino Faà di Bruno
Countess Lovignano	Carmel Eusepi

The Teachers

Headmaster Zeus	Franco Magno
Philosophy teacher	Mauro Misul
Professor Fighetta	Armando Villella
Math teacher	Dina Adorni
Science teacher	Francesco Maselli
Italian teacher	Mario Silvestri
Art teacher	Fides Stagni
Gym teacher	Marcello Bonini
	Olas

The Others

Blind accordian player	Domenico Pertica
Madonna, the coachman	Fausto Signoretti
Colonia	Fredo Pistoni
Town clerk	Mario Nebolini
The emir (also the beggar)	Vincenzo Caldarola
Owner of the Fulgor Theatre	Mario Liberati
Gradisca's sister	Fiorella Magalotti
Gradisca's little sister	Marina Trovalusci
The photographer	Milo Mario
The Federale	Antonio Spaccatini
Gradisca's bridegroom	Bruno Bartocci
The mutilated war veteran	Marco Laurentino
Sensale	Riccardo Satta
The prince	Marcello di Falco
Gigino Penna Bianca (gigolo at the	
Grand Hotel)	Costantino Serraino
Cafe owner	Clemente Baccherini
also:	Mario del Vago

365 1976 Casanova
      Screenplay: Fellini, Bernardino Zapponi, freely drawn
from Giacomo Casanova's The Story of My Life. Music: Nino
Rota, conducted by Carlo Savina. Cinematography: Giuseppe
Rotunno. Editing: Ruggero Mastroianni. Set Design and costumes: Danilo Donati. Scenography conceived by Fellini.
Post-production coordinator: Enzo Ocone. Set Designers: Giantito Burchiellaro, Giorgio Giovannini; Assistant: Antonello
Geleng. Building Supervisor: Italo Tomassi. Scene painters:
Rinaldo and Giuliano Geleng. Frescoes by Master Painter Mar-
io Fallani. Magic Lantern Designer: Roland Topor. Set De-
corator: Emilio D'Andria. Assistants to the producer: Ales-
sandro von Normann, Mario di Biase. Production Supervisor.
Giorgio Morra. Production Manager: Lamberto Pippia. Pro-
duction Services: The Casanova Company. Assistant Director:
Maurizio Mein. Assistants to the Director: Liliana Betti,
Gerald Morin, Anita Sanders. Production Secretary: Norma
Giacchero. English Dialogue Directors: Frank Dunlop, Christopher Cruise. Casting: Paola Rolli. Costume Assistants:

Gloria Mussetta, Raimonda Gaetani, Rita Giacchero. Sculptures: Giovanni Gianese. Special Effects: Adriano Pischiutta. Make-up Chief: Rino Carboni. Mr. Sutherland's Make-up by Giannetto de Rossi, Fabrizio Sforza. Hairstylist: Gabriella Borzelli. Choreographer: Gino Landi. Dialogue Consultant: Anthony Burgess. English Translation: Christopher Cruise. Continuity: Norma Giacchero. Assistant Production Managers: Gilberto Scarpellini, Alessandro Gori, Fernando Rossi. Assistant Editors: Adriana Olasio, Marcello Olasio, Ugo de Rossi. Costumes Executed by Tirelli and Farani. Jewelry: Nino Lembo. Wigs: Rocchetti-Carboni. The Italian Voice of Giacomo Casanova: Luigi Proietti. Sound Mixer: Fausto Ancillai. Dubbing Assistant: Camilla Trinchieri. Still photography: Pierluigi Praturlon. Produced by Alberto Grimaldi for P.E.A. (Rome). The film was photographed in its entirety at Cinecittà Studios, Rome. Technicolor, 165 minutes. Released in the United States through Universal in February 1977.

Cast

Giacomo Casanova	Donald Sutherland
Sister Maddalena (the nun)	Margareth Clementi
Annamaria (the pale girl with fainting spells)	Clarissa Mary Roll
Giselda	Daniela Gatti
Madame D'Urfe (the old lady who wanted to be reborn as a man)	Cicely Browne
Marcolina (whose presence helped make Casanova virile for Mme. D'Urfe)	Clara Algranti
Du Bois (the hunchback and "Praying Mantis")	Daniel Emilfork Berenstein
Henriette (the cellist)	Tina Aumont
Giantess	Sandra Elaine Allen
Lord Talou	John Karlsen
Prince del Brando (who bets that his coachman is more virile than Casanova)	Hans van den Hoek
Girl the coachman has for his love partner	Carli Buchanan
Duke of Wurtenberg	Dudley Sutton
Faulkircher	Reggie Nalder
The Pope	Luigi Zerbinati
Casanova's mother	Marie Marquet
Doll woman	Adele Angela Lojodice
Madame Charpillon (the English whore)	Carmen Scarpitta
Casanova's brother	Nicolas Smith
Entomologist	Mario Cencelli
His daughter Olimpia	Olimpia Carlisi
The hunchback girl	Angelica Hansen
Countess of Waldenstein (who keeps the old Casanova as her librarian)	Marjorie Bell

PART II

SECONDARY SOURCES

A. BOOKS ON FELLINI'S WORK AS A WHOLE

366 Agel, Geneviève. Les chemins de Fellini. Paris: "7e Art"
Editions du Cerf, 1956. 159 p.
    One of the earliest works on Fellini's work as a whole and
still one of the most important. When Fellini was once asked
which critical work he felt was on-target about his films, he
replied this one of Agel's. She deals with his life, his "artistic temperament," his "mythology," his early film collabora-
tions, and his own films through Bidone, as well as having sections on "Giulietta-Gelsomina" and Nino Rota. There is an interview with Fellini. Fellini is asked, "The idea of the 'party'--
is this your equivalent of Pascal's 'divertissement'?" Fellini:
"Yes. They are the culminations of solitude: the Vitelloni
carnival, the La strada procession, the Bidone New Year's
Eve." There is a friendly preface by Rossellini: "For several
years we worked together very closely.... He abandons, he
dreams, then suddenly he awakes, ready to make his dreams
concrete, to act." This edition includes Dominique Delouche's
Journal d'un bidoniste. See 424.

367 _____. Federico Fellini. Brussels: Club du Livre du Cinéma, collection "Les grand créateurs du cinéma."
    Cited in Salachas, 395. We do not know the publication
date.

368 Angelini, Pietro. Controfellini: Il fellinismo tra restaurazione
e magia bianca. Milano: Ottaviano, 1974. 309 p.

369 Bachelis, Tat'yana Izrailevna. Fellini. Moscow: "Nauka"
["Science"], 1972. 384 p.
    A long, well-documented study of the films through Giuli-
etta. There is some primary source material not available
elsewhere since she had conversations with Fellini during his
visit to Moscow in July, 1963. With an introduction by People's
Artist S. A. Gerasimov.

370 Betti, Liliana. Federico Fellini: Ein Portrait. Trans. , Inez
De Florio-Hansen. Zürich: Diogenes-Verlag, 1976. 302 p.

371 Budgen, Suzanne. Fellini. London: British Film Institute,
1966. 128 p.
    For many years the only original book-length study in Eng-
lish on Fellini's films as a whole, and still one of the most
illuminating and most professional. Fully documented, through

Giulietta. Contains long extracts from the interviews on Belgian
television as well as long extracts from a discussion held at the
Centro Sperimentale di Cinematografia on the occasion of the
showing of Dolce vita. To this day, these are available in English only here in Budgen's book. There is also a sequence from
the La strada screenplay and a very extensive listing of the cast
and credits of the films. With 33 small photos.

372   Reviewed: Callenbach, Ernest. Film Quarterly, 20 (Spring,
           1967), 56-57.
                "This staunchly sensible explication of Fellini. " She
           is concerned not with making judgments but with trying to
           understand what Fellini's work is about. "In film criticism
           (as in most other kinds) this sort of enterprise is rare. "

373   Dewey, Lang. Film (London), 46 (Summer, 1966).
                Gives detailed description of the book. Calls it "a
           very fine handbook. " His only disappointment is with the
           quality of the reproduction of the stills.

374   Hodgkinson, A. W. "Fellini," Film Society Review, (Decem-
           ber, 1966), 35.

374A   Morley, S. Films and Filming, 13 (November, 1966), 59.

375   Taylor, John Russell. Sight and Sound, 35, n. 4, (Autumn,
           1966), 205.

376 Cró, Mario and Stelio. La temática de Fellini y la poética de
     Ocho y medio. Mar del Plata, Argentina: Editorial de Cultura
     Moderna, 1963. 70 p.
          A detailed synopsis of $8\frac{1}{2}$, then the sections "El vuelo y la
     caida," "El mago de Guido y el hipnotizador de Cabiria," "La
     poetica," "La confesion," and "El problema cultural. "

377 Del Buono, Oreste. Federico Fellini. Monza: Circolo Mon-
     zese del Cinema, 1965. 48 p.
          A brochure of the Circolo Monzese del Cinema, listed as
     Cinestudio n. 14.

378 Entretiens avec Federico Fellini. Texte extrait des émissions
     télévisées "La Double vue. " Co-production de la Cinémathèque
     de Belgique et du Service cinéma de la Radiodiffusion, télévision
     belge. Scénario: Théodore Louis. Réalisateur: André Del-
     vaux.. Interviewer: Dominique Delouche. Brussels: Radio-
     diffusion télévision belge, 1962. 66 p.
          Transcripts of telecasts of one-hour broadcasts by Belgian
     television, January 19, February 2, February 16, and March
     2, 1961. Indispensable. The interviews are not only with Fel-
     lini but with Michelangelo Antonioni, Camilla Cederna, Ennio
     Flaiano, Yvonne Furneaux, Piero Gherardi, Otello Martelli,
     Giulietta Masina, Marcello Mastroianni, Alberto Moravia, Pier

Paolo Pasolini, Pegoraro, Tullio Pinelli, Nino Rota, Alberto Sordi, Leopoldo Trieste, Mario Verdone, and Cesare Zavattini. The interviews exhibit verve and charm and are cogent, entertaining, and illuminating. Asked, "What is Fellini?" some of the answers were--Masina: "A husband." Sordi: "A eunuch with the sweet life about him!" Pegoraro: "A good country priest--perhaps a 'monsignore,' who shows interest, who understands, who listens, who gives advice." Thirty excellently produced photos, mostly of Fellini, many of which are unobtainable elsewhere, including a striking white on black self-portrait. Contains also a number of drawings by Fellini.

379 Federico Fellini: Articles, interviews, reviews, and reminiscences. Selected and with commentary by G. Bogemski'. Moscow: Iskusstvo, 1968. 286 p.
A large collection but with inadequate source data and no indication of what and where anything has been left out of some selection. In Russian translation. Useful, as everything is, when it comes to source material by or about Fellini, where so much has either not been collected systematically or is unavailable in the original. Especially valuable here for material on Fellini's 1963 visit to Moscow for the $8\frac{1}{2}$ showing. The 73 photos are very poor in quality, but here too, some are not easily available elsewhere: Fellini in 1938; Fellini and Riccardo Fellini in 1947; at the time of Paisà and Il miracolo; Giulietta and her Oscars; Fellini and Rota; Fellini and Mastroianni on the beach at the time of Dolce vita; Fellini and Giulietta in Moscow.

380 Fellini. L'Arc n. 45, Aix-en-Provence: L'Arc, 1971. 88 p.
The entire issue devoted to Fellini. Contains a foreword by Roger Borderie: "Dieu et son clown." (They wanted to show that Fellini has his own "discipline, way of working, a solid, necessary knowledge of technical imperatives belonging to the cinema."); "Fellini par lui-même" (44 statements by Fellini); "Rimini," Fellini's personal remarks about his home town; Jean Roudant, "Cortèges," his "walk" through the studios of Cinecittà; two questions from Alain Resnais, answered by Fellini; J. M. G. Le Clezio, "L'extra-terrestre" ("All his films relate the same drama: the discovery of the shame and corruption of the world of the adolescent. The adolescent isn't really a man; he is a kind of being from another world, who has come from the end of the universe with all his innocence, and whom the human-bestial-world simultaneously attracts and repels."); René Micha, "Toby Dammit"; comments and letters by Bernardino Zapponi, Henry Miller, Georges Simenon, and Max Born; a long study on Fellini's themes, "Le clair et l'obscur" by Micha; Robert Lapoujade, "Du montage au montrage"; Catherine Backes-Clement, "Le sanglier, ou une érudition déplacée" (on Satyricon); Marcel Martin, "Un artiste sous le chapeau: perplexe"; a brief filmography through Clowns; several drawings by Fellini, including a very striking one of Terence Stamp as Edgar Allan Poe; and a cover photo of Fellini wearing a clown's nose. Some

of the Fellini statements have been translated and reprinted in
Fellini on Fellini (see 112).

381   Reviewed: Ciment, Michel. Positif, n. 131 (October,
        1971), 78-79.

382 Goldberg, Toby. Federico Fellini: A Poet of Reality. Boston:
     Broadcasting and Film Division, Boston University, 1965. 115
     p.

383 Ketcham, Charles B. Federico Fellini: The Search for a New
     Mythology. The Imagemakers Studies in Religion and Arts Ser-
     ies. New York: Paulist Press, 1976. 94 p.
         A short, splendid, carefully documented study by a profes-
     sor of theology explicating and taking most seriously what he
     feels is the central theme of Fellini's films: "that the old sym-
     bols which have structured the lives and thoughts of Western
     culture are now ineffective and powerless, that we are beginning
     a new era in which these old symbols must be redefined or in
     which new symbols must be created or discovered." Ketcham
     includes along with Fellini, Buñuel, Bergman, Kubrick, and
     Pasolini, and adds, "In either case, such thinking on the part
     of such creative artists has prophetic implications for the re-
     ligious structures of Western culture and for those of us who,
     like these directors, feel the 'shaking of the foundations.'"

384 Kornatowska, Maria. Federico Fellini. Warsaw: Wydawnictwa
     Artystyczne i Filmowe, 1972. 212 p.
         Critical study in Polish of the films through Clowns. Syn-
     opses of La strada, Cabiria, 8½, Giulietta, and Satyricon. Ex-
     cerpts (in Polish translations) from various interviews with Fel-
     lini. Excerpts, also in Polish, from various critics, on Fel-
     lini's films. Contains a number of photos not easily available
     elsewhere.

385   Reviewed: Kino, 8 (June, 1973), 39.

386 Murray, Edward. Fellini the Artist. New York: Frederick
     Ungar, 1976. 256 p.
         A film-by-film analysis from Sceicco Bianco through Amar-
     cord. (He does not treat Luci del varietà or the short films.)
     The book is meant to appeal to "film students," "movie buffs,"
     and the "general reader." Very valuable for the very large
     number of pertinent, illuminating quotations from Fellini for ex-
     plicating the central meaning of the films. There is no docu-
     mentation--the quotes appear helter-skelter--but he has read
     most of Fellini's interviews and other writings in English, and
     many of Fellini's remarks are not easily available elsewhere.
     Demonstrates the value of collecting and organizing what Fellini
     says about his films, taking what he says seriously, and using
     his comments to explicate his films.

387   Reviewed: Limbacher, James L. Library Journal, 101
        (August, 1976), 1655.
            "Fellini is portrayed as a sensitive and observing ar-
        tist and the almost complete auteur of his films, despite
        the fact that cinema is a collaborative art. "

388 Pecori, Franco. Fellini. Firenze: La nuova Italia, 1974.
    133 p.
        He begins with eleven pages of quotations from Fellini,
    which he titles, "The Myth and the Rite: A Self-portrait. "
    Then he goes on to "The Rite and the Myth: Life and Works. "
    He uses a number of early Italian periodical sources that are
    not easily obtainable. He refers to Moraldo in città as "more
    than a story--a theme. " Cabiria is "Gelsomina on the streets. "
    He has a brief section on Fellini in the hospital ("The Crisis
    of 1967") and its significance for his films at the time. His
    last section is called "Moraldo Returns to Rimini: Amarcord. "

389 Personale di Federico Fellini. Rome: Cineforum Romano,
    1966.
        A brochure.

390 Renzi, Renzo. Federico Fellini. Parma: Guanda, 1956. 63 p.
        Short but very important. By an editor of several of Fel-
    lini's screenplays, a long-time authority on the films, and a
    personal friend. "If there is an Italian director whose own life
    story we need right at the start to relate, it is Fellini, who has
    made his own life the direct source of his films. " Everything
    in Fellini's life has been as though "lived for the sake of telling
    stories about. " About a third of the material is on Fellini's
    life and career prior to Dolce vita. The rest goes through Ca-
    biria. The book was reissued in 1961 with an added section on
    Dolce vita.

391 _____. Federico Fellini. Trans. P. L. Thirard. Lyon:
    "Premier Plan" n. 12, 1960.
        French translation of 390, with an added section on Dolce
    vita.

392 Rondi, Brunello. Il cinema di Fellini. Rome: Edizioni di
    Bianco e nero, 1965. 418 p.
        By far the longest study (in any language) of Fellini's work.
    Rondi has been associated with Fellini in one way or another,
    on La strada, Dolce vita, $8\frac{1}{2}$, and Giulietta. He says in his
    preface, "I have refused, on purpose, to deal in biographic in-
    discretions or anecdotal nonsense, since on Federico Fellini
    there are already too many of these circulating in the world. "
    He has also declined to write anything on culture in general
    that doesn't firmly reside in the living body of each film and
    that isn't connected, from film to film, specifically, to the cre-
    ative history of their creator. Except for two introductory
    chapters on Fellini as a man and personality, he has preferred

to let the films speak for themselves. He handles the films,
chapter by chapter, from Luci del varietà through Giulietta.
There are 80 photos, some of them not easily available elsewhere, also a concise filmography.

393 Rosenthal, Stuart. The Cinema of Federico Fellini. South
Brunswick, N. J. and New York: A. S. Barnes, 1976. 190 p.
   One of the longest single studies of Fellini's work as-a-
whole in English (though not very long, and a third of the book
is photos, which indicates the state of serious book-length work
on Fellini even after a career that spans thirty years.) Rosenthal regards his study not as an "exhaustive analysis" but "rather a guide." He does not handle Fellini film-by-film but through
interweaving themes, approaches, camera style and--really--
whatever; so that the book is in fact a long unorganized commentary. It is, however, chock full of insights. He maintains
that Fellini's films are not repetitive but "in a continuous state
of growth and evolution." Fellini is fond of all the people he
uses in his films, and it is his consistent belief that "every
human life is valuable and interesting." In the ecclesiastical
fashion show in Roma, Fellini is attacking a definite group of
people who are "recognizable" (at least to Italian audiences)
down to individuals. The apparition at the end is Pius XII. In
Dolce vita there is an automobile leitmotif: "Cars, their oc-
cupants and styles of driving become clues to Marcello's relationships."
   Rosenthal interviewed Fellini shortly after Roma was released. Earlier, Fellini had had much hope for the hippie
movement: "Remember, I lived through fascism, and here was
a group of people to which those ideas were completely foreign.
But look at them. What are they doing? Where are they
going?" Rosenthal says that Fellini's treatment of hippies in
Roma is "his most flagrant dismissal of a phenomenon he does
not understand." The fading of the frescoes is the film's
"centerpiece" and is a metaphor for Fellini's fear of the new
values undermining and replacing the old ones. Rosenthal interprets Amarcord as a hardening of Fellini's attitude toward
the people of his youth "as he recognizes the roots of fascism
in their smallmindedness." Amarcord is a "hostile satire."
In the attitudes of the townspeople Fellini sees "the roots of an
empty, dangerous, intolerant chauvinism." The entire community is "ensconced in stupid, childish illusions" and so fascism
can easily thrive there. He finds most of the characters in
Amarcord "contemptible." But he says that Fellini's values
have not changed; he is still concerned about the individual.
The film is not really political or ideological, but Fellini here
has begun to deal "with larger problems." There are 120
black-and-white, non-glossy stills and a filmography that includes one of the most complete listings of cast and characters
yet published.

394 Salachas, Gilbert. Federico Fellini. Paris: Seghers, 1963.
224 p.

A Cinéma d'aujourdhui collection. See English translation, 395.

395 _____. Federico Fellini. Trans. Rosalie Siegel. New York: Crown, 1969. 224 p.

Small in format, it is still one of the most extensive and exceptionally illuminating collections of remarks by and about Fellini available in English. (Original edition was 1963.) About a third of the book is a long essay on Fellini by Salachas. About a fifth is a "Critical Spectrum," excerpts from critical writings on Fellini and his films: by Agel, Solmi, Aubier, Bazin, Renzi, and others, plus "witnesses" of Fellini at work: Martelli, Mastroianni, Périer, Pinelli, and Rossellini. The rest of the text consists of remarks by Fellini himself and excerpts from various of his screenplays. There is some very important source material not easily available elsewhere: parts of Il Matto's speech in La strada not included in the film; the Man with the Sack scenes omitted from Cabiria; and a project for an unrealized film, The Free Women of Magliano.

396 Reviewed: Crowdus, Gary. Cinéaste, 11, n. 4 (Spring, 1969), 22.

397 Harcourt, Peter. Cinema Journal, 9 n. 2. (Spring, 1970), 48-51.

398 Mamber, Stephen. Cinema, 5, n. 2, 43.

399 Rehrauer, George. Cinema Booklist. Metuchen, N. J.: Scarecrow Press, 1972, No. 407.

"The quality of the writing throughout is exceptionally high. The long essay is quite objective, but most respectful."

400 Publishers Weekly, 195 (January 27, 1969), 98.

"M. Salachas knows Fellini personally, and his essay provides insight into the films through many little personal touches."

401 Film Quarterly, 23 (Fall, 1969), 62.

A short, unfavorable review. Calls the lead essay "rhapsodic" and "idiotic". The rest of the book is deemed "readable" but "hardly essential."

402 International Film Guide, 7 (1970), 395-396.

403 Sega, Ercole. Federico Fellini: amico e regista. Bologna: 1963. 14 p.

A brochure of the Rotary Club of Bologna.

404 Solmi, Angelo. Storia di Federico Fellini. Milano: Rizzoli, 1962. 237 p.

See English translation, 405.

405   _____. Fellini. Trans. Elizabeth Greenwood. Atlantic
Highlands, N. J. : Humanities Press, 1968. 183 p.
         Though not oriented to film technique and though not a high-
brow approach (perhaps, indeed, because of these characteris-
tics), Solmi's is probably the best book-length introduction to
Fellini available in English to date (1977).   From the beginnings through $8\frac{1}{2}$.   Part I gives Fellini's biography, career, the
themes of his films.   Part II, besides giving in some detail the
history and background of each film and Fellini's problems with
producers, gives a detailed synopsis of each film, and the critical and commercial reaction to the film.   There is no foot-
note reference material, in either the Italian or English edition;
and the book gives the impression of almost having been written
off the top of Solmi's head.   But this is not so.   He has made
use of many sources, secondary and primary, many in Italian
publications not easily available to American critics, or at least
not used by them.   An early admirer of Fellini's work, Solmi
has been personally close to Fellini; and his book is studded
with valuable, non-hifalutin, insights, many of which are butt-
ressed by confirmatory conversations with Fellini alluded to
throughout the text.   With 28 very clear photos, several of Fellini as a young man and child not easily available elsewhere.

406   Reviewed: Times Literary Supplement, June 22, 1967, 557.
         "The original Italian version of Signor Solmi's book is
a good, straightforward, bio-critical study of Fellini and
his work. "

407   Film Quarterly, 21 n. 4 (Summer, 1968), 56.
         "Badly designed and printed, yet probably the best book
on Fellini so far. "

408   Action, 3 (November-December, 1968), 6, 46.

409   Choice, 5 (1969), 1458.
         "A thoroughly respectable book by a man who has been
close to Fellini. " Solmi's "moderate tone" about a "flamboyant film personality" is "refreshing. "

410   Film Comment, 6, n. 1 (Spring, 1970), 75.
         A short favorable review. A "welcome addition" to the
expanding literature on Fellini.

411   Harcourt, Peter. Cinema Journal, 9, n. 2 (Spring, 1970),
48-51.

412   McDonald, Gerald D. Library Journal, 93 (October 1, 1968),
3575.
         "A superb introduction to the films and to their crea-
tor. "

413   Manchel, Frank. Film Society Review, 4, n. 8, 42-43.

414   Morley, Sheridan. Films and Filming, 13, n. 12 (Septem-
           ber, 1967), 46.

415   Rehrauer, George. Cinema Booklist, Metuchen, N. J. :
           Scarecrow Press, 1972, no. 408.
               "The biographical portion of the text is affectionate,
           respectful, and tends to be factual rather than analytical. "

416   Tauber, Christian. Federico Fellini--Rom. Julien Green--
       Paris. Zürich: Juris-Verlag, 1971. 152 p.
           A professional Jungian analysis: "an investigation into the
       unconscious of artists with a strong mother-relationship. " (Tau-
       ber's study is in two parts: one on Fellini, one on Julien
       Green.) Many men remain tied to their mothers or to a mother-
       substitute. In such cases there can develop on the one hand,
       homosexuality, on the other, a Don Juan complex, and some-
       times impotence. "This vicious circle, whereby the effeminate
       man attaches himself to the dominating personality of the woman,
       obviously is part of the problem of the present age and appears
       most clearly and conspicuously in centers of culture like Rome
       and Paris. "

B. BOOKS ON INDIVIDUAL FILMS

417 Benderson, A. E. Critical Approaches to Federico Fellini's
8½. New York: Arno Press, 1974. 239 p.
    Indispensable. A Ph. D. dissertation. The longest published
professional study of a single Fellini film in any language. A
close "reading" of the film, replete with insight upon insight.
Contains too a section, "The Pinocchio Motif in 8½," which documents most effectively this aspect of the film. His Chapter
III is a Jungian, archetypal analysis. He points out that according to Jung, Maya is the name of Buddha's mother and takes
on the aspect of an archetypal mother figure; and the Magician's
mind-reading assistant in the film is named Maya. His last
chapter relates 8½ to Fellini's other films through Roma.

418   Reviewed: Geduld, Harry M. Quarterly Journal of Speech,
         61 (December, 1975), 476.
             "Benderson's treatise on Fellini's 8½ supplies us with
         a full-length methodology of critical interpretation. "

419 Boyer, Deena. The Two Hundred Days of 8½. Trans. , Charles
Lam Markmann. New York: Macmillan, 1964. 218 p.
    Surely one of the most fascinating works written about Fel-
lini's work and a delight in its own right. She had complete
on-the-set freedom from April, 1962, through January, 1963.
After this book it is surprising that anyone can fail to get things
straight about 8½. She gives a number of illuminating descriptions of variant sequences for the film. Fellini keeps turning
away young people looking for parts: "This picture is full of
old people. " The importance of the space ship idea and of man
leaving earth: "It's a way of saying that Guido's own troubles
are part of a much broader crisis that touches everyone, and
that under these conditions there's nothing to do but abandon
earth and start over elsewhere. " Carla is Saraghina transposed
to the time of Guido's manhood. The music heard at the Spa
is the kind heard in every Italian spa in the 30s. The people
are dressed in the style of 1930 as a way of projecting into the
present, Guido's childhood memories, with which he is presently
obsessed. The statue of the cardinal in the court is modeled on
that of the cardinal in the film; the statue of the Virgin, on
Caterina Boratto. The words that constantly recur in Fellini's
instructions to Saraghina for her second meeting with young
Guido are "warm" and "motherly. " An alternate line that Guido
says for the finale is, "I would like to kiss you all, and ask
your forgiveness. " There are fifty photos and an Afterword by
Dwight Macdonald (see 1015).

419A   Reviewed: Film Comment, 2 (Fall, 1964), 61.

420   Halpern, Henry. Library Journal, October 1, 1964.
          The book is a "skillful" report and a "valuable addition"
          to understanding film.

421   Rehrauer, George. Cinema Booklist. Metuchen, N. J. :
          Scarecrow Press, 1972, n. 1392.
          The book has a "certain importance" as a "well-pro-
          duced" diary of the making of a film classic.

421A   Weinberg, Herman. Film Culture, 38 (Fall, 1965), 73-
          75.

422   _____. Die 200 tage von $8\frac{1}{2}$. Hamburg, 1963.
          The German version of 419. Boyer writes in both French
          and Italian, and presumably there is a French and/or an Italian
          version too.

423   Casanova. Zürich: Diogenes-Verlag, in preparation 1976.
          Fellini's "most hateful and most heralded" ladies' men.
      With an essay by Stefan Zweig, selections from Casanova's Mem-
      oirs, writings from D. H. Lawrence through Fellini, and inter-
      views with modern Casanovas and social scientists.

424   Delouche, Dominique. Journal d'un bidoniste. In Geneviève
      Agel, Les Chemins de Fellini. Paris: "7e Art," Editions du
      Cerf, 1956.
          Indispensable, especially since there is so little on this neg-
      lected film of Fellini's. Fellini personally invited Delouche to
      be with him while he made the film. He interviews a real swin-
      dler (whom Fellini calls Lupaccio), on whom Fellini modeled
      Augusto. Delouche asks him, "What do you expect from life?"
      He answers, "A piece of work. " "What do you think of death?"
      "Being set free. A life like mine is not a thing of joy. You
      are not a Bidoniste for pleasure. " Delouche asks Fellini what
      actor he would have liked to direct. Fellini: "Charlot. " Whom
      would he have liked to meet? "Jesus, Cagliostro, St. Francis,
      Satan. "

425   Estève, Michel, ed. Federico Fellini: $8\frac{1}{2}$. Etudes Cinéma-
      tographiques, n. 28-29, (Winter, 1963), 86 p.
          A model of criticism both in judgement and scholarship,
      priceless in value when it first came out (within months of the
      release of the film!) and still splendidly illuminating. Replete
      with references to remarks by Fellini and citations from special-
      ized sources, all with full footnoted documentation. Particularly
      valuable for placing Fellini in the framework of literary and ar-
      tistic culture in general and not simply in the area of cinema.
      The entire double issue is devoted to $8\frac{1}{2}$. Estève: "From the
      very start" it won back to Fellini a great number of those who
      had progressively abandoned him after loving Sceicco bianco and

Vitelloni. For ten years his early critical success had slowly
declined and reached its lowest point with Dr. Antonio. "Now
$8\frac{1}{2}$ has demonstrated, magisterially, that we had been mistaken
in thinking that Fellini had no more to say." The articles contained are Barthelemy Amengual, "Itineraire de Fellini: du
spectacle au soi-même"; Alain Virmaux, "Les limites d'une
conquête"; Guido Aristarco, "L'intellectuel, l'artiste et le télé-
pathe"; Nicole Zand, "Mauvaise conscience d'une conscience
chrétienne"; Jean Collet, "Le plus long chemin"; and Christian
Jacotey, "Bilan critique." There are also selections from critics from Italy, Russia, and Uruguay, and a filmography,
through $8\frac{1}{2}$, by Vincent Pinel.

426   Hughes, Eileen Lanouette. On the Set of Fellini Satyricon: A
       Behind-the-Scenes Diary. New York: William Morrow, 1971.
       248 p.
           Indispensable for any study of Satyricon, or for Fellini's
       films in general, for that matter, and fascinating to read in its
       own right. She spent six months on-and-off the set with Fellini,
       taking down just about everything he or his crew said, including
       much of Fellini's scatalogical phraseology. Fellini seemed to
       like her personally and gave her very full freedom. She notes
       variant scenes shot but not included in the final film. She gives
       details on Fellini's near-fatal 1967 illness. She quotes Zapponi
       on Mastorna: "For Fellini, a film of death. He became ashen
       whenever we talked about it." Fellini on Encolpius and Ascyltus:
       "two breakneck kids with completely unhinged lives and panero-
       tic dreams." To Max Born (Giton): "You are evil and vulgar
       and cynical, and you lay everything in sight." Fellini is said
       to have included the suicide scene because the history of that
       period is full of suicides: not only Petronius himself but Seneca
       and even some of the emperors. Hughes to Fellini: "Why are
       there so many monsters in this picture?" Fellini: "But they
       are not monsters. They are innocent. You are less innocent."
       Fellini describes Born (Giton) as "a whore with the face of an
       angel." Fellini says that the Trimalchio's banquet scene was
       inspired by Fellini's childhood memories "of certain appalling
       dinners of the peasants of Romagna." Alain Cuny, asked if
       there was a connection between the character of Steiner and
       Lichas, replies: "I believe Steiner was a homosexual who mar-
       ried only to give a certain legitimacy to his position, but he was
       an unconscious homosexual. Lichas knows he is a homosexual
       and is happy with it, and that is the difference between the two
       civilizations."

427   Reviewed: Choice, 8 (June, 1971), 568.
           "Fellini is as much a mystery after reading the book
       as before." The book is "tedious" and basically "uninforma-
       tive."

428   Palmer, J. W. Library Journal, 96 (January 1, 1971), 96.
           This book has "value" as a "historical record." But
       much of it is "trivial" and is a "bore."

429 Perry, Ted. Filmguide to 8½. Bloomington: Indiana Univer-
     sity Press, 1975. 89 p.
        Indispensable. The single most concisely useful explication
     of the film in English. Indispensable from another aspect too:
     to show how splendidly one can provide insight upon insight into
     a work of art and then to conclude by missing the artist's point
     completely. (He thinks that 8½ may legitimately have two end-
     ings: Guido's suicide and Guido-in-the-finale and that this is
     not only "quite acceptable" but "helps to illuminate the work.")
     There is a credit and cast listing (exceptionally complete),
     a scene-by-scene outline, a brief description of Fellini's career,
     production notes, an annotated bibliography, and a long, close,
     splendid analysis, scene-by-scene, explicating the film. Guido
     is "a man surrounded." The central concern of the film is
     Guido's "confrontation with himself." He has fine original in-
     sights into the strange buzzing sounds throughout much of the
     film. (They are like the buzz of motion picture arc lights;
     they give a disturbing effect and function "as an event in the
     film and about the process of filmmaking itself.") He lists and
     partly explicates every instance of the various musical themes
     used in the film. Questions are continually being asked in the
     film by someone or other but not answered. The camera often
     holds Guido relentlessly within the confines of the frame. At
     other times, it is a case of the camera-as-Guido. For the
     most part, Guido remains "trapped by the moving camera."
     He is being "pursued by people who make demands upon him,
     pushing for decisions and commitments." In the film Guido's
     prowess as an artist is equated with Guido's prowess as a lover.
     For Guido "to be creative is to be potent." The harem is
     "not just the place where there is peace and order" but where
     Guido is "able to perform, to choose, to decide ... the way in
     which he directs the dance ... at the end of the film." But he
     interprets the scene with the Cardinal (in the steam room) as
     "blatantly comic" and maintains that the choice that the Cardinal
     demands, between the City of God and the City of the Devil,
     "has nothing directly to do with Guido as an individual human
     being."

430   Reviewed: Kauffmann, S. New Republic, 173 (July 26,
     1975), 35.
        Perry's Filmguide to 8½ is one of the more "worth-
     while" filmguides that have been issued. It is written "with
     feeling and insight." A big asset is its "scene by scene"
     description of the film.

431 Price, Theodore. Fellini's Penance: The Meaning of Amar-
     cord. Old Bridge, N. J.: Boethius Press--Cinema Division,
     1977.
        A scene-by-scene commentary and explication. "The whole
     movie is in fact the 53-year-old Fellini's form of prayer, his
     Our Father and Hail Mary, asking forgiveness for his pranks
     (his little acts of unkindness) against the old and the middle-

aged (who are now dead or dying), committed when he was too young to know better, to know the sorrows and hardships that older folk are subject to, but which he can now appreciate all too well, since he is now one of them. " It is "the work of a middle-aged man, thinking about winter and wishing for spring. "

432 Renzi, Renzo, ed. I clowns. Bologna: Cappelli, 1970. 406 p. Indispensable source material. In three parts. Part I contains: Fellini's "Un viaggio nell' ombra"; Oreste Del Buono's, "Da Fortunello a Giudizio, passando per Little Nemo"; Bernardino Zapponi "A Parigi, una recherche del circo perduto"; Tristan Remy, "Splendore e decadenza dei clowns"; Liliana Betti, "Un' entrata di Federico e le rivelazioni di un maghino intrance"; and Ornella Volta, "Breve dizionario enciclopedia dei clowns. " Part II: Anthology of writings on clowns, including Dickens, Grimaldi, Gautier, Baudelaire, Appollinaire, Cocteau, Jarry, Kafka, Copeau, the Fratellinis, J. L. Barrault, Chaplin, Groucho Marx, Red Skelton, and Marcel Marceau. Part III: The screenplay of Clowns. Profusely and beautifully illustrated with hundreds of large-format illustrations, in color and black-and-white, of circus clowns and scenes from Fellini's film. Introduction by Renzo Renzi, "La testa nel secchio. "

C. SECTIONS OF BOOKS ON FELLINI'S WORK AS A WHOLE

433 Agel, Henri. "Federico Fellini," Le Cinéma et le Sacré.
Paris: "7e Art" Editions du Cerf, 1961, 120-127.
An important study, too often neglected by American film
critics. Although the selection on Fellini is brief and treats
his films only through Dolce vita, the whole book, (including an
Afterword by Father A. Ayfre), casts light on Fellini's work.
La strada, says Agel, is most of all the expression of the
Christian theme, "the fruitfulness deriving from innocence
crushed." The film retraces "the mission of the completely
compassionate, completely bruised being who has to take up this
suffering in order to redeem, according to the logic of the
saints, Zampanò's soul, the prisoner of his own dark ignorance."
It is the same in Bidone. The only thing that can save Augus-
to's soul is "the suffering of the innocents" (the poor people on
whom he has preyed), especially the paralytic girl. Cabiria is
in one sense "an apotheosis of Fellinian dialectic and mythology."
But the Fellinian anguish of Dolce vita would be for Agel noble
and moving only if it "maintained an equilibrium between horror
and fascination." But here Fellini "hands himself over to his
private demons so that they may devour him."

434 Baldelli, Pio. Cinema dell'ambigvità: Rossellini, De Sica e
Zavattini, Fellini. Rome: Samona e Savelli, 1969. 400 p.

435 Bazin, André. "Cabiria: the voyage to the end of neorealism,"
What Is Cinema? Vol. II. Trans. Hugh Gray. Berkeley and
Los Angeles: University of California Press, 1967.
English translation of the essay in 436. Bazin calls the
final shot, where Cabiria turns toward the camera and her glance
crosses ours, "the true equal" of Chaplin's best inventions.
"As far as I know, Chaplin is the only man in the history of film
who made successful systematic use of this gesture, which the
books about filmmaking are unanimous in condemning."

436 _____ . Qu'est-ce que le Cinéma? IV. Une esthetique de la
Réalité: le néo-realisme. Paris: "7e" Editions du Cerf, 1962.
Contains five essays on Fellini's films by this very famous
and influential French critic. (The whole volume, has relevance
to Fellini.) "La strada" (Esprit, May, 1955); "Il bidone ou le
salut en question" (France-Observateur, March, 1956); "Cabiria
ou le voyage au bout du néo-réalisme" (Cahiers du Cinéma, n.
76, November, 1957); "La profonde originalité des Vitelloni"
(Radio-Cinéma-Télévision, October, 1957); and "L'Amour a la
ville" (Cahiers du Cinéma, March, 1957). Of La strada: As

113

with Chaplin's Limelight, "we could say that cinema was the
only adequate incarnation, that it was inconceivable in any other
medium, and that yet utterly transcended the technique of a particular art form. " Of Bidone: Although this film didn't quite
come off, it left him convinced of the Fellini genius manifested
in La strada. Fellini's latest film left him with a feeling of
"a poetic and moral vision in no way inferior to La strada or
Vitelloni. " If he had to compare the Fellinian universe to that
of a novelist's, it would be to that of Dostoyevsky's. Cabiria:
See 435. Vitelloni: He's just seen the film again. It has not
only "not gone out of style" but has "ripened" in perspective "as
if the message that it bore then hadn't managed to reveal to its
time its full worth and that we had to weigh its import. " Agenzia matrimoniale: Fellini is good "without being purely Fellinian. "

437 Bory, Jean-Louis. "Pour et contre Fellini," Les Yeux pour
     Voir: Cinéma I. Paris: Union Générale d'Editions, 1971.

438 Carpi, Fabio. Cinema Italiano del Dopoguerra. Milano:
     Schwarz, 1958, Chapter 7.

439 Chiarini, Luigi. Panorama del Cinema Contemporaneo (1954-
     1957). Rome: Edizioni di Bianco e Nero, 1957, 139-148.

440 Cowie, Peter. 50 Major Film-Makers. New York: A. S.
     Barnes, 1975.

441 Fallaci, Oriana. "Federico Fellini: Famous Italian Director,"
     Limelighters. London: Michael Joseph, 1967.

442 Favazza, Armando. "Fellini, Analyst without Portfolio," Man
     and the Movies, ed. W. R. Robinson, Louisiana: Louisiana
     State University Press, 1967.
         Favazza is a professional psychiatrist. The "upside-down-
     horse-on-the-raft symbol" in Giulietta, he says, is derived
     from Picasso's Guernica. The theme of La strada is "sadomas-
     ochism (complete with chains.)" Dolce vita is "a confused pro-
     jection by Fellini on a society that never was. " In 8½ Fellini
     has relieved his own pathological depression, thereby regaining
     respect, reassurance and affection, "a form of public approval
     of a personal illness. " As Fellini progresses, he will confess
     more, "with the audience as priest-absolver. " But his films
     will probably seem duller and less interesting. Fellini is typical
     of most Latin males. Favazza says that in Northern Italy there
     is a strong anti-clerical feeling and a notion that priests carry
     the mal occhio, the Evil Eye, which can be warded off "only by
     touching one's testicles. " That's why, says Favazza, "so many
     Italian men have their hands in their pockets when they pass a
     priest. "

443 Gregor, Ulrich. "Federico Fellini," Wie sie Filmen. Guter-
     sloh: Sigbert Mohn Verlag, 1966, 54-78.

444 Gregor, Ulrich and Enno Patalas. Geschichte des Films. Mu-
     nich: C. Bettelmann Verlag, 1973, 333-336.
        From Luci del varietà through Dr. Antonio. In Vitelloni
     a "Chekhov-like melancholy" hovers over the story of unevent-
     ful loves. The protagonists of Vitelloni and La strada too are
     less characters of an objective reality as they are personifica-
     tions of an inner attitude, a materialization of a spiritual re-
     ality. Cabiria also is a figure of allegory. She suffers not so
     much from being a prostitute or from being poor, but from a
     kind of spiritual emptiness. The waitress in Dolce vita is a
     "sister" to Gelsomina and Cabiria. And that film too mirrors
     the loneliness found in Vitelloni, La strada and Bidone: The
     frantic searching by the crowd for miracles "is only the other
     side of the loneliness of the individual. For Fellini's charac-
     ters the only way out of the prison of their isolation lies
     through God, the recourse to grace."

445 Haller, Robert. Three Motion Picture Directors. Notre Dame,
     1964.

446 Harcourt, Peter. Six European Directors: Essays on the
     Meaning of Film Style. Baltimore, Md.: Penguin, 1974, 183-
     213.
        An analysis of the films from Vitelloni through Roma. Fel-
     lini's fears seem "largely sexual." In all his films he has been
     attracted to the "androgynous" figure of the clown. Even his
     wife Giulietta looked this way in La strada. And in Giulietta
     the heroine loses her husband "because she cannot play her sex-
     ual role." In Toby Dammit for the first time there is an evil
     child that lures the central character to his death. And this
     child, with her eerie smile, bears "an uncanny resemblance"
     to Gelsomina. He notes the "slightly sinister Gioconda smile"
     that Fellini's characters have assumed over the years. It ap-
     pears on the young suicide in Giulietta, who killed herself for
     love. It appears on Giton and on others in Satyricon. After
     sex, disaster often strikes. After Encolpius and Giton's night
     of love the building collapses and "stones its inhabitants to
     death." In general, he calls Fellini "a great muddle-headed
     irrationalist with very strong feelings and no clear thought."
     In the latest films, but especially in Roma, there is "imagina-
     tive emptiness." He points out the significance of the final ti-
     tle of $8\frac{1}{2}$, coming as it does after Guido's becoming free to
     direct his films: "Fellini $8\frac{1}{2}$. Created and directed by Federi-
     co Fellini."

447 Joseph, Rudolph S., ed. "Der Regisseur Federico Fellini,"
     Hervorragende Filmgestalter. Munich: Münchner Stadtmuseum.

448 Kinder, Marsha and Beverle Houston. Close-Up: A Critical
     Perspective on Film. New York: Harcourt, Brace, Jovano-
     vich, 1972.
        A matter-of-fact retelling of the story of $8\frac{1}{2}$, with some
     explication. This is a popular textbook for college film courses.

449 Leprohon, Pierre. The Italian Cinema. Trans. Roger Greaves
     and Oliver Stallybrass. New York: Praeger, 1972, 117-118,
     141-147, 168-170.
        Contains a long, on-target, quotation by Fellini about Dolce
     vita. He was trying to "dedramatize" aspects of the world we
     live in and so get us used to "facing up to our monsters, one
     after the other. " He wanted to get "outside" of our own times.
     Once he arrived at his original title, Babylon 2000, "everything
     fell into place. " Dolce vita ties in with all his previous films.
     He has always been "passionately interested in human anguish. "
     He is fascinated by modern man's contradictions: "a frenzied,
     anguished, exciting life--and a terrible, hidebind motionless
     void. " In all the apparent excitement, "there is no room for
     faith. " He intended Dolce vita as "a cry of anguish" that would
     shake modern man from his "lethargy. " He unfolded his film
     against a panorama of funerals and ruins. "But these ruins
     are swathed in a light so splendid, so joyous, and so golden
     that life acquires a peculiar and endearing sweetness, even if
     the ruins collapse and block our paths. " Leprohon describes
     Dolce vita as "different scenes in a series of frescoes. " The
     meaning emerges "from the sum rather than from the parts. "
     The characters "flutter around Marcello like the figures and
     contradictions of the modern world. " The book contains brief
     biographical notes on Claudia Cardinale, Gianni di Venanzo,
     Aldo Fabrizi, Ennio Flaiano, Otello Martelli, Giulietta Masina,
     Tulio Pinelli, Nino Rota and Alberto Sordi.

450 Linden, George W. Reflections on the Screen. Belmont,
     Calif. : Wadsworth Publishing Co. , 1970, 10, 231, 258-263.

451 Lizzani, Carlo. ["The Problem of Fellini,"] Storia del Cinema
     Italiano 1895-1961. Firenze: Parenti Editore, 1961.

452 McAnany, Emile G. and Robert Williams. The Filmviewer's
     Handbook. Glen Rock, N. J. : Deus Books, 1965.

453 Munzi, Ulderico. Matusa. Roma: Il Sagittario, 1968.
        Contains a biographical profile on Fellini.

454 Nemeskürty, Istvan. A Filmmüveszet Nagykoruságe. Budapest:
     Gondolat, 1966.

455 Ortmayer, Roger. "Fellini's Film Journey," Three European
     Directors: Truffaut, Fellini, Buñuel. ed. James M. Wall.
     Grand Rapids, Mich. : Wm. B. Eerdmans Publishing Co. , 1973,
     65-108.
        Fellini's films as films, not as literature, stage drama, so-
     ciology, psychology, "or-heaven help us-theology. " Gelsomina
     "is as water," which in La strada has "a sacramental pres-
     ence. " She is "a holy one, being born from the waters and
     returning to them on death. She hears secretive sounds. She
     is aware of fire. She is close to the soil, planting tomatoes,

though she will not be around to harvest them. " He compares Fellini's aristic progression to Michelangelo's: "The difference between the Sistine Chapel ceiling and The Last Judgement is something like the jump from Sceicco bianco to Satyricon. Satyricon is not easy to take; neither is The Last Judgement. . . . Like the popes of the Council of Trent, who found The Last Judgement too carnal and too disturbing, many critics have assigned Fellini to oblivion for being both too sensual and too esoteric. "

456 Rondi, Gian Luigi. Cinema Italiano Oggi. Rome: Bestetti, 1966.

457 ____. Italian Cinema Today. New York: Hill and Wang, 1966, 92-111.

458 Sarris, Andrew, ed. The Film. Indianapolis: Bobbs-Merrill, 1968.

459 Schickel, Richard. Movies: The History of an Art and an Institution. New York: Basic Books, 1964, 153-155.
   Fellini is "something of a simpleton and something of a vulgarian," but the spectacular success of his films at least restored interest in the Italian film after the decline of neo-realism. La strada and Cabiria are "two wretched movies" that "tried to make tragedy out of stupidity, but had no discernible point except that mental retardation can lead to unhappiness. " Dolce vita is "vulgar, witless, and intellectually bankrupt;" and the bankruptcy is confirmed by $8\frac{1}{2}$.

460 ____. Second Sight: Notes on Some Movies 1965-1970. New York: Simon and Schuster, 1972, 289-291.

461 Schlappner, Martin, ed. Von Rossellini Zu Fellini. Zurich: Origo, 1963.

462 Solomon, Stanley J. 'Structuring an Expanding Visual Idea: Fellini Satyricon," The Film Idea. New York: Harcourt, Brace, Jovanovich, 1972, 370-376.
   An example of how a popular college film text handles one of Fellini's more difficult films. Quotes Fellini on characterizing Encolpius and Ascylto as the equivalents of hippie students of our own times. Satyricon is "the most striking example in the recent cinema of a film taking its structure from a series of images gradually unfolding around a central theme. The audience does not arrive at any realization of the theme of the decline of a civilization as a result of the progressive unravelling of the story. Rather the implications expand from sequence to sequence as new images of a dehumanized world appear to us. "

463 Sontag, Susan. Against Interpretation and Other Essays. New York: Farrar, Straus and Giroux, 1966.

464 Stephenson, Ralph and J. R. Dibrix. <u>The Cinema as Art.</u>
    Baltimore, Md.: Penguin, 1965.

465 Taylor, John Russell. <u>Cinema Eye, Cinema Ear.</u> New York:
    Hill and Wang, 1964, 15-51.
    Top-notch overview--one of the best in any language--of
    Fellini's films through $8\frac{1}{2}$. Says that up to <u>Vitelloni</u> it would
    have been possible "if increasingly odd" to regard Fellini as a
    realist. "But <u>La strada</u> makes it clear ... that he is nothing
    of the sort and never has been: his forte, even when his films
    have nearly all the trappings of external reality in their ex-
    pected places, is symbolic fantasy of almost baroque elaboration
    and artificiality." There is "nothing noticeably documentary"
    about <u>Agenzia matrimoniale</u> at all: "It is a fully-fledged Fellini
    film in miniature. The theme is humility and human suffering."

466 Yutkevich, S. I., ed. <u>Kinoslovar' v dvukh tomakh.</u> [Dictionary
    of the Film in two volumes.] Moscow: Soviet Encyclopedia,
    1966-1970, 742-744.
    Brief treatment of the films through <u>Giulietta</u>. "In contrast
    to the prose language of the neo-realists, the film language of
    Fellini is more metaphoric. He perceives as a metaphor the
    shots with the figure of Christ flying over Rome, and the final
    shots of the sea monster, as well as the image of sterility,
    falling down the stony hill, in <u>Bidone</u>."

D. UNPUBLISHED DISSERTATIONS

467 Burke, Francis Martin. Fellini's La Dolce Vita: Marcello's
Odyssey to Annulment. Gainesville: University of Florida,
1974. 289 p. Order No. 75-16, 364.
Says that Fellini sees Western man as "condemned to live
in a post-rational, post-Enlightenment world of relativity, dis-
continuity, and random energy quanta ... with the inadequate
equipment left over from a rationalist, Enlightenment tradition. "
This "casting off of rationalism" results in Marcello's "odyssey
to disillusionment. "

468 Reynolds, Lessie Mallard. An Analysis of the Non-verbal Symbolism in Federico Fellini's Film Trilogy: La Dolce Vita, $8\frac{1}{2}$,
and Juliet of the Spirits. Ann Arbor: University of Michigan,
1969. 207 p. Order No. 70-21, 769.
Considers Dolce vita, $8\frac{1}{2}$, and Giulietta to be a trilogy.
They use the archetypal metaphor of the Journey--through Hell
and Purgatory, towards Paradise. Marcello in Dolce vita travels spatially through "a modern Babylon. " Guido travels
through time: his present life, his past, his "future condition-
al. " Giulietta travels through "confused perceptions of substance. " There are archetypal representations of the Father,
Woman (Temptress, Ideal, and permissive Mother), and there
is the "recurring figure of the archetypal Old Magician. " The
camera eye is emphasized in Dolce vita in association with the
Christ statue and the eye of the dead fish, and becomes a
Christian symbol. In $8\frac{1}{2}$ there is the movie spotlight symbol;
in Giulietta the television represents a "fairy-tale view of reality. "

E. BOOKS (SELECTED) WITH PASSIM MATERIAL

469 Armes, Roy. Patterns of Realism: A Study of Italian Neo-Realist Cinema. New York: A. S. Barnes and Co., 1971.
Passim remarks on Fellini through Vitelloni. The latter shows "a desire to get beyond the confines of neo-realism and extend the scope of Italian cinema." The plight of the vitelloni "is symbolized by the use of landscapes and setting to convey the essential isolation of this situation." The camera style is clearly "an anticipation of Fellini's mannered baroque."

470 Bobker, Lee R. Elements of Film. New York: Harcourt, Brace and World, 1969.
Really a text for a basic film course. Brief synopsis of Fellini and his work. Also includes an excerpted reprint of J. R. Taylor's article on Fellini from his book Cinema Eye, Cinema Ear (see 465).

471 Clurman, Harold. All People Are Famous. New York: Harcourt, Brace, Jovanovich, 1974.
Brief reminiscences of three meetings with Fellini in 1971. When Fellini was shooting Roma, Clurman had the chance to see Fellini's doodlings in a notebook. The drawings were all of tumescent penises.

472 Cowie, Peter, ed. International Film Guide 1965. New York: A. S. Barnes, 1965.
A brief but sensitive and informed run-down of Fellini's career through 8½. In Vitelloni the characters, besides being rebellious and dissatisfied, are "spiritually starved." In the carnival sequence, each character "adopts the disguise that approximates to his ideal." In Dolce vita Fellini shows that "he is, and always has been, a romantic." The power of the film stems from "its fusion of realist and romantic elements." In 8½ Guido is viewed "a beaten man."

473 Durgnat, Raymond. Films and Feelings. Cambridge, Mass.: M. I. T. Press, 1967, 111-112.

474 Gromo, Mario. Film visiti. Rome: Edizioni di Bianco e Nero, 1957, 376-377, 470-472, 522-524, 537-539.

475 Jarrett, Vernon. The Italian Cinema. New York: Arno Press.

476 Kael, Pauline. Kiss Kiss Bang Bang. New York: Bantam
     Books, 1969, 398, 442, 460, 460-462, 463-464.
        In the section "Notes on 280 Movies" she gives her 1968
     verdicts on five films. Luci del varietà: "Though Fellini deals
     with 'artists', he never deals with talent or artistry. . . . His
     specialty is revealing the shoddiness of theatrical life. " For
     Fellini "the magic of show business (and this is the magic of
     his films) is in self-delusion. . . . The failure--the dreamer
     fooled by his dreams--is the poetic center of Fellini's films. "
     Sceicco bianco: "Perhaps the most gentle and naturalistic of
     Fellini's films. " It was not a success "perhaps because the
     target of the affectionate satire on glamour and delusion is pre-
     cisely the kind of people who go to the movies. " Vitelloni:
     Fellini's treatment is ambiguous. "He never suggests that these
     men should adjust to anything; he observes the farce of their
     aimless lives without condescension. " La strada: "The strange
     thing about this movie is that even if one rejects its concepts--
     and I do reject them--the mood and details of scenes stay with
     one; suddenly a year or two later, a gesture or a situation
     brings it all back. " Cabiria: "I think this is Fellini's finest
     film, and a work in which Giulietta Masina earns the praise
     she received for La strada. " (Kael had written that she thought
     the comparison of Giulietta Masina as Gelsomina to Chaplin,
     Langdon, Laurel, Barrault, and Marceau was "too just. ")

477 _____. Reeling. New York: Little, Brown and Co. , 1976,
     171-172.

478 Scott, James F. Film: The Medium and the Maker. New
     York: Holt, Rinehart and Winston, Inc. , 1975.
        An analysis of the way Fellini used the scope lense in
     Dolce vita. He quotes Martelli: "Fellini wanted to use per-
     spective according to his fantasy, often completely in contra-
     diction to the principles governing the use of certain lenses. "
     To which Scott remarks, "Instead of principles, Martelli might
     have said habits, since his further comments show how taste-
     bound were the supposed ultimates involved. "

F. ARTICLES ON FELLINI'S WORK AS A WHOLE

479 Agel, H. "Fellini," Etudes, 295 (December, 1957), 405-414.

480 "Alex in Wonderland," Village Voice, December 31, 1970, 39-40.

481 Alpert, Hollis. "Dream and Reality," Saturday Review, 44 (May 20, 1961), 37.

482 Amiel, Mireille. "La (très) pudique agonie de Federico Fellini," Cinéma '74, n. 190/191 (September/October, 1974), 224-230.
    Singularly interesting article on Fellini, from an issue dedicated to sixty years of Italian cinema, in which Fellini has a "special place." Of all the great modern filmmakers, Fellini is the most aware of being at the death throes of Western civilization--as well as at the dawn of something different. Babylon 2000, which he almost used as the title of Dolce vita, could indeed be the title for all of his work since. He is acutely aware that he is a witness of a world coming apart. "Think of that scene in Roma where the frescoes fade away after being exposed to the light of another epoch. An obsession that we find throughout his films now--Giulietta, or the end of a certain Conception of Woman, The Satyricon Apocalypse, Rome, or our very own death."

483 Bachmann, Gideon. "Stenografia wspomnien," Kino, 9 (May, 1974), 57-59.

484 Bawden, Liz-anne, ed. The Oxford Companion to Film. New York: Oxford University Press, 1976, 243-245.
    Brief, informative overviews of Fellini's career and of Sceicco bianco, Vitelloni, La strada, Cabiria, Dolce vita, $8\frac{1}{2}$, and Giulietta. Very brief biographical sketches too of Giulietta Masina and Marcello Mastroianni.

485 "Bergman-Fellini Film on Love," Times (London), January 6, 1969, 5.
    Announcement that Fellini and Bergman plan to collaborate on a new film--the theme is love.

486 "Biofilmographie," L'Avant-Scène, n. 102, April, 1970, 57.

487 "Biofilmographie," L'Avant-Scène, n. 129, October, 1972, 71-72.

488 "Boom in Campus Fellinis," Macleans Magazine, 79 (February 5, 1966), 41-42.
Article is not about Fellini, but about young Canadian film-makers who are striving to become great filmmakers like Fellini.

489 "Both Sides New," Show, April, 1970, 20.

490 Boussinot, Roger, ed. "Fellini," L'encyclopédie du cinéma. Bordas, 1967.
Noteworthy, illuminating summing-up of Fellini's films, through Giulietta, from the "autobiographical" point of view. It's a commonplace to say that a filmmaker is always making the same film and is always talking about himself in his works, but rarely are these truisms so marked as in Fellini's case. We can't help considering his entire work as one long attempt at unravelling his dreams and fantasies. His persistent themes and religious symbols, which assume the character of an obsession, deal with "the insoluble love-hate conflict that occupies many agnostic intellectuals, especially Italian." The article carefully relates the themes and stories of all the films to something in Fellini's life. E. g. : In La strada and Cabiria Fellini has "written a kind of love-poem" to his wife. "Let us not deceive ourselves, Fellini has here used his wife to express his most secret feelings, to reveal himself as intimately as possible." His films should not be confused with those of Antonioni's. Antonioni's characters "never cry"; their despair is irreversible. Gelsomina and Cabiria "achieve grace through tears."

491 Bouteillier, J. -P. Cinématographe, n. 9 (August/September, 1974), 43.

492 Calvino, Italo, trans. Sylvette Legrand. "Autobiographie d'un spectateur," Positif, n. 181, May, 1976.
This is a French translation of the introduction to Quattro Film (see 6) written at the request of Fellini.

493 Carroll, Paul. "Ode to Fellini on Interviewing Actors for a Forthcoming Film," Chicago Review, 18 (1966), n. 3-4, 98.
Splendid poetic tribute to the maestro (excerpt).
"what
if everything comes from the sea? The angels
are ecstatic fish. Or helicopters.
And you, Fellini, are
a deep-sea diver, searching for the sex
of God. Good luck."

494 Castello, G. C. Cinema (nuova serie), n. 116 (August 31, 1953), 109.

495   Cavicchioli, Luigi. Oggi, n. 30, 1954, 26-28.

496   Coote, Anna. "Roman Lunchtime with Fellini," Observer (London), September 27, 1970, 58-59.

497   Di Giammatteo. Comunità, 9 (December, 1955), 35.

498   Doty, Robert C. "Fellini and Bergman Plan Joint Film," New
      York Times, January 6, 1969, 38.
            Details press conference in Rome during which Fellini and
      Bergman announced Love Duet. Universal put up the money.
      Asked if they would see each other's script Fellini said, "Well,
      it isn't really a question of scripts. But it will not be a poker
      game, either, in which we hide aces up our sleeve. The only
      person we may hide things from is the producer." The project
      came out of mutual respect for each other's work.

499   Eason, P. "Notes on Double Structure and the Films of Fel-
      lini," Cinema (London), 2 (March, 1969), 22-26.

500   Enciclopedia dello Spettacolo. Roma: Le Maschere, 1958.
            A model encyclopedia article: ample, excellently documen-
      ted, authoritative data, tying in each film commented upon with
      all the others, chock full of objective information but exhibiting
      a viewpoint of its own. Through Cabiria.

501   "Federico Fellini," Cahiers du Cinéma, n. 84, June, 1958.

502   "Federico Fellini," Der Filmberater (Lucerne), n. 15, 1957.

503   "Fellini, bouffon de Dieu," L'Express, August 20, 1973.

504   "Federico Fellini to Make Film with Ingmar Bergman," News-
      week, January 20, 1969, 51.

505   Fitzgerald, J. "A Fellini Notebook," Critic, 22 (October-Novem-
      ber, 1963), 59.

506   Friendly, Alfred Jr. New York Times, April 2, 1970, 42.
            Says that Fellini has recently signed to do a series of spe-
      cials for the State owned TV network in Italy. Discusses the
      slump in the Italian films--no money to make them--and how
      this has affected some directors.

507   Garrett, G. P. "Fellini: A Selected Checklist of Available
      Secondary Materials Published in English," Contempora, Jan-
      uary/April 1971, 33+.

508   Gelinas, M. F. "Le cinéma Fellini est-il quêtaine?" Le Ma-
      clean 13 (April, 1973), 62.

509   "The Giants of Today's Cinema," Times (London), January 2,
      1963, 11.

Deals only superficially with Fellini.   The other directors
included are Hitchcock, Bergman, Antonioni, and Bresson.

510   Gray, M. Films and Filming, 7 (January, 1961), 47.

511   "The Great Lover," Parade, March 27, 1977, 7.
Mastroianni's various mistresses: Faye Dunaway, Jacque-
line Bisset, Catherine Deneuve. Now, at fifty-two, he is said
to be in love with a thirty-year-old press agent from Rome.
His wife, Flora Carabella Mastroianni, is supposed to be "a
most understanding wife who permits him to take mistresses
at will." The wife: "I know that in the end Marcello will
always come back to me. He is hopelessly sentimental." They
have a twenty-four-year-old daughter. He is supposed to be a
strong advocate of fidelity in marriage, but "Unfortunately, I
don't have the strength of character for it."

512   Grisolia, Michel. "Sous le plus beau chapiteau du monde sur
Federico Fellini," Nouvelle Revue Française, n. 245, 1973,
110-115.

513   Harcourt, P. "The Loss of Community: Six European Directors," Cinema Journal, 12 (Fall, 1972), 2-10.
Substantially the last chapter of Six European Directors
(see 446).

514   Hawkins, Robert F. "Close-up on Neo-Realism," New York
Times, November 25, 1956, Section II, 5.
Fellini's life has provided "data" for his important films.
Fellini interprets life in poetical and imaginative ways while
keeping within the realm of reality.

515   Herman, D. "Federico Fellini," American Imago, 26 (Fall,
1969), 251-268.
A psychoanalytic analysis of Fellini and his films, at times
illuminating, at times not.   Very good at presenting known material about Fellini's life but usually not highlighted or seen as
psychoanalytically revealing.   Fellini is a "narcissist ... in a
state of continual failure in relation to his idealized self."   The
Maddalena/echo chamber sequence in Dolce vita conveys "the
psychological mood that permeates every film Fellini has
made. ...   Marcello's helpless situation reflects the isolation
of the infant.   Exposed and vulnerable, he is humiliated by the
caprices of a female figure."   Fellini's fears of heights are
revealed time and time again in the "ubiquitous vertical lines"
of the films.   (The sheik on the swing, Guido as a kite etc.)
The women in the films fall into "rigid stereotypes," either big
and menacing or, like Gelsomina, "angels" who are "harmless
imbeciles."   Behind all this lies Fellini's "narcissistic ambiva-
lence."   Ultimately both types are dismissed by Fellini as "too
threatening or too vulnerable."   Claudia is the one exception,
but Guido can't deal with her.   Fellini's interviews are typical

of the chattering monologues of narcissists.   The cameras of
Dolce vita are symbols for "the eye and the penis," as is the
fish at the end.   It is "at once the reincarnation of parent-
swallowed-whole and at the same time a graphic rendering of
the breast and the penis embodied in one awesome entity."

516   Horizon, May, 1959, 99.

517   Horizon, May, 1960, 51.

518   Horizon, November, 1962, 110-111.

519   Hughes, Eileen Lanouette.   "La dolce vita of Federico Fellini,"
      Esquire, August, c. 1961.
           Long, detailed, exceptionally informative data, not easily
      obtainable elsewhere (if at all) on Fellini's career through Dolce
      vita.   Quotes Fellini as saying that Dolce vita is "a newspaper
      or rotogravure" on film.   The false miracle episode was based
      on an incident that took place in 1958.   Quotes Jesuit Professor
      of Theology at university in Genoa and longtime confidant of
      Fellini (Father Angelo Arpa): "Never has the cinema included
      in sin such a profound sense of bitterness and weariness, of
      misfortune and desolation."   Quotes also from L'Unità (pro) and
      Lo Specchio (anti).

520   Image et Son, n. 246, January, 1971.

521   "Importance et portée de l'oeuvre du réalisateur Federico Fel-
      lini dans l'histoire du cinéma, recension de ses principaux
      films," Nouvelle Revue Française, n. 159, 1966, 505.

522   Issac, D.   "Films About Films; Hooray for Hollywood," Dimen-
      sions, 5 (Summer, 1971), 47-51.   (Alex in Wonderland)

523   Jeune Cinéma, n. 41, October, 1969.

524   Johnson, Ian.   "Dreams, Fantasy, and Reality," Motion, n. 1
      (Summer, 1961), 10-13.

525   Kael, Pauline.   "Alex in Wonderland," New Yorker, 46 (January
      9, 1971), 62-64.   Reprinted in Deeper into Movies.   New York:
      Bantam Books, 1974, 283-287.
           Fellini appears in this take-off on $8\frac{1}{2}$.   "The flattery of Fel-
      lini is so severe and single-edged that after Mazursky and Tuck-
      er went through God knows what machinations to get Fellini ...
      they failed to provide him with good material."   Fellini's pres-
      ence does not work "magic" and he adds "nothing."   Fellini is
      "very tight" and "very dull."

526   Karkosch, K.   "Die vier Karrieren des Federico Fellini," Film
      und Ton, 19 (February, 1973), 30-32.

527   Knight, Arthur and Hollis Alpert. "History of Sex in Cinema.
      Part XIII: The Fifties. Sex Goes International," Playboy,
      December, 1966, 250+.

528   _____. "History of Sex in Cinema. Part XIX: The '60s--
      Eros Unbound in Foreign Films," Playboy, July, 1968, 191+.
          Outlines briefly the stories and themes of Dolce vita, Dr.
      Antonio, 8½, and Giulietta. Quotes Fellini on Dr. Antonio:
      A metaphor to show "how man's imprisoned appetites can finally
      burst their bonds and bloat into an erotic fantasy that comes to
      life, takes possession of its creator, and ultimately devours
      him. "

529   Lauder, R. "Fellini: Hopeful Humanist," US Catholic, 35
      (February, 1970), 16-22.

530   Mangini, Cecilia. "Le Cas Fellini," Cinéma '55, March 3,
      1955.
          Quotes Fellini as saying of Vitelloni: "It was always my-
      self speaking through my characters, only in another voice. "

531   "Mastermind with Makeup," Life, 73 (December 15, 1972), 74.
          Shows several photos of Fellini "in disguise," which Fellini
      concocted from an FAO Schwarz Deluxe Disguise Kit. Life had
      the kit sent to Fellini, who agreed to put on the make-up.
      Part of a whole series in this issue where Life also shows a
      famous architect who created something from children's building
      blocks.

532   Mastroianni, Marcello. "Marcello Mastroianni: A Candid Con-
      versation with Italy's Urbane Star of International Cinema,"
      Playboy, July, 1965, 56+.
          Indispensable. Mastroianni's comments about his own feel-
      ings and the age in which he lives prove tremendously illumi-
      nating of both the Fellini films in which he plays and those in
      which he does not. The interviewer remarks that all the films
      he's made are one way or another about weak men, often sex-
      ually impotent. Is that he? Mastroianni: "It's part of me;
      and I think it's part of many other men today. Modern man
      is not as virile as he used to be. Instead of making things
      happen, he waits for things to happen to him. He goes with
      the current. Something in our own society has led him to stop
      fighting, to cease swimming upstream. " One of the sources of
      trouble is that women are changing into men, and men are be-
      coming women. At least, they are getting weaker. He re-
      members his grandfather, who lived to be ninety: "I used to
      watch him and admire his authority. Where has all that gone?
      What's happened to that kind of man? Whatever it was that
      buried him, it took with it a whole era, a whole way of life. "

533   Mida, Massimo. "Fellini, Diogene del cinema," Cinema (nuova
      serie), n. 95 (October 1, 1952), 163-165.

534   "New Group Signs Four Noted Directors," New York Times,
       October 7, 1973, 79.
              States that Film Makers Associated have signed Fellini,
       Antonioni, Ken Russell, and Terence Young to a new contract.
       The others will do three films each, and Fellini will do one.

535   "New Names," Sight and Sound, Winter, 1955/1956, 120.
              Brief, early, thumb-nail sketch of Fellini, a "new name"
       among Italian filmmakers. His very early films "promised an
       interesting new talent." Since then, he has followed "a less
       rewarding path, (La strada and Bidone)--to a strained, uneasy
       combination of 'poetry' and melodrama. Will he commit, and
       find, himself?"

536   New York Times, June 3, 1973.

537   Newsweek, January 11, 1965, 40.

538   Nicholls, R. "La noia with Federico," Lumière, 20 (January-
       February, 1973), 4-6.

539   Nowell-Smith, Geoffrey. "Showman and Shaman," Times Liter-
       ary Supplement, October 31, 1975, 1311.
              Review of Quattro Film (see 6). "What the text loses in
       explosiveness it gains in interiority ... the text becomes an
       object of scrutiny rather than the power house of exhibitionistic
       pyrotechnics." Discusses the script as literature, the script
       as more of a "guide" or "aide-mémoire" to the film. Is very
       unhappy that Quattro Film leaves out the names of Pinelli,
       Flaiano and Rondi, who collaborated with Fellini on these
       scripts. "It is hard to see why they receive no acknowledge-
       ment in the book and authorship is attributed to the emperor
       alone." Also includes a brief commentary on the preface to
       Quattro Film, which was written by Italo Calvino.

540   Oliva, L. Film A Doba (Czech), 20 (May, 1974), 290.

541   Paolucci, A. "Italian Film: Antonioni, Fellini, Bolognini,"
       Massachusetts Review, 7 (Summer, 1966), 556-567.
              Splendidly illuminates Fellini's work by placing it in the
       context of other directors, and against the sociological back-
       ground of the Italian scene irrespective of the cinema. Also
       provides insights into several of Fellini's individual films. The
       procession in La strada, "like Dante's pageant at the top of
       Purgatory, is recognizable in all its details, but the final effect
       is strange and nightmarish." The party in Dolce vita is per-
       fectly clear, but "the surrealistic Matelda-like encounter at the
       end, jolts us into perplexity." In $8\frac{1}{2}$ an interview with the car-
       dinal is an "Augustinian encounter." What strikes us is "the
       despair of skepticism which hears the profoundest truths as
       mere, rote-like quotations." Of that picture as a whole, "The
       innocent love of the past and the rote-like lust of the present

are shown side by side in an expressive juxtaposition that is grim and sad and beautiful all at once."

542 Pechter, William S. "Alex in Wonderland," Commentary, 51 (April, 1971), 79+.
A film modelled after $8\frac{1}{2}$, about a director who can't decide what his next film should be. Pechter calls it "marked down from $8\frac{1}{2}$," and describes much of the film (which he deplores), but fails to mention that Fellini appears in the film very, very briefly.

543 "People Are Talking About," Vogue, 131 (January 15, 1958), 56.

544 Positif, n. 28, April, 1958.

545 Renzi, Renzo. "Federico Fellini," Premier Plan, n. 12, 1960.

546 _____. "Fellini Qui Va, Fellini Qui Vient," Jeune Cinéma, n. 41 (October, 1969), 1-8. Translated from Federico Fellini, Il Primo Fellini, Renzo Renzi ed. Bologna: Cappelli, 1969, 13-19.

547 _____. "Gli antenati di Federico Fellini," Cinema Nuovo, May/June, 1964. Reprinted in La Mia Rimini. Bologna: Cappelli, 1967, 13-16.

548 Rhode, Eric. "Fellini's Double City," Encounter, 23 (June, 1964), 44-49. Reprinted in The Emergence of Film Art: The Evolution and Development of the Motion Picture As an Art, from 1900 to the Present, Lewis Jacobs, ed. New York: Hopkinson and Blake, 1969, 341-352.

549 _____. "Gherardi in London," Sight and Sound, 39 (Winter, 1969-1970), 16-17.
Interview with Gherardi, who was the designer for La strada, Dolce vita, $8\frac{1}{2}$, and Giulietta. Valuable for interesting bits of information that only someone like Gherardi would know about. Says that Fellini got the idea for parts of $8\frac{1}{2}$ from a visit to the grave of Fellini's father. The bath-tub ritual of $8\frac{1}{2}$ was based on one that Gherardi remembered from his childhood and was filmed at his farm near Florence. Gherardi owns several houses in Bangkok and likes the East; hence the many oriental touches in Dolce vita. The fantasy scenes in $8\frac{1}{2}$ are tinted green. Says that it is the Fellini principle to use locations in an unusual way.

550 "Rival Young Directors," Newsweek, February 21, 1966, 98.

551 Rizzo, Eugene. "Fellini's Musical Alter Ego, Nino Rota: How They Work," Variety, May 21, 1975, 28.
An interview in Rome, also an account of Rota's "double

life" in classical music and in film scores. "If Fellini always
insists that I include a march, it is because of his extended
metaphor of the circus representing all life. "

552 Ross, T. J. "The Dance of the Homeless: On the World of
Fellini's Films," December, Spring, 1966, 103-116.
The essay is evidenced by a remarkably close and sensitive
attention to detail in the films treated (through Giulietta). The
last close-up of Zampanò is Fellini's "main device for leading
us to discover in the natures and dilemmas of his character
those of Everyman. " He finds that each film is patterned to
the way someone is "placed in the lead of, or set apart from,
or above, or below, the rhythm of procession, parade, or
dance. " The dance represents "the anguish of an abrupt, what-
the-hell shrug" which the characters seek to transcend. The
problem that Fellini poses is that "home-centered values, sen-
timents, ground rules are no longer tenable, since there is no
longer a world of homes. " Giulietta's husband is a "caterer,"
a professional party-giver who leads a dance. Saraghina's
rhumba is a "dance-initiation to sex. " He interprets the "twin-
kle" in Paola's eye in the last scene as suggesting "her ardor
to join in the dance and carousings of Marcello and his gang
across the way. " $8\frac{1}{2}$ takes up the "idea of Art" as transcending
the fate of the dancers and ends up "a qualified homage to
them. " Ross says that "height and water" are "polarizing symbols" of the Fellini landscape, and he includes a careful and illuminating analysis of the "height" metaphors in the films.

553 Sadoul, Georges. Dictionnaire des Cinéastes. Paris: Editions
du Seuil, 1968, 85-86.
Brief but pithy comments, often with a telling quotation from
Fellini: "In Cabiria, Cabiria (a sprightly character who won't
give up, who clings to life) became a Don Quixote, struggling,
lance upraised, against the monstrosities of a corrupt world,
of which La dolce vita gave a vast tableau. "

554 Samuels, Charles Thomas. "Movie Theatre Without Walls,"
New York Times Book Review, Part II, February 13, 1972, 2.
"There is no excuse, particularly with a public sophisticated
enough about cinema to want to buy scenarios, for omitting
sound effects.... Such 'impediments' are instead crucial re-
minders of the nature of cinematic achievement. " A review of
Early Screenplays (see 1).

555 Schaer; R. "Vom Untergang der Menschheit," Film und Ton,
19 (December, 1973), 38-39.

556 Setlowe, Rick. "Ask Fellini About Symbolism," Variety, January 21, 1970.

557 Shales, T. "Fellini: Everything Is Possible," Biography News,
2 (January, 1975), 81.

558 Skolsky, Sidney. "Tintyped: Anita Ekberg," New York Post
     Magazine, June 30, 1963, 3.
       A Dolce vita type interview of the real Anita Ekberg.
     Through it we learn that she likes corned beef sandwiches,
     sleeps in the raw, and owns a Ferrari.

559 Solmi, Angelo. "Fellini," Oggi, n. 7, 1963.

560 ____. "Fellini," Oggi, n. 9, 1963.

561 Stafford, Jean. "Neo-realismo Revisited," Horizon, March,
     1961, 98, 100.
       Just a few remarks on Fellini. She quotes Fellini on why
     his pictures "never end" because he doesn't want to offer so-
     lutions to problems and thereby beguile the spectator into think-
     ing that he has solved his problems too. Stafford comments,
     "This is a solemn creed, and it limits the uses of fiction; it
     eliminates the impossible, the castle in Spain." But she grants
     that it is "a creed of integrity."

562 Stanbrook, A. "The Hope of Fellini," Film, 19 (January/Feb-
     ruary, 1959), 17.

563 Sterritt, David. "Filmmaker Who Hates Going to Movies,"
     Christian Science Monitor, January 29, 1975, 5.
       Fellini was in the U. S. to help promote his latest hit
     Amarcord. Asks Fellini why he doesn't like to see his pictures
     once he's done with them. Fellini says, "I have reasons to be
     disappointed with myself ten thousands times a day. Why add
     another reason more?"

564 Stoop, N. M. After Dark, 7 (November, 1974), 68.

565 Sturgis, Norman. "On the Road to Hong Kong," Theatre Arts,
     46 (December, 1962), 60-61.
       Two American expatriates, with theatre background, visit
     Fellini's office in Rome. (Only one paragraph of the article
     is about Fellini, but good background comments on the Rome
     film world of that time.) They found Fellini "large, dynamic,
     and extremely responsive." His simple office suite was lined
     with pictures of Giulietta (whom Sturgis describes as "a former
     school teacher.") Good photo of Fellini in scarf and stocking hat.

566 "Thieves Break into Home of Fellini," Times (London), June
     1, 1974, 4.
       News item. Thieves stole paintings, antique lithographs, and
     other items from Fellini's home in Rome.

567 "Three Screenplays," Best Sellers, 30 (October 1, 1970), 265.
       Book review.

568 "Three Screenplays," Choice, 8 (September, 1971), 852.

"For film historical purposes, the screenplay opus of Fellini should be available. " "Sadly, there is no introduction to the book, nor are there commentaries, either descriptive or critical, for each work. The three screenplays have simply been glued together instead of molded into a helpful work. "

569 Thulin, Ingrid. "Comments on Fellini," Dialogue on Film, 3 (1972), 16.

570 Times (London), March 27, 1961, 14.

571 Times (London), April 20, 1967, 1.
     Brief note that Fellini is suffering from pneumonia and pleurisy.

572 "Twenty-fifth Cannes Film Festival Opens with Glitter and Pomp," New York Times, May 13, 1971, 50.
     Gives details of the festival. Former Golden Palm winners --Fellini included--were honored at Cannes. Fellini received a special gold medal. Clips were shown from the former prize-winning films.

573 "Unger-Fellini-John Milton Parlay," Variety, March 17, 1975, 46.
     Oliver Unger claims to have a "handshake deal" with Fellini to film Milton's Paradise Lost.

574 Walter, E. "Federico Fellini: Wizard of Film," Atlantic, 216 (December, 1965), 62-67.
     A mélange of tid-bits of information, mostly second-hand. (Walter played the journalist in 8½ who kept asking Fellini stupid questions.) But he did visit Fellini's mother and sister. Fellini's mother said she cried during 8½ when Guido asked the ghost of his father to stay awhile and talk because they've never really had a talk. The mother tells Walter, "Because, you see, Federico and I have never had a talk.... We're good friends--but I don't feel I really know him. " In 8½ Carla talked mostly in "comic-stripese. " There are private jokes in Fellini's films. In 8½ all the old people at the luxury hotel at the spa were actually inmates of a Roman old folks' home. And the employees of the hotel were titled aristocrats.

575 Weiner, B. "Fellini, Truffaut, Rise of Louis XIV," Northwest Passage, 5 (April 26, 1971), 22.

576 Weismann, G. "Fellini," Nola Express, 1 (June 12, 1970), 11.

577 _____. "Fellini," Nola Express, 1 (June 26, 1970), 26.

578 Wolf, William. "Italy's Movie Greats," Cue, November 6, 1965, 14.

579 Zorkii, A. "Fil'my i dialogi iul' 1973-go," Iskusstvo Kino (U.S.S.R.), n. 12 (1973), 22-42.

G. ARTICLES ON INDIVIDUAL FILMS, INCLUDING FILM REVIEWS

Luci del varietà

580 Aristarco, Guido. Cinema (nuova serie), n. 55, February 1, 1951, 49-50.

581 Ave Maria, 101 (May 22, 1965), 9.

582 Bassan, R. "Les feux du Music-Hall," Télécine, n. 191/192 (September/October, 1974), 37.

583 Cervoni, Albert. "Les feux du Music-Hall," Cinéma '74, n. 190/191 (September/October, 1974), 310-311.
On seeing the film again after a period of almost twenty-five years; so far as early post-World War II Italy is concerned, "everything has changed and nothing has changed." The film possesses "an unquestionable air of bitterness." It previsions the atmosphere and themes of $8\frac{1}{2}$, Clowns and Roma. It is a universe "laced with sex, uncomfortable about it, and with a misogyny obsessed with women."

584 Crist, Judith. "'50 Fellini: Bite and Wit in Vignettes," New York Herald-Tribune, May 7, 1965, 12.
"Somehow old-fashioned in the best sense."

585 Cue, May 8, 1965.
"Fifteen years was too long to wait." "There are wonderful scenes, simultaneously hilarious and sad, etching the contrast between the assumed self-importance of members of the seedy troupe and the pitifully ineffective lives they lead."

586 Davies, B. J. Film Journal, n. 20 (August, 1962), 84.

587 Durgnat, Raymond. Films and Filming, 7 (December, 1960), 33.

588 Gili, J. A. "Les feux du Music-Hall," Ecran, n. 29 (October, 1974), 77-78.

589 Gill, Brendan. "Beginnings," New Yorker, 41 (May 8, 1965), 167.
"A first novel notoriously reveals its author's deepest pre-

occupations (not yet having learned from critics what their pre-
occupations are), the poor fellow marches them up and down
his pages as naked as jay birds. " It is "fascinating" to observe
in the film "the introduction of certain themes that, disguised
and enriched, provide the matrix" for much of Fellini's later
works. The film is a "continuously charming affair, mingling
comedy and pathos with Chaplinesque dexterity (the Tramp hov-
ers over many scenes like an instructive guardian angel.)"

590   Guarino, Ann. "Early Fellini Film Is About Show Business,"
      New York Daily News, May 7, 1965.
            Enjoyed the humor. "The picture is dated, but the photo-
      graphy is clear. "

591   Hull, David Stewart. "Not Yet in Release," Film Quarterly,
      15 (Fall, 1961), 48.
            "Most of the Fellini trademarks are already in evidence.
      The individual is solitary and must realize the fundamental ri-
      diculousness of his existence. The woman is the eternal agent
      of consciousness, patient but vigilant. Checco in many ways
      is a sketch of Fausto in Vitelloni, and the bored delinquents of
      that film can be clearly seen in the provincial youths who give
      rousing Bronx cheers to the weary performers. "

592   Kauffmann, Stanley. New Republic, 152 (May 15, 1965), 33.
      Reprinted in A World on Film. New York: Dell Publishing
      Company, 1966, 325.
            "An undistinguished backstage story of a poor Italian touring
      troupe of vaudevillians, but the soggy story is well told. "
      There are "felicities of execution" throughout the film "that lift
      it out of the ordinary. "

593   "Limelight," Newsweek, 65 (May 17, 1965), 104.
            Although co-directed with Lattuada, the film is "unmistak-
      ably Fellini's, in concept, in feeling, in small moments of per-
      sonal signature; and its release, now, is an occasion for cheer-
      ing and glee. " Elements of the film "looking forward to $8\frac{1}{2}$ "
      are "animated by Fellini's idea of providence and divine grace. "

594   Mida, Massimo. "Fellini fra le luci del varietà," Cinema
      (nuovo serie), n. 47, October 1, 1950, 171.

595   Mishkin, Leo. "Variety Lights, Fellini's First, A Schmaltzy
      Effort," Morning Telegraph, May 7, 1965.
            Luci del varietà is nothing more than "a heavy-breathing
      comedy drama overflowing with soap suds. "

596   Sarris, Andrew. Village Voice, May 6, 1965, 21-22.
            He doubts that had the film been reviewed in America when
      it was first released it would have been treated "as any-
      thing more than a declassé version of All About Eve. "

597   Times (London), October 10, 1960, 7.
            Luci del varietà is ten years old and is "not necessarily
      the worse for that." Compares the film briefly to Osborne's
      The Entertainer.

598   Weiler, A. H.   "First Fellini Picture Seen on Double Bill."
      New York Times, May 7, 1965, 34.
            Likes the film even though it is "a little dated." Calls it
      "wholesome corn" and claims "no offense intended."

599   Winsten, Archer. "Two Fine Films at the New Yorker," New
      York Post, May 7, 1965.
            "This is good work, sharply observed, very characteristic
      Fellini, and consistently entertaining." Noticed that even in
      this early film Fellini showed the contrast between people with-
      out money and those with.

                              Lo sceicco bianco

600   Castello, G. C.   Cinema (nuova serie), n. 99-100, December
      15-31, 1952, 335-337.

601   Crowther, Bosley.   New York Times, April 26, 1956, 37.
            Wants to see more Fellini before saying what his capabili-
      ties are.   He'll not count Sceicco bianco against Fellini since
      this is "just a practice swing."

602   del Fra, Lino.   Bianco e Nero, n. 6, 1957.

603   Ghelli, Nino.   Bianco e Nero, n. 9-10, 1952.

604   Simon, John.   "Favorites," Private Screenings.   New York:
      Berkley Medallion, 1971, 31-33.
            Calls this and Vitelloni Fellini's "early masterpieces."
      The film is "a model of a comédie larmoyante in which laughter
      and tears are blended in perfect proportions." We are "con-
      tinually aware both of how Wanda sees the events and how they
      really happen." His interpretation of Wanda's final line "You
      are my White Sheik!": 'Wanda has learned that in a world
      where illusions crumble into reality, the only happiness is to
      raise reality to the level of illusion by seeing it with loving,
      forgiving eyes, grateful that it is at least as much as it is.
      White Sheiks do not fall into our laps ready-made; we must
      fashion them patiently and fondly out of the brown or grey one's
      life provides."

605   Solmi, Angelo. "The Misunderstood Lo sceicco," Fellini. Atlantic
      Highlands, N. J.: Humanities Press, 1968, Part II, Chapter 4.
            Tells of the problems Fellini had in casting the film (Fel-
      lini had to fight to have Sordi play the white sheik), describes
      the public's negative reaction when the film came out.   The

early critics didn't like it either. Solmi liked it from the
start, feels now that it is not one of Fellini's minor works.
As time goes by the film's impact grows and "one becomes
aware of the richness of tones, the subtle magic that reveals
the melancholy vein beneath the comedy."

606 _____. Oggi, n. 15, 1952.

607 _____. Oggi, n. 33, 1961.

I vitelloni

608 Archer, Eugene. Film Culture, 2 (1956), n. 4, 24-25.
      Splendid articulation and explication of the theme of the
film. Calls the film "great" and a "model of progressive film
technique." Its distinction lies in Fellini's understanding of his
characters and "his unusual sympathy for their problems."
The rich comedy is "intensified by the compassion of the director's approach."

609 Crowther, Bosley. "Italian Drama Delves into Social Problem,"
New York Times, October 24, 1956, 43.
      Generally liked the film, but claims that the film's weak-
ness is in its "weak conventional end." Thinks Fellini simply
"got tired" and "called it off." Believes that the Italian dialogue is "livelier" than the English titles translate.

610 Fellini-Flajano-Pinelli. Cinema (nuova serie), n. 99-100, December 15-31, 1952, 289-293.

611 Film Society Review, 5 (May, 1970), 24.

612 "Italian Film About 'Spivs,'" Times (London), March 27, 1956,
3.
      The other names for the vitelloni are hobbledehoys, drones
or spivs. Vitelloni was billed as Spivs in London. Fellini is
a "penetrating and witty social critic."

613 Knight, Arthur. "Everybody Talkin' 'Bout Heaven," Saturday
Review, 39 (November 10, 1956), 28-29.
      Excellent presentation of the film's theme. The vitelloni
are "the sons of lower middle-class families who feel that they
are too good for manual labor. Not rich enough to be called
wastrels or poor enough to be bums, they drift along aimlessly,
hoping for the break that will give them a definite status in society."

614 McCarten, John. New Yorker, 32 (November 3, 1956), 175.
      "...the theme seems hardly worth this full-length treat-
ment, even though the acting is admirable throughout."

615 Marks, Louis. Films and Filming, 1 (December, 1954), 21.

616 "Marty--Italian Style," Newsweek, 48 (November 12, 1956),
     130.
         Vitelloni is "a meandering movie which does not tell a story
     so much as take a long look at a human situation. Americans
     are likely to get the feeling that it is a great deal longer than
     it actually is."

617 Michalek, Bolesław. Nowa Kultura, n. 38, 1958.

618 Murray, William. Village Voice, 2 (November 21, 1956), 8.

619 "The New Pictures," Time, 68 (November 5, 1956), 110.
         "It is a finer piece of work than La strada in every way."
     "The nimbleness, the knowingness, the irony, the sharp obser-
     vation of small-town life ... has hardly been surpassed on the
     screen." In Fellini's hands, "people sometimes seem more
     important than the screen has made them appear for years:
     they seem larger, somehow, even than the lowliest and most
     helplessly lost among them."

620 Quigly, Isabel. "Desolate Sympathy," Spectator, 196 (April 6,
     1956), 443.
         Vitelloni is "stronger" than La strada but "less exotic."
     "This is one of the profound social commentaries I have met
     in the cinema--the portrait, piercingly accurate, of a genera-
     tion and a country's dilemma; and the story, sour-sweet hope-
     less, and always human, of five well-nourished, spiritually
     starved, not-so-young men."

621 Simon, John. "Favorites," Private Screenings. New York:
     Berkley Medallion, 1971, 34-37.
         Fellini's "most beautiful" film. The vitelloni are indolent
     youths living in a provincial town "in which there seems to be
     no place for them." One of the most brilliant features of the
     film is the score by Rota: "The quick-silver switches in the
     music ably support the changing moods of the story." The iron-
     ies in the film "are so delicate that they can perch comfortably
     on the razor's edge between laughter and tears."

622 Solmi, Angelo. Oggi, n. 40, 1953.

623 _____. "Retaliation with I vitelloni," Fellini. Atlantic
     Highlands, N.J.: Humanities Press, 1968, Part II, Chapter 5.
         Fellini fights to keep the original title of Vitelloni. They
     are what good-for-nothings are sometimes called in Romagna.
     Fellini and his friends had been called that by an old woman
     when they had pestered her. Moraldo "is clearly Fellini him-
     self," but the others too "are part of Fellini." Fellini may
     sometimes condone his vitelloni but there is also "a severe
     moral condemnation, which is evident in the finale." They are

more "insensitive" than guilty or "without hope of redemption."
They are not "dead souls," just "torpid ones who can be awak-
ened when they come into contact with the harsh reality of life."

624   Sufrin, Mark.   Film Society Review, 5 (May, 1970), 42-45.

625   Times (London), September 5, 1953, 5.
        The Venice Film Festival awarded the Silver Lion to Vitel-
loni.

626   Weightman, J. G.   "In Praise of Fellini," Twentieth Century,
        June, 1956, 598-600.
            Fellini's subject is the "poetry of human relationships in
        an old, poor, and contracting society, and he never allows the
        breath of commercialism to cloud his exact vision of things as
        they are."   The vitelloni are "always talking in a Chekhovian
        way, of leaving to make their fortunes elsewhere."

627   Willing, Diana.   Films in Review, 7 (December, 1956), 527-
        528.
            The film is an incompetent and irresponsible mode of work.
        "Fellini does not seem to know from one sequence to the next,
        where the film is going, and, in the end, he winds up abruptly
        and improbably."   She says she never liked Italian neo-realism
        anyway and found it rather a rationalization for lack of skilled
        scriptwriting, the lack of cinematic know-how and equipment,
        and the lack of "energizing beliefs."

628   Young, Vernon.   "La strada: Cinematic Intersections," Hud-
        son Review, 9 (Fall, 1956), 437.   Reprinted in On Film, Chi-
        cago: Quadrangle Books, 1972, 59-67.
            Although primarily on La strada, this article includes an
        exegesis of Vitelloni (61-63).   "Narrated with an almost novel-
        istic abundance of detail, the film is seldom allowed to relin-
        quish its visual melody of the five.   Arms linked abreast, the
        wastrels dance down the street at night, or split up and pair
        off (Moraldo always odd man)."   "And always the distance, be-
        hind the lonely, short-sighted figures of men: the sea, the
        railroad track and street."

Un' agenzia matrimoniale

629   Amengual, Barthélemy.   "Amore in Città," Section 6 of Chapter
        6, "Six Films Exemplaires," Le Neô-Réalisme Italien: bilan de
        la critique, Etudes Cinématographiques, n. 32-35, Summer,
        1964, 171-174.
            "The whole of Fellini is in Agenzia matrimoniale: powerful
        realism of his chance characters (here the owner of the agency),
        the Gelsomina-Cabiria type, the feeling for just the right back-
        ground--now urban and neo-realist, now rural and religious, the
        dark glasses that the 'villains' put-on, childhood and its certain-

ties, the unusual in the everyday, and that vain cruelty of the
artist--here the newspaper man--that imposes itself so force-
fully in Luci del varietà. " Above all, what stands out is "the
accusation of our social life: a particular world has given
birth to Gelsomina and her sisters, and instead of looking
toward heaven, the way he too often suggests, Fellini here fo-
cuses on our unjust social world. "

630 Castello, G. C. Cinema (nuova serie), n. 123, December 15,
1953, 339-342.

631 Tozzi, Romano. "Love in the City," Films in Review, 10
(June-July, 1959), 358-359.
     Gives brief background of the multi-episode film, Amore in
Città, "touted in Europe as a new kind of neo-realism"--drama-
tizing incidents lifted out of the daily papers. Fellini's pre-
sumed satirization of matrimonial agencies is "downright absurd. "

632 Vogel, Amos. "Limits of Neo-realism," Film Culture, 3
(1957), n. 2, 17-20.
     Indispensable. One of the best, most lucid, and most in-
formative articles on the background of Amore in Città of which
Agenzia matrimoniale is one of the segments. The film was
produced by Cesare Zavattini, the ideologist of neo-realism,
"as an artistic manifesto of the school. " Vogel goes on to quote
Zavattini in a brief, clear, cogent outline of what Zavattini
means and intends by the neo-realist approach. Vogel goes on
to a devastating critique of Zavattini's logic and performance.
Yet Agenzia matrimoniale he finds has "elements of genuine
pathos and flashes of the lyrical talent that has stamped Fellini
as one of the true poets of neo-realism. "

                              La strada

633 Aliaga, Joseph. "Fellini's Mystery," Medium, 1 (Summer,
1967), 27-37.

634 Aristarco, Guido. Cinema Nuovo, n. 46, 1954.

635 _____. Cinema Nuovo, n. 46, December 10, 1959.

636 _____. "Guido Aristarco Answers Fellini," Film Culture,
4 (February, 1958), 20-21.
     Answers Fellini's interview with Bluestone (see 230). Fel-
lini had said 'Oh, well, if you want to understand my work,
don't read Cinema Nuovo. They have called La strada--called
me--a traitor to neo-realism. In Italy, it is very difficult to
find honest, objective criticism about directors. There are too
many special interests. " Aristarco doesn't say that La strada
is badly directed, only that "it is wrong; its perspective is

wrong. " There is one viewpoint, that of Fellini's film, "full
of mystery, grace--that is mysticism. " Then there is the
other, of Cinema Nuovo, "faith in man's ability to dominate and
modify his world"--in a word, "realism. "

637 Aubier, Dominique.   Cahiers du Cinéma, n. 49, July, 1955.
      Saint Francis of Assisi has more than an "influence" on the
film, rather a case of "brotherhood. " The film deals not with
monks or religion but surely with "the sacred. "

638 Bazin, André.   Esprit, n. 5, May, 1955.   Reprinted in Qu'est-
ce que le Cinéma?   Paris: 7e Editions du Cerf, 1962.

639 Benayoun, Robert.   Positif, n. 13, 1955.

640 Borneman, Ernest.   Films and Filming, 1 (December, 1954),
20.

641 Bort, L.   Kaleidoscope (Milwaukee), 5 (February 11, 1971), 61.

642 Bovasso, Julie.   Village Voice, 1 (August 1, 1956), 6.

643 Cabrera, G.   (G. Cain) "El camino del calvario," Un Oficio
del Siglo 20, Barcelona: Biblioteca Breve, Editorial Seix Bar-
ral, S. A. , 1973, 130-136.

644 Castello, Giulio.   Cinema (terza serie), n. 141, 1954.

645 Cinema (nuova serie), n. 139, August 10, 1954, entire issue.

646 Cross Currents, 6 (Summer, 1956), 200.

647 Crowther, Bosley.   "Some Thoughts on Baby Doll and the Italian Film La strada," New York Times, January 6, 1957, Section II, 1.
      Basically a review of Elia Kazan's Baby Doll, which Crow-
ther thought was not very good.   He compares and contrasts
Baby Doll to La strada, which is a "commendable foreign film. "

648 Cue, 43 (October 28, 1974), 36.

649 De Baroncelli, Jean.   Le Monde, March 15, 1955.
      Like "a transfiguration of neo-realism.   Everything is
everyday, familiar, perfectly plausible. " And yet we are "at
the other end of the spectrum, in the confines of the strange,
even the fantastic. "

650 De Laurot, Edouard.   "La strada--A Poem on Saintly Folly,"
Film Culture, 2 (1956), n. 7, 11-14.   Reprinted in Renais-
sance of the Film, ed. Julius Bellone.   London: Collier-Mac-

millan, Ltd. , 1970, 264-276, and in the Hudson Review, 14 (Autumn, 1961).

"The Angel-Fool, the Poverella-Gelsomina, the sinner but, as Gelsomina calls him, 'poveracio' Zampanò, are all loved and excused in this lyric in praise of saintly folly, where madness is a blessing, and poverty a virtue. " La strada may not be a great work, but it is an "exquisite" one, a poem of "bitter and tender beauty. " "Between the triumphant chant of Man in the revolutionary epic and the morbid howling of egos in the psychological drama, Gelsomina will be heard intoning the plaint of a soul and offering up an inarticulate plea for mercy. "

651 Dent, Alan. Illustrated London Newsletter, 227 (December 24, 1955), 1110.

He finds "little good" to say of a film that has been hailed a masterpiece. (Giulietta is "surpassingly" good.) "All that happens in this limp and listless film" is that the strong man murders the tight-walking clown, at which the girl "goes out of her mind. " He agrees soundly with an earlier critic who said, "It is not so much neo-realism as melo-realism. "

652 Elley, Derek. Focus on Film, n. 10, Summer, 1972, 46.

653 Flaiano, Ennio. Cinema (nuova serie), n. 139, 1954.

654 Gautier, Jean-Jacques. Le Figaro, September 8, 1954.

Gelsomina is a fake child, a fake Chaplin, whom she laboriously strives to imitate.

655 Genêt. New Yorker, 31 (March 26, 1955), 115-116.

La strada is "made of odd pieces of Italian life indissolubly put together in terms of characters, and is a film not to miss. " The film was seen in Paris, a year before the New York opening.

656 Gow, Gordon. Films and Filming, 16 (October, 1969), 58.

657 "A Grim Italian Film," Times (London), November 25, 1955, 3.

Discusses neo-realism and where it is headed in Italy. "In directing this piece of vagabondage, Federico Fellini spares the audience nothing in the way of bestiality and degradations; this is realism crowing on a dung-hill. "

658 Hartung, Philip T. "Pilgrim's Progress," Commonweal, 64 (August 3, 1956), 441.

He doesn't know "how American audiences, used to a success story and conventional boy-gets-girl ending," will take to the film, but it is certainly "for the discriminating. " If ever a film is "ever flowing with the love for man, be he saint or sinner," it is La strada. Fellini's "magnificent conception" is that of "the road of life down which, no matter how fast one runs, one cannot escape the Hound of Heaven. "

659   Hatch, Robert.   Nation, 183 (August 4, 1956), 106.
      Fellini's theme is "a parable about the intercourse of strength, tenderness, and wit in this world and about the terrible loneliness that comes when they cannot relate to one another. "   He is reminded of the "comforting theory that God in His mercy endows His fools with a special sweetness, goodness, and exquisite perception, " but he doubts that Fellini intends "anything so sentimental. "

660   Jubilee, 4 (October, 1956), 52.

661   Knight, Arthur.   "Italian Realism Refreshed, " Saturday Review, 39 (June 30, 1956), 23-24.
      Lovely, sensitive review.   La strada is neo-realism on a new plane, a mixture of realism and poetry.   What makes the film "completely extraordinary is the way its poetry, its symbols, its modest philosophy all flow from incidents so commonplace that only in this juxtaposition do they begin to acquire significance. "   The images created have a clarity "of a Cartier-Bresson photograph come to life. "   Gelsomina is like the "foolish, warm-hearted innocent" that Langdon used to play.

662   McCarten, John.   "Protracted Parable, " New Yorker, 32 (July 28, 1956), 48.
      Finds the ideas of the film "elementary" and Fellini's characters and situations "odd. "   The characters, moreover, have "a good deal of monotony" about them.   Giulietta Masina, "who has been done up to resemble Harry Langdon, has a limited range of expression, registering joy and sorrow but nothing in between. "   Richard Basehart, however, "helps out considerably when everybody else becomes too leaden for comfort. "

663   Mannock, P. L.   Films and Filming, 2 (January, 1956), 22.

664   Martin, Andre.   Cahiers du Cinéma, n. 45.

665   Mayer, Andrew.   Quarterly Film Radio and Television, 11 (Spring, 1957), 276-279.

666   Media and Methods, 11 (December, 1974), 36.

667   Mida, Massimo.   Il Contemporeneo, n. 15, April, 1955.

668   Morris, Herbert.   "The Road, " Kenyon Review, 19 (1957), 203-204.
      A poem inspired by the film (excerpt):
          "Not in a root, or stone, but in a man
          she found a thing to hold her tenderness.
          I like her dedication after that,
          her saying, if she spoke, I live by this. "

II: Articles on Individual Films   143

669 "Movie Milestone," Harper's, 213 (August, 1956), 81-82.
     Finds the film "low-life in context, somber in tone, and
     without hope in message." The film's technicians "build an en-
     tire picture around the sort of equivocal ambiguity that film
     conveys as no other medium can."

670 National Parent Teacher, 51 (October, 1956), 38.

671 Redi, Riccardo. Cinema (nuova serie), n. 130 (March 31,
     1954), 163-165.

672 Reichley, James. "The Beauty and the Best," New Republic,
     135 (December 31, 1956), 22.
     Much is a plot summary. Then compares La strada to
     Born Yesterday. Knows that La strada is a superior film but
     isn't exactly sure why.

673 Sadoul, Georges. Les Lettres Françaises, March 17, 1955.
     The only similarity between Giulietta Masina and Chaplin
     is that each wears a bowler. "For the rest, I don't see any
     connection."

674 Solmi, Angelo. "The Lonely Heroes of La strada," Fellini.
     Atlantic Highlands, N. J.: Humanities Press, 1968, Part II,
     Chapter 6.
     Even though Vitelloni was enormously successful, Fellini
     still had difficulty launching La strada. (Producers didn't want
     either Giulietta Masina or Anthony Quinn to play the leads.)
     Tells how Fellini, during shooting of Luci del varietà saw two
     nomads, like Zampanò and Gelsomina, who ate supper together
     without speaking a word to one another. This triggered off Fel-
     lini's idea for the film. The true meaning of the film is in its
     ending. Zampanò, "who does not think and lives only through
     his senses, becomes a human being again through anguish and
     suffering" as he remembers Gelsomina. In La strada Fellini
     has tried to make a film along Chaplin's lines, "with all the
     bitter desolation of The Tramp, The Circus, and City Lights."

675 _____. Oggi, n. 39, 1954.

676 "The Strong Grow Weak," Newsweek, 48 (July 16, 1956), 84.
     "As the girl, Giulietta Masina is extraordinarily touching
     and gives a performance hard to forget, though one does dis-
     cover as time goes on that one can tire of something touching.
     It is an unusual movie. But Americans are very apt to get the
     feeling, again and again, that now THE END is at hand, only
     to find themselves wrong." Sums up--"Novel and arguable."

677 "The Strong Grow Weak," Time, 68 (July 23, 1956), 84.
     Devotes itself for the most part in telling the incidents of
     the plot. The film is a beautiful allegory "of innocence and
     the artist and the brute--in which no one wins." Giulietta has

a little of Imogene Coca and Stan Laurel plus "something more:
a vernal innocence that is as ageless as it is rare. "

678 Swados, Harvey. "La strada: Realism and the Comedy of
Poverty," Yale French Studies, 17 (Summer, 1956), 38-43.
    Splendid, informative, appreciative study of the film as an
example of the "cinema of poverty. " To Swados this is the
"real meaning of realism, neo--or any other variety" as por-
trayed in Open City, Paisan, Shoeshine, Bicycle Thief as well
as in Chaplin's masterpieces The Gold Rush, City Lights, Modern Times. "These anonymous figures are universal, as poverty is universal and glamor is not; because most people
throughout the inhabited world live like this, in streets like this
and not in an infinitude of endlessly mounting sequined MGM
staircases. "

679 Szczepański, Jan Józef. Tygodnik Powszechny, n. 7, 1957.

680 Times (London), September 8, 1954.
    La strada wins Venice Film award--the Silver Lion, which
ranks below the grand prix.

681 Times (London), November 8, 1955.

682 Times (London), March 29, 1957, 3.
    La strada, "the Italian drama about itinerant circus per-
formers," won the Oscar for best foreign film.

683 Tyler, Parker. Classics of the Foreign Film: A Pictorial
Treasury. New York: Citadel, 1962, 216-218.
    Outlines briefly Neo-realist and State apprehensiveness
about the film and attempts at censorship lest foreign audiences
think that "sordidness" prevails among the Italian lower classes.
Considers the moral of the film true, beautiful, and lucid:
"Gelsomina is technically a starved butterfly, defenseless; but
like Christianity when it first opposed armed paganism, wins
out by happy, clear-souled surrender. " Has five captioned
photos briefly and intelligently outlining the plot of the film.

684 Weightman, J. G. "Evil in the Cinema," Twentieth Century,
159 (January, 1956), 69-72.
    Reviewed with Rififi and Les Diaboliques. "In all three we
are treated to the spectacle of a man beating a woman, and in
all three the beating precedes a kind of rape. " Finds the film
as good as the best Russian films. "If Giulietta Masina is not
a natural half-wit, either she or Fellini must be a genius. "
But he finds fault with the ending: where, in a "concession to
sentimentality, the strong man looks up to heaven and repents. "
The rest of the film is "ruthless" and "absolutely sound. "

685 Weiler, A. H. "La strada Is Tender, Realistic, Parable,"
New York Times, July 17, 1956, 19.
    Fellini "has used his small cast, and, equally important,

his camera, with the unmistakable touch of an artist. His vignettes fill his movie with beauty, sadness, humor and understanding. "

686 _____. "A Fine La strada Again Illustrates Values of the Neo-
Realistic Film," New York Times, July 22, 1956, Section II,
1.
Longer than the review on July 17, 1956. Compares Giuli-
etta Masina's performance to that of Chaplin and Langdon.
Bravos also for Quinn and Basehart.

687 Whitebait, William. "An Italian Strong Man," New Statesman,
50 (November 26, 1955), 705.
On seeing the film a second time. "It plants itself. Story,
characters, landscape are all firmer than I remember. " Zampanò is The Strong Man; Gelsomina, The Female Clown; Il Matto is The Tightrope Artist, "a bit cracked, a bit taken by her
and fascinated by him, as the matador is by the bull. " Here
then, "is a time-honored theme. "

688 Willing, Diana. Films in Review, 7 (August-September, 1956),
351-352.
An early appraisal of Fellini, written after the New York
City premiere. Fellini is a "comparatively new Italian director. " She finds the film a "not too professional film" about
human loneliness, and "since our loneliness is an omnipresent
fact we scarely need to be reminded of it amateurishly. " The
film has been shot with too much improvisation. Zampanò,
Gelsomina, and Il Matto seem to her like examples of "those
curses of the human race called ignorance, stupidity, and
a-morality. " She finds it inexcusable that Fellini uses "the
feeble-minded girl's a-morality" to titillate the audience. As
for Giulietta's performance as Gelsomina "the less said about
her the better. "

689 Woodtli, S. Reformatio, 17 (May, 1968), 310-311.

690 Young, Vernon. "La strada: Cinematic Intersections," Hudson
Review, 9 (Fall, 1956), 437. Reprinted in On Film. Chicago:
Quadrangle Books, 1972, 59, 67.
Briefly characterizes Sceicco bianco, extensively critiques
Vitelloni, then goes on to give a detailed encomium of La strada, which he cannot praise too much: "the most uncompromising fable yet evoked from the material of Italian naturalism. "
The film is not cinematically remarkable but is "metaphysically
astounding; longitudes of implication extend as awesomely as
the ocean, on the strand of which it begins and ends. " He
finds Giulietta Masina's performance "fabulous. " She is to be
linked with the great clowns, her art to be "apprehended, not
subsumed, by the relation it brings to the art of Chaplin or
Barrault or Marceau. "

Il bidone

691   Aristarco, Guido.   Cinema Nuovo, n. 67, (September 25, 1955),
      925-955.

692   Bazin, André.   France Observateur, March, 1956.

693   Bianchi, Pietro.   "Federico Fellini: Il bidone," L'occhio del
      cinema, Milano: Garzanti, 1957, 57-62.

694   Borde, Raymonde.   Cinéma '56, n. 11, 1956.

695   Castello, G. C.   Il cinema neorealistico italiano.   Milano: Ed-
      izioni RAI, 1956, 54-61, 71-76.

696   Cocks, John.   Film Quarterly, 18 (Fall, 1964), 55-57.
            The film is "an interesting addition to the Fellini canon and
      a flawed but vital second part" of the La strada, Bidone, Ca-
      biria trilogy.   Sees in the film "the disquieting, almost painful
      struggle of one of the major film poets of our time to make a
      statement about which he seems uncomfortable."   Interprets
      Augusto's stoning and death at the end as Fellini's "plea for the
      accepting of man, evil and deceitful though he may be."

697   Crowther, Bosley.   New York Times, November 20, 1964, 42.
            "It is, in short, an obvious cheap-crime picture, very much
      on the sentimental side, and therefore thematically inferior to
      the two films it fell between [La strada and Cabiria].   But it
      contains some very strong Fellini phases and accumulations of
      moods that make it well worth seeing."

698   "Fellini's Inferno," Newsweek, 64 (November 23, 1964), 117.
            Calls La strada, Cabiria, and Bidone a trilogy.   Zampanò
      on the beach is Purgatory; Cabiria·s smile at that film·s end
      "suggests Paradise"; Augusto·s death is the Inferno.   Charac-
      terizes the stoning of Augusto as a Biblical symbol.   The film
      has "great power, and moments of wonderful life and beauty."

699   Fulford, Robert.   Saturday Night Publications Ltd., 80 (Feb-
      ruary, 1965), 29-31.
            Augusto looks for a way to express his love to his daugh-
      ter; he does this the only way he knows, by cheating his fellow
      conmen of the few hundred thousand lire that would pay for his
      daughter's education.   In the 1950's many Italian directors,
      especially Fellini, began looking for a heightened "sense of
      character."   Says that Fellini says, "In doing this they did not
      abandon social realism of the 1940's.   Italian post-war films
      started out saying: this is how people live; this is how it
      looks.   They have never stopped saying this, but in the 1950's,
      and much more so today, they've also been saying; this is how
      people feel; this is why they laugh: this is why they lose hope."

700 Furrow (Ireland), 10 (January, 1959), 31.

701 Ghelli, N. Bianco e Nero, 16 (September/October, 1955), 9-10.

702 Hartung, Philip T. "Compulsive?" Commonweal, 81 (December 11, 1964), 389.
Short "run-down" of some of the current foreign films, which includes Bidone. "Even old and not-the-best Fellini is better than no Fellini." The story is "somewhat contrived, especially in the conversion finale. But Il bidone is still worth seeing, and is a must for Fellini enthusiasts."

703 Jackiewicz, Aleksander. Film Jako Powieśĉ XX Wieku [Film as Novel in the 20th Century], 1966.

704 Mangini, Cecilia. "I due bidoni," Cinema Nuovo, n. 66 (September 10, 1955), 174-175.

705 Ojetti, Pasquale. Cinema, n. 151, 925-951.

706 Pathé Magazine (Paris), n. 11, 1955, "special issue."
A promotion booklet for Pathé Co. --includes black-and-white and color illustrations.

707 Prouse, Derek. Sight and Sound, 26 (Winter, 1956/1957), 153-154.
With all the criticisms, the film is still "the work of a sharp and fascinating talent." But there is "a typical Fellini dichotomy: one law for the bad and another for the good. While greed, lust and general depravity are enthusiastically scrutinized, goodness remains merely an abstraction." But perhaps Fellini is content that this is so: "that decadence should evoke his shrewdest satire while good remains only a vague, symbolic, and mystical force." Says that the final sequence is considerably cut in the version shown. Franco Fabrizi is a wholly convincing Roberto: "a glibly handsome and slippery fraud."

708 Quigly, Isabel. "Sharp Practice," Spectator, 197 (November 16, 1956), 682.
Fellini's "most remarkable" film to date, (1956), better than Vitelloni: "its morality is stronger, its direction sterner and more confident; its use of the grotesque ... more assured and pointed."

709 Rotha, Paul. Films and Filming, 3 (January, 1957), 23. Reprinted in Rotha on the Film. London: Faber and Faber, Ltd., 1958.

710 Sarris, Andrew. Village Voice, 10 (November 19, 1964), 13, 18.

711 Solmi, Angelo. "A Step Backwards--Il bidone," Fellini. At-
     lantic Highlands, N. J. : Humanities Press, 1968, Part II,
     Chapter 7.
     Fellini had met a swindler in a restaurant who told him the
     story of his life. Bidone is a slang term for a trick played
     upon those "who will not denounce it for fear of looking stupid. "
     Says that the film was hurriedly made and even more hurriedly
     edited--to get it ready for a film festival showing, and he points
     out what he feels are various defects in the film. But it is
     "in no way unworthy of the great trilogy of loneliness, that
     opens with La strada and ends with Le notti di Cabiria. " Bi-
     done is "a defective link in the chain" but is still "a link of
     iron, difficult to break despite the most violent attacks. " Fel-
     lini, at least when the film first came out, strenuously defended
     it.

712 Times (London), November 12, 1956, 3.
     "Fellini has moved away from the severe realism of the
     Italian cinema of the middle forties and a kind of drama, which,
     while it does not cut itself adrift from realism, seeks to com-
     bine that quality with an outlook at once satirical and poetic. "

713 Weightman, J. G. "Out and About," Twentieth Century, 160
     (December, 1956), 557.
     The theme is the tragedy of an ageing confidence man who
     longs to bring off a swindle "that will set him off for the rest
     of his life. " The film is not bad but a "disappointment. " It's
     partly like La strada and Vitelloni "without the intensity of
     either. . . . Poetry and irony have declined, while pathos has
     been allowed to increase. " Hopes that Fellini will be able to
     arrest this tendency towards "thickening and softening. "

                           Le notti di Cabiria

714 Baker, Peter. Films and Filming, 4 (March, 1958), 23.

715 Bazin, André. Cahiers du Cinéma, n. 76, 1957.

716 Benedetti, Benedetto. ["Cabiria--the Sultan's Guest, "] Cinema
     Nuovo, n. 25, December 15, 1956.

717 Cabrera, G. (G. Cain). "Del amor y del dinero," Un Oficio
     del Siglo 20. Barcelona: Biblioteca Breve, Editorial Seix Bar-
     ral, S. A. , 1973, 352-354.

718 Corbin, Louise. Films in Review, 8 (December, 1957), 529.
     Only a 150-word review but quite to the point. The film
     is "ineptly written" and "synthetic. " There is no realism,
     "neo or other. " Masina's performance is one of "feeble-minded
     insouciance which constitutes her acting style. " The talk that
     her Cabiria is like Chaplin's tramp "was started by Italian
     press agents. " The film "is of no consequence. "

719 Crowther, Bosley. New York Times, October 29, 1957, 34.
Says that there are "two weaknesses in Cabiria. It has a
sordid atmosphere and there is something elusive and insuffi-
cient about the heroine. Her get-up is weird and illogical for
the milieu in which she lives and her farcical mannerisms clash
with the ugly realism of the theme." "The film runs for an
hour and fifty minutes, which is too long for the little it has
to tell."

720 Digest Religiso, 3 (Autumn, 1957), 54.

721 Gorbman, Claudia. "Music as Salvation: Notes on Fellini and
Rota," Film Quarterly, 28 (Winter, 1974/1975), 17-25.
Tight, detailed, brilliant article on relationship of the musical score to the central meaning of the film. (Also contains
a brief exegesis of the musical leitmotifs in La strada.) Spec-
ifies four musical themes and the fifth theme, silence. "Music prevails so much in Cabiria that its absence is quite notice-
able." Every element of the film has demonstrated, says Gorbman, a search for salvation. The music of the young people
at the end of the film "is salvation: unmotivated, gratuitous,
ubiquitous." Cabiria "joins the procession with a mixture of
grief and joy, aware of herself, of those around her, and of
the renewed possibility of life."

722 Hartung, Philip T. "More About les Girls," Commonweal, 67
(November 22, 1957), 202-204.
"Instead of having a conventional plot, it relates a series
of episodes which, though fascinating and highly dramatic in
themselves, seem at first to be disconnected." Fellini is "en-
amored" of his subject matter and takes "too long" to end the
story. The last scenes are "heartbreaking" and "redeemed"
only by the finale which "although ambiguous, shows the survival
of the spirit in spite of man's inhumanity to man."

723 Hatch, Robert. Nation, 185 (November 23, 1957), 396.
Wonders whether Masina is an actress or a clown, suspects
she is no clown but an actress typed by her director-husband
"who perhaps knows her strength and weaknesses too well and
who is too eager for her success." The film permits Masina
to continue wooing us but "with a very small bag of tricks."
He regrets that he doesn't much care what keeps happening to
Cabiria in the film.

724 "An Italian Cinema Clown in the Great Tradition," Times (London), April 7, 1958, 10.
Cabiria is "a rare and a moving experience." Simply gush-
es with bravos for Giulietta Masina and her portrayal of Cabiria. She is compared to Chaplin's tramp.

725 "It's Rich and Subtle," Newsweek, 50 (November 4, 1957), 114-
115.
"Even better than the powerful La strada." Calls Masina

"the best tragi-comedian on film since Chaplin. " The movie's
message, "time-honored--worn to a frazzle ... and particularly
by the Italians" is "that life kicks some people in the face as
often as it caresses others, and only a few of the kicked can
come up smiling. "

726 Jackiewicz, Aleksander. Film Jako Powieść XX Wieku, [Film
     as Novel in the Twentieth Century], 1958.

727 Kerans, James. Film Quarterly, 12 (Fall, 1958), 43-45.
     Very sensitive exegesis, of the film as a whole but parti-
     cularly of its opening and closing sequences. The opening epi-
     sode (Cabiria pushed into the river by her early lover) is "al-
     most a parody of neo-realismo melodrama. " The rest of the
     film undertakes "to transfigure this formula, to invert it, to
     give it religious, humane, and artistic dignity. " "Grace, really,
     is the subject of the film. The sense that Cabiria is 'chosen,'
     whether as victim or redeemed.... "

728 Knight, Arthur. "Noblest Roman of Them All, " Saturday Re-
     view, 40 (November 9, 1957), 28.
     Says the film "glows with the affirmation of life" and calls
     the 36-year-old Fellini "without question Italy's greatest film
     artist today. " Not so much a review of the film as an assem-
     blage of exceptionally valuable comments from a Fellini inter-
     view that illuminate the film and Fellini's attitude toward making
     films. Fellini tells about the real-life prostitute Wanda, whom
     he chanced upon while making Bidone and who ultimately served
     "as a sort of technical advisor" in Cabiria. She was "an in-
     dependent creature with a hard cover of anger for her terrible
     lonely pride. " Fellini cannot see how American directors can
     take someone else's script that has been written for some spe-
     cific star and make of it "something personal. " He cannot di-
     rect just any script. "In all my films I try to send out the
     inner realization of something. I cannot work otherwise. "

729 Lane, John Francis. "No Road Back, " Films and Filming, 4
     (October, 1957), 10, 32.

730 McCarten, John. "Dreamy Doxy, " New Yorker, 33 (November
     9, 1957), 109.
     "Cabiria is as firm as Dr. Pangloss in the conviction that
     everything is for the best in this best of all possible worlds. "
     He thinks that maybe something is to be said for this attitude,
     "just what I can't think offhand. " He thinks Masina's acting is
     sometimes too clownish to sustain the realist mood of the film,
     but he feels Masina's performance is "sturdy" and Perier's
     "superb" and that there are in the film some "highly effective
     episodes. "

731 Martin, Marcel. Cinéma '57, n. 22, 1957.

732 National Parent Teachers, 52 (January, 1958), 38.

733 Playboy, January, 1958, 9.
Just a comment that the film is "a must-see follow-up" by
the director and star of La strada.

734 Quigly, Isabel. "Instead of a Miracle," Spectator, 200 (April
11, 1958), 456+.
Cabiria is, in a way, a small capitalist: she owns her
house, gas stove, furniture. Everything is paid for. And just
as the house sets her apart from the other streetwalkers so
the future holds, in her dreams, the impossible mirage of re-
spectability: marriage and a home. The film's whole point is
that "faith makes no miracles at all, but that the courage and
perkiness, toughness, and resilience that make it possible for
Cabiria to go on believing in them are worth more, in the end,
than any miracle." But the film is too bitty, too anecdotal, at
times too repetitive of past triumphs, mannerisms, to rank with
Fellini's best films.

735 Revue Nouvelle (Belgium), 26 (November, 1957), 462.

736 Sarris, Andrew. Film Culture, 4 (January, 1958), 18-21.

737 _____. Village Voice, 14 (April 10, 1969), 51, 54.

738 Solmi, Angelo. "A Message of Hope in Cabiria," Fellini. Atlantic Highlands, N. J. : Humanities Press, 1968, Part II, Chapter 8.
Tells how Fellini, while shooting Bidone, chanced on the
real-life prototype of Cabiria, a little prostitute whose "wild,
violent behavior," said Fellini, "hid an enormous need of affection." Tells too how Fellini and Gherardi walked through
the quarter of Rome frequented by prostitutes to get ideas for
settings. Cabiria, says Solmi, is more representative of poor
people in general than is Gelsomina. This makes Cabiria "of
greater value" than La strada and represents a "reconciliation"
between Fellini's poetic universe and the old tendencies of neo-
realism. Compares the "delicacy" and "humiliation" of the
film's finale to those of the films of Chaplin.

739 _____. Oggi, n. 43, 1957.

740 Times (London), May 18, 1957, 8.
Cannes Film Festival awards. Giulietta wins the award for
her performance in Cabiria.

741 Times (London), May 20, 1957, 3.
A short comment on the film and on the Giulietta Masina,
who won the Cannes' award. Considers Cabiria "sentimental"
and "monotonous for all its elaboration of surface detail." Fellini is a "facile" director, but one whose "feelings do not go
deep."

742 Viazzi, Glauco. Contemporaneo, October 12, 1957.

743 Wort und Wahrheit, 13 (January, 1958), 50-52.

La dolce vita

744 Alicata, Mario. Cinema Nuovo, n. 150, 1961.

745 Allen, Roderic. Film, n. 29 (Summer, 1961), 11-12.

746 Alpert, Hollis. World, 1 (August 29, 1972), 53.

747 _____. "Adventures of a Journalist," Saturday Review,
     44 (April 22, 1961), 33. Reprinted in Fellini, Federico. La
     dolce vita. Trans. Oscar DeLiso and Bernard Shir-Cliff. New
     York: Ballantine Books, 1961.
        "The most brillant of all the movies that have attempted to
     portray the modern temper." Its message is that "the modern
     loss of faith has resulted in a sapping of what the nineteenth
     century called the will." "But there is a surprising lack of
     anger in Fellini's camera. It is almost as though he has come
     upon a pageant of life that is, for all its irony, haunting and
     strangely beautiful."

748 Andrews, Nigel. Monthly Film Bulletin, 39 (September, 1972),
     184.

749 "Angry Cry Against a Sinful City," Life, May 12, 1961, 54.

750 Aristarco, Guido. Cinema Nuovo, n. 143 (January-February,
     1960), 39-44.

751 Ave Maria, 93 (June 17, 1961), 17.

752 Ave Maria, 94 (August 26, 1961), 15.

753 Baragli, Enrico. "Dopo La dolce vita I: Tra realtà, arte e
     religione," La Civiltà Cattolica, 3 (September 17, 1960), 602-
     617.

754 _____. "Dopo La dolce vita II: Critici, registi e pubblico,"
     La Civiltà Cattolica, 4 (October 15, 1960), 159-176.

755 Beckley, Paul V. New York Herald-Tribune, April 20, 1961.
        Long review. Raves for Fellini and the cast. Claims that
     Dolce vita may be "the most exciting film of the year."

756 Bergtal, E. "Lonely Crowd in La dolce vita," America, 106
     (October 7, 1961), 13-15.
        Written by a sociologist, who feels, now that the first wave
     of reviews has passed, that "a more reflective study of some
     of the film's sociological insights may be in order." Reflecting
     on the religious aspects of the film, he asks and answers,

"Does Fellini mean that of its nature religion is of no use in the City of Man? Or rather does he want to say that much of what passes for religion in Italy is irrelevant? Or is the film an apocalyptic sermon, warning man of what happens when he deliberately cuts himself off from the Supernatural? From the movie itself it is hard to say just what Fellini intends. "

757   Blackfriars, 42 (February, 1961), 83.

758   Cameron, Kate. "La dolce vita Is a Disturbing Picture," The Daily News, April 20, 1961, 73.

759   Canby, Vincent. "They Even De-Dolce'd La vita!" New York Times, November 8, 1970.
      Canby re-saw Dolce vita recently and was shocked to find so many scenes missing from the film. Gone were: the helicopter taking Christ to Rome, the fake miracle, Steiner's literary party, and all reference to murder and suicide. The reason--he later found out--was that he saw a dubbed, cut TV version.

760   "Cannes Award for La dolce vita," Times (London), May 21, 1960, 7.
      News item. States that Dolce vita won the highest prize at the Cannes film festival.

761   Cederna, Camilla. "Confesso Fellini," Espresso-mese, July, 1960, 54-63, 108-109.

762   Christian Order, 2 (January, 1961), 62.

763   Cleaves, Henderson. "La dolce vita Stirs Controversy," New York World-Telegram and Sun, April 15, 1961.
      Brief descriptive background of the "controversy" surrounding Dolce vita. Written the week the film was to open in New York.

764   Cook, Alton. "La dolce vita Revels Brought to America," New York World Telegram and Sun, April 20, 1961.

765   Cousins, Norman. "Meaning in the Human Arena," Saturday Review, 46 (March 9, 1963), 22.
      Dolce vita "caricatures life; it loses contact with the capacity of men to preserve and indeed enlarge their dignity under stress or attack. " If the characters in Dolce vita are indeed searching for a meaning in life, he's unhappy with them because they lack credentials for the search. They have no real insight into life. "The main question before humanity is not the meaninglessness of life but rather how to mobilize human intelligence and feeling into making a better and safer world. "

766   "Critical Reactions," Commonweal, 74 (May 26, 1961), 221.
      'Reactions" to the classification Dolce vita got from the Legion of Decency.

767   Crosby, John.   "La vita Decadente," New York Herald Tribune,
      April 24, 1961.
          Dolce vita "expresses the temper of the times more vividly
      and succinctly than anything I have seen. ...   One serious flaw
      is the central character. ..." Claims that Dolce vita is mis-
      sing a "central overriding purpose" or "it's hidden. " But in-
      spite of all this finds that Dolce vita has "warmth, freshness,
      vigor," and "originality. "

768   Crowther, Bosley.   New York Times, April 20, 1961, 30.
          This is a long, favorable review.   "In sum, it is an awe-
      some picture, licentious in content but moral and vastly sophis-
      ticated in its attitude and what is says.   An excellent cast per-
      forms it. " Says Fellini "is nothing if not fertile, fierce and
      urbane in calculating the social scene around him and packing
      it onto the screen. "

769   _____ .   "Fellini's Urbane Film Looks Askance at Life,"
      New York Times, April 23, 1961, Section II, 1.
          A most favorable review.   Gives a long description of epi-
      sodes in the movie with an analysis.   Talks about the rich
      "rendered lax by luxury, by the confusions of politics and the
      evidences of injustice that have knocked the props out from un-
      der their faith, they are without morals or conscience, seeking
      sensations or a way of gratifying their libidos and their restless
      minds. " Says that Fellini has done a "brilliant job" and says
      that Fellini's understanding of "the scene" emerges the "most
      moral and sobering exhibitions ever put on the screen. "

770   Cue, 43 (September 23, 1974), 35.

771   "The Day of the Beast, " Time, 77 (April 21, 1961), 72.
          "In conception" the film is "noble and profound, and its vi-
      sualization of the principal symbols--particularly the apparitions
      of Christ and antichrist--was stunning. " But "for all its vitali-
      ty, the film is an artistic failure. " Fellini thinks he has put
      "a thermometer to a sick world; but it may be that he has sim-
      ply taken his own temperature. "

772   "Denunciations and Box Office Boom in Italy for Sardonic Sweet
      Life, " Variety, February 17, 1960.

773   de Vecchi, Mario.   "The Sweet Life's Hard Knocks," New York
      Times, April 16, 1961, Section II, 7.
          Article written three days before Dolce vita opened in New
      York, by a close friend of Fellini.   Basically retells all the
      "problems" Fellini encountered before, during, and after the
      making of Dolce vita.   Says Fellini's first producer initially re-
      jected Dolce vita because it was too "chaotic," "depressing"
      and "realistic. " Because of the delay in finding a new producer,
      Fellini had to recast much of the film.   During the actual shoot-
      ing, money was the only problem.   When the film opened in

Rome, the censors charged that Dolce vita was an "insult." Hopes that now that Dolce vita is opening here--all Fellini's "problems" will be over.

774   "La dolce vita Blazes Subtitled Paths; May Mislead Showman Back in Italy," Variety, November 1, 1961, 19.
The Legion of Decency approved only the subtitled version of Dolce vita. Presumes that a dubbed version would have been "condemned." Too, because of Dolce vita's success, more theatres are willing to show subtitled pictures.

775   "La dolce vita Cannes Choice," Daily Telegraph and Morning Post, May 21, 1960, 10.

776   "Dolce vita Gets Approved," New York Times, April 19, 1962, 35.
Dolce vita got the Motion Picture Association of America approval. This means that Dolce vita will now get wider distribution privileges. Some theatres don't book foreign films without this approval.

777   "La dolce vita Stirs Fuss with Reds: 'Tain't Wholesome for Cuban Workers," Variety, February 12, 1964, 2, 58.

778   "Dolce vita to Astor Globally for $1,350,000," Variety, March 14, 1962.
Astor films acquires all rights--worldwide--from Rizzoli Films for Dolce vita.

779   "La dolce vita, with 200 U.S. Prints, Assumes Model Role for Linguals," Variety, October 18, 1961.

780   Discussion, 46 (March 30, 1963), 30.

781   Duprey, Richard A. "Bergman and Fellini, Explorers of the Modern Spirit," Catholic World, 194 (October, 1961), 13.
Fellini views the world in critical condition. Dolce vita's vision is "clearly apocalyptic" with Rome as the new Babylon. The reporter and photographer who "haunt" the film indict us all. "The accusation of La dolce vita is clear. If we are products of the age in which we live, we are also responsible for it." In the film, each dawn brings a "reckoning." "For Fellini's picaresque hero, this Italian Peer Gynt, dawn brings the harsh light that dismembers dreams and delusions." The seven dawns remind us of the Book of the Apocalypse. Each dawn points out a new truth and "each time Marcello fails to profit by the lesson.... As dark falls and temptation multiplies temptation, the once moderately idealistic young man becomes a prime inhabitant of this earthly hell."

782   _____. "La dolce vita," Catholic Mind, 60 (March, 1962), 38-42. Reprinted from Critic, 20 (November, 1961), 26-28.
Fellini "recreated the modern Babylon in which we live so

as to enable us to see our own image spread before us on the
wide black-and-white screen." The film reminds him of a re-
treat master or confessor's warnings "that grace refused--un-
heeded over and over--may not be offered again." Marcello
is an "unwitting Faust" who makes no deal with Mephistopheles
but who strolls into the area of self-indulgence which the devil
conjures up before him. The God of Dolce vita is not an aven-
ging God but one "who waits and lets depravity prove its own
punishment for those who would embrace it."

783 _____. "La dolce vita; Fellini's Diagnosis of the Modern
World," Critic, 20 (November, 1961), 26-28. Reprinted in
Catholic Mind, 60 (March, 1962), 38-42.
        See 782.

784 Durgnat, Raymond. Films and Filming, 7 (January, 1961), 31-
32.

785 _____. "Some Mad Love and the Sweet Life," Films and
Filming, 8 (March, 1962), 16-18, 41.

786 "Federico Fellini: veni, vidi, vita," Playboy, March, 1962,
84.
        "His harrowing, mesmeric pawn play of ennui and eroticism
in Roman cafe society." The "fatal flaw" of others has been
Fellini's strength: "egocentric self-assurance."

787 "Fellini's Powerful Film of Decadence in Rome," Times (London), December 7, 1960, 15.
        Dolce vita opened in London on December 8, 1960. Gives
a brief synopsis of the "controversy" that has attached itself to
Dolce vita. Quotes another critic, who said that Dolce vita is
a "poem in verses and stanzas making up an apocalyptic fresco
of seven nightmarish nights and seven sobering dawns." States
that Dolce vita is well-planned and well-built: "The whole is
built up in a series of blocks, so solid do they seem, each
making its own distinctive contribution to the whole." Calls it
a "condemnation of a society which has lost its way, lost its
hope, lost its faith."

788 "Fellini's Sequel to Moraldo," Times (London), March 24, 1959,
6.
        Brief survey of what Fellini has done since Vitelloni. Talks
also about Fellini's new film--Dolce vita. Tells that Dolce vita
is akin to Moraldo in città, which Fellini had planned after Vitelloni and has long since dropped. Fellini has called Dolce
vita a "great panorama of a society in decadence, an anguished
journey through spiritual ravines where every myth is reduced
to a desolate emptiness, where are broken into tiny fragments
the major ideals and institutions, from love of one's country to
marriage, from honesty to respect for one's work."

789 Filmfacts, 4 (1961), 101.
        Perhaps the most complete listing of credits and cast,

identifying precisely who plays whom, plus a short objective
synopsis of the story and sample selections of several reviews
of the film.

790 Flaus, John. Film Journal, n. 19 (April, 1962), 44-49.

791 Franchi, R. M. Film Quarterly, 14 (Summer, 1961), 55-57.
"What is most wrong with the film is its obviousness, its
perverse insistence on saying the same thing over and over."
Fellini has chosen "to recreate a giant cross-section of modern
civilization and what is more to make a moral judgment con-
cerning that cross-section. Frankly, he is not up to the task."
Of the characters: "No motivations are attributed, no atmosphere is created; we are forced to assume that all these people
act this way for no good reason." The scene in the castle is
"so blatant, that it might have been written by Stanley Kramer."

792 Genêt. New Yorker, 36 (August 13, 1960), 93-94.
Gives a good synopsis of the film. Then concedes that perhaps Fellini's "loose, stylistic method" has a legitimate use in
this film. Quotes a French critic who called Dolce vita "un
beau poème cinématographique." Thinks maybe that's what Dolce vita is.

793 Gerasimov, Sergei. Films and Filming, 7 (March, 1961), 7,
38.

794 Gibbs, Patrick. "Muck-Rake's Progress," Daily Telegraph,
December 10, 1960.

795 Gilbert, Justin. "Fellini's Vita a Bold Achievement," New York
Mirror, April 20, 1961.
"Fellini paints with people, using a tar brush and a smudge
pot for his portraiture." Then, he gives them a "Dorian Gray-
ish overlay" so that they emerge "handsome, seductive" or
"honestly human." Then Fellini strips them bare to "expose
their moral and spiritual putrescence."

796 Grandi, Libero. "Filming La Dolce Vita in Black-and-White
and Wide-Screen," American Cinematographer, 41 (April, 1960),
234-235+.
About the cinematographer of Dolce Vita--Otello Martelli.

797 Hart, Henry. Films in Review, 12 (June-July, 1961), 352-354.
"A three-hour peep-show--a carelessly written and directed
hodge-podge of skits." Really just an exploitation film, which
can be promoted to attract sensation-seekers. Refers to Fellini's "racketeering instincts." The hero is played "without any
characterization" by Mastroianni. The scene with Steiner in
church "has little point." The whole film is a "meaningless
mess."

798   Hartung, Philip T.   "The Waste Land," Commonweal, 74 (May
      12, 1961), 177.
          Not an unfavorable review, but to him the film is a "cold"
      picture.   It doesn't draw you into it the way L'Avventura does,
      which treats a similar theme.   Dolce vita "aloofly displays the
      evils" and makes you draw your own conclusions.   It generally
      has neither the compassion nor the universality of La strada
      and Cabiria.

799   Hatch, Robert.   Nation, 192 (April 29, 1961), 379-380.
          "...La dolce vita is a great crowd of actors behaving with
      listless impropriety and no attempt at a sustained idea.   When
      it comes to debauchery, this picture isn't in the same class
      with Rain. "

800   Hawk.   Variety, February 17, 1960.
          Review of Rome-showing on February 10.   The film is ul-
      timately "very moral. "   All the while Marcello "refuses the ad-
      vances of the only woman (Emma) who really loves him. "   Fel-
      lini's direction is "a natural talent of poetic stature. "

801   Hawkins, R.   Sight and Sound, 29 (Spring, 1960), 66.
          By a correspondent in Italy.   One of the early statements
      in English (before the American opening) of the apocalyptic as-
      pect of the film: 'What may impress the casual viewer as an
      episodic film is actually a poem in verses and stanzas, making
      up an apocalyptic fresco of seven nightmarish nights and seven
      sobering dawns.   The film permits no halfway reactions....
      One is asked to accept, or not....   This particular world is on
      the brink of catastrophe, Fellini seems to be saying in this an-
      ticipatory film.   Its personages, knowing it or not, fighting it
      or not, are waiting for disaster to strike. "

802   "Headmaster Deletes Boy Critic's Dolce Review; Young Editors
      Resign," Variety, January 2, 1962.
          Headmaster John J. Doyle said that the film received an
      "adult only" classification from the Legion of Decency, and he
      felt it was not "a fit subject. "   The Superintendent of the Boston
      schools had asked Doyle for his "prompt action in suppressing
      a review of an exotic film. "   The review appeared in the Boston
      Latin School Register.   Boston Latin is the oldest public school
      in America.

803   Hen, Józef.   Film, n. 30, 1964.

804   Holland, Norman N.   "The Follies Fellini," Hudson Review, 14
      (Autumn, 1961), 425-431.   Reprinted in Bellone, Julius, ed. ,
      Renaissance of the Film.   New York: Macmillan, 1970.
          Calls Dolce vita's theme and mythic dimension: "men over-
      powered ... by the gorgon-like image of woman. "   "Men become
      mere consorts, lover-kings, ridiculous, impotent. "   "The women
      are goddesses, mythical, unreal belles dames sans merci, the
      sight of whom bewitches men.... "

805 _____. "The Puzzling Movies: Three Analyses and a Guess
at Their Appeal," Journal of Social Issues, 20 (January, 1964),
71-96.
Contains a modified version of his 1961 explication of Dolce
vita. Wants here to try and answer why people like the kind
of film that is difficult, that baffles and puzzles them, and
sometimes even frustrates them. (The other films treated are
Seventh Seal and Marienbad.) Holland offers a series of dis-
organized insights, some that ring false, some true, some obvious, some not, all generally based on mythology. Dolce vita's
leading theme is "the subjugation of men." The key symbols
of the film are sights and sounds. What Fellini likes to do in
Dolce vita and in his other films is to "dehumanize" people.
Some representative insights of Holland: the Miracle is about
"the traditional mating in the fields of sun-god and mortal woman." Cabiria is a "tawdry and pathetic image of Venus" who
renews herself in water "after venal Adonises have chosen and
abused her." The young girl at the end of the film is "the
virgin by the sea, image of a renewed innocence, a kind of
Aphrodite Urania." Polidor is a "doddering Pied Piper, awed
by images of woman about him" whose trumpet is "limp." He
feels that the film gives no particular reason for Steiner's suicide. Why do puzzling pictures give pleasure? They take us
back to a childhood situation of puzzlement, but present it now
as an intellectual puzzle "rather than an emotional one in real
life." Also: while we try to puzzle out the intellectual content,
we are allowed to enjoy "the forbidden content" of the film
(usually sensual).

806 Horizon, Autumn, 1970, 47.

807 Hughes, Eileen Lanouette. "La dolce vita of Federico Fellini,"
Esquire, August, 1961. See 519.

808 Illustrated London News, 238 (January 7, 1961), 34.

809 "Italian Government's Refusal to Ban Film," Times (London),
February 19, 1960, 8.
Signor Magri, Under Secretary for Entertainment, rejects
the "demands" of those who wished Dolce vita to be withdrawn.
Says that Magri didn't like Dolce vita; he called it a "sombre
fresco which clashed with the sensibilities of healthy persons
sometimes arousing disgust by scenes of a raw and ruthless
realism." But he ordered the film to be released with no cuts.
Under existing law Magri could not do otherwise--but wished
that the "new Bill" under consideration would be hurriedly
passed. Magri wished film producers would show a "greater
artistic and moral sensibility."

810 "An Italian Multi-Prizewinner Arrives," Cue, April 22, 1961.

811 Jubilee, 9 (July, 1961), 47.

812 Kael, Pauline. "The Sick-Soul-of Europe Parties: La notte,
     La dolce vita, Marienbad," Massachusetts Review, 4 (Winter,
     1963), 378-391. Reprinted in I Lost It At the Movies. Boston:
     Little, Brown and Co. , 1965, 179-196.
          She doesn't think that Fellini is "simply exploiting the inci-
     dents and crimes and orgies of modern Rome in the manner of
     a Hollywood biblical spectacle, but Dolce vita is a sort of a
     Ben Hur of the more, but not very much more, sophisticated. "
     Dolce vita "wants to be a great film--it cries out its intentions
     --and it's frequently clever ... and it's sometimes effective. ...
     And that is all it is. ... Perhaps we need to see some intelli-
     gent, hardworking or creative people who nevertheless have the
     same outlets--or vices, if you will--as these shallow people. "

813 Kałużyński, Zygmunt. Polityka, n. 32, 1964.

814 Kauffmann, Stanley. "A Catalogue of Deadly Sins," New Repub-
     lic, 144 (May 1, 1961), 22-23. Reprinted in A World on Film.
     New York: Dell, 1966, 320-322.
          "About half-way through ... I found myself thinking: What
     next? We've had Exhibits A, B, C, of decadence. How many
     more?" "Fellini has set out to move us with the depravity of
     contemporary life and has chosen what seems to me a poor
     method: cataloguing sins. Very soon we find ourselves think-
     ing: Is that all?" "Fellini's indictment becomes increasingly
     glib the more he slugs away at it. The execution is excellent;
     the concept is superficial. "

815 Lane, John Francis. "La (The) dolce (Sweet) vita (Life),"
     Films and Filming, 7 (June, 1961), 30+.
          Deals with the English dubbing of Dolce vita.

816 Lanier, S. "Wine of the Country--Sweet and Dry," Christianity
     and Crisis, 21 (May 15, 1961), 76-78.
          Reviews together Dolce vita and Antonioni's L'Avventura,
     (which were released in America at about the same time.) "Two
     remarkable sermons are being preached daily in New York City.
     One is extravagant, vivid, sprawling across its subject with all
     the superficiality and sudden, stark shock of picture-magazine
     journalism; the other is slow, spare, taking its time to lay bare
     its mystery with surgical precision. " The first--Dolce vita,
     the second is L'Avventura. He characterizes Dolce vita as
     "puritanical. " It is filled "with a naivete that is very American,
     middle-class American, ... that sees sin as predominantly sex-
     ual and always somehow ugly, dirty, and repulsive. "

817 "Legion Decides Shocks Are Moral in Dolce vita," Variety,
     May 17, 1961.

818 Lejeune, C. A. "Black Week for Rome," Observer (London),
     December 11, 1960.
          It is a masterpiece "of its kind" but a very "dreadful kind.

I should not like to send anyone to see the picture unpre-
pared.... " Some of the scenes are "the most sickening exhi-
bitions of human degradation and depravity ever shown on a
public screen. "

819   Lusso, Joyce. "Sladkaya Zhizn' and Yego Khuliteli," ["La dolce
      vita and Its Disparagers"], Literaturnaya Gazeta, April 28,
      1960.
         Letter from Italy. Talks of the reaction to the film in
      Milan, where Fellini was spat upon and threatened with a beat-
      ing, and in Rome, where someone challenged him to a duel.
      He was also called a Bolshevik.

820   Macdonald, Dwight. "Three Italian Films, and a Reprise,"
      Esquire, 55 (April, 1961), 18+. Reprinted in On Movies. New
      York: Berkley, 1971, 383-385.
         For all its human insights, Dolce vita is a sensational film;
      that is, it goes in mostly for effects. The "orgy" at the end
      is "embarrassingly dull as screen orgies usually are. " Most
      of the episodes are too long. Fellini makes a point, sometimes
      brilliantly, but then goes on to make it all over again. He is
      "fumbling around, not sure of what he wants to say, and so he
      'covers' himself on the shotgun principle. " The film is a "ser-
      mon against upper-class corruption, but one that exploits its
      gamy subject matter as much as it exposes it. "

821   Martin, Body. "Movie of Rome's Decadent Youth Will Open
      Louisville Run on Friday," Courier-Journal (Louisville), Amuse-
      ment Section, 1.
         Gives background of the "controversy" over Dolce vita in
      Rome. Says that in New York the audience "took the film in
      stride. "

822   Mekas, Jonas. Village Voice, 6 (April 27, 1961), 13.
         He never liked Fellini, but Dolce vita is Fellini's best film.
      "It shows that Fellini is a great man. That doesn't make the
      film great. But it doesn't have to be. A great man today is
      better than a great film. " Fellini's view of rich people is "a
      poor man's fish eye simplified point of view. He doesn't know
      how to portray rich people. " Dolce vita is "all surface and no
      inside. " It is "Cecil B. De Mille at his best-worst-best. " It
      is a "very great bad film which I will never forget. "

823   Melik, Peter. "Fallen City of Man," National Review, 10 (June
      17, 1961), 392+.
         A sweet, gentle, loving review. "An ambitiously conceived
      and wholly serious piece of work, very moral though never di-
      dactic, and as unmendacious a venture in a mass entertainment
      medium as we've had since Shoeshine. " "His basic attitude is
      neither apologetic nor cynical--only astringently watchful. He
      does not preach or harry, he shows. " Views the photographers
      as a modern equivalent of the Furies. "Rossellini's sense of

landscape and Chaplin's instinct for visual narrative are still
the two poles on which Fellini's own creative axis turns. " Finally, Fellini reminds us "that the Kingdom of Heaven and
'grace abounding' are as available to the man who wants them
as they ever were. "

824   Mishkin, Leo. "Dolce vita Vivid, Fascinating Film," Morning
      Telegraph, April 20, 1961.
            "There is no getting away from the fact that this latest work
      from the man who made La strada, 1 vitelloni, and Nights of
      Cabiria, ... stands as one of the screen masterpieces of the
      year. "

825   _____. "Sight and Sound," Morning Telegraph, April 24,
      1961, 2.
            A review of both The Apartment and Dolce vita. Discusses
      their similarity of theme--"a survey of contemporary manners
      and morals" and "a study of the state of modern civilization. "
      The difference between The Apartment and Dolce vita is that the
      first is asking you to "enjoy" the "moral corruption" while Dolce
      vita found the corruption "tragic. "

826   Morandini, Morando. "Year of La dolce vita," Sight and Sound,
      29 (Summer, 1960), 123-127.
            A well-informed run-down of films, mostly by young direc-
      tors, on the Italian film scene about the time of Dolce vita's
      release. Virtually all the films are unknown or unavailable to
      English-speaking audiences, and the run-down gives at least
      some sort of context for Fellini's film. Also valuable for in-
      formed insights into the background and substance of Italian neo-
      realism. "The initiators of neorealism are all now in their
      fifties, or older. In this finest period, soon after the war,
      problems could be honestly simplified and the alternatives of
      Fascism or anti-Fascism were clear to see. It is not so now.
      Many social and economic distinctions appear to be vanishing;
      many illusions (including the Communist dream) have crum-
      bled. ... " Comments favorably on the length of films like Dolce
      vita (three hours): "The directors are beginning to show a bold
      and unaccustomed respect for the film with time to develop and
      to motivate its characters on the scale of a good novel" (Fellini,
      Visconti, Antonioni).

827   Moravia, Alberto. Les Cahiers R. T. B. , 1962.

828   Morgan, W. John. "The Squalor That Was Rome," New States-
      man, 60 (December 10, 1960), 924.
            Only one-sixth of the review is devoted to Dolce vita. "The
      pace is electric except that one feels one is going around in
      circles. " The rest of this review deals with Spartacus.

829   "Movies: Three From Italy. La dolce vita, L'Avventura and
      Rocco and His Brothers," Show, 1 (October, 1961), 117-118.

830 Navone, John J. "Fellini's La dolce Italia," Commonweal, 77
     (March 15, 1963), 639-641.
        Brilliant, indispensable article, not simply for insight into
     Dolce vita but into the entire Fellini canon. "In Italy many of
     the old traditions are now breaking up; and with them has gone
     much of the old instinctual certitude. Western 'social pro-
     gress,' which has everywhere produced unsatisfying emancipa-
     tions and a complete urbanization of the soul, is a relatively
     recent force in Italy. Finding themselves committed to the vi-
     sible benefits and the concealed contradictions of the modern
     world, the Italians have experienced shocks of revolution and
     alarm at every social level. In the motion picture, these
     shocks have been expressed in that rising scream of torment
     which had its climax in what the German Catholic press hailed
     as the most Christian film in years, Fellini's Dolce vita. "
     But "Fellini is too Christian for despair, too convinced, even
     in the face of the worst human perversity, that God is love and
     cares for us through those ministering angels which find their
     way into every Fellini film. "

831 Neville, Robert. "Poet-Director of the Sweet Life," New York
     Times Magazine, May 14, 1961. Section VI, 17.
        Fellini had Gherardi make the sets look "as if they had been
     flash-photoed and printed in rotogravure: black-and-white con-
     trasts, few half-tones, combinations of sharp focus and blurs. "
     The costumes were not to be literal but a special "line" of
     Gherardi's own. The dresses were not to be dresses but rather
     flash photos of dresses. Says that when Mastroianni asked Fel-
     lini what Dolce vita "meant," Fellini answered, "It's a kind of
     baroque merry-go-round, a dancing of images that move here
     and there without meeting and thus composing something like a
     fresco of modern society. " Says that Fellini had no share of
     the foreign profits of Dolce vita and received only $50,000 as
     total pay for making the film.

832 _____. "The Soft Life in Italy," Harper's, 221 (Sep-
     tember, 1960), 65-66+.
        By an American journalist living in Rome. Particularly
     valuable for background to the film that practically every Italian
     would have but not most Americans. Says that the incident of
     the gilded Jesus borne to Rome by helicopter actually happened
     on May 1, 1950. Says that Moravia, in reviewing Dolce vita,
     called Fellini a cinematic Petronius, "thus implying that in Mor-
     avia's opinion the present times corresponded to the bittersweet
     life under Nero described in the Satyricon. " The words of the
     film's title are "loaded with irony that needs little interpretation
     here. Fellini, like so many other Italians, has been very much
     aware of the American slogans about the 'abundant life,' 'the
     good life,' 'the full life,' which have been waved constantly at
     Europeans during the postwar years. This is his reply. "

833 New York Times, September 20, 1975, 59.
        News item. Dolce vita will be shown for the first time on

Italian television after fifteen years. It will be part of a series
entitled "Great Moments in Italian Cinema."

834   "No Holds Barred," Observer (London), May 15, 1960.

835   O'Connor, Jim. "Dolce vita Sale a Record," New York Journal
American, April 15, 1961.

836   Oliver, Edith. "The Soft Life," New Yorker, 37 (April 29,
1961), 126-128.
"My suggestion ... is just to ignore the forced irony and
fumbling symbolism, and take the movie as it comes. What
difference does it make if the shadow cast by a statue of Christ
... falls on a terrace of some pretty girls sunbathing in bikinis? What is wrong with sunbathing in bikinis?"

837   "Out and About," Twentieth Century, 169 (January, 1961), 81-84.
Splendid explication, bulging with insights. Especially good
on pinning down the function of the characters in the design of
the film: Marcello, Steiner, Sylvia. Steiner, for example, is
the modern deraciné eclectic, "the man with only intellectual
allegiance." For him life has meaning "only as he can contem-
plate it as a work of art." He records natural sounds, the wind
and the sea, and listens to them like music. He delights in his
child because of the child's fondness for words, its instinctive
gift for poetry. For Steiner real life is too insistent to contem-
plate in the raw. "Here, as elsewhere in the film, a number
of questions remain unanswered, though not, I am sure, through
any carelessness on Fellini's part. His wish is to shock us
into seeing the total vacuity and negative life that such an existence may involve, and to suggest that it is not through art or
the abstracting of the intellect that salvation is to be found."

838   Pasolini, Pier Paolo. Filmcritica, n. 94, 1960.

839   Pechter, W. S. "Two Movies and Their Critics," Kenyon Review, 24 (Spring, 1962), 351-356.
"In the ... final shot, we see the angel in gigantic close-
up as slowly, very slowly, she turns her head and fixes on us
that gaze of innocence...." "The movement is ... one of those
disturbing instances of the screen's ability to move us emotionally by what we know is bad; and it is bad." It's a mistake to
judge Fellini by Dolce vita or La strada. His "masterpiece"
is Vitelloni. Dolce vita is a "failure" but not a "disreputable"
one.

840   Pelswick, Rose. "Sin, Sex, and Sensation," New York Journal
American, April 20, 1961.
"Unquestionably an unusual film, and an arresting one in its
down-beat way."

841   "Picture Grosses," Variety, July 12, 1961, 10.

842 <u>Playboy</u>, July, 1961, 16.
      "As an inventory of our era's errors the script seems some-
   what lopsided. What, not <u>one</u> noble Roman left in Rome?"

843 <u>Positif</u>, n. 35, July/August, 1960.

844 Quigly, Isabel. "Lump-of-Life," <u>Spectator</u>, 205 (December 16,
   1960), 990+.
      Compares it to <u>L'Avventura</u> beside whose "marvelous man-
   nered seriousness of eye" it has "the kick and superficiality of
   a strip cartoon. " It has "only one thing to show and shows it,
   repetitively" (the corruption and commercialization of modern
   life). The Jesus/helicopter opening scene sets the film's tone:
   "sacred and profane brought together with shock tactics. " A
   sprawling, disappointing film that "cannot be summed up. "

845 Rhode, Eric. <u>Sight and Sound</u>, 30 (Winter, 1960/1961), 34-35.
      Thoroughly caustic, a useful compendium of anti-Fellini,
   anti-<u>Dolce vita</u> cliches. Fellini likes to "improvise. " But "the
   artist is no camera. He is an interpreter involved in his material and culturally discriminating. In this sense art is always
   didactic and this discriminating is a hard, thoughtful job, not
   easily improvised. Fellini's attempt ... to catch spontaneously
   'the way life is' can be seen as naive. " Martelli's camera-
   work is "exciting," Gherardi's sets "mood evoking," and Rota's
   score "clever. " They help Fellini to build up images that are
   "swirling" and that have a rhythm that is "compelling. " But
   the ballet-like procession to the sea at the end of the film (after
   the party) has "no relevance" to the action and is injected "ty-
   pically" just because it is "pretty. " And the ending (the young
   girl waving at Marcello) is "of course" unmotivated.

846 Richardson, Robert. "Wastelands: The Breakdown of Order,"
   <u>Literature and Film</u>. Bloomington: Indiana University Press,
   1969, 106-116.
      Detailed and carefully reasoned essay showing similarity of
   theme in T. S. Eliot and Fellini (as well as in much of modern
   literature) "that this is a dry time, a barren and sterile place,
   that we lead empty and futile lives. " Both <u>The Waste Land</u> and
   <u>Dolce vita</u> have seized the imagination of a large audience, become "almost an epitome of the outlook of a generation," whose
   titles have entered common speech. Eliot's practice leans toward cinema style, Fellini's toward poetic style. Both the poem
   and the film are made up of scenes and images that are incom-
   plete but which build up impressions cumulatively. Marcello is
   a Tiresias-like spectator. Poem and story tell a modern story
   against an older background. The endings of some of Eliot's
   poems are remarkably close "to the ending of some of Fellini's
   films. " (Prufrock and Marcello both end up on a beach.) The
   Paola character is like Eliot's hyacinth girl: "in both poem and
   film, innocence is a magic movement when things seem a little
   better, if only for a moment. "

847   Roemer, Michael.   "Three Hours in Hell," <u>Reporter</u>, 24 (March
      30, 1961), 40, 42-44.
         "Implicit in the film is the suggestion that if most of us
      had money, and therefore time, we too would stand face to face
      with the unresolved emptiness in which we live; that it is only
      the strait jacket of the daily struggle that saves many of us
      from a continuous experience of chaos. "

848   Ross, Don.   "The Anatomy of Decadence," <u>New York Herald-
      Tribune</u>, April 16, 1961.
         Summarizes some of the critical responses to <u>Dolce vita</u>,
      before the New York City opening.   Moravia called it the great-
      est film ever made in Italy.   Rossellini was greatly disappointed.
      Quotes a distributor, long-time friend of Fellini's, as saying
      that in the film Fellini is "crying out for a reawakening of mor-
      als, of what is beautiful in life. "

849   Sarris, Andrew.   <u>Village Voice</u>, 13 (November 23, 1967), 31.
         A review on re-seeing <u>Dolce vita</u> at the Bleecker St. The-
      atre after several years.   "<u>La dolce vita</u> and 8½ would have
      been complete disasters without Mastroianni's personality to
      hold them together. "   "Much of <u>La dolce vita</u> remains a mess. "

850   _____.   "The Auteur Theory and the Perils of Pauline," <u>Film
      Quarterly</u> 16 (Summer, 1963), 26-33.
         Unreadable account of Sarris's view of the auteur theory,
      mostly based on French sources and in answer to an article by
      Pauline Kael.   In <u>Dolce vita</u> Fellini "enlarged his material with-
      out expanding his ideas" and so the film is "as bloated as the
      fish which terminates the orgy sequence. "   But in social im-
      pact <u>Dolce vita</u> is "the most important film ever made. "   It
      "contributes to an awareness of the hypocrisy of so-called so-
      cial morality which denies to the peasants and the proletariat
      the sweet Faustian decisions of the Kennedys and the Rockefel-
      lers," and so "can be forgiven for its intellectual and formal
      failures. "

851   Schleifer, Marc.   "La <u>Dolce vita</u> and <u>L'Avventura</u> as Contro-
      versy: <u>L'Avventura</u> and <u>Breathless</u> as <u>Phenomenalist</u> Film,"
      <u>Film Culture</u>, 26 (Fall, 1962), 59-62.
         More on <u>L'Avventura</u> than on <u>Dolce vita</u>.   In <u>Dolce vita</u>
      "like back woods there are continuous stretches of boredom
      while he gathers his breath for the next breathtaking onslaught. "
      <u>Dolce vita</u> is more ambitious than <u>L'Avventura</u>.   But it is also
      "repetitious, erratic, stuffed with Christian confusions about
      flesh and innocence. "   Antonioni, on the other hand, is not con-
      fused.

852   <u>Sign</u>, 40 (July, 1961), 43.

853   <u>Sign</u>, 41 (July, 1962), 49.

854   Simon, John. "The Sour Truth About the Sweet Life," Horizon,
      4 (September, 1961), 110-112. Reprinted in Acid Test. New
      York: Stein and Day, 1971, 17-22.
          (In Acid Test the article is retitled "To Live in Pieces,"
      and is "slightly altered" from the original.)
          Dolce vita's "most important point: there is no cure for
      human insufficiency and unhappiness. Too much money destroys
      as much as too little; the loving woman is as much of a bore
      as the intelligent one is a whore; the intellectual life and the
      life of the senses are only different facades erected before the
      ... identical void." The film implies with "unforgettable images
      the impossibility of loving."

855   Smith, Millborn, "La dolce vita," The Theatre, May, 1961, 14-
      15.
          "La dolce vita is a film of anguish, and Fellini has caught,
      as perhaps no one before him has, the special quality of pathos
      in these people, who, unable to feel emotion, seek that special
      ephemeral emotional experience which, if it does nothing else,
      will at least assure them that they are alive." "Their reaction
      to the fish is our natural reaction towards them."

856   Sobolev, R. "Tozi t 'n' k sviat ma chuvstuata," Kinoizkustvo,
      28 (November, 1973), 52-68.

857   Solmi, Angelo. Oggi, n. 48, (November 25, 1959).
          Stresses the ethical value of the film and calls the film a
      "masterpiece."

858   ____. "The Universal Vision of La dolce vita," Fellini, Atlan-
      tic Highlands, N.J.: Humanities Press, 1968, Chapter 9.
          Marcello is the new Moraldo of Fellini's old plan for Mor-
      aldo in città. From the first, Fellini has Mastroianni in mind
      as the film's protagonist. Reactions to the film at its Italian
      release. Fellini tells Solmi that official clerical reaction to
      the film ("unsuitable for all") completely misinterpreted Fellini's
      aim in making the movie. Solmi of Marcello: he "mirrors
      Fellini's own curiosity, and is a reflection of Fellini himself
      with his virtues and faults." Dolce vita is a solemn warning,
      a sermon, a "passionate accusation" against those who think
      they can do without God and who think they can find safety in a
      materialist philosophy of life.

859   "Soviet Hails Dolce vita But Public Can't View It," New York
      Times, April 20, 1962, 19.
          The Soviet newspaper Izvestia "deplored" the fact that the
      United States did not give sufficient recognition to Dolce vita.
      Dolce vita won two minor Oscars while West Side Story won ten
      major ones. An Associated Press reporter found this amusing
      since the Soviet government won't allow their people to see
      Dolce vita.

860 "Spain Still Bans La dolce vita," International Herald Tribune,
     May 30, 1972.
         News item. Spain's Supreme Court upholds the ruling that
     has prohibited the showing of Dolce vita in Spain for the last
     twelve years. The ban was imposed because the film was
     "critical of the Church" and because it "displayed certain im-
     moral acts without sufficiently condemning them. "

861 Steel, Ronald. "Fellini: Moviemaker as Moralist," Christian
     Century, 78 (April 19, 1961), 488-490.
         Report from Rome. Romans queue up for hours to see the
     film. Same is true in the provinces. Says that more Italians
     have seen Dolce vita than any film ever shown. "Fellini has
     taken four years of newspaper scandals and fused them together
     into a moving ... indictment of the malaise of a society floun-
     dering for values in a sea of 10,000 lire notes. " Gives an
     overview of the reaction to the film among various groups in
     Italy. The Vatican first allowed the film, then denounced it.
     Says that Rossellini declared on TV that Dolce vita was the
     work of a provincial. To which Fellini replied, "The reason
     I'm castigated by other Italian directors is because I've un-
     masked their world, because I've acted like a priest who has
     unveiled the mysteries they've tried to keep hidden from the
     faithful. "

862 Steinman, Sam'l. "What Soured La dolce vita?," Variety,
     January 10, 1962.
         Fellini "concocted" the whole idea for Dolce vita by "putting
     together a lot of things that did happen" and mixed in some
     things that "might have or could have or should have happened. "

863 Stonesifer, R. J. "O Lost, Again: La dolce vita in the Class-
     room," College English, 25 (January, 1964), 294-296.
         Claims that in Dolce vita Fellini "unendurably documents
     themes which he, and others, have taken from the literature of
     the Lost Generation. " Notably, from The Wasteland, The Great
     Gatsby, A Farewell to Arms, and The Sun Also Rises. You
     have to judge for yourself whether the parallels Stonesifer cites
     are convincing. Sylvia, for example, he says, is "something
     like a grandaughter to Hemingway's Lady Brett, one of a whole
     host of ladies descended from that bitch goddess of non-success.
     She is also akin to Eula of Faulkner's The Hamlet and a host
     of other doxies created by authors who wanted females to rep-
     resent more than just females. "

864 Tablet, 214 (December 10, 1960), 1145.

865 "Total Decay," Newsweek, 57 (April 24, 1961), 98.
         Very short review. "... has been called both the most
     exciting movie ever made and perverted sensationalism. In
     fact, it is as controlled an indictment as a prosecutor in the
     arts has ever offered. " The story is "not deep" but "strong,
     striking, and complete. "

866 Tyler, Parker. "La dolce vita," Classics of the Foreign Film.
New York: Citadel, 1962, 244-249.
Fellini's film is basically autobiographical, "a sort of public
confession and moral critique." Its strength comes from the
"eloquence and breadth of vision" it evokes from the basic metaphor derived from a journalism that panders to scandal-monger-
ing the adulteration of society. He points out that none of the
participants in the final party episode seems to have gone to
bed with one another during the night. Has eight captioned photos that give a brief synopsis of the film's story.

867 _____ . "La dolce vita and the Monster Fish," Sex
Psyche Etcetera in the Film. New York: Horizon Press, 1969,
106-113.
Labels Steiner the "disillusioned 'Catholic' liberal who regrets his worldliness so acutely that he kills himself." Concen-
trates mostly on the wild party sequence at the end, the "pace
and verve" of which "should make Orson Welles pale with envy
and von Stroheim wince in his grave." The monster fish em-
bodies the moral of the film: "an image of the wild-partiers'
lust for entering the animal sensations." Thought Fellini the
"foremost commercial film director of our time." (Later
changed his mind after seeing Bergman's The Silence and Per-
sona.)

868 "Vatican's Wrath Over New Film," Times (London), February
15, 1960, 15.
From their Rome correspondent. There has been "furious
reaction" to Fellini's latest film, Dolce vita. Says that a neo-
fascist agitator "spat" on Fellini at the Rome premiere. The
communists have thus asserted that the "liberty of the cinema
is at stake" and asked for support for "freedom of artistic expression." Claims what the big controversy has done is
"pack" the cinemas all over Rome. People stand for the three
hours to see the film and cars are left triple parked outside the
theatres. Fellini has "offended" because he shows the decadent
ways of Rome's "cafe-society." Says that the miracle episode
is based on an event the year before, when two children said
that the Madonna had appeared to them.

869 Vie Spirituelle, 104 (June, 1961), 636-641.

870 Walker, Alexander. "The Sweet Life--Really It's a Living
Hell!," Evening Standard, December 8, 1960, 10.
"It is by turns exhilarating and exhausting. It grips and it
bores."

871 Walsh, Moira. America, 105 (May 27, 1961), 382-384.
This is a preamble to the movie review of Dolce vita.
"The objection ... that the critic's reaction to a film is funda-
mentally different from that of the mass audience seems to me
to be largely invalid." Argues against the censorial attitude,

"What will the effect of this film be on someone without my advantages of intelligence and moral training?"

872 _____. America, 105 (June 3, 1961), 410-411.
"There is no doubt in my mind that Fellini intends his film as a salutary moral warning."

873 Weaver, W. "Letter From Italy," Nation, 190 (March 19, 1960), 260-261.
Tells of what happened to Fellini in Italy when Dolce vita opened there and is written as preview/review of the movie which hadn't opened here yet. Says that Fellini took a print to Genoa (because he was worried about the touchy subject matter) and had a private showing for Cardinal Siri, who approved the film. Claims that Fellini has half the population in Dolce vita. "So Fellini has made a family album of Rome (with some of the portraits touched up and brightly colored, as they often are in albums), and the Romans are flocking to look at it." The rest of the article is devoted to movie-making in Italy and where it is headed.

874 "What Did Fellini Say?," Saturday Review, 46 (March 30, 1963), 30.
Printed here are three letters to the editor in reply to the March 9th editorial, "Meaning in the Human Arena." One letter says that you can only understand Dolce vita if you accept Dante as its base. See 765 for the editorial of March 9.

875 Winsten, Archer. "La dolce vita at the Henry Miller," New York Post, April 20, 1961, 51.
A long favorable review. Talks about the Steiner suicide. "If you accept it as the ultimate commentary on what modern existence must mean to the sensitive ... then La dolce vita can be ... the cinematic sum-up of our time."

876 Wood, Robin. "The Question of Fellini Continued," December, 9 (Summer/Fall, 1967), 140.

877 Woodtli, S. Reformatio, 17 (May, 1968), 311-313.

Le tentazioni del dottor Antonio

878 Alpert, Hollis. "Images and Experiments," Saturday Review, 45 (July 7, 1962), 16.
Dislikes all three episodes of Boccaccio '70. Of Fellini's episode says, "Nothing done by Federico Fellini can be wholly without interest, but here he has strained himself." "Fellini caricatures a vice crusader ... and punishes the poor doctor severely for his objections to a huge billboard that provocatively displays the face and proportions of Anita Ekberg." "But Mr. Fellini's broad joke is a letdown after La dolce vita."

879 Beckley, Paul V. New York Herald Tribune, June 27, 1962.
     Dr. Antonio is "less satire than burlesque." "I won't say
     nothing of Fellini's genius comes across; what hurts isn't the
     hyperbole but the lag from one horse laugh to the next."

880 "Boccaccio Opens Cannes Festival," New York Times, May 8,
     1962, 45.
     News item from Cannes. Tells of the opening of the festi-
     val. Says that the last segment, directed by Mario Monicelli,
     was left out of Boccaccio '70 because the film was too long.
     Monicelli tried to stop the Cannes showing. But Boccaccio '70
     will open with only three segments--Visconti, Fellini, and De
     Sica.

881 "Chick Boccacciatore," Time, 79 (March 23, 1962), 75.
     Dr. Antonio is "some kind of religious nut who spies on
     lovers in public parks, then denounces them vehemently; he car-
     ries a prayer book in one hand and pinches pretty bottoms with
     the other." The film (Boccaccio '70) grossed more than
     $200,000 in its first ten days in Italy.

882 Cinema, v. 1, n. 2, 1963, 4-7.

883 _____. v. 1, n. 3, 1963, 34.

884 Coe, Richard L. "Shapely But Shoddy," Washington Post, Oc-
     tober 4, 1962, D10.
     Says that Dr. Antonio is "worth, at best, about six minutes
     and consumes some forty-five." Boccaccio '70 is "overlong,
     overblown and over its head in crass commercialism...."

885 Coleman, John. "Pro Dolce vita," New Statesman, 65 (April
     5, 1963), 499.
     "It's the most clearly satirical, the most evidently inventive,
     the most choppy and enigmatic." Was aware that Fellini's epi-
     sode had been cut radically. There are "limping hints" through-
     out of what Fellini intended. "Amazing then, with such a po-
     tentially fecund subject, how little Fellini extracts from it, how
     crude and slow his development proves."

886 Crowther, Bosley. New York Times, June 27, 1962, 40.
     Liked Fellini's episode best. Says, "... it could be almost
     a preface or apologia for the other two, for it is a withering
     demolition of the kind of prudery that takes exception to material
     that lays stress on the magnificence and voluptuousness of the
     female figure."

887 Cue, June 30, 1962.
     Claims that the Italian triptych is, "despite inherently solid
     entertainment values," too long. All three segments are "frank-
     ly presented, exuberantly played, and embellished by lively Ital-
     ianesque background music."

888   Deglin, Paul. Ciné, August 30, 1962, 8-9.
      A "Don Quixote", a "cross-grained obsessive" whom des-
      tiny goes out cruelly to punish--this is Dr. Antonio.

889   "Every Italian a Stallion?" Time, 79 (June 29, 1962), 60.
      Likes Visconti's episode best. Gives a half column des-
      cription of each segment. Then sums up all three by saying,
      "Technically, the film strains against the cramping conventions
      of a dying realism. Fellini's episode, especially, with its ear-
      bruisingly inane drink-more-milk jingle ('every Italian can be
      a stallion') and its massive billboard ... displays a brilliant
      sense of how the surreal now impinges on, and modifies the
      real."

890   Filmfacts, 5 (1962), 145.
      Cursory, brief summary of the story, chief credits, and
      inadequate listing of cast. Ample excerpts from six reviews.

891   Fitzpatrick, Ellen. Films in Review, 13 (June/July, 1962),
      363-364.
      Like Dolce vita, shows "the intellectual and moral nihilism
      of those currently in control of Italian filmmaking." Fellini
      "not only directed but wrote this puerility." Among other things,
      she spells Boccaccio's name wrong.

892   Fratini, Gaio. "Foglietti di diario: Le tentazioni del dottor
      Antonio," Boccaccio '70, eds. Carlo Di Carlo and Gaio Fratini.
      Bologna: Cappelli, 1962.
      Anecdotes and conversations with Fellini, Anita Ekberg, and
      others, about the film. The billboard of Anita was so large
      and had to stay up so long that people who lived in buildings
      nearby and could see it--like Dr. Mazzuolo in the film--com-
      plained to the authorities that it was indecent. Asked if the
      film had a moral, Fellini answered, "If people are so obsessed
      with the female image it's because there is often placed between
      men and women an atmosphere of taboo equal in proportion to
      that between the little De Filippo and the giant Anita."

893   Gill, Brendan. "Overstuffed," New Yorker, 38 (July 7, 1962),
      64.
      Doesn't care much for any of the three episodes. Of Fel-
      lini says, "... he is avenging himself on those who have found
      his movies too risqué, but the revenge is self-indulgent and
      uninventive, and to me there is something cruel in the use to
      which he puts Miss Ekberg, who is on a sufficiently formidable
      scale as God made her."

894   Gilliatt, Penelope. "Mammary Madness," Observer (London),
      March 31, 1963.
      Not fond of three-part movies where one can "catch only a
      breath of the tone of a director's voice." Says Fellini's is the
      best contribution because it is "the most vernacular and vulgar."

895 Hartung, Philip T. Commonweal, 76 (July 13, 1962), 401.
"This subject of the sex-obsessed fanatic ... has been done
before...." "Or is Federico Fellini, who directed, trying to
tell off censors who stepped on his La dolce vita? In any case,
no episode of his lengthy film had the objectionable bad taste of
this short."

896 Hawkins, Robert F. "New Activities on Italy's Film Front,"
New York Times, July 30, 1961, Section II, 5.
Article was written during the shooting of Dr. Antonio.
Says that Fellini's favorite time to film is midnight. Gives a
capsulized version of Dr. Antonio. Tells that some spectators
stop by to watch the filming, and Fellini sends chairs over for
them and gives them some hot espresso from his own trailer.
Fellini stops "shooting" just before dawn.

897 Hodgens, R. M. Film Quarterly, 16 (Spring, 1963), 58.
A very short review. None of the episodes of Boccaccio
'70 fare well. Says that at least Visconti's is "smooth"; Fellini has some "fine touches"; and, de Sica has "Miss Loren."

898 Illustrated London News, 242 (April 13, 1963), 556.
Miss Ekberg's "personification of Temptation" is "very gen-
ial as well as very large."

899 "Italian Film Director in the Steps of Boccaccio," Times (London), February 14, 1962, 15.
According to their special correspondent from Rome, Fellini is known as "the great mystificator." This review likes
Fellini's episode a lot and says that it "is the sort of cinema
we have not seen for many a day."

900 Johnson, Ian. Films and Filming, 9 (April, 1963), 29.
"A refinement of style from the semi-realism of La dolce
vita to the sharp and clear lines of Mondrian with a dash of the
baroque and the fascinating and dazzling tempo of Zazie." The
early "zaniness" is not questioned, and Fellini slackens his pace
almost irretrievably; but "quite a lot remains."

901 Kauffmann, Stanley. "Picaresque and Picturesque," New Republic, 147 (July 16, 1962), 28-29.
A favorable review. Of Fellini's episode says, "The story
is more naught than naughty, but Federico Fellini's direction is
dazzling; a tour de force that makes up in baroque casting and
swift, satirical editing for what the script lacks in freshness.
The virtuosity of the direction in La dolce vita ... is intensified here, suitably and delightfully, in a story of not even al-
leged depth." Fellini's episode treats "with cynical frankness"
the main reason for getting these three beauties together in one
film--"a stroll down Mammary Lane." (The three beauties are
Miss Ekberg, Miss Schneider, and Miss Loren.)

174   Federico Fellini

902 "Letters Force Cancellation," New York Times, November 24,
     1962, 15.
         News item states that the manager of the Paramount The-
     atre in Stapleton, Staten Island, cancelled the future booking of
     Boccaccio '70. The film was cancelled because of letters writ-
     ten to the theatre protesting the "condemned" rating from the
     Legion of Decency.

903 Life, March 16, 1962.
         Full-page photo of the billboard from Dr. Antonio.

904 Mallett, Richard. Punch, April 10, 1963, 534.
         In Dr. Antonio Fellini shows "comic imagination" and "flash-
     es of excellent character and incident; but one feels that much
     of the thing is exaggerated, overdone, hammed-up for an audi-
     ence bright-eyed at the prospect of fun concerned with sex. "
     Mallet saw the sub-titled version and is amazed at the number
     of people who are willing to "regard a dubbed version as the
     same film. "

905 Mishkin, Leo. "Boccaccio '70 Most Engaging Film Fare," New
     York Morning Telegraph, June 27, 1962, 2.
         Boccaccio '70 is "the kind of adult, civilized motion picture
     fare that may very well prove the high point not only of the
     summer, but of this year and maybe even the next eight years
     anyway, as well. "

906 Month, May, 1963, 311.

907 Movie, n. 9, 35.

908 Pelswick, Rose. "Twin Houses Open with Lavish Film," New
     York Journal-American, June 27, 1962, 26.
         Dr. Antonio may be interpreted as Fellini's answer to
     "raised eyebrows" over Dolce vita. Calls Dr. Antonio an "amu-
     sing spoof. "

909 Playboy, August, 1962, 26.
         "A free wheeling fantasy about a professional prude. "

910 Pitman, Jack. "Now: A Two-Intermission Roadshow," Variety,
     November 15, 1961, 18.

911 Schumach, Murray. "Legion of Decency and Chain in Rift, "
     New York Times, October 18, 1962, 49.
         The Legion of Decency gave a rating of "C" for Condemned
     to the movie Boccaccio '70, which was being distributed to all
     the Loew's chain. Monsignor Little, Executive Secretary of the
     Legion of Decency, was upset with Loew's. In the past they
     did not distribute films that received a "C" rating. Loew's dis-
     tributed this film because of a "shortage" of American feature
     films.

912 "Short Stories Filmed by Three Directors," Times (London),
     March 29, 1963, 15.
          Claims that Boccaccio '70 is intended to please all. It has
     "stars," "sauce," and "Fellini, Visconti, and de Sica." Accord-
     ing to this report, Fellini's episode was cut thirty minutes from
     what Fellini had intended. He calls Dr. Antonio "scrappy and
     disjointed as it stands."

913 Solmi, Angelo. "From Le tentazioni del dottor Antonio to $8\frac{1}{2}$,"
     Fellini. Atlantic Highlands, N.J.: Humanities Press, 1968.
     Part II, Chapter 10.
          "It is a light-hearted, paradoxical film on the surface, but
     deep down it is bitter and dramatic." Dr. Antonio "joins the
     gallery of Fellini's characters who are isolated and incapable
     not only of true charity towards their neighbor, but of genuinely
     communicating with the outside world."

914 "Summitry," Newsweek, 60 (July 9, 1962), 73.
          "Fellini has got some wildly hilarious moments out of this
     gargantuan fantasy, but has taken this theme too seriously.
     When the spoof turns into a sermon on prudery ... the fun dries
     up; when the puritan gets his comeuppance, many people are
     likely to feel that he is really the victim of an adult trick."

915 Tablet, 217 (March 30, 1963), 345.

916 Taylor, John Russell. Sight and Sound, 32 (Spring, 1963), 91-
     92.
          The film is "peculiar" and "strange": "there seems to be
     something there, struggling to get out" but which doesn't manage
     to emerge. Suggests that the fault may be that Fellini had orig-
     inally edited the film to run for an hour and a half but had to
     shorten it to fit the three-episode Boccaccio '70. The longer
     version might have made clear such "mysterious" figures as
     Dr. Antonio's sister who has fits and the "demonic little girl"
     who regulates the game.

917 "Tells Censors They Wish to Delete Dialog Which Favors Their
     Views; Lawyer's Anatomy of Anita Ekberg," Variety, November
     7, 1962.
          An uproarious (and illuminating) deadpan account of the ex-
     change of views between Ephraim London, the attorney who once
     defended Lenny Bruce, and a member of the Kansas State Board
     of Review, which wanted deletions made in Fellini's film. Lon-
     don said that to censor Dr. Antonio's remarks would be like
     censoring the pronouncements of the Board. He quotes the Bi-
     ble, using the same words Dr. Antonio uses, and says "The
     Lord's words cannot be described as obscene." Finally, when
     the Board objected to "the extreme bobbling" of the breast "on
     the billboard girl," London pointed out that the billboard girl
     was Anita Ekberg, "who, as you noticed is well endowed," and
     that when she ran, "bobbling" was "unavoidable."

918   "Three-Part Trifle," <u>Christian Science Monitor</u>, July 25, 1962,
      6-7.
          This is a short review.   Not one episode is seen favorably
      by this reviewer.   He calls Boccaccio '70 a "three-part trifle
      determined to preoccupy itself with sex...." Says that Dr.
      <u>Antonio</u> is a "demi-fantasy ... plays the old game of bait-the-
      Puritan...."

919   <u>Times</u> (London), December 21, 1961, 3.
          A short article on the "almost complete" Boccaccio '70.
      Included also is a brief synopsis of each episode of the film.

920   Ulanov, Barry.   "A Note on the Italian Films," <u>Catholic World</u>,
      195 (August, 1962), 319-320.
          The irony is "Italian" and "fine," but it "lumbers" across
      the screen.   The hero is "the popeyed little man with the un-
      governable lusts." Fellini makes his point well but too often,
      and by the fourth time around his ingenuity and the viewer's
      patience are exhausted.   Out of his criticism of Western society
      Fellini is content to make "a long series of exemplary tales ...
      with morals as neatly delivered in each one as in an Aesopian
      fable."

921   <u>Variety</u>, May 16, 1962.
          Says it is obvious Fellini is getting back at those who in
      Italy criticized <u>Dolce vita</u>'s "outspokenness." In <u>Dr.</u> Antonio
      Fellini's approach is "at times overloud, obvious, and repetitious
      in his barbs, but there's no gainsaying the overall impact of the
      piece...."

922   Walsh, Moira.   <u>America</u>, 107 (September 8, 1962), 697-698.
          Believes that Fellini made the film to get back at the cri-
      tics in Italy who denounced <u>Dolce vita</u>.   And because Fellini is
      attacking a censor doesn't mean that Fellini is approving what
      the censor is against.   <u>Dr. Antonio</u> is "a travesty of a particu-
      lar and familiar type of misguided, would-be censor, against
      whom every sensible civic-betterment committee the world over
      has to be constantly on guard."

923   Winsten, Archer.   <u>New York Post</u>, June 27, 1962, 34.
          Claims that there is an "occasional giggle," but the joke
      and the audience "wear out long before this jest draws to its
      end."

                              Otto e mezzo

924   Acconci, Domenico.   <u>Cinema Nuovo</u>, 12 (July/August, 1963),
      n. 164.

925   "Actress in 8½ Finds It Pays to Be a 'Full-Bodied Woman',"
      <u>New York Post</u>, July 26, 1963.
          Shows photo of Edra Gale (who played Saraghina) as a very

attractive blonde. She had gotten the role by answering a Fellini ad in a Milan paper for a "full-bodied woman. "

926 Alemanno, Roberto. "Gli equivoci culturali del festival di Mos-
ca," Filmcritica (Rome), 14 (July/August, 1963), n. 135-136.

927 Alesandrov, Gregori. "8½ ," Sovetskaya Kultura [Soviet Cul-
ture], July 27, 1963.

928 Alpert, Hollis. "From ½ Through 8½ ," New York Times Magazine, July 21, 1963, 20.
A photo essay with at least one photo from each movie,
totalling 8½. Under each there's a one- or two-sentence description of each film. Says that Fellini has "...a profound
feeling for the savor and anguish of living, and an almost over-
flowing warmth for the people of his stories. "

929 _____. "The Testament of Federico Fellini," Saturday Review,
46 (June 29, 1963), 20. Reprinted in Film As Film: Critical
Responses to Film Art, eds. Joy Gould Boyum and Adrienne
Scott. Boston: Allyn and Bacon, 1971.
For the most part, just a précis of the story. "Dream
and reality merge in one love-filled final scene. The people of
his life become his performers, the performers become his
people, and he joins them. "

930 Andrews, Nigel. Monthly Film Bulletin, 39 (September, 1972),
184.

931 Aristarco, Guido. Cinema Nuovo, n. 162, 1963.

932 _____. "Vosem' s polovinoy," ["8½ ,"] Iskusstvo Kino, n.
11, 1963.

933 Ave Maria, 98 (August 10, 1963), 21.

934 Baker, Peter. Films and Filming, 10 (October, 1963), 28-29.
Several captioned photos giving the story of the film.

935 Batten, Mary. Film Comment, 1 (Summer, 1963), 61-62.
Guido is "a pouting adolescent, seeking protection and love,
demanding much, giving nothing, searching for an abstract purity ... rather than human understanding. " If the magician at
the end is meant as a force for good, then "Fellini has withdrawn art from social involvement by associating the artist with
commercial magic. " Is not sure whether the suicide at end is
meant to be real or fantasy. The film from the press confer-
ence on is "inconsistent and weak. " If the final ending is taken
seriously, "then Guido's problem becomes a big joke, a spoof.
If Guido's problem is taken seriously, then the instant-pudding
ending is at best, inadequate and vulgar. "

936 Bennett, Joseph. "Italian Film: Failure and Emergence," Kenyon Review, 26 (Autumn, 1964), 738-747.
     "I think that $8\frac{1}{2}$ is the worst film ever made by a major Italian film director. It is a disgusting piece of self-exhibitionism; it wallows in self-indulgence and self-abuse. Its pretentiousness is totally gagging; it is witless and senseless, a public indiscretion."

937 Bianco e Nero, n. 4, 1963.

938 Borde, Raymond and Marcel Bouissy. Nouveau Cinéma Italien (Lyon), "Premier Plan," 1963, n. 30.

939 Bory, Jean-Louis. "Un Freudisme simplet et un surréalisme démodé," Arts, n. 919.

940 Branigan, Alan. "Fellini Film Fantastic," The Evening News (Newark), February 2, 1964.

941 Cameron, Kate. "$8\frac{1}{2}$ Is Film Title--Honest," Sunday News, Section II, 1.

942 Carey, Gary. "Eight and a Half: Director in Mid-journey," Seventh Art, 1 (Fall, 1963), 12+.
     The film's ending excites us "not because Fellini has told us something significant about the creating process, but because he has found such a visually exciting method for his idea that it doesn't matter if this idea isn't quite first-rate."

943 Carroll, Walter J. Villager, August 8, 1963.
     "If Fellini, like the director in the film, decides to duck under a table because he has nothing to say, let him. I myself prefer an artist who does say something, however violently I may disagree with it."

944 Casty, Alan. Development of the Film: An Interpretive History. New York: Harcourt, Brace, Jovanovich, 1973, 291-301.

945 Cervoni, Albert. "De Visconti à Fellini," France Nouvelle, n. 922, (June 19-25, 1963).

946 Chapier, Henry. Combat, May 25-26, 1963.

947 _____. Combat, June 1-2, 1963.

948 Charensol, Georges. "Le miroir du diabole," Les Nouvelles Littéraires, June 6, 1963.

949 Cinema, 1 (August/September, 1963), 19-22.

950 _____. 1 (November/December, 1963), 44.

951 Coe, Richard L. "$8\frac{1}{2}$ a Poem in Images," Washington Post, August 2, 1963.

952   Cohen, Roberta. "A Fresh Interpretation of Fellini's $8\frac{1}{2}$," Film
      (London), n. 38 (Winter, 1963), 18-19.

953   Coleman, John. "The Entertainer," New Statesman, 66 (August
      23, 1963), 233.
            Says that Vitelloni and its success "over here" has to do
      mainly with Fellini's reputation as a filmmaker. Talks of Fel-
      lini's talents. Calls him a "poet of the second-rate: of the
      dancer stumbling through a routine, the itinerant strong-man
      scowling for pennies, the vulnerable starlet playing cool and in-
      tellectual at a party." Claims that the nicest thing anyone could
      say about Fellini is that he had the "guts to try and show this
      particular form of lachrymose sexuality in the environs of art."
      Calls $8\frac{1}{2}$ an "autobiographical oddity."

954   Comuzio, Ermanno. "La colonna sonora di Otto e Mezzo,"
      Cineforum, 3 (March, 1963).

955   Conti, I. "Fellini's $8\frac{1}{2}$," Ikon, 22 (January-March, 1972), 43-
      76.
            Part I of a Jungian analysis of $8\frac{1}{2}$.

956   ____. "Fellini's $8\frac{1}{2}$," Ikon, 22 (July-December, 1972), 123-
      170.
            Part II of a Jungian analysis of $8\frac{1}{2}$.

957   Cook, Alton. New York World Telegram and Sun, June 26,
      1963, 26.

958   "Countdown Till $8\frac{1}{2}$ at Fellini's Cape," New York Herald Tri-
      bune, April 21, 1963.
            From a Rome correspondent. Fellini built a tower for a
      new film, and because of its proximity to the airport he needed
      government clearance. The tower could be seen for miles; and
      once everyone knew its purpose, it was dubbed "Fellini's Cape
      Canaveral."

959   Crist, Judith. New York Herald Tribune, June 26, 1963. Re-
      printed in The Private Eye and the Cowboy and the Very Naked
      Girl. Chicago: Holt, Rinehart and Winston, 1968, 14-16.
            An intellectual and artistic "exercise" of the first rank but
      an "in movie," "strangely cold and uninvolving ... for the non-
      devout." At the end she instantly realizes "that the heart has
      not been touched or the spirit moved." She "admires" Fellini's
      work but it is as if she has been "eavesdropping on the psycho-
      analysis of a comparative stranger--there's nothing that makes
      us care very much about him."

960   Cross Currents, 13 (Fall, 1963), 514.

961   Crowther, Bosley. New York Times, June 26, 1963, 36.
            A long review. Says that Fellini has compressed "so much
      drollery and wit," and "so much satire on social aberrations,

so much sardonic comment on sex and ... even a bit of a tra-
vesty of Freud, that it pains me to note that he hasn't thought
his film through to a valid end. "

962   _____. "Digging Fellini," New York Times, June 30, 1963,
Section II, 1.
        Different from the earlier review. Gives a description of
$8\frac{1}{2}$ and talks about Dolce vita too. Claims that since Fellini
brought Dolce vita to a "cynical end," Fellini "yielded" to his
"romantic nature" and ended $8\frac{1}{2}$ happily.

963   Cue, 43 (January 7, 1974), 39.

964   De Baroncelli, Jean. Le Monde, 1-4, 1963.

965   "Director on the Couch," Time, 81 (June 28, 1963), 82.
        Fellini has a problem that troubles him! Why is he so pre-
occupied with making movies that speak of the emptiness of life?
But unless this problem has been preying on our mind too, we
may not care to take on Fellini's "doubts and confusions. "
Guido in the steambath scene is a "sheet-wrapped Dante," led
down into a "fumey inferno. " Fellini has himself said that
making $8\frac{1}{2}$ was a "liberating" experience to him. But, asks the
Time reviewer, is that a reason for showing the film publicly?

966   "Dizzy Doings on a Set," Life, 55 (July 19, 1963), 95.
        A photo essay of the cast in costume for $8\frac{1}{2}$ during its mak-
ing. There is a photo of Fellini and Mastroianni together--like
twins. Says, "$8\frac{1}{2}$ is considered autobiographical because the
film's hero is a movie director. "

967   "La dolce far niente," Time, 81 (March 1, 1963), 46.
        Supercilious comments on occasion of release of the film in
Italy. Says the picture's first audience "sat in polite, astounded
silence" while Mastroianni wandered about the screen in a sub-
jective story that was "at best, out of reach. " In the premiere
there was scattered applause but no shouting for the director.
In answer to highbrow critics who said Fellini was influenced by
other critics and directors, Fellini is quoted as saying he never
read Ulysses, saw Marienbad, knew nothing of Proust, and had
seen only one film by Bergman. Guido, says Fellini, is just a
man who accepts his own confusion and sees "that this chaos is
the real fire out of which his creativity comes. "

968   Dorigo, Francesco. Cineforum, n. 23, March, 1963.

969   Dort, Bernard.   "Fellini juge de Fellini," France-Observateur,
June 6, 1963.

970   ____. "Superproductions à la première personne," Les Temps
Modernes, n. 207-208, August-September, 1963.

971 Dyer, Peter John. Monthly Film Bulletin, 30 (October, 1963),
     140.

972 "8½ Sets Mighty Box Office Pace in Art Spots," Variety, Sep-
     tember 11, 1963.

973 El Kaïm, Arlette. Les Temps Modernes, n. 207-208, August-
     September, 1963.

974 Etudes, 318 (September, 1963), 254-259.

975 Extension, 58 (October, 1963), 38.

976 "Federico Fellini in Search of Himself," Cue, June 29, 1963.
         "All works of art are, in a sense, self revelations. In
     Fellini's films the confessional has always been present. " Now
     in 8½ Fellini may be said to be "studying himself. "

977 "Fellini's 8½ Wins Top Prize at Moscow's Film Festival," New
     York Times, July 22, 1963, 19.
         8½ was awarded top honor for its "outstanding creative dir-
     ecting. "

978 "Fellini's Film about Making a Film," Times (London), August
     22, 1963, 12.
         Says that what is great about Fellini is that once the "shock"
     of a new film by him has "worn off," you see how nicely it fits
     into the pattern of "what has gone before. " This reviewer com-
     pares Fellini's work (8½) to a "conventional film," the same way
     that Gide's Les Faux Monnayeurs is related to a "conventional
     novel. "

979 "Fellini's Masterpiece," Newsweek, 61 (June 24, 1963), 112-
     114.
         Long, splendid, informative, on-target review, from which
     many later articles seem to have been cribbed. Calls 8½ "be-
     yond doubt, a work of art of the first magnitude, dealing with
     the raw material of experience and the way an artist adjusts to
     it. " Draws sharp parallel between 8½ and Dante's poem. The
     traffic jam is the dark wood in the opening line of Dante. The
     critic is the Virgil-like guide; Claudia is Beatrice. Guido is
     pursued by "the whole swarm of lost souls who are the modern
     world. " The article contains many first-hand comments by Fel-
     lini from a Fellini interview that illuminates this and other Fel-
     lini films: 'Woman is mother, sister, saint, and virtue; and
     the other side is whore, corruption, and sin. " 'When we make
     too many problems, we lose ourselves. It is only when Guido
     gives up his problem that he's saved. " In the film's finale,
     says the reviewer, "the earlier danse macabre is transformed
     into a dance of life. " Noting that Fellini has spoken of being
     "absolved" when he is making a film, the reviewer says, "It is
     the most natural thing in the world for him that a religious state
     of grace should be expressed in a director picking up a mega-
     phone. "

980   "Fellini's New Film in Rome Première Tonight," Times (Lon-
      don), February 13, 1963, 13.
          From their Rome correspondent.   Calls $8\frac{1}{2}$'s ending a "let-
      down." Says that Mastroianni is "hampered by the fact that he
      has apparently to imitate Fellini in speech and gesture," there-
      by resulting in "an anonymous performance which fails to
      move us." The "best" performance is given by Sandra Milo.
      Raves also for Gherardi's sets and di Venanzo's photography.

981   Filmfacts, 6 (1963), 127.
          Another in the series (unfortunately intermittent) of useful
      compilations of factual data on individual films.   Data on $8\frac{1}{2}$ not
      as extensive as those on Dolce vita.   Lengthy (though incom-
      plete) listing of cast, full credits, and short synopsis.   Long
      quotations from reviews of the film in the New York Times,
      New Republic, Variety, New York Herald Tribune, Time, and
      Saturday Review.

982   Furrow, 14 (November, 1963), 712.

983   _____, 17, (January, 1966), 37.

984   Gessner, Robert.   The Moving Image.   New York: E. P. Dutton
      and Co. , 1968, 259-261.

985   Gilbert, Justin.   "$8\frac{1}{2}$ Is Another Superb Fellini," New York
      Mirror, June 28, 1963, A2.
          Calls $8\frac{1}{2}$ a "psychiatric casebook--with each word and each
      illustration an arresting example of man baring his soul and
      teeth at hostile hordes."

986   Gill, Brendan.   "Without a Net," New Yorker, 39 (June 29,
      1963), 62.
          $8\frac{1}{2}$ is a comedy, and "the hero's plight and eventual salva-
      tion are to an uncanny degree, disorganized manifestations of
      joy.   Life, Fellini seems to be saying, is often very hard as
      well as absurd, but oh, how desirable it is!   How eager I am
      to come to terms with it, and how sorry I shall be to bid it
      goodbye. "

987   Gilliatt, Penelope.   "Fantastic Fellini," Observer (London),
      August 25, 1963, 17.   Reprinted in Unholy Fools: Wits, Com-
      ics, Disturbers of the Peace.   New York: Viking Press, 1973,
      344-346.

988   Graham, Peter.   International Film Guide, 1 (1964), 66.

989   Greenberg, Harvey R.   "$8\frac{1}{2}$--The Declensions of Silence," The
      Movies on Your Mind.   New York: Saturday Review Press/E. P.
      Dutton and Co. , 1975, Chapter 7.
          Greenberg is a professional, fairly orthodox psychoanalyst.
      He finds $8\frac{1}{2}$ "incontrovertibly superb" but Fellini's films after

that are a fatal decline, and the "spurious joy" that concludes
$8\frac{1}{2}$ ends in the "barren declensions" of his later films. "Dae-
dalus is dashed down; Orpheus torn asunder; Promethius de-
voured." Guido's mother is the "impossible Mom--self-pitying,
guilt-provoking ... bewildering, frighteningly sexed." Saraghina
is "the awesome apotheosis of pre-adolescent sexual hopes and
fears." The Cardinal is "a complex symbol of failed paternal
authority and inadequate maternal sustenance." There is a
"splitting" of the female image: Guido is either "immersed in
lavish care or savagely menaced." Woman either "feeds him
into a state of blissful satiety or devours him. He must be her
absolute master or she will turn on him and tear him apart."
Guido can't tolerate older women because "they remind him of
his own declining charms." Guido and Fellini ask us to accept
them for what they are in return for their movies. The can-
nibalization of Eumolpus in Satyricon is "surely the ultimate
ferocious assault of the audience-mother upon the artist." With
Amarcord, "the exhausted magician is still reaching into his
worn-out bag of tricks to run through his act numbly, by rote."

990   Guttuso, Renato. Cinema Nuovo, n. 170, 1964.

991   Hale, Wanda. New York Daily News, June 26, 1963, 62.

992   Hartung, Philip T. "We Are Such Stuff," Commonweal, 78
      (July 12, 1963), 425.
          Calls $8\frac{1}{2}$ "a work of art." Says that as Fellini moves us
      from incident to incident in "a mixture of dreams, daydreams,
      fantasies, and realities ... the viewer has to decide for him-
      self which is which and where the seemingly unrelated episodes
      are going. But they all relate to the whole--trust Fellini for
      that." The final scenes show the entire cast dancing by with
      Guido "apparently at peace with the Church" and accepting every-
      one "as they are." $8\frac{1}{2}$ provides "an exhilarating and stimulating
      experience--one that continues long after its final scene."

993   Hatch, Robert. Nation, 197 (July 27, 1963), 59-60. Reprinted
      in Film as Film: Critical Responses to Film Art, eds. Joy
      Gould Boyum and Adrienne Scott. Boston: Allyn and Bacon,
      1971.
          The film is "a work of egotism so striking as to guarantee
      its notoriety and almost to assume its success." The film's
      strategy is "not unlike the shabby ruse of writing a paper en-
      titled, 'Why I Have Nothing to Say.'" He thinks that Guido first
      suffered his nervous collapse in the traffic jam depicted in the
      film's opening sequence. Not every episode explains itself to
      him. Characters appear without explanation. Doesn't think that
      there is much autobiography in the film. He cannot seriously
      believe that Fellini "is so plain-souled that he could throw off
      melancholy by reminding himself that a man must be taken for
      what he is, not for what others would have him be." He doubts
      that the film's finale, "the giant ring-around-a-rosie, to the
      music of a clown band" stands for anything but "a good camera
      shot."

994 Hawkins, Robert F. "Fellini Activates an Unorthodox Project
in Rigid Secrecy," New York Times, August 26, 1962, Section
II, 7.
An account of a visit to the set of $8\frac{1}{2}$ in the making. Describes all the secrecy which surrounded it. Hawkins had it
on "good authority" that the secrecy was just a hoax of Fellini's and that he has never been more sure of himself in his
life.

995 Helman, A. "Federico Fellini: albo autotematyzm filmu,"
Kino (Poland), 9 (October, 1974), 60-63.

996 Hirschman, Jack. Film Quarterly, 17 (Fall, 1963), 43-46.
"The motion picture, motion pictures have been waiting
for. It contains--without parody, with almost loving strokes
of homage--virtually everything that has been aspired to in
films from Griffith to 1963. " It is "perhaps the first film
that has about it the kind of personal touch of autobiography
that one finds ... in poems. " The ending is a "moment of
epiphany" on which the very characters who have bugged Guido
"and who have had to bug him, appear in the light of this essentially untouchable existence, purged, seeable, that is,
loved. "

997 "His Movie $8\frac{1}{2}$; Note and Scene," Show, 3 (December, 1963),
49.
Very short. Says that Fellini "stole the 1963 show" with
his "brilliant" $8\frac{1}{2}$.

998 Holland, Norman. "Fellini's $8\frac{1}{2}$; Holland's 11," Hudson Review,
16 (Autumn, 1963), 429-436.
Much of the article is a supercilious retelling of the
film's plot. (To Claudia's offer to create order and cleanli-
ness, Holland remarks that this is Guido's problem and "a
chambermaid would seem to be just the one to solve it for
him. ") Dolce vita succeeds while $8\frac{1}{2}$ fails because Dolce vita
has "memory" and $8\frac{1}{2}$ does not. In $8\frac{1}{2}$, as in other Fellini
films, men "try to rise, but sink down, grow old and die; wom-
en offer life. " The clown-magician is "satanic" and "death-
like. " Connocchia is like Guido's father in the dream and tries
to make him fail. Guido's speech to Luisa at the end is "ham-
my" and "Tennessee Williams-like," and is "parodied" by the
finale, which Holland calls a "Todtentanz" led by the "death-
like" mind-reader.

999 Horizon, January, 1963, 38.

1000 Huss, Roy and Norman Silverstein. The Film Experience:
Elements of Motion Picture Art. New York: Dell, 1968, 46-
47, 94-98.
Says that at the end when Guido joins the dancers it shows
that he has "come to terms with those forces of his past who
are dancing about him and with whom he conjoins. "

1001 Hyman, T. "$8\frac{1}{2}$ as an Anatomy of Melancholy," Sight and
      Sound, 43 (Summer, 1974), 172-175.
      Takes as a starting point Fellini's description of $8\frac{1}{2}$ as
      "melancholy, almost funereal, but also resolutely comic" and
      a study, Saturn and Melancholy. The melancholic is both a
      sick man and a visionary artist. Sums up Fellini's theme in
      $8\frac{1}{2}$: "Liberation consists in our acceptance of the interdepen-
      dence of contrary states within our experience; only his failure
      to accept distinguishes the impotent man from the creative in-
      dividual." (If this "summing up" seems both turgid and vapid,
      it is representative of the style of the article.) The structure
      of $8\frac{1}{2}$ is like the Eucharistic Mass, from descent to "a real-
      ization of spiritual death," to a state when we are ready to
      receive Grace, finally to partake of the communion, which cor-
      responds to the film's ending. Likens Guido to Peer Gynt and
      claims, without documentation, that about the time Fellini was
      making $8\frac{1}{2}$, he was "undergoing analysis by the Jungian, Dr.
      Bernard."

1002 Jackiewicz, Aleksander. Film Jako Powiesc, 1965.

1003 Jubilee, 10 (September, 1963), 48.

1004 Kael, Pauline. "$8\frac{1}{2}$: Confessions of a Movie Director," I
      Lost It At the Movies. New York: Little, Brown and Co.,
      1965, 261-266.
      Finds the film "surprisingly like the confectionery dramas
      of Hollywood heroines, transported by a hack's notion of Freud-
      ian anxiety and wish-fullfillment." She disagrees with Fellini's
      views that $8\frac{1}{2}$ is like the experience of a movie director, which
      is "most likely to be solitary, concentrated hard work." She
      views $8\frac{1}{2}$ as a satire on big expensive movies, and since $8\frac{1}{2}$
      is itself a big expensive movie, she asks how we can distin-
      guish it from its target. The film is "too big and impressive
      to relate to lives and feelings." The sequence of the screen
      tests for the mistress and the wife, is "one of the most night-
      marish" episodes in the film.

1005 Kast, Pierre. "Les petits potamoge'tons," Cahiers du Cin-
      éma, n. 145, July, 1963.

1006 Kauffmann, Stanley. "A Jolly Good Fellini," New Republic,
      149 (July 13, 1963), 28-29. Reprinted in A World on Film.
      New York: Dell, 1966, 322-325.
      Says that $8\frac{1}{2}$ is about a director "stuck" for a story, an
      artist in a "creative slump." "The film is thickly laced with
      fantasy--with recollection, projection, wish fulfillment, and a
      dream girl who reappears throughout." Calls $8\frac{1}{2}$ a "brilliant"
      film. "In image, visual ingenuity, subtlety of pace, sardonic
      humor, it is stunning. We see a wizard at the height of his
      wizardry...." Starts at the beginning and gives a description
      and critique of many of the "marvelous" episodes in $8\frac{1}{2}$. Com-

pares the opening scene with Guido in the car suffocating and
then floating up to the sky to Dali's Crucifixion. Doesn't like
the ending. Calls it "a somewhat hollow convenience to end
the film pleasantly. " In general, "I don't think $8\frac{1}{2}$ 'says' very
much, but it is breathtaking to watch. "

1007   . "Landmarks of Film History," Horizon, 18 (Spring,
1976), 40-47.
          An informed, appreciative analysis of what is happening
in the film and why Kauffmann likes the film so much. Ap-
plaudes Di Venanzo's photography, whose "incredibly sensitive
gradations of black and white" seem to have "more color than
many films shot in color" yet the film "revels" in its black
and whiteness. Gherardi helped transfigure Fellini's wish
"from the look of life to the look of life as theatre. " The
look of the film is unique: "No one who has seen $8\frac{1}{2}$ could
ever mistake a minute of it for any other film. " Calls the
famous ending of the film Guido's "last fantasy," that states
his resolution and "prophesies the film he will make. " $8\frac{1}{2}$ is
"the quintessence of romanticism," where the artist becomes
the subject of his artwork. In $8\frac{1}{2}$ the artist is pilgrim, warrior, and battlefield. Draws a likeness between $8\frac{1}{2}$ and Six
Characters in Search of an Author, only in that Pirandello's people were "imagined," Fellini's "remembered. "

1008   Kuhn, Helen W. Films in Review, 14 (August/September,
1963), 433-435.

1009   Lane, John Francis. "A Case of Artistic Inflation," Sight and
Sound, 32 (Summer, 1963), 130-135.
          "However fond we are of the director of I vitelloni we
are not really deeply concerned about his intellectual and sexual fetishes.... He has made a film director's notebook,
and I am not surprised that directors everywhere (even those
who usually hate Fellini's films) love this picture. "

1010   . "The Face of '63--Italy," Films and Filming, April,
1963, 11.
          A rundown of the films made in Italy in 1963. $8\frac{1}{2}$ is one
of the big "colossals" along with The Leopard and Cleopatra.

1011   . "The Shake Up," Films and Filming, 9 (May, 1963),
55.
          Only about one fourth of the "review" is on $8\frac{1}{2}$. Mostly,
he is commenting on Pasolini's La Ricotta in the light of whose
importance he finds it difficult "to have very deep feelings"
about $8\frac{1}{2}$. He's not sure that anyone can call Fellini's film
"finished. " The ending is "inconclusive, a confession ... that
Fellini doesn't really have anything to say. Fellini admits
this. " The film is "coated with superficial elegance but empty
and shallow beneath. "

1012   Lerman, Leo.   "Catch Up with $8\frac{1}{2}$, " Mademoiselle, September,
       1963, 62.
             Quotes Fellini that all the episodes of the film "were tak-
       en, more or less, from my own life. " "This film, " says Fel-
       lini "is more than a confession.   It is my testament. "   In
       Dolce vita, says Lerman, Fellini "saw sensationally.   In $8\frac{1}{2}$
       he sees beautifully, technically, with realism raised to poetry,
       albeit his world is peopled by beauty flawed by time. "

1013   Levinger, Larry.   Playboy, 19 (August, 1972), 127.

1014   Lewalski, Barbara K.   "Federico Fellini's Purgatorio, " Mas-
       sachusetts Review, n. 3, 1964, 567-573.
             Indispensable.   Splendid, illuminating, systematic presen-
       tation of the correspondence of Dante's Inferno to Dolce
       vita, and the Purgatorio to $8\frac{1}{2}$ and the probable influence of
       Dante's great work on Fellini's films.   Suggests that Fellini
       "has consciously undertaken in these two films a contemporary
       Divine Comedy in a modern medium for modern times. "   In
       Dolce vita, Marcello is Dante; Steiner, a false Virgil.   Mar-
       cello undertakes a journey through the various circles of Hell.
       Steiner's pseudo-intellectual circle of friends exemplifies "the
       intellect turned parasitically inward upon itself" divorced from
       nature, society, reality.   The little waitress is a Beatrice-
       figure.   The monster fish is an "inversion" of the traditional
       Christ symbol, "a transposition of the Satan figure seen at the
       pit of Dante's hell. " $8\frac{1}{2}$ is a continuation of the Dante sym-
       bolism in Dolce vita.   The film is "a symbol for remaking a
       life (the proper activity of Purgatory.)"   Daumier too is a
       false-guide.   Claudia is the Beatrice-figure.   Carla is flesh,
       Luisa is mind, Claudia is spirit.   Guido is like Dante "who
       questioned and sought to learn from various eminent men he
       met in Purgatory. "   The magician is the new guide: grace.
       The final dance is Dante's "great symbol of the Church as
       Communio Sanctorum transposed to a Communio Humanorum
       and is thus an appropriate close for the modern Purgatorio. "

1015   Macdonald, Dwight.   "$8\frac{1}{2}$: Fellini's Obvious Masterpiece, "
       Esquire, 61 (January, 1964), 149-152.   Reprinted and consider-
       ably expanded as the afterword to Boyer, Deena, The Two Hun-
       dred Days of $8\frac{1}{2}$.   New York: Macmillan, 1964.   The expanded
       version is also in On Movies.   Englewood Cliffs, N. J. : Pren-
       tice-Hall, Inc. , 1969, 15-31.
             Although the theme, symbolism, structure, and meaning
       of the film is to Macdonald "delightfully obvious" (everything
       in the film is "all there, right on the surface"), he delayed
       writing the original Esquire review until he read up as much
       criticism as he could explicating the movie.   In this rave ar-
       ticle--he "can't see any way not to recognize" $8\frac{1}{2}$ "as a mas-
       terpiece"--besides explicating the film himself he answers the
       arguments of various "high-brow" critics of the film (J. F.
       Lane, N. Holland, G. Carey, J. Coleman, J. Simon.)   To

Macdonald, "this portrait of the artist as middle-aged man"
is the "most brilliant, varied and entertaining film" he has
seen since Citizen Kane. Compares Guido to Prospero, and
$8\frac{1}{2}$ to The Tempest, "another drama with a most implausible
happy ending." All through the film Guido and Fellini "are
escaping from one kind of reality, but only ... to rush boldly
and recklessly into another kind, the artist's kind. In this
sense the finale is consistent with what has gone before--and,
in fact, its logical conclusion." With $8\frac{1}{2}$ Fellini has become
"the greatest master of social comedy since Lubitsch." Macdonald, to whom Fellini has not been "one of my favorite directors," comments unfavorably on the earlier films. Sceicco
bianco is "crude" compared to Antonioni; La strada leaves a
"sentimental aftertaste" (mostly because of Giulietta Masina
whose miming "put me off"); Dolce vita is "sensationalized,
inflated, and cinematically conventional"; Dr. Antonio "ster-
torously labors a hackneyed theme"; Vitelloni, formerly exciting, is now "pedestrian, faded." His favorite up to $8\frac{1}{2}$,
the Dickens-like Cabiria. His applause for $8\frac{1}{2}$ is great, but
in it Fellini is a "Latin Bergman, sensuous and dramatic and
in no way profound."

1016   Maddocks, Melvin. "Fellini Again: $8\frac{1}{2}$," Christian Science
       Monitor, June 26, 1963, 6.
          "$8\frac{1}{2}$ is hard to resist. For after all the undeniably shab-
       by ups-and-downs it traces, it is finally an act of buoyancy,
       in which the filmgoer--feet off the ground--will also find him-
       self sharing."

1017   Maintenant, 2 (October, 1963), 315-316.

1018   Mandara, Lucio. "Un'avanguardia con la vocazione della re-
       troguardia," Cinema '60 (Rome), 4 (March, 1963).

1019   Martin, Marcel. Cinéma '63, n. 78, July-August, 1963.

1020   Mauriac, Claude. "Huit et demi ou les catoblepas entre eux,"
       Le Figaro Littéraire, June 8, 1963.

1021   Mekas, Jonas. "Movie Journal," Village Voice, 8 (June 27,
       1963), 13.
          Written after having seen $8\frac{1}{2}$ for the second time. "It
       is a beautifully free film. It is a first-person film, an auto-
       biography, a magnificent notebook."

1022   Metz, Christian. "Mirror Construction in Fellini's $8\frac{1}{2}$,"
       Film Language: A Semiotics of the Cinema, trans. Michael
       Taylor. New York: Oxford University Press, 1974, 228-234.
       French edition, Essais Sur la Signification au Cinéma. Paris:
       Editions Klincksieck, 1968, 223-229. Originally appeared in
       Revue d'Esthétique, 19 (Janvier--Mars, 1966), 96-101.
          Becoming one of the most influential essays on $8\frac{1}{2}$. The

"mirror construction" is a metaphorical translation for construction en abyme, which Metz takes from André Gide, whose
Paludes, as Metz points out, is artistically similar to $8\frac{1}{2}$ because it is about a novelist writing Paludes. Guido's problems
are those of Fellini reflecting on his art. $8\frac{1}{2}$ is like no other
previous film in this respect: "It is not only a film about a
director, but a film about a director reflecting himself about
his film." Fellini's $8\frac{1}{2}$ is all that Guido "would have liked to
have put into his film." When, during the screen test sequence, someone says to Guido, "Why, that's his own life,"
we are to apply the remark to Fellini himself. The film that
Guido will make is Fellini's $8\frac{1}{2}$. Guido and Fellini made a
film out of the confusion of their lives, but $8\frac{1}{2}$ is a well-con-
structed film, "as little confused as possible."

1023   Mishkin, Leo. "$8\frac{1}{2}$ Technical Feat That's Odd, Baffling,"
       Morning Telegraph, June 26, 1963.
              Long review. Calls $8\frac{1}{2}$ "technically brilliant" and a "fas-
       cinating achievement."

1024   Moravia, Alberto. Espresso, February, 1963.

1025   _____. "Le film qui a empêché Fellini de se suicider," Le
       Nouveau Candide, June 6-13, 1963.

1026   Myers, Fred. "A Movie Director's Dream," Christianity and
       Crisis, 23 (October 14, 1963), 184-185.
              A favorable review. Has only raves for Mastroianni as
       Guido and loves Fellini's direction. Says, "An artist who has
       achieved success, maturity, mastery of his craft and an avid
       public, and who suddenly discovers he has nothing important
       left to say, has turned his dilemma into a work of art." Calls
       the harem sequence "extravagant" and "delicious."

1027   Newton, J. M. "Fellini's $8\frac{1}{2}$ and the Poor English Film Cri-
       tics, " Cambridge Quarterly, 3 (Winter, 1967/1968), 3-27.

1028   Pechter, W. S. "$8\frac{1}{2}$ Times Two," Twenty-Four Times a Sec-
       ond. New York: Harper and Row, 1971, 77-84.
              He likes the film much better now that he's seen it a
       second time. The "revelation" is one of form, structure, and
       unity, which he now sees. "The pieces fit together ... they
       cohere; the fabric is whole." He is now "not at all convinced
       that $8\frac{1}{2}$ is not a masterpiece." Earlier he thought the film
       lacked "mind." Before, he thought the ending was weak; now,
       the film's meaning "is altered by an apprehension of its form."
       Guido's imagined suicide he calls a "comic fantasy." He thinks
       the film is so personal "as to be almost unparalleled in the
       history of film." But although the film runs "torrentially" it
       does not run deep and is an "impressive case for the virtue of
       a luxuriantly imagined, superficial art." Half of Fellini's films
       seem to him to be "serious failures," including Dr. Antonio
       and Dolce vita, both of which presumably he has seen only once.

1029   Pelswick, Rose. "Fellini's Film Interesting in Arty Way,"
       New York Journal-American, June 26, 1963, 23.
            Says that $8\frac{1}{2}$ is "interesting in its arty, shrewdly disor-
       ganized way."

1030   Perry, Ted. "Signifiers in Fellini's $8\frac{1}{2}$," Forum Italicum, 6
       (March, 1972), 79-86.
            A careful, useful explication of various scenes or shots
       in the film, offering many insights, some valuable and telling,
       some obvious and dull, some silly and useless. Guido's "es-
       trangement" from the world is "signified" by letting the camera
       see what Guido sees and by having people stare into the cam-
       era. Claudia works for Guido as though she were his mother.
       The lamp that Claudia uses to set a table for Guido in one of
       his fantasies is the same that appeared earlier in his childhood
       home and the one Luisa carries in the harem sequence. The
       ending of the film seems tacked on but is really "the natural
       outgrowth of Guido's personality." He engages the world in
       the only way he knows--by directing people.

1031   Philippe, Pierre. Cinéma '63, n. 78, July-August, 1963.

1032   Playboy, September, 1963, 35.
            "Maybe you'll be hungry for substance after it's over,
       but while it's going on, it ranges from diverting to disturbing."

1033   Podestà, José-Maria. "$8\frac{1}{2}$, un discutido film de Fellini,"
       Cuadernos de Cine Club (Montevideo), n. 9, April, 1963.

1034   Price, James. "$8\frac{1}{2}$: A Quest for Ecstasy," London Magazine,
       3 (November, 1963), 58-62.
            Pregnant with insights explicating the film, he ends up
       disliking it. Dolce vita was "necessarily" left unresolved be-
       cause its "exposed electric ends plug into $8\frac{1}{2}$, which is both
       a continuation and a recapitulation of Fellini's work as a
       whole." Fellini's attitude toward his Church "has never been
       more fully exposed for an English audience." Guido's confron-
       tation with the cardinal may be seen as "modern agnosticism
       versus catholicism, but this is a trap. Guido is not modern
       agnostic man, but modern catholic man. He may be a bad
       catholic, but a catholic he remains." Price finds the proces-
       sion at the end a "standard Fellini cliché" that has now been
       so overworked by Fellini that it is no longer of much value.

1035   Qualietti, Lorenzo. Cinema 60, n. 334, March, 1963.

1036   Rabine, Henry. La Croix, June 6, 1963.

1037   Reiner, Eric. Film Comment, 2 (Winter, 1964), 48.
            Letter to the editor--in answer to Mary Batten's review
       of $8\frac{1}{2}$ (see 935). Includes an important quote from Fellini.

1038 Renzi, Renzo. "La mezza età del socialismo," Cinema Nuovo, n. 162, March/April, 1963.

1039 Revue Nouvelle, 38 (September, 1963), 243-246.

1040 Rhode, Eric. Sight and Sound, 32 (Autumn, 1963), 193.
The Cardinal gives Guido "the uncompromising choice: civitas dei or civitas diaboli." Guido chooses the latter "but rightly so, perhaps, for he does find a sort of happiness in an image of innocence, of a girl called, almost inevitably, Cardinale." He doesn't think that Fellini confronts the fantasies easily: when they are at the center of the screen 8½ "thins out and the mechanism of the plot begins to show through." Fellini doesn't "face-up" to the total case, but what he does present, he presents with "flair and exuberance."

1041 _____. "Federico Fellini," Tower of Babel: Speculations on the Cinema. London: Weidenfeld and Nicolson, 1966, 121-134.

1042 Sacchi, Filippo. "Fellini, sempre più difficile," Epoca, February, 1963.
He pleads for a rope and a hangman's knot. He too thinks he should be hanged, like the critic in the film, because he confesses that he hasn't been able to understand the masterpiece. "It must surely be a personal deficiency of mine in as much as all my colleagues understand it." The film is a superb example of cinema, but he finds it "neither fish nor fowl."

1043 Sadoul, Georges. "Une révision infernale," Les Lettres Françaises, n. 981.

1044 Salari, Tiziano. "Fellini e Il Tasso," Cinema Nuovo, n. 164, July-August, 1963.

1045 Sarris, Andrew. Village Voice, 8 (September 19, 1963), 16, 19.

1046 _____. Village Voice, 15 (December 31, 1970), 39, 49.

1047 Schickel, Richard. Movies: The History of an Art and an Institution. New York: Basic Books, 1964, 153-155.

1048 "The Screen Answers Back," Films and Filming, May, 1962, 12.

1049 Senior Scholastic, 83 (September 27, 1963), 6T.
Says, "After the great Italian movie director Federico Fellini startled his audiences in 1960 with La dolce vita, his critics and admirers wondered where he'd go next. Where he goes in 8½ is up--artistically and thematically." Gives a good description of what takes place in the film, and calls 8½ a "work of art." Recommends 8½ to all adults and mature teens.

1050 "Shameful, Villainous Films Hit by Vatican," New York Herald
      Tribune, February 19, 1964.

1051 Sherman, William, and Leon Lewis, eds. , "Fellini: The Psy-
      chology of Self," The Landscape of Contemporary Cinema.
      Buffalo, N. Y. : Spectrum Press, 1967, 9-12.

1052 Shivas, Mark. Movie, n. 11, 25.

1053 Sign, 43 (September, 1963), 44.

1054 Silke, James. Cinema, 1 (November/December, 1963), 44.

1055 Simon, John. "Fellini's $8\frac{1}{2}$ ¢ Fancy," Private Screenings. New
      York: Berkley Publishing Co. , 1967, 86-91. Reprinted in
      Film as Film: Critical Responses to Film Art, eds. , Joy
      Gould Boyum and Adrienne Scott. Boston: Allyn and Bacon,
      1971.
            Despite two or three good scenes (unnamed), $8\frac{1}{2}$ is a "dis-
      heartening fiasco. " The tone is "never sure, faltering between
      irony and self-pity ... shame-faced poeticism and tongue-tied
      self-mockery. " The dance-of-life ending is "foreign" to the
      film's matter. Guido's foibles are recognizable, his neuroses
      "exemplarily Freudian," but "there's little about him that is
      specific, interesting, compelling enough to make us care. "
      To all the metaphysical questions raised by Guido and about
      Guido in the film, Fellini's only answer is the "corybantic"
      dance of life, which, says Simon, was "undoubtedly" suggested
      to him by the dance of death at the end of The Seventh Seal.

1056 Solmi, Angelo. "From Le tentazioni del dottor Antonio to $8\frac{1}{2}$,"
      Fellini, Atlantic Highlands, N. J. : Humanities Press, 1968,
      Part II, Chapter 10.
            Fellini to Solmi: $8\frac{1}{2}$ is such a "shameless" and "brazen"
      confession that it's no use to try and make people forget that
      the film is about "my own life. " He makes a film to please
      himself first of all, then the public. Solmi of the Cardinal:
      he is "the image of Fellini's primitive religious faith, a mix-
      ture of catholicism and superstition, to which Fellini has al-
      ways remained attached in his films, with almost childish in-
      sistence. "

1057 "Soviet Outcry Over Moscow Film Award," Times (London),
      July 30, 1963, 9.
            News item states that the Soviet cultural establishment is
      outraged over the awarding of the grand prix to the Italian
      film--$8\frac{1}{2}$. Moscow claims that $8\frac{1}{2}$ is "alien" to the communist
      doctrine.

1058 Stempel, Hans and Martin Ripkens. "Afterword," Acht und
      Halb. Hamburg: Schröder, 1963.
            In $8\frac{1}{2}$ Fellini has taken himself as the object of his delin-

eation. "He has filmed a monologue with his own image. "
"The mystic half-darkness of the earlier Fellini films has been
banished. Bright are the faces, brighter still is most of the
background and after the sharpest altercation the picture is
invested with brightness, which the finale of the film, with its
promise of redemption, anticipates. " And the finale is the key
to the film. "Reject the ending, and you reject the whole
film. " The film is like an "inverted pyramid," and it is on
the final scene that it rests.

1059 Stubbs, J. C.   "$8\frac{1}{2}$," Journal of Aesthetic Education, 9 (April,
1975), 96-108.
    Actually an excellent overview of Fellini's work from
Luci del varietà through Giulietta, including comments on
Clowns and Roma. (Much of the material is a workman-like
précis of Solmi's material.) Of Luci del varietà: "The tacky
side of vaudeville has never been better detailed. " Marcello,
of Dolce vita, is an "artist manqué. " Guido is "more fully
Fellini's portrait of the artist. " Contains a useful "sequence
outline" of $8\frac{1}{2}$ and thirteen excellent study questions for film
classes using the film.

1060 Szkłowski, Wiktor.   Filmcritica, n. 183/184, 1967.

1061 Tablet, 217 (August 24, 1963), 918.

1062 "Talk of the Town," New Yorker, 39 (July 6, 1963), 19-20.
    Bits of an interview with Fellini at the New York opening
of $8\frac{1}{2}$. Fellini apologizes for his English but this reviewer
finds Fellini's English, which Fellini says he learned from the
GIs right after World War II, "eloquent enough" for practical
purposes. Fellini on $8\frac{1}{2}$: "It is a picture about all men, and
therefore about me. In any event, I could hardly say ... that
it was a picture about me, and therefore about all men. "
Once Fellini decided to make Guido's occupation that of a movie director, "like me," everything fell into place. "Never
have I had so easy a time with a picture. " He has the feeling
that this picture has "set him free" and that he'll now be able
to make a dozen different kinds of pictures, "or a hundred. "

1063 Tarare, Claude.   "La fête et l'enfer," L'Express, June 6,
1963.

1064 Tebano, Nerio.   "$8\frac{1}{2}$ e l'ultimo Antonioni," Cinema Nuovo, n.
164, July-August, 1963.

1065 Thirard, Paul-Louis.   Cinéma '63, n. 78, July-August, 1963.

1066 _____ .   "Documents sur un film," Cinéma '63, n. 75, April,
1963.

1067 Torök, J. -P.   Positif, n. 54-55, July-August, 1963.

1068   Toti, Gianni. "E mezzanotte dottor Fellini," Cinema '60, n. 33, March, 1963.

1069   Tusiani, Joseph. "Fellini's $8\frac{1}{2}$," Catholic World, 197 (September, 1963), 395-396.
       The story is "fundamentally a soliloquy," and Guido Anselmi is Fellini "speaking for and about the world of Federico Fellini." The thought of the Cardinal in the film, who represents religion, "haunts the director of films in search of a film." Guido is an eauton timoroumenos (self-punisher). He carries his "moral dualism" from his childhood memories "always to re-emerge with greater restlessness on the surface of his present need." The "suicide" at the end is to let death show Guido "how simple life could have been."

1070   Variety, April 4, 1963.
       From their Rome correspondent. "The author-director picture par excellence." Like Dolce vita it is bound to divide its viewers "into rabid partisans and 'I-don't-get-it' detractors." "One of the most visually striking of all films, yet it has heart and inner impact."

1071   Walsh, Moira. America, 109 (July 13, 1963), 61-62.
       An "embarrassingly candid psychological autobiography," and "a stimulating visual and intellectual double crostic" that does not come across to her as an "integrated work of art" and which does not seem as successful as some of Fellini's earlier movies. She attests, however, to the realism of the Catholic school scene where there is a reading from the life of St. Aloysius.

1072   Weismann, G. Nola Express, July 10, 1970, 22.

1073   Winsten, Archer. New York Post, June 26, 1963.

1074   Winston, Douglas Garrett. The Screenplay as Literature. Rutherford, N.J.: Fairleigh Dickinson University Press, 1973, 140-161.

1075   Wood, Robin. "The Question of Fellini Continued," December, 9 (Summer/Fall, 1967), 140.
       Compares Fellini's film to the works of Mahler, who said "A symphony should be like the world--it should contain everything." Guido echoes him. But $8\frac{1}{2}$ suffers in comparison to Mahler because "the grandeur of spirit is almost entirely lacking."

1076   Wuilleumier, Marie-Claire. "La fête fellinienne," Esprit, November, 1963.

Giulietta degli spiriti

1077 Adler, Renata. "Fellini Casts a Color Spell," Life, 59 (No-
      vember 26, 1965), 18+.
      Says that Fellini has "abandoned" the "conventional dra-
      matic line" and takes the "conjurer's" as his model. This,
      she says, "frees the camera to explore its own possibilities."
      In Fellini's earlier films he reached the conclusion that most
      modern drama reaches--that there is "no way out." Feels
      that Giulietta is a way out for Fellini. "Acknowledging the
      dead end, Fellini turns his camera to something funny or beau-
      tiful. Turns it so frequently ... that although Giulietta may
      not be his most rigorous film, it is certainly, visually, his
      richest."

1078 Alpert, Hollis. "Carnival of Spirits," Saturday Review, 48
      (November 20, 1965), 55.
      Says, "Touching and often delightful as Masina is, the
      'spirits' she calls up are more interesting than she." It is
      the faces--"haunting", "bizarre", and "expressive"--that Fel-
      lini uses that give the film its "greatest strength." They help
      the story and add an "almost poetic depth and richness" to it.
      "Bad spirits or good, it is they who turn the movie into a gor-
      geous human circus."

1079 Argentieri, Mino. "Fellini," Rinascita, October, 1965.

1080 Arkadin. "Film Clips," Sight and Sound, 35 (Spring, 1966),
      97.
      Sums up the British reviews of the film: most were anti,
      but a few were very pro. Good selection of quotations from
      papers and periodicals not easily obtainable. The Daily Worker
      critic found the film "the strongest and most positive expres-
      sion in people Fellini has ever made: his richest and most
      valuable film to date." (Nina Hibbin.) Alexander Walker in
      the Standard: In 8½ and Giulietta "the camera has found its
      His and Hers of exquisite banality." Arkadin closes with the
      intelligent question whether perhaps "exact description and less
      violent view-mongering, one way or another, would not be more
      useful in the long run."

1081 Ave Maria, 103 (February 12, 1966), 15.

1082 Blum, Ralph. "Juliet of the Spirits, 'Touching and Daring,'"
      Vogue, 147 (January 1, 1966), 70.
      Gives a good synopsis of the film. States that Dolce vita
      was not Fellini's first autobiographical film--Vitelloni was.
      The autobiography has continued through each succeeding film,
      including Giulietta. In Giulietta Fellini has "assumed public
      responsibility for his own dreams, his 'unconfessed desires'."
      Says, "To suggest that in Juliet Mr. Fellini does for Mrs.
      Fellini what he did for himself in the character of Guido An-

selmi in $8\frac{1}{2}$ is sheer twaddle. What he does do ... is to give
her another cruelly honest look at himself. " Asks, what woman "fantasizes up flotillas of naked ladies!" Giulietta's fantasies, says Blum, are really Fellini's. "It would be a disser-
vice to Fellini if we failed to recognize the real secret agent. "

1083   Brustein, R. "La dolce Spumoni," New York Review of Books,
       5 (December 23, 1965), 22-24.
           An exquisite diatribe, a compilation of all the arguments
       against the post-Cabiria Fellini, of those who liked Vitelloni
       but hated Dolce vita, and $8\frac{1}{2}$, and now Giulietta. The latest
       film is "a huge helping of Italian ice cream, covered with
       marshmallow topping, chocolate sprinkles, butterscotch sauce. "
       You emerge from the theatre as from a debauch, "glutted and
       bleary eyed, yet with a curiously empty feeling in the /stomach
       and a flat taste in the mouth. " The film is specious, hollow
       and boring. Fellini's films are indebted "less to true percep-
       tion than to carnival showmanship. " And in $8\frac{1}{2}$ Fellini acted
       out an auto-erotic fantasy "resolved by an outrageously dis-
       honest conclusion. " Giulietta's dream sequences owe "less to
       Strindberg than to soap opera. " The film is most successful
       as an "ocular feast. " Brustein adds some explication by re-
       ferring to the child-Giulietta as the adult Giulietta's "tutelary
       spirit. " During "a good part of the film" he couldn't make
       out whether Suzy, her treehouse, her villa, and her entourage
       were supposed to be an hallucination or the real thing--which
       he blames on Fellini.

1084   Canby, Vincent. "Sandra of the Flesh," New York Times,
       November 28, 1965, Part II, 11.
           An interview with Sandra Milo for the New York opening.
       She is dressed "in her work clothes: two baby-blue feather
       boas, a large smile and not much else unless you count shoes. "
       Present are her husband, a publicity man, a lady translator,
       a reporter, and a photographer. She confirms that Fellini will
       even change a role so that it fits the person he is using.

1085   Castello, Giulio, trans. Geoffrey Nowell-Smith. Sight and
       Sound, 35 (Winter, 1965/1966), 18-19.
           A generally unfavorable, but not a hostile review, excep-
       tionally well-informed, and informatively analytical. The film
       is "an overabundant and uneven work, a jumble of odds and
       ends, sometimes splendid in their own right, thrown out by an
       imagination which seems a prisoner of itself. " It's all right
       for an artist to keep returning to congenial motifs, but here Fel-
       lini seems to be repeating his whole repertoire of effects,
       and the effects are beginning to look worn out. In both $8\frac{1}{2}$ and
       Giulietta what strikes one is "the lack of balance between the
       complex and dazzling phantasmagoria Fellini desires and a
       'message' which is by comparison slight and obvious. " Fellini
       has reached a crucial point in his career, a "dead end" from
       which he can escape only by making films quite different from
       the last two.

1086 Chapin, Louis. Christian Science Monitor, January 10, 1966,
      6.
          Generally a pro review. Deals mostly with the color in
      Giulietta. Says that although Fellini has previously not used
      color--because of its "static influence"--here color "lives"
      and "moves" as part of his "whole virtuosity." Fellini quite
      often "understates" color with near-neutral lights and darks.
      Other times he "flourishes" it. Giulietta is about "a mature
      woman's inward groping from married disillusionment toward
      rediscovery of herself." Fellini "loads her precarious odyssey
      with festoons of the bizarre, the psychic, and the erotic. At
      several points ... he risks being bewildering as well as some-
      what tasteless."

1087 Crowther, Bosley. "Cinema of the Spirits," New York Times,
      November 28, 1965, Part II, 1.
          Talks about Giulietta and the Japanese film Kwaidan direc-
      ted by Masaki Kobayaski. Discusses why these two films are
      alike even though the Japanese film is a mystery. Says they
      are alike because of their "conspicuous departure from strict
      reality" and the "deliberate incursion into realms that are dom-
      inated by forces that seem intangible and beyond control."
      Also, Kwaidan's ghosts are the "phantoms of man's fearful im-
      aginings before Freud, and the spirits of ... Giulietta are sim-
      ply those that Freud identified." Wonders why two films such
      as these can't be made in Hollywood.

1088 _____   "Fellini in a Psychic Wonderland," New York Times,
      November 7, 1965, Part II, 1.
          Much different from his earlier review of November 4.
      Talks basically of the "color" in Giulietta, and about what is
      and is not "new." Says that Giulietta is not as complex as
      Dolce vita or $8\frac{1}{2}$. Feels that Fellini was more interested in
      the visual--the color--and what he could do with it. Fellini
      is just having fun with a "soap opera character." Claims that
      color becomes the "psychic signals" and "sly devices" for Giu-
      lietta's "feelings", "moods", and "erotic stimuli." Fellini
      uses color "like a circus designer on a binge." Loves espe-
      cially the treehouse scene and a memory visit to the circus
      as a child.

1089 _____ . "Juliet of the Spirits Is Here," New York Times,
      November 4, 1965, 57.
          Says, "Mr. Fellini has reared back and truly passed a
      cinematographic miracle, in this gaudy, surrealistic rendering
      of the fantasies of a wealthy bourgeois wife when her mind is
      aroused by the suspicion that her husband is cheating on her."
      Giulietta Masina is "still appealing" in her "Harry Langdon
      way." Since this is Fellini's first feature-length color film,
      he uses his "palette" well. Nino Rota's score is "brilliant."

1090 Cue, 43 (February 25, 1974), 36.

1091 Ellison, Harlan. Cinema, 3 (July, 1966), 46.

1092 Extension, 60 (April, 1966), 38.

1093 Färber, Helmut. Filmkritik, n. 12, 1965.

1094 Farber, Manny. "The Wizard of Gauze," Negative Space.
      New York: Praeger, 1971, 165-169.
      Using his arcane and precise knowledge of old Hollywood
      movies, all the bad points of which Fellini supposedly copies
      and none of the good ones, Farber excoriates the director and
      his films. Fellini revives the "chiclet colors that didn't work
      for George Sydney when he directed MGM musicals." Giulietta
      Masina has a Spring Byington ability to "exude goodness, pa-
      tience, and domestic cleanliness with a raspberry valentine
      smile." "The key scene in Spencer Tracy cycles--a gliding
      fox trot through admiring ballroomates while someone plays
      their song--is stylized into glossiness, made creepy by leng-
      thening the moves." Mario Pisu wears more eye-work make-
      up than his Giulietta. The "gauze" of the article's title is the
      "Gauze Wonderland of meaningless decor."

1095 "Fellini in His Element with Supernatural," Times (London),
      February 10, 1966, 16.
      Gives a precise, accurate, and perceptive synopsis of
      the plot action of Giulietta. Then addresses himself to the
      film as film and especially to Fellini's use of color. Calls
      Giulietta "visually thrilling ... with some of the most beauti-
      ful bizarre and altogether astonishing use of colour yet seen
      on the cinema screen...." Fellini does not "launch" an attack
      on our senses. Giulietta is "slow and quiet" and with many
      horror sequences "underplayed with a precision and subtlety
      [of which] one might have thought Fellini ... quite incapable."
      Says that you can't argue with those who don't like or can't
      accept Giulietta. But if you do and can--then "the experience
      is unique in its vividness and intensity."

1096 Fieschi, Jean-André. "Cabiria Trépanée," Cahiers du Cinéma,
      n. 174, January, 1966, 77-78. Also in Cahiers du Cinéma
      (English), n. 2, 1966, 76-77.
      Everyone is free to refuse to be interested in the family
      upsetments, terrors, and devils of a middle-class Roman
      housewife "not very young, not very good-looking, and not very
      intelligent." Its neo-realism consists of the most banal every-
      day acts, the most unheroic characters, the most undramatic
      situations. But the film is in a strange way dear to him.

1097 "Flight of Fancy That Will Cost Fellini £900,000," Times
      (London), September 25, 1964, 16.
      News item about Fellini's first color film. The Rome
      correspondent saw Fellini's wardrobe list for Roman soldiers,
      African warriors, angels, a Buddhist monk, and a medium.

Therefore, the correspondent believes that Giulietta "has a theme rather than a story and its theme is imagination, woman's imagination. "

1098 Films and Filming, 11 (August, 1965), 52-53.

1099 "Fitful Genius of Fellini Film," Times (London), October 25, 1965, 15.
Was written on the Rome opening of Giulietta. Says that Giulietta is the "biggest event in the Italian cinema. " The film has opened and it is a little bit of a "let down. " Giulietta is "a constant delight to look at. It has the controlled extravagance of design, the mixture of reality, of caricature, the confident flamboyance which go to make so important a part of the showmanship of Fellini. " But this is "not enough. "

1100 Gibbs, Patrick. "One Fantasy Too Many," Jury, n. 7, February 28, 1966, 225.
Claims that Fellini concentrated on the color at the "expense" of all other "essential elements"--namely, the "writing. "

1101 Gill, Brendan. "Married Misery," New Yorker, November 6, 1965.
"Fellini's beautiful ... new movie. " Giulietta, in the prime of life, "presides over a charming house outside Rome and has ... 'everything to live for', but in fact she fears that she has nothing to live for. "

1102 Gow, Gordon. Films and Filming, 12 (March, 1965), 52-53.

1103 ____. Films and Filming, 12 (April, 1966), 52-53.

1104 "Happy Medium," Newsweek, 66 (November 15, 1965), 124-124A+.
Gives a description of plot and theme and how Giulietta's problem is resolved. "If the film sounds enthralling and ridiculous at the same time, it is precisely that. Fellini is such a virtuoso of visualization that he can get away with almost any script or theme. His sets are gorgeous, his costumes superb, his imagination unrivaled. " Loves what Fellini does with color in this film. Says that Fellini uses it to show Giulietta's sexual progression in her clothes from "pure, saintly white to a mixture of white and passionate red.... "

1105 Hart, Henry. Films in Review, 16 (December, 1965), 643.

1106 ____. "Kaleidoscopes," Films in Review, 17 (January, 1966), 46-47.
Groups the film with others of the rank of Thunderball as using old forms to seem new and to be just one mess. No plot: just a "mish-mash of fantasy, satire and contingency as

to baffle esthetic analysis. " Science-fiction gadgets, aerial photography, high-speed film, telescopic lenses that try to bring back the novelty of the old travelogue. Nudity, fast-cutting, color, electronic sounds, and a dialogue of whatever happens to be fashionable for the moment. In short, a "mélange" that he suggests calling kaleidoscopic.

1107   Hartung, Philip T. "Fellini, Freud, and Frills, " Commonweal, 83 (November 26, 1965), 244.
        Compares Giulietta's story to Alice in Wonderland's: Fellini is conducting Giulietta on a wild, mad, hilarious and often touching tour similar to Alice's except that this story is "a fantasy for adults. " Giulietta may be a modern upper-middle class wife, but she is still an unsophisticated woman. At the close of the film, when Giulietta learns to rise above her husband's betrayal and she dismisses "her unsettling spirits, " he is reminded of the close of The Tempest. "Our revels are ended. These our actors ... were all spirits and are melted into air. "

1108   Harvey, James E. "Fellini's Juliet--A Masterpiece for Filmhaters?" Flint Journal (Michigan), June 1, 1975.
        It may be the movie for people who don't like movies. "It crystallizes for these indifferent and infrequent moviegoers impressions of the film medium's consistent lack of artistic stature. "

1109   Hatch, Robert. Nation, 201 (November 15, 1965), 371-372.
        Feels that Giulietta is a waste of time and that it could be boiled down into a "fifteen-minute production number with little loss of content. " "It is expensive, derivative, self-indulgent and a bore. I have no doubt that Fellini intends his new film to be ironic and sophisticated, but it turns out arch and chic. "

1110   Hawkins, Robert F. "Focus on Fellini's Giulietta, Woman and Movie of Mystery, " New York Times, October 4, 1964.
        During the shooting of early sequences of the film. Fellini says that he is really "ashamed" of talking about a film that he has not shot yet. Until it's on the screen, "it's a very personal thing. " He compares a shooting script to a novelist's "outline": "no one asks a writer what he's after when he's still on Chapter One. " Says that Fellini has called the story a blend of One Thousand and One Nights and the everyday.

1111   "Hors d'Oeuvre, " Films in Review, 19 (December, 1968), 626.
        Quotes Sheilah Graham that Fellini actually consults mediums. Says that one of them told him that his next two films would die; the prophecy caused actors to refuse to work for him until after his next two pictures.

1112   International Film Guide, 4 (1967), 107-108.

1113   Jubilee, 13 (December, 1965), 56.

1114   Karaganow, A.   Kinematograficzeskije Wstrieczi

1115   Kast, Pierre.   Cahiers du Cinéma, n. 164, March, 1965.
       With Fellini during the shooting of the film. Fellini
       says, "I am always making the same film in so far as what
       evokes my curiosity, what really interests me, what sets off
       my inspiration, is all the time to tell the story of people in
       search of themselves, looking for a more genuine way of liv-
       ing, for a direction, for a way to live their lives that will
       best match the true roots of their individual personalities. "

1116   Kauffmann, Stanley.   "$8\frac{1}{2}$ --Ladies' Size," New Republic, 153
       (November 13, 1965), 28-30+.   Reprinted in A World on Film.
       New York: Dell, 1966, 325-329.
       What the spirits symbolize is "the opening of Juliet's
       senses to a more complex world than the one of husband, chil-
       dren, and canalized friendships to which she had been limited. "
       The parallels with $8\frac{1}{2}$ are "obviously intended to be obvious. "
       The film is its female counterpart--"Hers to hang next to His. "
       But the character Juliet is "pallid," and Miss Masina is not
       satisfactory.   Juliet's fantasies "seem neither to spring from
       her nor to affect her or us as they are meant to. " Kauffmann
       goes on to discuss at length the problem of color in film, Fel-
       lini's use of it in this film, and Fellini's work in general.
       What distinguishes Fellini from other important directors is
       his humor. $8\frac{1}{2}$ was a "cascade" of bitter, funny, scintillating
       jokes on himself.   Giulietta is not nearly impudent enough.
       It is almost as if Fellini "were inhibited," as if he did not
       feel free "to make the same cynical fun about a woman, about
       a wife, about a woman's life, as he did about himself. "

1117   Kaziragi, Hugo.   "Dzhul'etta i dukhi" ["Giulietta degli spiriti"],
       Iskusstvo Kino, n. 5, 1966.

1118   Lamb, S.   "Where the Girls Are: The Socio-psycho Soap
       Opera," Montrealer, 40 (March, 1966), 52-53.

1119   Liber, Nadine.   "New Fantasy by the $8\frac{1}{2}$ Man," Life, 59 (Aug-
       ust 27, 1965), 50-54.
       The first three pages of this article contain photos and a
       brief synopsis of Giulietta.   The last page deals mainly with
       Fellini and contains many quotes from him.   Fellini says,
       "The best moment of the day for me is when I go to sleep.
       I dream and a fiesta starts. " Fellini talks about the problems
       involved in making a color film.   Says that maybe someday
       color will wind up being more important than faces.   "But
       what worries! Every morning, I feel like a police inspector,
       checking to see if there isn't a yellow character hiding in a
       green corner. " "I suppose I should have shot the whole film
       as a test, and then again for good. " About the film--none of

the cast seems to know what Giulietta is about. All they know
is that Fellini is "off on another mystical tangent as he filmed
scenes showing ghastly horses, a cargo of repulsive human
flotsam, and a woman discovering a silver chute which leads
to--well somewhere.... " According to this article, several
endings were shot.

1120   Macdonald, Dwight. Esquire, March, 1966. Reprinted in On
       Movies. Englewood Cliffs, N. J.: Prentice-Hall, Inc., 1969,
       385-390.
              In $8\frac{1}{2}$ Fellini was Prospero; here he's the sorcerer's ap-
       prentice "unable to control the demonic spirits he has conjured
       up. " The crisis of the heroine of this film is not in itself
       less interesting than Guido's crisis in $8\frac{1}{2}$, but it is "obviously"
       less interesting to Fellini: "he doesn't care as much about
       her problems as about his own, and the movie shows it. " The
       casting of Giulietta Masina in the lead was a "major mistake. "
       She is "extremely limited" as an actress. Movie directors
       should "stop confusing their loved ones with their leading la-
       dies.... A director's private feelings about an actress has no
       necessary relation to what his audiences see on the screen. "

1121   Marszalek, Rafal. Powtórka z Zycia, 1966.

1122   Meehan, Thomas. "Fantasy, Flesh and Fellini, " Saturday
       Evening Post, 239 (January 1, 1966), 24-28.
              Exceptionally informative, chock full of information, often
       first-hand. Giulietta is the "painfully autobiographical" but
       "symbolic" presentation of the Fellinis' marriage from Mrs.
       Fellini's point of view as $8\frac{1}{2}$ was from Fellini's. Quotes Fel-
       lini as saying that casting is the "most important single ele-
       ment in filmmaking. " Fellini wants to find "the one person"
       who will play the part better than anyone else. Tells how Fel-
       lini studied 5,000 photos for the Paola girl in Dolce vita be-
       fore chancing on her at a friend's home. On the set, in need
       of a shave, a cigarette dangling from his lips, Fellini looks
       like "a slightly down-at-the-heels confidence man. " Tells how
       Fellini works with his co-writer building an idea into a story.
       Fellini, on directing his wife in Giulietta, as opposed to her
       performances in La strada and Cabiria: "I want you to play
       yourself.... Do what you always do. Feel what you always
       feel. " Says that Fellini himself composed the main musical
       themes for La strada, Cabiria, and Dolce vita, humming them
       to Rota, who then transcribed them. Gives intimate biographi-
       cal details about Fellini not easily found elsewhere. It is not
       evident exactly what data came first hand, what was borrowed,
       and there is no documentation. But a wealth of information
       appears in the article.

1123   Michener, Wendy. "Even at Dinner Fellini Is the Total Di-
       rector, " Maclean's Magazine, 78 (December 15, 1965), 49.
              She is invited to a private party at a Chinese restaurant

where she talks to Fellini for the Montreal opening. "In some
ways, it was like having dinner with a camera. Fellini's
prominent eyes zoomed suddenly to examine and record the
gesture of a hand. Abruptly he reached out and adjusted a
lock of my hair. " She says that Giulietta is "about a woman
getting free, growing up--like those beautiful Roman pines,
deeply rooted and secure in their own existence. "

1124   Moravia, Alberto. Espresso, n. 44, 1965.

1125   _____. "Quando Fellini sali sul trono," Espresso, n. 51,
       1965.

1126   Péter, Rényi. "Fellini: Es A Szellemek" ["Fellini and the
       Spirits"], Filmélet (Budapest), 1967/I, 396-403.
       The monsters are beautiful, yet "they are still monsters. "
       They symbolize the powers facing man and which Fellini in-
       corporates in some concrete demon or vampire. They are in
       all of Fellini's mature works, and this film "is really swarm-
       ing with them. " They are "politely" called spirits. But the
       film could have been entitled Giulietta and the Monsters. Fel-
       lini is a "neo-Catholic" who does not give an answer to the
       problems he poses. But his own "humanism is a bourgeois
       protest against the life style of modern imperialist society. "
       He is a "good-willed man with genuine compassion" as well as
       a great master of his art.

1127   Playboy, February, 1966, 33.
       Fellini is a wizard, but the film has "more sparkle than
       substance. " It is all "somewhat feeble, because Juliet is a
       bit pallid as written and played, and her problems a bit banal. "

1128   Price, James. London Magazine, April, 1966, 88-92.
       The film is "a wonder to behold," not so much because
       it is "sophisticated and ingenious" but because "the objects and
       characters which pass across the sets and the sets themselves
       are products of a wildly hipped-up imagination. " He says of
       Giulietta Masina, 'We don't really love her as much as we
       did; her reactions are conventional, her smile too royal and
       indulgent, her movements lacking spontaneity. There is an
       accuracy in the characterization which is disconcerting. " He
       has two ample, informative quotations from Fellini on the im-
       portance of "first myths" in an artist's life and on Fellini's
       way of working with actors.

1129   Quigly, Isabel. "Meet the Wife," Spectator, February 11,
       1966, 167. Reprinted in Jury, n. 7, February 28, 1966.
       We know that Fellini "was one of his own vitelloni; we
       know 8½ was a piece of public psychotherapy.... We know
       his wife is Giulietta Masina, and he now makes a film about
       a woman called Giulietta in matrimonial troubles (we know they
       have matrimonial troubles). " The film, "like all Fellini

films," is too long, "even the eternally intriguing triangle of circus-brothel-convent ... has, after all, only three angles on the world and as a quizzing-glass tends to be repetitive."

1130   Reporter, 33 (December 16, 1965), 45-46.

1131   Robinson, Robert. "Spirit Willing, Flesh Weak," Jury, n. 7 (February 28, 1966), 229.
         Claims that the film's motive is "split," its impulse is "divided," its technique "brilliant" yet "indulged." But says that "to be left unsatisfied by a master is an experience nobody can afford to miss."

1132   Roud, Richard. Jury, n. 7, February 28, 1966.
         "I don't think I have ever seen a film that is quite as silly as this one." It is a "Reader's Digest version of Freud dressed up in what a small town shopkeeper might think of as the height of chic...." Says that only in a "second-rate capital as Rome could such nonsense be taken seriously."

1133   Sadoul, Georges. "La Tentation de Sainte Giulietta," Les Lettres Françaises, November 4, 1965.

1134   Sarris, Andrew. Village Voice, 11 (November 11, 1965), 23. Reprinted in Confessions of a Cultist. New York: Simon and Schuster, 1970, 215-219.

1135   _____. Village Voice, 11 (November 18, 1965), 23. Reprinted in Confessions of a Cultist. New York: Simon and Schuster, 1970, 215-219.

1136   Simon, John. "Wherefore Art Thou, Juliet?," Private Screenings. New York: Berkley Medallion Edition, 1971, 223-225. (The original review appeared in the New Leader in 1965.)
         Includes a reply to Dwight Macdonald, who commented on Simon's $8\frac{1}{2}$ review. "A dreadful film: a little less arrogant, but no less vacuous and even tawdrier than $8\frac{1}{2}$." Vitelloni is a "masterpiece, one of the ten or twelve great films ever made." All of Fellini's films from Luci del varietà to Dolce vita contain strokes of genius. But somewhere in the middle of Dolce vita Fellini had to go and discover Intellect "and the harm ... was done. Thus fell Fellini." Finds it bad taste to film your wife's story, have her play herself in it, add the moral that if the husband cheats on her she has to endure it stoically, and in accepting his conduct find her own liberation. Giulietta's freeing herself at the end, with just one dream, from a lifetime's guilts and fears, is "the final cop-out."

1137   Tablet, 220 (February 12, 1966), 194.

1138   Tallmer, Jerry. "Juliet and Freddy," New York Post, November 9, 1965.
         Fellini and his wife are in New York City to attend the

opening of the film. Off-screen Giulietta is "thoughtful, cogent, fully grown-up in black lace and blonde coiffure. " The
ages he seems to have gotten are that Fellini is 45 and Giulietta is 39. [She was born in 1921.] Fellini surprises her
with a gift, a golden clutch bag from Bergdorf's. She kisses
him and touches him tenderly. Fellini tells him that Giulietta
is an outgrowth of an idea he had a long time ago for a film
in which Giulietta would be "a little nun" whose visions are
investigated by a Roman Catholic priest after "people begin to
talk about her miracles. " The religious motif is now changed
to a psychological one. Fellini thinks that psychology "can do
better than all the other things for man. " Fellini says that
he has never been psychoanalyzed. "My way of psychoanalyz-
ing myself is to make movies. "

1139   Tassone, A.   Revue du Cinéma/Image et Son, n. 286 (August,
       1974), 93-98.

1140   Trombadoni, Antonello.   "Giulietta degli spiriti, " Via Nuovo,
       October 28, 1965.

1141   Tynan, Kenneth.   "Gaudy Chic, " Jury, n. 7, February 28,
       1966, 224.
       Calls Giulietta an "ecstasy of chic self-indulgence"--a
       "parcel that conceals, beneath layers of gaudy wrapping, a
       fragment of old rope. " Claims that Giulietta is an "immensely
       pretty film of monumental triviality. "

1142   Walker, Alexander.   "How to Say Nothing and Say It Beautiful-
       ly, " Jury, n. 7, February 28, 1966, 228.

1143   Walsh, Moira.   America, 113 (December 18-25, 1965), 786.
       Feels the film somewhat superficial, with nothing like the
       "artistic balance and stature" of $8\frac{1}{2}$. Fellini "characteristical-
       ly" finds hope in his heroine's final ability to face reality and
       to be true to herself. Nevertheless, "the film is making a
       pretty depressing statement about life, much of which remains
       painfully true even if we think the heroine's plight is highly
       specialized and at least partially her own fault. "

1144   Walter, E.   "Private Jokes of Federico Fellini, " Vogue, 146
       (September 1, 1965), 274-275.
       On the set of Giulietta. In real life the Fellinis live in
       a villa at Fregene, feed dozens of cats in their garden, have
       a maid called Fortunata, entertain hordes of people, and are
       interested in games of charades and in spiritualism. In the
       film Giulietta lives in a villa at Fregene, feeds many cats,
       has two maids named Fortunata, entertains hordes of people,
       plays at psychodrama in the garden, and holds seances. But
       neither $8\frac{1}{2}$ nor Giulietta is really autobiographical. "Private
       joke": in Giulietta forty nuns are played by young boys re-
       cruited from the beach at Fregene. "They walk more like
       nuns than nuns do, " explains Fellini.

1145 Weismann, G. Nola Express, July 10, 1970, 22.

1146 "A Wife Betrayed," Time, 86 (November 12, 1965), 114+.
      "Fellini puts on a psychic three-ring circus that promises
      profundity and delivers only a stunningly decadent freak show."
      Gives a good plot summary of the film. Concludes that,
      "Though Giulietta offers a bizarre and enticing spectacle, it is
      transparently a gaudy intellectual shell game that expends awe-
      some amounts of energy to discover a pea."

1147 Williams, Forrest. "Fellini's Voices," Film Quarterly, 21
      (Spring, 1968), 21-25.
      The dialogue is used to characterize and satirize the
      world of the haute bourgeoisie, to whose superficiality the real
      Giulietta is finally opposed. Almost every utterance that falls
      on Giulietta's own ears "is affected, phony, humanly meaning-
      less." Fellini's theme is the conflict between Giulietta's hu-
      man responses "however ingenuous and even hallucinatory" and
      the triviality of her milieu. Dante would have placed Giuliet-
      ta's entourage "with his famed sense for the really relevant
      fault ... deep in the malbowges, where are punished abusers
      of words."

                              Toby Dammit

1148 Arnold, Gary. Washington Post, August 14, 1969.
      All three episodes of Spirits of the Dead are concerned
      with "worldly, dissolute people who find themselves drawn ir-
      resistibly toward suicide." Fellini's episode is "within hailing
      distance of being classic."

1149 Armstrong, Michael L. Films and Filming, 20 (November,
      1973), 54.
      "Serves to show everybody what film-making is all about."
      The film's theme is that of "human desolation within a world
      of a tawdry fanfare, inhabited by sycophantic freaks."

1150 Bahrenburg, Bruce. The Evening News (Newark), September
      4, 1969, 20.
      Compared to the other two segments Fellini's looks like
      "a work of art." But Fellini has done this before and better
      in Dolce vita and 8½. Claims that Fellini has "a great eye
      for the extravagant posturings of inhabitants of a decaying aris-
      tocracy.... But he is not a profound social satirist, and even
      in his best films deep social insights are usually missing."

1151 Black, George. "The Devil and LSD in Fellini Come-back,"
      Observer (London), (December 31, 1967), 4.

1152 Blumer, Ronald. "Tales of Mystery and Imagination," Take
      One, 1 (July/August, 1968), 22-23.
      Aside from his imagery, Fellini's strong point is "his

way of capturing snatches of truths almost en passant through his extraordinary use of extras. " The opening sequence is a "hash-like quintessence of everything great he has ever done. When, however, he is called upon to get on with it and tell his story, the film suffers. " The ending is drawn out and poor, tacked on to keep Poe in the episode. Says that in the opening sequence many of the characters are actually painted backdrops.

1153 Canby, Vincent. "Three Unrelated Stories by Poe," New York Times, September 4, 1969, 51.
Calls Toby Dammit "marvelous. " Discusses Fellini's adaptation of the Poe story and suggests that Terence Stamp looks like a blonde version of Poe.

1154 Comuzio, Ermanno. Cineforum, n. 8, 1968.

1155 Crist, Judith. "After Many a Turkey Dies the Summer," New York, 2 (September 22, 1969), 55.
Calls the Vadim segment "ludicrous" and the Malle segment "tedious. " Fellini's Toby Dammit "proves Fellini to be the master he is. His satiric, surrealistic view of contemporary society has never been more mordant, his artist's eye more penetrating.... " "This segment should be freed from the first two-thirds of the movie and retitled 9-5/6 ... it would redound ever more to Fellini's glory. "

1156 Filmfacts, 1969, 494-499.
Credits, synopses, and selection of reviews of the Vadim and Malle episodes in the tri-partite film as well as Fellini's episode. Summarizes various reviews and gives the "score" of representative reviews covered: 12 favorable, 1 mixed, 2 negative. Gives lengthy quotations from New Republic, New York Times, Village Voice, and Newsweek.

1157 Fuksiewicz, Jacek. Kino, n. 8, 1968.

1158 Gili, Jean A. Cinéma '68, n. 129, 1968.

1159 Gilliatt, Penelope. New Yorker, 45 (September 13, 1969), 143-144.
"An instantly recognizable Fellini fantasy about what the Devil now is. " The short film is, for Fellini "nothing much, which is to say that it is ten times as interesting as most: fluently comic, sober, barbed, a little desperate with a droll and perfectly earnest belief in Heaven and damnation. "

1160 Gross, Robert A. "The Telltale Heart," Newsweek, 74 (September 15, 1969), 102.
Fellini gives us "a harrowing experience of obsession and terror by projecting the inner fantasies of his protagonist on the screen. " Fellini is "a master of cinematic psychoanalysis. " The little-girl/Devil-figure seems to suggest "that purity and corruption are inextricably tied together. "

1161 Kauffmann, Stanley. New Republic, 161 (September 27, 1969),
      22. Reprinted in Figures of Light. New York: Harper and
      Row, 1971, 196-198.
         "Go to see Spirits of the Dead about an hour after it be-
      gins. It's a three-part film--three Poe horror stories made
      by three different directors. The first two are silly bores,
      by the justly disregarded Roger Vadim and the greatly over-
      rated Louis Malle. The third is by Federico Fellini and his
      horror story is joyous. "

1162 Kovacs, S. "Toby Dammit: A Study of Characteristic Themes
      and Techniques," Journal of Aesthetics and Art Criticism, 31
      (Winter, 1972), 255-261.
         Analyzes the relation of Fellini's films to his life and to
      his attitude to his surroundings. The films are personal,
      though not autobiographical. The world he depicts is one in
      which he is deeply involved. He works with many of the same
      technicians and actors, and writes his own stories. Thus he
      makes his own personal statement "over and over again. "
      Toby represents the archetypal media-hero of the mid-sixties,
      based on the Beatles and Rolling Stones. Stamp's role "con-
      tinues the myth of the brilliant drunken English artist, a type
      created and perpetuated by men such as Byron, Dylan Thomas,
      and Richard Burton. "

1163 Mishkin, Leo. "Spirits of the Dead Weird Trio," New York
      Morning Telegraph, September 4, 1969, 3.
         "There's little sense to be made out of any of these tales
      of horror, of course. " But Vadim, Malle, and Fellini have
      "invested them with some splendid trappings, impressive color
      effects, and in the final Fellini item, strange faces, strange
      masks and strange accents that may remind you of both Juliet
      of the Spirits and $8\frac{1}{2}$. "

1164 Monthly Film Bulletin, 40 (April, 1973), 76.

1165 "New Movies: Two Dead Spirits Out of Three," Time, 94
      (September 12, 1969), 96.
         Toby is "hounded by his own self-contempt and haunted
      by a vision of a corrupt cupid from hell. " There is almost
      too much in this short film. "Fellini's sometimes too prodigal
      genius threatens to overwhelm the story, which he apparently
      agreed to do only on the advice of his astrologer. "

1166 "Notes sur 'Non Scommettere la Testa col Diavolo' (Il Ne Faut
      Pas Parier sa Tête avec le Diable), Realisé par Federico Fel-
      lini, et sur 'La Sequenza del Fioredi Carta' Realisé par Pier
      Paolo Pasolini," Cahiers du Cinéma, n. 199, 1968, 47.

1167 Observer (London), September 23, 1973, 34.
         "Only Fellini's surrealist fantasy retains any imaginative
      sweep, and that is diminished by his recent Roma, many of
      whose sequences are in the earlier film in a more coarsely
      embryonic form. "

1168 Sarne, M. "Fellini's Toby Dammit," Films and Filming,
      19 (November, 1972), 20-23.
            An imaginative, chi-chi retelling of the film that is use-
      ful since he retells, chronologically, every sequence in detail.
      In the film Fellini "is totally concerned with subjectivity. The
      whole film is a point of view film, Toby Dammit's. "

1169 Sarris, Andrew. Village Voice, September 11, 1969, 51, 55.
            "Once more we are treated to the spectacle of media-
      manacled man blinded by the glare of modern publicity and
      now there is not even the innocence of a little girl to serve
      as a moral beacon. " Sarris is "appalled" by the film. "If
      Fellini can trot out the same old satirical routines at the drop
      of a hat or an option, what possible meaning could they ever
      have had?" He feels that the ultimate question of film criti-
      cism, applicable to Renoir and Hitchcock as well as to Fel-
      lini, is, "At what point does a personal cinematic language
      become a tired cliche?"

1170 Schickel, Richard. "A Sandwich of Baloney and Fellini," Life,
      67 (September 5, 1969), 12.
            The short film exhibits "an economy and a clarity of in-
      tent often missing in Fellini's full-length, self-indulgent" fea-
      tures. The film seems to Schickel a statement of Fellini's
      "satisfaction" with the manner he has evoked through his vari-
      ous filmmaking experiments.

1171 Simon, John. New Leader, September, 1969. Reprinted in
      Movies into Film. New York: Dial Press, 1971, 188-189.
            A "real disappointment," "vastly inferior to the good old
      Fellini, who, it seems, will never come back. " He likes the
      TV interview, which he finds "genuinely funny and knowingly
      directed. " The award dinner is a "neon-lit stereotype. " The
      idea of the Devil as an impudent little girl "seems to be
      cribbed from Buñuel's Simon of the Desert. "

1172 Verdone, Mario. Bianco e Nero, n. 11/12, 1968.

                         Director's Notebook

1173 Booklist, 69 (December 1, 1972), 338.

1174 Gardella, Kay. "Fellini's Satyricon Film Touched on in NBC
      Spec," New York Daily News, April 12, 1969, 10.
            "To watch a master like Fellini at work was a creative
      experience. "

1175 Limbacher, James L. Sightlines, 6 (March/April, 1973), 17.
            Just a listing of the film.

1176 McBride, J. "The Director as Superstar," Sight and Sound,
      41 (Spring, 1972), 78-81.
            Not a review but a study of Director's Notebook, an in-

vestigation into Fellini's work and especially into Satyricon.
Points out that this short film has been almost completely ig-
nored by critics since it appeared in 1969. Almost the only
study of the film, carefully and sensitively analyzing its design
and artistic value. McBride says he enjoys it more than 8½
though less than Cabiria. Says that though there are parts of
the film that are "frankly awful," there are parts that match
Fellini's best work. "The long concluding sequence, a series
of bizarre characters auditioning for roles in Satyricon, moved
me more than anything else he has done." Includes many ample comments by Fellini from the film.

1177 Micciche, Lino. Film, July, 1969.

1178 Variety, April 16, 1969.
        "Were it not for Federico Fellini's unswerving instinct
for lyricism and innate discipline, this hourlong show ... could
have been an exercise in self-indulgence."

                              Satyricon

1179 Albrecht, J. Philadelphia Free Press, 3 (May 25, 1970), 11.

1180 Arnold, Gary. "Mississippi Mermaid, The Damned, Zabriskie
        Point, and Fellini's Satyricon," Film 70/71, ed. David Den-
        by. New York: Simon and Schuster, 1971, 191-193.

1181 Askew, E. View from the Bottom, 1 (June 20, 1970), 3.

1182 Aubriant, Michel. Le Journal du Dimanche, December 21,
        1969.
        It reaches heights that even the most gifted of filmmakers
never attain. What they lack and Fellini's film has are "a
sense of the extravagant, of fable and myth, a dimension of
tragic derision and a seeking after great and desperate adven-
ture."

1183 Audience, n. 80 (August, 1972), 6.

1184 Balber, G. Times Now, 1 (August 6, 1970), 17. (This pub-
        lication has since changed its name to the Gold Coast Free
        Press.)

1185 Baldini, Gabriele. "Fellini minerale," Il Dramma, 44 (Novem-
        ber 1968), 13-17.
        He was on the set with Fellini during the shooting of Sat-
yricon. Fellini told him that just as he had stuck a card on
the camera (during the shooting of 8½) that read, "Remember
that this is a comic film," he had thought of sticking on a new
card for Satyricon that read, "Remember that this is a mineral
film." Baldini interprets "mineral" here to mean "what is re-

mote and set while at the same time has deep natural roots: everything that attains final truth ... but also everything that such truth conspires to cancel out and to reject by presenting it to our eyes in forms entirely unusual and questionable. "

1186 Barker, Paul. "A Set of Caricatures," New Society, September 16, 1970, 506.
Belittles the film's satirical or moral content or design. It is "a film about images, not stories." The second half is inferior to the first because it "tries somewhat hard to have a plot." The film "oozes caricatures," and he likes this. Throughout the film, figures simply sit and stare at the camera. The faces and gestures are extraordinary. He finds Fellini's intellectual justification of the film "flawed. "

1187 Baudry, Pierre. "Un Avatar du sens," Cahiers du Cinéma, n. 219, April, 1970, 56-57.
Full cast and credits. One-line summary quotations from various contemporary French reviews. Says that many contradictory reviews mirror Fellini's own statements about the film. On the one hand the film is seen as a true view of ancient Rome--the Romans were "certainly" like that. On the other, Fellini seems to take the Roman world as a metaphor for present-day society (although the film itself doesn't say so). Says there is a castration theme in the film; Oenotea is not a mother figure. Rather is she like Saraghina of $8\frac{1}{2}$, who initiates Encolpio. The story of the film is that of the sexual education of the hero. Something to think about: whether the presence in the film of Alain Cuny and the fact that he played Steiner in Dolce vita have a symbolic effect on Fellini and on us in connection with Satyricon.

1188 Baumgold, Julie, ed. "All the Elegance of Decadence," New York, 3 (March 9, 1970), 4.
Satyricon is recommended in a column called "Best Bets." "They call it Fellini Satyricon and it couldn't be anyone else's. Not with those unearthly colors, steamy mist, kohl eyes in red-lipped flour faces.... Early viewers are calling it a great trip movie. "

1189 Bear, G. Photon, n. 23, 1973, 8-9.

1190 Bory, Jean-Louis. Nouvel Observateur, December 15, 1969.
Fellini has once again mobilized "his magicians, his acrobats, his wild beasts, his monsters, his hippopotamus woman." But why complain about the repetitions and the obsession when the film is so extraordinary?

1191 Cameron, Ian. Movie, n. 17 (Winter, 1969/1970), 36.

1192 Canby, Vincent. "Fellini's Magical Mystery Tour," New York Times, March 15, 1970, Section II, 1.
Much different from and longer than his earlier review of

March 12 (see 1193). Quotes Fellini, who had spoken years
earlier of his desire to make a costume picture. Says that
Satyricon is the "quintessential Fellini film." It is a respectful, intelligent, screen translation of the classic. Satyricon
is in the style of Dolce vita but less disguised. There is no
"surrogate Fellini-figure" like Marcello of Dolce vita. Calls
Satyricon a "travelogue through an unknown galaxy." Says,
"As if to obtain his ultimate revenge on the Roman Catholicism
that he has satirized in so many of his earlier films, Fellini
has imagined a world without Catholicism, and, ironically,
comes up with a strong argument for it, or, at least for something. "

1193 ____. "Surreal Epic Beyond the Sea," New York Times,
March 12, 1970, 48.
Deals with the source of Fellini's idea, Fellini's cast,
and especially with the "special place" that the sea plays in
"almost" every Fellini film. Says that La strada, Dolce vita,
and Satyricon all end by the sea's edge. Fellini is not stopped
by the sea, and there are times when one may wonder if Fellini has "fallen over the edge" into the "cinema of the ridiculous." But then Fellini arrives at a "magnificently realized
movie of his--and our--wildest dreams." Satyricon is a "sub-
terranean Oz. "

1194 Capdenac, Michel. Les Lettres Françaises, December 17,
1969.
Fellini transposes Freaks into antiquity. Through his
sensibility and tortured genius he has created "a nightmare
Rome, a decomposing body, swarming with vermin, like the
charogne of Baudelaire's. "

1195 Cat, J. Berkeley Tribe, 2 (May 1, 1970), 12.

1196 Catholic Film Newsletter, 35 (March 30, 1970), 24.

1197 Caviglioli, François. Paris-Match, November 15, 1969.
This is a dangerous film for Fellini, who here says aloud,
without perhaps knowing it, what he has been thinking since his
childhood in Rimini: "What do I have in common with this
world? What am I doing here with these people?"

1198 Chapier, Henry. Combat, December 18, 1969.
"Only Eisenstein perhaps has such a fresco-like mastery. "

1199 Chauvet, Louis. Figaro, December 18, 1969.
An "astonishing," "sultry" film. To be seen even though
it means "the ordeal of a long and sombre voyage. "

1200 Cluny, Claude-Michel. Nouvelle Revue Française, n. 205,
1970, 123.

1201 Collet, Jean. Etudes, 332 (February, 1970), 239.

1202 _____ . Télérama, December 13, 1969.
_____ This "grand guignol blister, this festival of hideous wind-
baggery, of aggressive bombast, of wild colors, and of horror. " He hasn't the least feeling for the world of Rome.
When he sees Satyricon, he feels like "going down into the
catacombs. "

1203 Corbuzzi, Gianfranco. Cinema Nuovo, n. 201, 1969.

1204 Corliss, Richard. "From Satyric to Sublime," National Review, 22 (May 19, 1970), 521-523.
_____ A long, unfavorable review. The reason for the title
Fellini Satyricon is to distinguish Fellini's movie from a
"cheapie" movie made at the same time. Says that only a
tenuous connection exists between Fellini Satyricon and Petronius' Satyricon. Fellini "is actually the side-show barker who
(literally) parades an endless line of freaks, frumps, fools,
and phonies before our presumably gaping child's eyes. " Satyricon lacks the "anchor of reality" in the form of a "rela-
tively normal protagonist" who can dream or hallucinate aspects of the other characters. 'Satyricon is painfully, obviously the work of an artist in decline.... " The flirting he
has done with a film form that one critic has called "neo-sur-
realism,' an oil-and-water blend of De Sica and Dali, is ...
a flirtatious exploitation both of people ... and of a film genre
that peaked beautifully with $8\frac{1}{2}$.... " Compares Fellini to
James Joyce--both ex-Catholics who renounced their faith intellectually but not emotionally. Compares $8\frac{1}{2}$ to Portrait of
the Artist as a Young Man. But with Joyce his art came
first, while Fellini lets his "obsessions" get in the way of his
art. Sums up Satyricon as "Thumbs down and eyes closed. "

1205 Cowie, Peter. International Film Guide, 8 (1971), 185.
_____ "The richness of the imagery, the scope of Fellini's vision, is never in doubt, but it is hardly surprising that his
audience should be as bewildered by this tangled skein of a
plot as his two young men are. "

1206 Cox, Harvey G. , Jr. "The Purpose of the Grotesque in Fellini's Films," Celluloid and Symbols, eds. John C. Cooper
and Carl Skrade. Philadelphia: Fortress Press, 1970, 89-
106.
_____ By a Protestant theologian on the faculty of Harvard's
Divinity School, who idolizes Fellini. Quintessential example
of the expression, "Never mind my enemies, save me from
my friends. " Visited Fellini during the shooting of Satyricon.
Reason for decline in conventional religion is rise of bureau-
cratic, IBM-type technology. Fellini uses grotesque to try and
get back "our lost sense of the mysterious, the transcendant,
and the holy. " Fellini, like Hieronymus Bosch, pours on the
monsters and the grotesque because he wants "to zap us into
an encounter with another reality" and because he wants us

"to see perverts, cripples, idiots, sadists, and weak-kneed pushovers as our brothers and sisters." Cautions that it is a "known fact" that Fellini is "the biggest liar in Rome."

1207   Crist, Judith. "Fellini's Timeless Pagans," New York, 3 (March 16, 1970), 48.
       "It is the work of a master, a further enlargement upon the basics he has been considering and reconsidering throughout his career. And its value is in the essential heart-beat that brings the painted flesh to life and retains the sense of life on a fragment amid the ruins."

1208   Csicsery, G. Good Times, 3 (May 1, 1970), 16.

1209   Cue, 43 (January 14, 1975), 35.

1210   Culkin, Haskell. Show, April, 1970.

1211   De Baroncelli, Jean. Le Monde, September 6, 1969.
       Fellini's error is in thinking that just showing decadence is enough to give unity and interest to his story. In Petronius, Encolpius and Ascyltus are active agents; in Fellini, just passive witnesses. But the film is rich, complex, spectacular, and exceptional.

1212   Delahaye. Cahiers du Cinéma, n. 218, 1970.

1213   Dillard, R. H. W. "If We Were All Devils: Fellini's Satyricon as Horror Film," Contempora, 1 (January/April, 1971), 26.

1214   "Directors: Petronius, 20%; Fellini, 80%," Time, 94 (September 12, 1969), 96-97.
       On the film's opening at the Venice Film Festival. Reports that the "normally reserved" press corps gave it a five-minute ovation. Says that the film "may be the most glorious bacchanal in the history of cinema." Says that Fellini is attempting "to render this vast fresco as a giant metaphor for the 1960s, and quotes Fellini, "The film is ... an allegorical satire of our present-day world." Festival tickets, normally about $3.20, were being black-marketed at $100.

1215   "Dossier-Film #4," L'Avant-Scène, n. 102, April, 1970, 55-62.
       Full cast and credits, a synopsis, background information on Petronius and his work, excerpts from Fellini's interviews about the films, excerpts of representative reviews.

1216   Duran, Michel. Le Canard Enchaîné, December 17, 1969.

1217   Espresso, February 23, 1969.

1218   "Expert Dub," Times (London), September 19, 1970, 12.
       About the dubbing of Satyricon into English. Seems that

Lord Birkett did the dubbing along with a Mr. Wood, who worked on the English version of the script. Fellini approved the effort. It took four weeks to dub, and the mixed final soundtrack, with music and other special effects, was done back in Rome. Fellini's aim was a "distanced effect, half-way between dialogue and commentary, which allowed considerable freedom in synchronization of lip movement."

1219 "Fellini Casts Mae West in Film on Debauchery," New York Times, August 10, 1968, 17.
    News item from Rome. States that Fellini has signed Mae West for his new movie--Satyricon. Says that the new film will be "...a vast fresco of comedians old and young portraying the bawdy days of Petronius Arbiter in ancient Rome." Plans to have Groucho Marx and Jimmy Durante in Satyricon too. The Beatles will compose some of the music and perhaps be in a few scenes.

1220 "Fellini Satyricon for London," Times (London), August 27, 1970, 9.
    Announces the coming of Satyricon to London on September 10, 1970.

1221 "Fellini to Make Film of Satyricon," Times (London), September 28, 1968, 19.
    Fellini announces his intention to film Satyricon.

1222 La Fiera Letteraria, August, 1968.

1223 Film Daily, 136 (February 26, 1970), 6.

1224 Film Information, 1 (April 15, 1970), 1.

1225 Films and Filming, 16 (November, 1969), 26-31.

1226 Fischer-Homberger, E. Reformatio (Zürich), 19 (April, 1970), 301-302.

1227 Geyrhofer, Friedrich. Neues Forum, July 17, 1970.

1228 Gow, Gordon. Films and Filming, 17 (November, 1970), 47-48.

1229 Gower, Roger. "Old World or New?," Cambridge Quarterly, 6 (1972), n. 1, 59-63.
    A review of the Italian and English screenplays of Satyricon. Finds the film "a window and a mirror, where, out of ourselves, we may see both past and present at the same time." At one moment we get an intimate glimpse of an alien world. But this slips away, and when we see a world of extravagance and greed, "we wonder whether it is ourselves we are watching."

1230   Harcourt, Peter. Queens Quarterly, 77 (Autumn, 1970), 447-
       452.
           Thoughtful, illuminating essay integrating Satyricon into
       the body of Fellini's other films. Says that the "surrealist"
       elements evidenced in the earlier films dominate in Satyricon.
       These have now "assumed the center of the stage while the
       more human elements have been pushed to one side." There
       is a preoccupation with the confusions and pain associated with
       sexual love "and something like a crescendo of fear." The
       earlier films very often ended with images of children "as if
       to imply the possibility of fresh life." In Satyricon there are
       few children, and as a result, "given Fellini's private store
       of metaphor, there is little sense of hope."

1231   Harper, T. Great Speckled Bird, 4 (September 20, 1971), 26.

1232   Hart, Henry. Films in Review, 21 (April, 1970), 239-241.
           "Just what, in addition to making money, was Fellini
       doing when he was concocting this film? Propagandizing for
       homosexuality? Yes. Deliberately abetting for political pur-
       poses, social disintegration? Yes. Enhancing his reputation
       among today's anarcho-nihilists? Yes. Anything else? My
       guess: regurgitating a personal, life-long anti-humanism."

1233   Hatch, Robert. Nation, 210 (March 23, 1970), 347. Reprinted
       in Film 70/71, ed. David Denby. New York: Simon and
       Schuster, 1971, 182-184.
           "Fellini makes wickedness seem leadenly repellent; that
       may be good doctrine, but it is no way to win laurels."
       "Many of the great scenes lie idle, while he improvises from
       hints and holes in the text." "This is laborious, I'm afraid
       pretentious work, and it's a pity."

1234   Helix, 2 (May 21, 1970), 19.

1235   Hibben, M. People's World, 33 (September 26, 1970), 5.

1236   Highet, G. "Whose Satyricon, Petronius's or Fellini's?"
       Horizon, 12 (Autumn, 1970), 42-47.
           Indispensable. The best, most complete comparison be-
       tween Fellini's film and Petronius' original work, illustrating
       what Petronius had in mind and what changes Fellini made.
       Fellini had the problem "of making a continuous work of art
       out of a scarred, fragmentary torso with its head and limbs
       knocked off. This he has done very well." The episode of
       the wizard who punished Oenothea is not a classical story but
       a medieval tale, where the wizard was Virgil, then conceived
       not as a poet but as a magician. Suggests that some of Fel-
       lini's sources for what is not in Petronius are from Suetonius,
       Ovid, Tacitus, and Juvenal. The film pre-figures the post-
       Christian world "that is now lurching toward its birth." The
       violence that punctuates the film pre-figures "the irrational

savagery of our own era. " Fellini's view is essentially and
profoundly pessimistic. He thinks this is "the worst of all
possible worlds, endurable only through intense irresponsible
pleasure followed by interminable escape. In such a world the
only real people are exiles. "

1237   Hofsess, John. Take One, 2 (July/August, 1969), 29.

1238   Hughes, Eileen. "Old Rome a la Fellini," Life, 67 (August
       15, 1969), 56-59, 61.
       A short essay about the making of Satyricon. Donati
       talks about designing for Fellini, but mainly these pages are
       filled with photos. Quotes Mario Romagnoli, the sixty-nine-
       year-old Roman restaurant owner, who plays Trimalchio--
       "Fellini pestered me to do it, and now my clients tease me
       and my wife complains, 'All these years you have lived a clean
       life. Now in your old age you have ruined your reputation and
       become a dirty old man. '" Someone asked Fellini if Satyricon
       is a study in degradation. Fellini replied, "Not at all. The
       purpose of my film is not to show vice or corruption--this,
       to me, would be vulgar. So far as I am able, my intention
       is to give an unbiased look at this world. "

1239   Kael, Pauline. "Fellini's 'Mondo Trasho,'" New Yorker, 46
       (March 14, 1970), 134-140. Reprinted in Deeper into Movies.
       New York: Bantam, 1974, 160-166.
       Fellini is a latter day DeMille equating sexual vice with
       apocalypse. "The idea that sticks out in every direction ...
       is that man without a belief in God is a lecherous beast. " She
       thinks it's "a really bad--a terrible movie. " The freaks in
       the film hark back to the childish superstition that ugliness
       was "God's punishment for disobedience. " The homosexual
       boys "with gold dust in their hair" are "the painted women of
       naughty novels. It's the most simple-minded and widespread
       of all attitudes toward sin. " Fellini is "like a naughty Chris-
       tian child" who thinks "it's a ball to be a pagan, but a naughty
       ball. " She finds Giton memorable, "the complete whore, who
       takes pleasure in being used. " But for the very most part,
       the movie is "tired. " Fellini's idea of a movie seems to be
       to gather and exhibit "all the weird people he can find. " Sat-
       yricon is a "parade of leering, grinning cripples. " As an ar-
       tist, Fellini "draws upon the imagination of a Catholic school-
       boy and presents us with a juvenile version of the Grand In-
       quisitor's argument. "

1240   Kaleidoscope-Milwaukee, August 7, 1970, 7.

1241   Kanfer, S. "Rome, B. C. , A. F. ," Time, 95 (March 16,
       1970), 76-79+. Reprinted in Film 70/71, ed. David Denby.
       New York: Simon and Schuster, 179-182.
       Quotes Carl Jung: "If I had taken these fantasies of the
       unconscious as art, they would have carried no more conviction

than visual perceptions, as if I were watching a movie." Kanfer says that <u>Satyricon</u> is probably the first and certainly the
most important <u>Jungian</u> film. Takes us through the film, episode by episode, describing the visual images. "The catalogue
of images is not as unrelated as it seems. At its best, the
scenario synthesizes art, moving like music and spreading out
like a suite of paintings. In this, <u>Fellini Satyricon</u> exceeds
the original."

1242 Kauffmann, Stanley. <u>New Republic</u>, 162 (April 11, 1970), 24,
      38. Reprinted in <u>Figures of Light</u>. New York: Harper and
      Row, 1971.
          <u>Satyricon</u> is "elegiac, joyless, reasoned." Kauffman
      doesn't believe Fellini's interpretation of the film as a pre-
      Christian film for a post-Christian era. Nor is the purpose
      to show parallels in decadence. "Fellini is not as superficial
      as that." Fellini is still wrestling with the type of personal
      crisis with which $8\frac{1}{2}$ and <u>Giulietta</u> were concerned: the "ex-
      panded consciousness (within) and amplified communication
      (without)" of contemporary culture, with which Fellini does not
      feel he can deal. <u>Satyricon</u> is the condition of life that forced
      Fellini to make that film. The film has no characters, story,
      or drama. It depends "entirely on its look." The static, in-
      dividual scenes of the film are but "pictures from the dream
      of a man who once had exuberance and now has only dreams."

1243 Lachize, Samuel. <u>L'Humanité-Dimanche</u>, December 14, 1969.
          Fellini's anguish and obsessions demand great intellectual
      effort on the part of the viewer. But the cinema isn't just for
      having fun.

1244 Langman, Betsy. "Working with Fellini," <u>Mademoiselle</u>, 70
      (January, 1970), 74-75+.
          Not very illuminating but long and highly detailed account
      of how Miss Langman, a young American actress, got a part
      as an extra in the Trimalchio episode. During make-up ses-
      sions she notices that the make-up was used to exaggerate
      features of the actors: "The fat were made fatter, the thin
      thinner, the bald balder."

1245 Lefevre, Raymond. <u>La Revue du Cinéma/Image et Son</u>, n.
      232, November, 1969.
          "This apocalypse of sex, this demise of sensuality, this
      defeat of woman as erotic object." The film is "<u>Freaks</u> in
      a peplum."

1246 Lerman, Leo. "Catch Up With," <u>Mademoiselle</u>, March, 1970,
      70.
          Calls <u>Satyricon</u> "the biggest disappointment of the cinema-
      tic season thus far." Says that Fellini must be taken seriously
      because of his masterpiece--$8\frac{1}{2}$. Claims that the only "good"
      thing about <u>Satyricon</u> is its visual aspect. <u>Satyricon</u> is a
      "bloated flick" which we must suffer through the "cumulative
      boredom and ineptitude, the self-indulgences of."

1247   Lorraine. Kaleidoscope-Milwaukee, 3 (July 9, 1970), 9.

1248   Mara, Jan. Minute, December 18, 1969.
       "Fascinating like the waters of the Styx, hallucinating
       like a canvas by Bosch. "

1249   Mardore, Michel. L'Humanité-Dimanche, December 14, 1969.
       "Super-Fellini." "Hell replaces paradise. " Fellini, "a
       Christian moralist, tortured by modern anguish, projects his
       obsessions with more force than ever. "

1250   Martin, Marcel. Cinéma '69, n. 140, November, 1969.
       You can find in the film "every traditional ghost and ob-
       session in the Fellinian universe. "

1251   Mass Media, 12 (June 15, 1970), 3.

1252   Mauriac, Claude. Figaro Littéraire, December 15, 1969.
       "The film's rhythm, if it hasn't succeeded in being what
       we'd like it to be, is no less rich. " (He found that the shots
       of the film were somehow chained down.)

1253   Media and Methods, 6 (March, 1970), 10.

1254   Mekas, Jonas. Village Voice, 15 (May 14, 1970), 20.

1255   Michalek, Boleslaw. Film, n. 50/51, 1969.

1256   Moravia, Alberto. "Dreaming Up Petronius," New York Re-
       view of Books, 14 (March 26, 1970), 40-42.
       Beginning with an outline of Petronius' work as an "open"
       novel, episodic, where the characters proceed from place to
       place and adventure to adventure "just as happens in everyday
       life. " The connecting thread is Encolpius's "sexual prowess,"
       which starts out "above average," then is suddenly destroyed
       by the enraged and vindictive God, Priapus. 'Which, if one
       thinks about it, is just and meaningful. " Studies of antiquity
       led to various Renaissances, and the last Renaissance is like
       a "farewell. " Fellini's film bids farewell to Petronius' world.
       "For Fellini, antiquity is a dream whose meaning has been
       lost, while still being there and making its presence felt at
       all times. " Fellini neglects (purposefully and rightly) what has
       been written about the ancient world and sticks to what has been
       painted. It is from what Fellini has seen and examined (ra-
       ther than from what he has read) that he has drawn his inspi-
       ration. Fellini uses dissociation or "an alienated and inco-
       herent simultaneity" to create the atmosphere of a dream and
       why it was meaningful for Fellini to have said that the film
       was "the documentary of a dream. " Discusses the monstrous
       and the impure in Satyricon and points out that in the film
       "the monsters are the old, the sick, the infirm, the unattrac-
       tive; the impure, the young, and the beautiful. "

1257 Morgenstern, Joseph. "Roman Carnival," Newsweek, 75
      (March 23, 1970), 102. Reprinted in Film 70/71, ed. David
      Denby. New York: Simon and Schuster, 1971, 296-301.
            Calls Satyricon "repetitive and surprisingly solemn."
      Claims that it was as though Fellini were interested in the
      past as a "club with which to whack the present." If Fellini
      meant Satyricon to be a "fleshing-out of subjective decadence,
      a world gone awry in the skull of the perceiver, why couldn't
      he soak up enough variety of fantasy life to fill two hours
      without repeating himself?" Says that there must be "more
      ingenious ways to exteriorize decadence than to use circus.
      freaks and cripples...." Fellini's film has itself become dec-
      adent and "not as much fun as it should be."

1258 "Movies from Alfred to Zabriskie," New York, 2 (September
      15, 1969), 31.
            A short synopsis of Satyricon. Satyricon "...relates the
      sexual and political attitudes current during the last days of
      the Roman Empire in terms of an extended banquet conversa-
      tion."

1259 Myhers, J. "Fellini's Continuing Autobiography," Cinema
      (Beverly Hills), Fall, 1970, 40-41.
            Remarkable, fascinating interpretation of Satyricon as a
      film à clef--"a composite of events and relationships between
      Fellini and himself, his loves, his Church, his friends, and
      his country." Myhers claims a long-time acquaintance with
      Fellini that originated in his eleven-year stay in Italy. He
      quotes a remark of Fellini's that "My Satyricon is even more
      autobiographical than my $8\frac{1}{2}$." According to Myhers, Encolpio
      is Fellini, Vernacchio is Aldo Fabrizi, Eumolpo is Rossellini,
      Lica is Mussolini, and the triumphal war of the conquerors of
      Lica is that of the Allies invading Rome in 1944. The episode
      of the death of the hermaphrodite is "a subconscious dramati-
      zation of the birth and death of his own infant son circa 1945."
      Eumolpo rich, on his litter, is "the end of Rossellini's Film car-
      eer, his involvement with Howard Hughes, money, and Ingrid
      Bergman." Ascylto's death is "the symbolic death of homosexual
      desires in Fellini." The old man who happily eats Eumolpo's
      dead flesh is the prototype of the modern day producer: "I'll
      be nauseous for a few hours, but I'll be rich the rest of my
      life."

1260 Nels, Jacques. Annales Conferencia, n. 233, 1970, 55.

1261 New York Times, January 31, 1970, 36.

1262 O'Mealy, Joseph. "Fellini Satyricon: A Structural Analysis,"
      Film Heritage, 6 (Summer, 1971), 25-29.

1263 Oxenhandler, Neal. Film Quarterly, 23 (Summer, 1970), 38-42.
            Certainly one of the best exegeses of one of Fellini's more

difficult films. Very "pro": The film is "not an idle, arbitrary dream, as Moravia and Simon contend, but rather a carefully drafted masterwork designed to produce a special gamut of responses." Comments splendidly on the content, design, style, tone, and intent of the film. The film is a "fable" for our own times. Notes the victory by Encolpius via his beauty over opponents in various encounters. On this level, the film can be taken as "a wish-fulfillment dream of the adolescent who, confronting a terrible world, finds that he can wander through it unscathed, thanks to his youth and beauty." Calls the episodic structure of the film "picaresque" and compares it to that of Moll Flanders and Gil Blas. Categorizes Fellini as "a stoic who sees human destiny as part of a natural process of decay and renewal."

1264 Pandiri, T. A. "Movie Mailbag," New York Times, June 7, 1970, Section II, 6.
      Long letter in reply to Simon's review. Says that Simon's review is based on a "misunderstanding" not only of Fellini's purposes but also of Petronius'. Fellini's additions neither "contradict" nor "violate" but "further define" Satyricon. Gives several examples. Should be read.

1265 Paris-Match, December 13, 1969.
      "A dazzling recreation of a world collapsing."

1266 "Picked by Fellini," Times (London), January 21, 1969, 10.
      Martin Potter has been chosen to play Encolpius in Satyricon. Potter is a British actor. Potter says that Encolpius is "a totally free young animal." Max Born, a hippy from Chelsea, will play Giton. Born describes Giton as "a little whore with an angel's face."

1267 Positif, n. 3, 1969.

1268 Powell, Dilys. "Gallery of Obsessions," Times (London), September 13, 1970, 27.
      "A good deal of Federico Fellini's adaptation of Petronius' Satyricon--Fellini Satyricon, is boring, or so I thought at the end. Not at the start." "One had the feeling that the great wayward Italian director was bringing to life on his wide screen the figures of some Pompeiian wall painting...." Talks about what Fellini does with the story line. Admits a dislike for Petronius' Satyricon. Calls the film's ending "an unfinished sentence with the characters as if in a transfer pattern, frozen, plastered into wall-painting on broken masonry." The film is boring because it is disconnected and long. It is "a brilliant curiosity."

1269 Quattrocchi, Angelo, Neville, and Jill. Village Voice, 15 (January 22, 1970), 55, 57-59.

1270 Reed, Rex. "Cheers for the Fellini Satyricon, Ditto for Lov-
      ing, But for the Rest of This Month's Movies ... Murder!"
      Holiday, 47 (March, 1970), 32. Reprinted in Big Screen, Lit-
      tle Screen. New York: Macmillan, 1971, 265-266.
            Likes the film and claims that Satyricon will endure--at
      least for him. Openly states that he will make no attempt to
      explain Satyricon. Everybody's talking about Satyricon, but
      they're "saying the wrong things. Like most works of art
      nobody understands, lavish attempts are being made either to
      overintellectualize it or dismiss it as the creation of a sick
      mind." Claims that Satyricon should only be dealt with on the
      entertainment level. Says, "It is not Fellini's interpretation
      of Roman mythology any more than it is Fellini's projection
      of the end of the world, and if Fellini himself claims it is
      either then he's a bigger fool than I think he is."

1271 Regent, Roger. Revue des Deux Mondes, n. 1, 1970, 182.

1272 Revue du Cinêma Internationale (Lausanne/Paris), n. 3, May,
      1969.

1273 Rollin, Betty. "He Shoots Dreams on Film," Look, 34 (March
      10, 1970), 48-53.
            With Fellini during the shooting of some of the film. It
      is not clear that the quotations from Fellini are first-hand.
      Fellini: "I am too tender.... My father too, was unable to
      say no. He was soft. My mother was strong." "Often when
      I work, I am like Christopher Columbus with a crew who wants
      to go back."

1274 St. Anthony, 78 (September, 1970), 6.

1275 Samuels, Charles. "Puppets: From 'Z' to Zabriskie Point,"
      American Scholar, 39 (Autumn, 1970), 678-691.
            Blisteringly condemns the film. Says that the general
      meaning of the film is clear but does not state or restate his
      view of what the film says except that "we rarely know why
      any one of the characters goes anywhere or why he acts as he
      does," except that "his action is meant to be disreputable."
      The nymphomaniac episode tells us "that Roman hedonism is
      self-punishing"; the hermaphrodite episode "that Roman religion
      is futile." Nothing appears redundant to Fellini "if it can in-
      spire revulsion." Fellini is "in a sweat to show us that Rome
      is terrible, although that doesn't keep him from exploiting its
      vices." Asks question after question about why Fellini has
      various scenes in the film. His only answer: 'Because Fel-
      lini wanted the effect." The film is "heavy-handed in meaning,
      simultaneously garish and obscure in detail."

1276 Sarris, Andrew. Village Voice, 15 (March 19, 1970), 51.

1277 Saturday Review, 53 (March 14, 1970), 42+.

1278 Schickel, R. "Zabriskie Point, Fellini Satyricon, and The Damned," Film 70/71, ed. David Denby. New York: Simon and Schuster, 1971, 187-191.

1279 Schlesinger, Arthur, Jr. Vogue, 155 (April 15, 1970), 58. Like Bergman, Fellini too is a "genius." Fellini is unsurpassed as far as seeing more deeply into human faces, evoking vivid feelings of degradation and despair. Fellini searches "poignantly" for some trace of compassion and love, and converts emotion into cinematic image. He truly "understands and commands the medium." Satyricon is "an exercise in free confession, a dazzling rendition of private fantasy, an unconstrained release of all the things Fellini sees or imagines or wants or fears." "But the film leaves a sour taste." "One feels that Fellini's capacity for disgust has overpowered his sense of humanity."

1280 Sign, 49 (June, 1970), 46.

1281 Simon, John. "Fellini Satyricon," Movies into Film, New York: Dial Press, 1971, 211-219. (Incorporates his two reviews--the first is from the New Leader, the second from the New York Times.)
    Carefully compares Petronius's with Fellini's Satyricon, of which the latter is a "thoroughgoing vulgarization and subversion." To be expected when there is a film adaptation of a classic. First-rate film talents don't bother with adaptations. Fellini, too, was once first-rate, when he made Sceicco Bianco and Vitelloni "and left Petronius alone." Fellini and his co-scenario writer "pilfer from everywhere," without heed of integration or meaning. Even the continuity is faulty. It is a blistering, informed, carefully documented review.

1282 _____. "A Spanking For Fellini Satyricon," New York Times, May 10, 1970, Section II, 11. Reprinted in Movies into Film. New York: Dial Press, 1971, 211-219.
    What Fellini has done has been to dump his dreams into the film, "and what an uninteresting lot of dreams they are." The images are random, the dreams "undigested," raw material of the unconscious that do not make telling works of art. We shouldn't expect the film to make sense. It is just "idle, meaningless image-mongering." Many scenes just show off Fellini's and his co-writer's "homework in Classics 12B." The film is full of "grotesque, overpainted faces ... misconceived torsos and pointlessly preening behinds." It is "a gimcrack, shop-worn nightmare."

1283 _____. "Movie Mailbag," New York Times, June 28, 1970, Section II, 12.
    Replies angrily to the long letter by Miss Pandiri, who defended Fellini's movie (see 1264).

1284   . New York Times, July 12, 1970, Section II, 21.
          Correction of his letter.

1285   Sirkin. Harry, 1 (July 2, 1970), 15.

1286   Steele, L. Los Angeles Free Press, 7 (April 17, 1970) 37.

1287   Sweeney, Louise. "Fellini's Ancient Rome's Moral Decay,"
       Christian Science Monitor, March 11, 1970, 10.
          A short, favorable review. Points out that Satyricon is
       not Fellini's first exposé on decadence--he did it before in
       Dolce vita. Calls Satyricon "a handsomely photographed wal-
       low in degeneracy."

1288   Taylor, John Russell. Sight and Sound, 39 (Autumn, 1970),
       217-218.
          A "nightmare vision of a civilization on its last legs,
       over-rich, over-ripe, decorating its surfaces with a neurotic
       elaboration." The very "ornateness" of the film takes on a
       moral quality, by provoking a moral response. Dolce vita,
       "investing Fellini's private city of dreadful night with the face
       and features of modern Rome, showed us a few of the 120
       jours de Sodome and told us that they were a bore and a bane.
       Satyricon, disguising the same city of Fellini's mind as ancient
       Rome, not only tells us, but puts us through every grinding,
       asphyxiating moment."

1289   . "City of the Dreadful Night," Times (London), Sep-
       tember 11, 1970, 14.
          Compares Satyricon to Dolce vita. "Like La dolce vita,
       Fellini Satyricon is constructed massively, architecturally
       though this time as a stately progression from dark to light
       rather than as an alternation of one with the other." The film
       has been publicized as a "sexy romp" and notes that nothing
       could be further from the truth. Fellini forces us to "detach"
       from the "naked bodies," and "suggestive attitudes" and see
       it clearly and to judge it. Seeing a Fellini film--a Fellini
       "vision"--is like a "journey round his skull, seeing things as
       he sees them, sharing his most private passions, preoccupa-
       tions and fetishes, accepting, even if unwillingly, his mental
       furniture as our own."

1290   Teisseire, Guy. L'Aurore, December 23, 1969.
          Whatever one's judgment might be, "every frame of the
       film issues genius."

1291   Teissier, Max. Cinéma '70, n. 142, January, 1970.
          He loves Fellini, but what he finds in this film leaves
       him "sensually dissatisfied, with no sense of surprise."

1292   Times (London), September 15, 1969, 8.

1293 "Top Venice Prize Won by Fellini Satyricon. " New York
      Times, September 6, 1969, 33.
           News item. Satyricon is awarded the Critics Prize at
      the Venice Film Festival.

1294 Tyler, Parker. Screening the Sexes: Homosexuality in the
      Movies. Garden City, N.Y.: Anchor Press/Doubleday, 1972.
           Says that Fellini, against his desire, had to cut a scene
      from Vitelloni that indicated that one of the vitelloni "was real-
      ly homosexual. " Satyricon is the "most profoundly homosexual
      movie in all history. " The Minotaur is a "quasi-sexual sur-
      rogate" for Fellini himself, "sitting Jove-like in his office,
      receiving all the eager, flashy, amiable young men who desire
      to be in his films. " Lichas may be an "even more radical
      surrogate. " The hermaphrodite "looks like a chubby fourteen-
      year-old faggot who has been dressed for a drag party and
      collapsed because he has been sent on a trip. " Tyler's whole
      book is very illuminating, talking freely about matters and
      films that are usually never mentioned in formal criticism.
      This book should never be neglected in examining the films of
      Fellini (or perhaps those of other directors).

1295 Van Dyke, Willard. "Movie Mailbag," New York Times, June
      28, 1970, Section II, 12.
           Letter agreeing with Simon's review of Satyricon. Van
      Dyke was the director of the film department of the Museum of
      Modern Art.

1296 Veillot, Claude. L'Express, December 8, 1969.
           Fellini, though reluctant, is, in Satyricon, a Christian
      who is "more than ever Christian. "

1297 Walsh, Moira. America, 122 (April 4, 1970), 376.
           "The deliberate lack of continuity, however, with its at-
      tendant lack of contrast, irony, resonance or any other human
      attribute, leaves the spectator without a clue about how he is
      intended to construe the film or how to go about making any-
      thing of it at all. "

1298 Weinberg, Herman. "Triptych--Italian Style. " Take One,
      Spring, 1970. Reprinted in Saint Cinema: Selected Writings,
      1929-1970. New York: Drama Books Specialists, 1970.
           The three films are The Damned, Zabriskie Point, and
      Satyricon, and Weinberg is appalled by the lack of artistry and
      by the lubricity of each. Drawing on his vast and precise
      familiarity with films of the past, Weinberg excoriates the
      three films, finding little or anything good in any of them.
      Satyricon has nothing for the ears or the mind, only "for the
      eyes. " He has read all of Fellini's own commentary on Sat-
      yricon and that has not moved him. The directors of old
      "didn't have to 'protest' so much. ... They just quietly made
      masterpieces. Today, the plethora of interviews a director

gives ... become part of the film." We have to know them
too to fully understand the film. He prefers the Visconti of
La terra trema and the Fellini of La strada, "in the days of
their purity, before they became so successful, before they
became bloated with success." Though crotchety, this article
raises (very knowledgeably) issues of aesthetics that pro-Fel-
lini critics have to face up to.

1299 Willamette Bridge, 3 (May 14, 1970), 21.

1300 Winchester, J. Broadside, 9 (August 12, 1970), 9.

1301 Witt, Piotr. Kultura, 30, n. 8, 1970.

                              I clowns

1302 "Analyse du Film Les Clowns de Federico Fellini," Esprit,
      4, n. 3, 1971, 1031.

1303 Andrews, Nigel. Monthly Film Bulletin, 39 (September, 1972),
      184.

1304 Arnold, Gary. Washington Post, July 30, 1971.
            Arnold himself never liked clowns, only trapeze work,
      so he can't respond sympathetically to the passing of the clown.
      And without this special interest, he finds the film "hollow,
      tedious, and alienating." And anyway, he asks, what with
      having Bob Hope, Phil Silvers, Carol Burnett, and Jerry Lew-
      is, why all the fuss about the disappearance of the "atavistic,
      small town" circus clown?

1305 Bates, A. "Fellini-Grotesque," Gay, 2 (August 2, 1971), 15.

1306 Brudnoy, David. "Home on the Range," National Review, 23
      (October 22, 1971), 1191.
            Deals only superficially with the white clown and the au-
      guste clown. Says that, "The Clowns is another of Fellini's
      tolerant, loving, intimate probings into the nature of mankind,
      seen here through a warm and never cloying juxtaposition of
      the clown and ostensibly nonclown who is you and me." Fel-
      lini runs the "gamut of emotions" from "joyful hilarity" in the
      circus ring to the "pathos" of the old clowns lost in their
      memories. Clowns "awakens the child--and, I hope, the
      mensch--in us all."

1307 Canby, Vincent. New York Times, June 20, 1971, Section II,
      1.
            Doesn't like Clowns. Expected more from Fellini. Calls
      the mock-funeral ending "...very symbolic, not terribly funny,
      and ultimately looks like imitation Fellini."

1308 _____. "Fellini's Affectionate Memoir Unfolds," New York
Times, June 15, 1971, 50.
        Liked about one-third of the film. Was disappointed by
rest and expected more from Fellini. Gives an accurate account of each segment. When he saw the bucket plop on Fellini's head says, "The movie director, obviously, is not only
ringmaster and white clown, but also the ridiculous auguste."
"It's not that The Clowns is not a good deal of fun, or that it
is boring, it's just that--to me, anyway--this sort of coda
doesn't do justice to the entire career."

1309 Carroll, Kathleen. New York Daily News, June 15, 1971, 52.
        Doesn't "star-rate" the film because "documentaries are
not star rated." Finds that the "clumsy slapstick" of the clowns
"no longer amuses us."

1310 Coote, Anna. "Circus Dreams," Observer (London), January
3, 1971, Color Supplement, 18-21.
        Says that Fellini associates the strange creatures depicted
in the film with the monsters and freaks he knew as a boy in
Rimini: "the dwarf nun, the tramp with broken legs, the mad-
man obsessed with war stories." Quotes Fellini: "It's like a
young boy who goes to the church to become a priest. He has
a vocation--I have the same feeling about the circus."

1311 Crist, Judith. New York, June 14, 1971.
        The film is "classic," "austere" in construction, a "com-
plexity of insights and perceptions." It is the work of a master and of a piece with his greatest creations. She quotes
from Fellini's notes to the film: "The world is peopled with
clowns. During my research in Paris, I imagined a sequence
(never shot) in which I saw clowns everywhere in the street:
ridiculous old ladies with absurd little hats, women with plas-
tic sacks on their heads to protect them from the rain ...
businessmen with bowler hats and a bishop with the face of
an embalmed man."

1312 "Critique du Film Les clowns de Fellini," Séquences, n. 68,
1972, 32.

1313 Cue, 43 (March 11, 1974), 35.

1314 Etudes, 334 (May, 1971), 728.

1315 "Fellini Despre Clovnil," Cinema (Bucharest), 11 (March,
1973), 14-15.

1316 Filmfacts, 14 (1971), 372.
        The cast and credits; a sympathetic, informed synopsis
of the film; a compilation of the critical reaction (12 favorable,
3 mixed, 1 negative); and long excerpts from reviews by Judith Crist, Stefan Kanfer, Gary Arnold, and Stanley Kauffmann.

1317 Free, William J. "Fellini's I clowns and the Grotesque,"
      Journal of Modern Literature, 3 (1973) n. 2, 214-227.
           Indispensable. One of the most informative essays for
      understanding the intellectual background of Fellini's work.
      Relates the material in Wolfgang Keyer's The Grotesque in Art
      and Literature to Fellini. Contends that a major difference
      distinguishes Fellini's artistic vision and most 20th-century ar-
      tists (Kafka, Beckett, Genet, Ionesco, etc.). These "almost
      unanimously find in the grotesque, dark visions of the evil
      times upon which we have fallen." Fellini, on the other hand,
      though his world is no less grotesque, does not see a "dialec-
      tic of despair." Fellini's reaction to the absurd world is
      "joyous, his laughter optimistic."

1318 Friendly, Alfred Jr. "Now! In the Center Ring!! Fellini!!!"
      New York Times, July 19, 1970, Section II, 13.
           Written during the shooting of Clowns for Italian TV.
      Clowns was to be the first of five specials (each about 55 min-
      utes), but looks like this one may run much longer and be the
      only one Fellini makes. The day of his visit to the set Fel-
      lini was in a "foul mood." His assistants said that his "mood"
      was due to the 95-degree temperature and Fellini's low blood
      pressure. Fellini also had his hand bandaged from an accident
      in Paris when he put his hand through a "set" window. What
      the film is about: "The Clowns is to be ... a re-evocation of
      the three stolen days Fellini spent with a circus ... when he
      ran away at age eight." The circus is "seedy." The extras
      are costumed for 1925, and the performers are all Fellini's
      "favorites."

1319 Genêt. "Letter from Paris," New Yorker, March 27, 1971,
      96-97.
           A favorable review written on the French opening of
      Clowns. Gives a good description of the film and discusses
      the white clown and the auguste clown. Says that Clowns is
      "a great imaginative movie--a true creation in fine frenzy."
      "The finale is almost the handsomest part of it all, with the
      big top filled with shifting colored lights like fire works, and
      windblown ribbons being wafted up like sky rockets--a gala of
      colors and a carnival of magical movements."

1320 Gilliatt, Penelope. "Fellini Himself," New Yorker, 47 (June
      12, 1971), 96, 99-100. Reprinted in Unholy Fools: Wits,
      Comics, Disturbers of the Peace. New York: Viking Press,
      1973, 15-20.
           Deals with the two types of clowns. Calls Fellini the
      most "pre-Freudian" of all directors. The film's subject is
      "extravagant." "In the ring or out of it ... nothing is abso-
      lute." Fellini believes "profoundly in the redeemable, and
      clowning is the system where there is always another chance
      and where damage never matures. It is his native land, and
      we are in it." Quotes Fellini as having said that clowns are
      his "holy fools"--"sacred anarchists, convivial, without guilt."

1321 Guberinic, S. "Stvarnost in predstava--Federico Fellini Klovni
      (1970), Rim (1971)," Ekran, 12 (1974), n. 115/116, 273-279.

1322 Hart, Henry. Films in Review, 22 (June-July, 1971), 367-369.

1323 Hatch, Robert. Nation, 212 (June 28, 1971), 828-829. Re-
      printed in Film 71/72, ed. David Denby. New York: Simon
      and Schuster, 1972, 197-199.
          The promises of the film, the exhilaration and the mira-
      cle of a past recaptured, are not fulfilled. The film keeps
      losing momentum, letting the viewer escape. "There are in-
      stants of flashing and cheeky good humor, but overall, it has
      a vault-like chill. "

1324 Jaffe, Ira. Film Quarterly, 25 (Fall, 1971), 53-55.
          The circus as a ritual initiating the young into life
      "through the fierce mockery of bodily injury and death. " Finds
      a theme of the "confrontation of death" throughout the film.
      Although part of the problem of the old clowns is that a changed
      society can no longer appreciate them, the other problem is
      simply "the rush of time bearing old age and death. "

1325 Kanfer, S. "Pierrots and Augustos," Time, 97 (June 21,
      1971), 84. Reprinted in Film 71/72, ed. David Denby. New
      York: Simon and Schuster, 1972, 196-197.
          "Fellini's pretense is to restore the icons of his youth
      for the pleasure of today's children, but beyond the easy de-
      lights is a philosophy clearly aimed at adults. " Says Fellini
      implies "if the human condition is a melancholy joke, then
      death is its punch line and hilarity the only proper response. "

1326 Kauffmann, Stanley. New Republic, 165 (July 3, 1971), 22+.
      Reprinted in Living Images. New York: Harper and Row,
      1975, 59-61.
          Both likes and dislikes Clowns but doesn't really consider
      it a "real" Fellini film, even though many of the familiar Fel-
      lini "hallmarks" are there. Comments on the dialogue in the
      interviews with the old clowns, and claims that Fellini had
      them out of sync purposely to make us aware of different time
      levels. Sums up, "It's a job that Fellini did and did well,
      employing both his strength and his weaknesses. "

1327 Koch, John. Boston After Dark, August 3, 1971, 9.
          Compares Fellini to Mailer in that he explores the world
      in reference to himself. "The film is too much of a piece,
      so well knit ... it is hard to cite any pre-eminent virtue be-
      yond Fellini's informing vision. " "The Clowns is the very es-
      sence of Fellini, Fellini's logical extension of his imaginings
      as we know them on film. "

1328 Lahr, J. "Riddle of the Clowns," Vogue, 158 (August 1, 1971)
      90-91.

1329   Latil-le Dantec, Mireille. "Der Zirkus der Welt in der Welt
       des Zirkus: Versuch über Federico Fellini's Die Clowns,"
       Dokumente, J. 27, 1971, H. 2, S. 153.

1330   Lauder, Robert E. "A Priest Looks at Fellini," New York
       Times, July 4, 1971, Section II, 11.
              "There is a long tradition in Christianity of depicting
       Christ as a clown, infinitely vulnerable but never finally de-
       feated. " "The clown--by helping us to laugh at the apparent
       hopelessness that surrounds us--may lead us to hope once
       again. " Finds the film "almost a documentary in the meaning
       of man" and a "hymn to humanity. " What emerges in Fellini's
       films is his love for his characters.

1331   Mallett, Richard. Punch, July 19, 1972, 91.
              "It's altogether a minor work in the Fellini canon, but
       it's entertaining--and 'U'. "

1332   Manns, T. Chaplin (Sweden), 14 (1972), n. 6, 224-225.

1333   Melly, George. Observer (London), July 16, 1972, 28.

1334   Mulholland, L. Nola Express, 90 (September 24, 1971), 21.

1335   Paini, Dominique. "Lettre sur Les clowns," Cahiers du Ci-
       néma, n. 229, May, 1971, 64-65.
              A theoretical discussion with himself about the nature and
       meaning of the film, posing questions and suggesting answers.
       For example, if the clown, actually and symbolically, has dis-
       appeared, can he be found elsewhere than in the circus? Fel-
       lini finds the clown again "in actual fact, in life, and renders
       null and void the distinction between Art and Nature and re-
       turns to nature to find what we no longer find in Art. "
       "Reads" the film from a political and from a psychoanalytical
       point of view too.

1336   Pierre, Sylvie. "L'homme aux Clowns," Cahiers du Cinéma,
       n. 229, May, 1971, 48-51.
              Brilliant, provocative, illuminating analysis of the film
       from a psychoanalytic point of view. The opening sequence of
       Clowns "clearly" exhibits those characteristics of the kind of
       scene that Freud labelled "primal. " "The Clowns represents
       in regard to a primal scene the same reworking through fan-
       tasy as the dream of the wolves for Freud's patient. "

1337   Povse, J. "Klovni in Fellini," Ekran, 10 (1972), n. 98-99,
       320-323.

1338   "Recherche de la beauté derrière un apparence par Fellini
       dans Les Clowns," Pédagogie, 26 (1971), n. 8, 736.

1339   Reed, Rex. Holiday, 8 (July, 1971), 12.
              Describes some significant scenes and gives a good gen-

eral description. "In this simple, honest and beautiful study
of the end of clowns, Fellini tenderly touches the pulse of the
empty civilization we've become through our inability to smile,
even at the funny things around us, and stings the conscience
into awareness. "

1340 ____ "The Laughter Has a Cutting Edge in Fellini's Fine New
Film," New York Daily News, February 26, 1971, 50.
"A dazzling, affectionate work of the highest rank. "

1341 Sarris, Andrew. Village Voice, 16 (July 1, 1971), 47.

1342 Saviola, Kevin M. Women's Wear Daily, June 15, 1971, 14.
Fellini has created a new kind of movie: the director's
first person narrative.

1343 Schickel, Richard. "Pagliacci Plays Fellini," Life, 71 (July
9, 1971), 9.
Finds the film not very interesting on the intellectual
level. Likes the whirling sequences that make him forget "all
the posturing talk about the meaning of the clown figure. " He
especially dislikes Fellini's "constant intrusion of himself and
his camera crew, pratfalling around, in order to demonstrate
that there is a bit of the clown in everyone. " He feels we
know that, "and even if we didn't, such self-conscious adora-
bility is finally painful. "

1344 Sleezy. Seed, 7 (July 30, 1971), 19.

1345 Sweeney, Louise. "Yes, They're All There," Christian Science
Monitor, June 16, 1971, 4.
Calls Clowns "an extravagant, thrilling, and beautiful cir-
cus of a film with Fellini as ringmaster.... "

1346 "La Symbolique des clowns dans les films de Fellini," Nouvelle Revue Française, n. 221, 1971, 118.

1347 Taylor, John Russell. Times (London), April 2, 1971, 10.
A short synopsis of his review that appeared in this paper on September 2, 1970. "The overall effect is delight-
ful.... " Clowns "would be the Fellini film you like if you
don't like Fellini; but that does not prevent those who do from
liking it as well. "

1348 ____ . Times (London), July 14, 1972, 9.
The style of Clowns, Roma, and Director's Notebook is
a "fantasy documentary of the mind. " Breaks Clowns into three
sections: reconstructed autobiography of Fellini as a child; the
circus and a search for the circus clown carried out in a fantastic documentary style; and a Fellini extravaganza. Clowns
may appeal to us because of the nonchalance about it, but the
whole film "could hardly be more tightly, impeccably controlled. "

1349 _____ . "Fellini Goes to the Circus," Times (London), September 2, 1970, 7.
     "Fellini may not have much sense of discretion--in many
ways that is his greatest glory--but at least he has the sense
to let his films speak for themselves or not at all. "

1350 _____ . 'Roma and The Clowns," Sight and Sound, Autumn,
1972, 229-230.
     Not very long, but indispensable for understanding Direc-
tor's Notebook, Clowns, and Roma. With these films, says
Taylor, Fellini has created a new genre: the Fellini "essay"
film. Although the impression the film (Clowns) gives is ca-
sual, it is "shaped with precision and consciously created. "
The film is "a kind of exorcism for Fellini--but then so are
all his films, ways of dealing with his obsessions in various
ways, directly and indirectly, to work them out of his system. "
Despite this very personal aspect about these films, Fellini
manages to keep his aesthetic distance by "enshrining" a part
of himself in each film, "a skin which is sloughed off as he
moves on to something new. "

1351 V[rhovec], B. Ekran, 10 (1972) n. 98-99, 401.

1352 Werb. Variety, September 16, 1970, 14.
     There are "static moments" when the clown expert is
discussing clowns. And he sees no need to highlight Anita
Ekberg "as a man eater" or to put Victoria Chaplin in a film
about great clowns just "to recall her father's eminence. "

1353 Westerbeck, Colin L. Jr. "Ciao Pagliacci," Commonweal,
94 (September 24, 1971), 501-502.
     The mock-funeral finale "fits Pierre-Aime Touchard's
splendid phrase 'a song of despair'; clearly anyone who sings
about his despair also overcomes it. "

1354 Wilnblad, A. Kosmoroma (Denmark), June, 1972, 237.

1355 Wilson, T. Space City, 3 (October 7, 1971), 16.

1356 Winsten, Archer. "Fellini Looks at The Clowns," New York
Post, June 15, 1971, 57.
     "Uncommonly beautiful and evocative. "

1357 Zimmerman, Paul D. "The Nose-Thumbers," Newsweek, 77
(June ·21, 1971), 86.
     Clowns is sometimes "hilarious" and then at times "ter-
ribly sad. " What Fellini wants to do is "repudiate the death
of clowning, so he repudiates it and, like the clowns he cham-
pions, thumbs his nose at death itself. " Quotes Fellini: "This
show based on miracle, fantasy, jest, nonsense, fable, the lack
of coldly intellectual meanings--is precisely the kind of show
that pleases me. "

Roma

1358 "Actor Accused of Film-Set Fire," Times (London), October
      27, 1971, 6.
            News item. A frustrated actor who did not get a part in
      a Western sets fire to the Roma set to get revenge.

1359 After Dark, 5 (December, 1972), 61.

1360 Alpert, Hollis. World, 1 (July 4, 1972), 102.

1361 _____. World, December 5, 1972, 69.
            "It is Rome as only Fellini would show it to us. It may
      not be wholly true, but it's not false, either. "

1362 Amiel, M. "L'analyse d'un grand film: Fellini Roma," Ci-
      néma, 168 (July-August, 1972), 57-65.

1363 Andrews, Nigel. Monthly Film Bulletin, 39 (December, 1972),
      n. 647, 258.

1364 Armes, R. "Rome from Rimini," London Magazine, 12 (Feb-
      ruary/March, 1973), 116-122.
            The film is "clearly Fellini's masterpiece to date. " Gone
      is "the sentimentality of La strada, the pretension of La dolce
      vita, the self-conscious intellectualizing of $8\frac{1}{2}$. " Everything in
      the film is constructed, even the Fascist newsreel in the film,
      instead of using archive material. The fantastic elements of
      Fellini's early neo-realist films "that seemed to jar" were in
      fact the authentic roots of Fellini's genuine style. Says that
      there is a level of "personal illusion and private joke" in the
      film; e. g. , the old Roman aristocrat who "remembers" the ec-
      clesiastical fashion show resembles Giulietta Masina, and there
      are figures oddly resembling Visconti and Marco Ferreri.

1365 Axelsson, S. Chaplin, 14 (1972), n. 119, 279-280.

1366 Bachmann, Gideon. Film Quarterly, 26 (Winter 1972/1973),
      37-39.
            Reviews the film "with a certain ambivalent affection. "
      The mixture of fantasy and reality ("the thing Fellini does
      best") is so strong in the ecclesiastical fashion show sequence
      "that you are goaded into believing what you see. " But the
      question he asks of all of Fellini's detailing of his life and
      career in the film is "How relevant is this to the rest of us?"
      He finds "strictly additive style of cutting, the musical under-
      scoring for effect, fabulous decor often wasted by careless
      camera use" plus lack of social consciousness, story line, in-
      volvement, and "just plain compassion. " The mustiness of the
      subject matter permeates the form as well. "It is the nostal-
      gic odor of amazing talent. "

1367 _____. "Au paradis plus vite," Ekran, 10 (1972), n. 94-
      95, 196-198.

1368   Bory, Jean-Louis. "Les Trois Romes de Fellini," Le Nouvel
       Observateur, May 22, 1972, 69.
              The film is monumental: with its architectural fullness,
       proportional harmony, and vigorous originality in which is mir-
       rored the temper of its director-architect. The evening is
       magisterial: 'Rome at night, lit-up, spread out, dead, or
       rather etherized by night. Suddenly there is let loose a tor-
       rent of thunder and flame, an invasion of barbarians, a horde
       of motorcyclists, in helmets, thundering through, like a troop
       of Attila's cavalry, the whole city as if to take a final census
       of its beautiful stonery, before the last farewell, and the pal-
       aces and churches and triumphal arches tremble, the fountains
       become silent, the statues die standing up--this dog of a Fel-
       lini, he has had us take a night tour of Rome, as though we
       were tourists. But it is of the sound and fury of the Apoca-
       lypse. "

1369   Boyum, Joy Gould. "The Creative Egotism of Fellini," Wall
       Street Journal, November 8, 1972, 4.
              Starts with a discussion of film and its place in the world
       of Art. Then talks of Fellini and Roma. Calls Fellini a "su-
       premely honest artist. " Says that Roma is more than a view
       of Rome from the eyes of Fellini--calls Roma a "vision. " The
       traffic jam is filmed as a "mammoth circus parade of cars and
       lights, and clowns disguised in street clothes; its central fi-
       gure is a movie camera on a crane, the plastic sheets protect-
       ing it from a windy downpour flapping wildly against an El Gre-
       co sky. "

1370   Calendo, J. Inter/View, 27 (November, 1972), 40.

1371   Canby, Vincent. 'Roma--The Faces are Perhaps Too Famil-
       iar," New York Times, November 5, 1972, Section II, 1.
              An unfavorable review. Breaks Roma down into "items"
       that Fellini deals with in the film and gives descriptions of
       them. Some of these "items" are: whores, Fellini's child-
       hood, Roman food, and table manners. "If you admire his
       earlier films ... it's a little sad to see him spending so much
       time and effort in Roma, not re-exploring those concerns, but
       simply recycling them, along with camera shots and faces. "

1372   Catholic Film Newsletter, 37 (October 30, 1972), 102.

1373   Chapier, Henry. Combat, May 15, 1972.
              What Fellini thinks of the present age, "his shots of hip-
       pies, grouped together like monks in the Piazza di Spagna tell
       us sufficiently, as well as the fabulous final sequence of the
       motorcyclists hurtling across Rome at full speed straight into
       the camera. "

1374   Charensol, Georges. Le Nouvelles Littéraire, July 22, 1972.
              Fellini is here making his way along the same road that

he took up in Clowns and which has "only the semblance of
being a documentary." No one is less objective than Fellini.
What he gives us is "not a picture of Rome but his own portrait. He is writing a journal in time and he never stops projecting his obsessions on to the city, which he pretends to de-
scribe, but which, as seen by him, is one of complete unreal-
ity."

1375   Chauvet, Louis. Le Figaro, May 15, 1972.
       There are some weak spots in the film, but when Fellini
"unleashes the delights of his imagination, nothing can compare
to them. No one can resist them."

1376   Chazal, Robert. France-Soir, May 16, 1972.
       There are memories in the film full of a "painful nostal-
gia." In the film there is an unrehearsed scene where Fellini
tries to stop Anna Magnani late at night, who cuts him off
saying, "Oh go to bed, Federico. It's late." Chazal says that
this is the severest of criticisms, but it is Fellini himself who
has chosen it.

1377   Cinema '72, n. 168, 1972.

1378   Cocks, Jay. "Fellini Primer," Time, 100 (October 23, 1972),
       74.
       An unfavorable review. He doesn't like Fellini to re-use
ideas from his other, older films. Claims Fellini did his best
the first time around and only messed it up in Roma. Says,
"Lacking a sense of strong commitment or interest, Fellini's
Roma becomes an aimless side-show."

1379   Colaciello, R. Inter/View, 27 (November, 1972), 40.

1380   Cosmopolitan, 173 (December, 1972), 14.

1381   Crist, Judith. New York, 5 (October 23, 1972), 106.
       Gives a good description of the movie and details a few
of the episodes. Says, "In the gut and the people of Rome,
Fellini exposes the gut and people of all our cities, where the
grotesques make their mark on our memories and ourselves,
where time brings changes and only celebrities can talk seriously of the world's end as a macabre gang of cyclists whiz
past the treasuries of centuries."

1382   Cue, 43 (July 8, 1974), 34.

1383   Curtiss, Thomas Quinn. "Fellini's Masterful Roma," Inter-
       national Herald Tribune, May 17, 1972.
       "Here is a vast fresco of the Eternal City, intensely per-
sonal and constantly absorbing. There is not a dull moment
... and one wishes there were more."

1384   Damiani, B. "Il re è Nude," Cineforum, n. 115-116 (July-
       August, 1972), 140-143.

1385 Daniel, F. "Oerdoengos Fellini," Film Kultura, 9 (September/October, 1973), 27-33.

1386 De Baroncelli, Jean. Le Monde, May 16, 1972.
      The film is simultaneously "a portrait (perhaps falsified, certainly incomplete), a spectacle, a satire, a psychoanalysis, and an autobiography. " It mixes "the present with the past, reality with phantasmagoria. "

1387 Delain, Michel. L'Express, May 15, 1972.
      Rome: with its "fascist yesterday and its question-mark today, which we just catch a glimpse of in the light of exploding flares. "

1388 Denby, David. "Obsessions," Atlantic, 231 (January, 1973), 94-96.
      Liked the early Fellini of Vitelloni and Cabiria; but $8\frac{1}{2}$ was "a monstrous act of egotism. " Starts by telling us how in recent years the "director" has come to the foreground as the "star" of the film. Because directors are "caught-up" with giving their work their own "vision," it is no wonder that their films lack variety and development. Fellini is one such director whose "vision" has become more central to his films while the narrative and dramatic elements have become "feeble. " Roma is "a perfect rubbish of 'vivid' Fellini images piled one on top of another, a tedious catalogue of the fantastic and the bizarre.... When everything is so wild, we have no ground from which to judge whether a given sequence is meant satirically or whether that's the way Fellini naturally sees things and wants them to be. "

1389 Dooley, Roger. Villager, October 19, 1972, 9.
      Claims that Roma is the "most appealing" film by Fellini in recent years. Roma is not as "repulsive" as Satyricon, nor as "subjective" as Clowns.

1390 Duran, Michel. Le Canard Enchaîné, May 24, 1972.
      He admires the film, but what he personally holds against Fellini is his "taste for feminine ugliness. " If there is a pretty woman, either he passes her swiftly by or he has her made up in some loathsome way.

1391 Ebert, Roger. Chicago Sun-Times, January 12, 1973.
      "Fellini isn't just giving us a lot of flashy scenes, he's building a narrative that has a city for its protagonist instead of a single character.... The only sly thing is that the city isn't Rome--it's Fellini, disguised in bricks, mortar, and ruins. " In the film the prostitute, so often used as a symbol of fleeting moments, "becomes eternal; and the Church, always the symbol of the unchanging ... becomes temporal. "

1392 Ethier, J. -R. Séquences, 72 (April, 1973), 39-41.

1393 Etudes, 337 (July, 1972), 82.

1394 Film, n. 66 (Summer, 1972), 8.

1395 Film Information, 3 (November, 1972), 2.

1396 Filmfacts, 1972, 455-459.
        One of the most complete of the helpful, informed, and
informative Filmfacts compilations. We have the cast and
credits, a full analysis of the action of the film, a summary
of American critical reaction (7 favorable, 1 mixed, 8 negative), and lengthy excerpts from reviews in Variety, Chicago
Sun-Times, and Newsday. From the analysis: The ecclesiastical fashion show is meant to evoke "the ostentatious past
when the Church and the aristocracy co-existed in luxury and
harmony." Anna Magnani is regarded by Fellini as the quintessential "aristocrat and tramp" and so epitomizes Rome.

1397 Filmkritik, 17 (January, 1973), 42-43.

1398 Filmmakers, 5 (September, 1972), 20.

1399 Foley, Charles. "Fellini Films Sexy Hippies of Old Rome,"
Observer (London), September 15, 1968, 6.

1400 Gallery, 1 (November, 1972), 15.

1401 Gelmis, Joseph. Newsday, October 16, 1972.
        Finds the film a "bore." It has "no central focus for
our emotions. It is a dreamy travelogue...." Fellini's "en-
dorsement of young freaks who make love on the Spanish
Steps" makes him suspect that he is "courting young film go-
ers."

1402 Genauer, Emily. "Art and the Artist," New York Post, October 28, 1972, Magazine Section, 14.
        Claims that Roma is a "storyless, not quite documentary
montage of the sights, sounds and smells of Rome from the
time Fellini ... came there as a boy, to the present, when
we follow a crew of young film-makers making their own documentary of the city."

1403 Goodwin, M. and N. Wise. Take One, 3 (November/December,
1971), 30.

1404 Gow, G. Films and Filming, 19 (January, 1973), 46-47.

1405 Green, Benny. Punch, 264 (January 17, 1973), 93.
        Tells us what Roma is not about and discusses Fellini's
style since Dolce vita. Discusses and describes three episodes
in Roma that are most "memorable": the eating scene, the
brothels, and the music hall. Says that each is done with such
"utter brilliance as to leave the optic nerve drunk with sheer
delight."

1406 Greenspun, Roger. New York Times, October 16, 1972, 46.
      Says that in Roma "...Rome is not so much the subject
as the occasion for a film that is not quite fiction and surely
not fact, but rather the celebration of an imaginative collaboration full of love and awe, suspicion, admiration, exasperation
and a measure of well-qualified respect." Claims that Roma
was the most "enjoyable" Fellini film he's seen in a dozen
years. Calls the film "exuberant" and "beautiful." The audience that he saw Roma with kept interrupting the film with applause. Gives a good description of the story.

1407 Guberinic, S. "Stvarnost in Predstava--Federico Fellini Klovni
      (1970), Rim (1971)," Ekran, n. 115/116 (1974), 273-279.

1408 Hale, Wanda. "Federico Fellini Looks at Rome," New York
      Daily News, October 16, 1972.
      Long review. "When the powers that be were handing
out a sense of humor, sense of beauty, and a sense of the
serio-comic ... Fellini must have been first in line."

1409 ____. "Fellini's Rome and Losey's Trotsky," New York Sun-
      day News, Section III, October 8, 1972, 7.

1410 Hatch, Robert. Nation, 215 (October 30, 1972), 413.
      Roma looks a good deal like Clowns and Satyricon, and
he objects to Fellini's increasing obsession with "repugnant
human flesh." Knows that these "types" exist but wishes Fellini could find others to frequent his films. Says, "Fellini has
been developing a taste for overeaters," and that "his rhythm
is becoming predictable," and his "arrogance" is competing
with his talent. Feels that Fellini is now "exploiting" Rome
just as he "exploited those old friends of his, the clowns."

1411 Hayman, Ronald. "Noisy Dreams of a Fat City," Times (Lon-
      don), January 12, 1973, 10.
      "The ostensible purpose of Roma is to draw comparisons
between his experience and the experience of a young man arriving in Rome today. Without either narrative continuity or
coherent pattern, the film flashes backwards and forwards over
the intervening decades." The English version has cut out the
two interviews with Mastroianni and Sordi. Claims that Fellini
has gotten too "mechanical and has taken himself too seriously."
The film needs "irony" and more "humour."

1412 H[epner], I. Film a Doba, 18 (May, 1972), 228-230.

1413 Hjort, Ø. Kosmorama, 19 (March, 1973), 152-153.

1414 Hofmann, Paul. "Rome: Fellini's Not So Eternal City," New
      York Times, May 1, 1972.
      A picture of the political scene in Rome just before the
several elections, not long after Roma has opened, and with

emphasis on the relations between various artists and the So-
cialist, Communist, and Neo-Fascist parties. Says that the
official Communist line was that Fellini's Rome was only a city
of his imagination and, therefore, the film was of no sociologi-
cal interest. The film is doing well at the box-office, but the
reviews "are lukewarm at best. " He interprets advertising
posters for the film--Roma over the picture of a monumental
prostitute--to mean that the message of the film is that "the
Eternal City is a whore. "

1415 Inter/View, n. 23, July, 1972, 6.

1416 Ionescu, G. "Circul e o lume care moare....," Cinema
      (Bucharest), 11 (March, 1973), 14.

1417 Kael, Pauline. New Yorker, 48 (October 21, 1972), 135-140.
      Reprinted in Reeling. Boston: Little, Brown and Co. , 1976,
      25-27.
           Fellini appears to see himself "as official greeter for the
      apocalypse; his uxorious welcoming smile is an emblem of
      emptiness. " Whenever there is dialogue or thought, the movie
      is "fatuous. " In the film Fellini "interacts with no one; he is
      the only star, our guide ... and he often miscalculates our re-
      actions, especially to his arch, mirthless anti-clerical jokes. "
      Emotionally, he lives in the past. The scene of those vanish-
      ing frescoes "is so clumsily staged" that we become embar-
      rassed for him, and particularly "by the Sears, Roebuck quali-
      ty of the frescoes. The tragedy of their disappearance is a
      blessing. "

1418 Karcz, D. 'Rzym--logika p ozornie chaotycznej konstrukcji,"
      Kino (Poland), 9 (September, 1974), 41-47.

1419 Kauffmann, Stanley. New Republic, 167 (November 4, 1972),
      22. Reprinted in Living Images. New York: Harper and
      Row, 1975, 148-150.
           "The public agony of Federico Fellini continues, and con-
      tinues to be extremely sad. He is metamorphosing from an
      artist whose works can be judged, into an invalid whose symp-
      toms must be diagnosed. " Claims Fellini is "desperate" for
      material. That he "tacks" on scenes and "pads. " And he
      can't think of any other way to end Roma than to "follow a
      bunch of night-time motorcyclists as they vroom through the
      city. "

1420 Kissel, Howard. Women's Wear Daily, October 16, 1972, 22.
           Claims that what disturbs him most is that the personal
      moments in Roma seem "contrived, strained," and "without
      human warmth. "

1421 Knorr, W. Jugend Film Fernsehen, 17 (1973) n. 1, 37-38.

1422 L[ajeunesse], J. Image et Son, 262 (June-July, 1972), 156.

1423   Larsson, M.   "Brev fran Rom," Chaplin, 14 (1972), n. 3, 83-
       84.

1424   Leduc, J.   Cinéma Québec, 2 (January-February, 1973), 44-45.

1425   Legrand, G.   "L'apocalypse selon Federico Fellini," Positif,
       140 (July-August, 1972), 1-7.

1426   Lucato, C.   "L'autobiografia di Narciso," Cineforum, n. 115-
       116.   (July-August, 1972), 132-139.

1427   Maclean-Hunter Limited, 86 (January, 1973), 70.
            This short review claims that the "common view" of Fel-
       lini's career is that La strada, Dolce vita, and $8\frac{1}{2}$ are master-
       pieces; and that Satyricon, Clowns, and Roma are the "minor
       works of a burnt out artist." This reviewer disagrees with the
       "common view." Says, "It was Fellini's destiny to be elegant,
       superficial and splendidly entertaining."

1428   Mara, Jan.   Minute, May 24, 1972.
            "A film you can't pigeonhole--baroque, astounding, that
       sometimes makes you dizzy, often droll, always fascinating."

1429   Mayor, Francis.   Télérama, May 24, 1972.
            The film is Fellini, "what he has in his head and in his
       loins. It is a new parade of his obsessions. But this time
       without the pretext of a story, of anything make-believe. It is
       Fellinissimo."

1430   Meehan, Thomas.   "Temptations of St. Fellini," Saturday Re-
       view, 55 (November 18, 1972), 99.
            Says that despite what Kael and Crist say--the narrator's
       voice is not Fellini's. Knows so because he has interviewed
       Fellini. (Says that Fellini has a high-pitched voice that would
       be unsuitable.) Roma is "uneven" but it has some "brilliant
       parts" that "make the whole very much worth seeing." Roma
       is "an episodic jumble of fictionalized memories of the direc-
       tor's arrival in Rome as a young man mixed together with
       semi-abstract documentary footage of present-day Rome...."
       The film is "saved from being oppressive by the rich earthi-
       ness and ribald humor of the Romans themselves. Fellini's
       Roma is, in fact, hugely funny."

1431   Meisel, Myron.   Boston After Dark, January 2, 1973, 4.
            "The trouble with Fellini's Roma is that it is neither a
       real Rome nor a Rome of the imagination. Somewhat patheti-
       cally, it is only a Rome of the ego."

1432   Melly, George.   Observer (London), January 14, 1973, 32.

1433   Michałek, B.   "Festyn Felliniego," Kino, 7 (September, 1972),
       58-59.

1434   Millar, Gavin. "Prodigality," Listener, 89 (January 18, 1973),
        95-96.
            Of Rome the city: "The boy from the country is spell-
        bound by it all, and Fellini's exaggeration is a measure of his
        adult delight in it." Feels that it would be "less endearing"
        if Fellini had suggested to us that he had gotten Rome's "mea-
        sure," had seen through it. But no, he suggests rather that
        he is still spellbound "by a physical prodigality and a spiritual
        resilience that he will never quite match, however much he
        sheds his country ways."

1435   _____. "Self-Lovers," Listener, 90 (December 27, 1973),
        896.
            Recapping the films of 1973, one of the ones that sticks
        in his mind as "bound to last" is Roma, "as gargantuan and
        brilliant a circus show as usual."

1436   Motion Picture Herald, 242 (November, 1972), 640.

1437   "Murder Clue Sought in Film," Times (London), August 10,
        1971, 5.
            News item. Film of Rome's hippies taken by Fellini may
        hold clue to who shot a man in Rome. The Piazza Navona was
        filled with real and acting hippies when the man was shot. The
        witnesses will see film to see if they can spot killer.

1438   New Leader, 55 (November 27, 1972), 20.

1439   New York Times, December 13, 1972, 64.
            Roma chosen by the Motion Picture Arts Academy as the
        "official" Italian entry in the Best Foreign Film category.

1440   Nichols, Peter. "Rome: The City Which Shaped Fellini,"
        Times (London), September 16, 1972, 9.
            Article was written before the London opening of Roma.
        Consists mainly of quotes from Fellini about Rome. Fellini
        says that Roma is "a portrait of a relationship established with
        the city." Fellini says that a filmmaker must have something
        "of the magician, the prophet and the charlatan" in him. Fel-
        lini doesn't like to re-see his films once completed. He com-
        pared the experience to "looking at an old photograph of one's
        self with more hair." Nichols says that Roma was a big suc-
        cess in Paris--equal to that of Dolce vita.

1441   Parents, 47 (December, 1972), 79.

1442   Pechter, W. S. "America (The Emigrants), Rome (Fellini's
        Roma), and the bourgeoisie (The Discreet Charm of the Bour-
        geoisie)," Commentary, 55 (January, 1973), 83-86.

1443   P[eruzzi], G. Cinema Nuovo, 217 (May-June, 1972), 213-217.

1444 Playboy, 19 (December, 1972), 62.
      Calls Roma a "cinematic pearl. " "Those who view Fel-
lini's showmanship as a mere shell game may label Roma a
documentary about the Eternal City--but we prefer to compare
it with the etchings of Hogarth or Toulouse-Lautrec. "

1445 Powell, Dilys.   "Night in the City," Times (London), January
      14, 1973, 29.
      Fellini is a "great fantasy spinner" who gives us several
"trips" around Rome.   Roma is a "creation of an imagination
at once extravagant and strictly directed. " The film is "a
huge dream, an off-shoot of his Satyricon, grotesque, horrible,
beautiful. " Asks where Fellini can go from here--hopes that
perhaps, he'll go back to the mysterious organism, more complex than Rome--the human being.

1446 Prédal, R.   Jeune Cinéma, 64 (July-August, 1972), 18-19.

1447 Price, Theodore.   Quarterly, 45 (Fall, 1972), 24-26.
      'Rome is Fellini's grand passion, the love of his life.
She appears in (or casts a spell over) all his films.   He thinks
of her as a woman--who has had many lovers before him, who
may have other lovers even now, and who certainly will have
new lovers after him. "

1448 Q P Herald, January 6, 1973, 10.

1449 Racine, Robert W.   Mass Media Ministries, 9 (December 11,
      1972), 2.

1450 _____.   Mass Media Ministries, 9 (February 5, 1973), 4.

1451 Redbook, 140 (January, 1973), 52.

1452 Reilly, C. P.   Films in Review, 23 (November, 1972), 566.
      The film repeats itself "as most circuses do, and is oc-
casionally boring, but there are thrilling moments which take
one's breath away. " Fellini proves that there is nothing new
in the eternal city, "there is only the indestructable myth. "
There is a striking publicity cover photo of Fellini in a "directing" pose.

1453 Rice, R. Susan.   Media and Methods, 9 (March, 1973), 16.
      Claims that Roma is "marred" by the TV-like way it was
made.   The freaks, mannequins, clergy are all "cliches of
style. " Says that the film is "disappointing," and calls the
"sophomoric themes" that were so "fresh" in earlier Fellini
films "tired. "

1454 Ringe, P.   Show, 2 (January, 1973), 51-52.

1455 Rolling Stone, n. 124, December 21, 1972, 72.

1456 Rosenthal, Stuart. Focus on Film, 11 (Autumn, 1972), 8-9.
      Throughout the film we have new values undermining and
      displacing old ones. There is "a yearning for the equilibrium
      of the past." Feels that Fellini has been troubled by recent
      criticism that an artist's personal concerns and obsessions are
      of little interest and relevance in an era of political and social
      upheaval. The Ecclesiastical fashion show "must rate among
      the most inventive, mesmerizing and grimly hilarious pieces
      of film that Fellini has produced." Identifies the patron of
      that event as Cardinal Ottoviani, and one of the nobles as
      Count Orsini. In some prints, there have been some cuts from
      this sequence.

1457 Sar'ivanova, M. "Konfrontatsiia-Varshava '73," Kinoizkustvo
      (Bulgaria), 28 (August, 1973), 69-75.

1458 Saturday Review, 1 (January, 1973), 47.

1459 Schickel, Richard. "Mellowing of the Masters," Life, 73 (No-
      vember 17, 1972), 30.
            Calls Roma a "formless meditation." Roma is "good"
      when it recreates Fellini's youth and "bad" when he gives us
      his "stylized" vision of Rome. Fellini "ought to buy himself
      a house in the country. Or at the very least a long vacation,
      any place where the pasty-faced figments of his imagination
      can get a suntan."

1460 Sharples, W., Jr. "Fellini's Roma: The Audacious Image,"
      Filmmakers Newsletter, 6 (February, 1973), 51-52.

1461 Sign, 52 (April, 1973), 34.

1462 Somlyó, G. "Mi ez....? Fellini: Bohócok," Filmkultura,
      6 (November-December, 1972), 39-46.

1463 Stewart, B. "Civis Romanus est," Month, 6 (May, 1973), 188.

1464 Sweeney, Louise. 'Roma--Fellini's--Tone Poem of Traffic
      Jam," Christian Science Monitor, October 16, 1972, 8.
            "Fellini has subtitled his picture The Fall of the Roman
      Empire 1931-1972, so you can draw your own conclusions,
      particularly from the final shots of a roving band of motorcy-
      clists zapping through the city's streets like some invading
      horde." Claims that since there is so much to say about Ro-
      ma, and so much packed into the two hours of the film, it
      can't be dealt with here. Cites a New York Times dispatch
      as saying that the Romans couldn't see themselves in the film;
      but they figured that it would "go over big in America."

1465 Tassone, A. "De la Romagne a Rome: voyage d'un chroni-
      queur visionnaire," Image et Son, n. 290 (November, 1974), 15-
      38.

1466 Taylor, John Russell. Sight and Sound, 41 (Autumn, 1972),
      229-230.
          Roma is part of a new genre Fellini has created: the
      Fellinian "essay" film. It is "no more a documentary about
      Rome than The Clowns is a documentary about clowns." (See
      1350). Every set in the film is constructed including the ap-
      proach to Rome on a congested thruway, which meant laying
      two and half miles of road in Cinecittà. The film is "really
      about Fellini and Rome, with Rome in second place," how
      Rome has impinged upon Fellini's imagination. The motorcy-
      clists of the "visionary finale" are like the Four Horsemen of
      the Apocalypse.

1467 Tessier, M. Ecran, 6 (June, 1972), 26-29.

1468 Times (London), October 31, 1972, 11.
          Just a photo from Roma.

1469 Turroni, G. "Umano/Non umano/Disumano," Filmcritica, 23
      (March, 1972), 156-157.

1470 Vas, I. "Egy regi dal visszhangja," Film Kultura, 9 (Septem-
      ber-October, 1973), 23-26.

1471 Vogue, 160 (August 1, 1972), 40.

1472 Vogue, 160 (October 1, 1972), 76.

1473 Werb. Variety, April 29, 1972.
          The Rome opening. "A kaleidoscope film." It incorpor-
      ates "outstanding moments of intuitive showmanship, an unre-
      solved love-hate relationship for the city ... and Fellini's in-
      flexible search for self-challenging projects." It's too long
      and has its "limping moments," but "by any measure it is a
      fascinating film."

1474 Westerbeck, Colin L., Jr. "Arrivederci, Roma," Common-
      weal, 97 (November 10, 1972), 136.
          The cinema is truly "magic" under Fellini's direction.
      Hopes that Fellini's imagination is not "exhausted" already.
      "Some of the material that Fellini has used before--the vaude-
      ville theater, for instance--is beautifully renewed in this film,
      but some of it wasn't Fellini at his best in the first place and
      doesn't rework well here."

1475 Whitehorn, E. P T A Magazine, 67 (January, 1973), 6.

1476 Winsten, Archer. "Fellini Turns His Camera on Rome at the
      Ziegfeld," New York Post, October 16, 1972, 23.
          "It is incredible that a picture of this sort, a grab-bag
      of people and locations in a great city could be as consistently
      funny and fascinating ... as it is."

1477 Wolf, William. Cue, January 6, 1973, 2.

1478 Young, J. C. Film (England), May, 1973, 10-11.

1479 Yurenev, R. "Spory v Rime," Iskusstvo Kino, 9 (1973), 141-154.

1480 Zimmerman, Paul D. "Digging the Eternal City," Newsweek, 80 (October 30, 1972), 112.
      Roma is "a thrilling personal memoir, imperfect and sprawling only because it breaks so much new ground--its cavalcade of images, ideas and forms, all harnessed to a strangely exhilarating vision of impending doom."

Amarcord

1481 Allen, T. New York, 7 (September 23, 1974), 68-69.
      "Federico Fellini's sketchbook on a misspent youth in an Italian wasteland, begrudgingly puts back some of the warmth, compassion, and popular accessibility that the director has renounced in all his films since The Nights of Cabiria." Claims that Fellini is "confused" because he "shifts jarringly" from spurts of lyricism to encroaching realism.

1482 Alpert, Hollis. Saturday Review, 2 (October 5, 1974), 42.

1483 _____. "European Memories: Bitter and Sweet," Saturday Review/World, 2 (October 19, 1974), 41-42.
      Compared with Fellini's other films, this one is "minor, but this doesn't mean that it is not filled with the Fellini warmth and magic." In contrast to Vitelloni, which was "tender social satire," in Amarcord there is little sense of satire, no denunciation of decadence, "rather a tolerant understanding of, and sympathy with small lives and the pathos and humor they engender."

1484 Ankenbrandt, T. "Amarcord Melts False Images," National Catholic Reporter, 11 (January 31, 1975), 13.

1485 Arnold, Gary. "A Fellini Masterpiece," Washington Post, October 9, 1974, Section E, 1.
      Loves Amarcord and compares it to Thornton Wilder's Our Town. Discusses the "people," the "emotions" and the "spectacle" in Amarcord. Amarcord is "a work of art constructed from reminiscences ... the episodes appear to be casually arranged, but they add up emotionally."

1486 L'Avant Scène, n. 153, December, 1974, 58-60.

1487 Bachmann, Gideon. Take One, 4 (November/December, 1972), 35.

1488 _____. "Lettre de Rome: Amarcord est sorti," Cinéma
'74, n. 187, May, 1974, 28-30.

1489 _____. "Premiera filma Federica Fellini ja Spominjam
Se v rimu," Ekran, 12 (1974), n. 113/114, 189-191.

1490 _____. "Stenografia wspomnien," Kino, 9 (May, 1974),
57-59.

1491 Barnes, Clive. "Season of Mellow Fruitfulness," Times (London), September 28, 1974, 9.
        A commentary on the new season of the Arts in New York
City. The film hits are Bergman's Scenes from a Marriage
and Fellini's Amarcord. "All New York, or at least that part
capable of conversation, is discussing these two films."
Barnes had hoped to compare the two films in this article, but
at the time of writing his commentary had only seen Amarcord.
Amarcord is Fellini's "loveliest movie." It is "a garland of
memories" and you leave the movie theatre "in a state of sad
joyousness." The appearance of the peacock is "crazy, meaningless, incredible ... and unforgettable."

1492 Baumbach, J. "Going to the Movies: Pieces of the Masters,"
Partisan Review, 41 (1974), n. 4, 584-585.
        Doesn't know if Amarcord is a major film in Fellini's
canon "but at the very least it is a lovely minor one." It is
"a return to the concerns of I vitelloni" but in Fellini's later
"more flamboyant" manner. Gradisca is "the spirit of spring."
The Uncle Teo episode is "a piece of Fellini's vision at its
most eloquent."

1493 Bonitzer, Pascal. "Memoire de l'oeil," Cahiers du Cinéma,
n. 251/252, (July/August, 1974), 75-76.
        The subject of the film is "delight," where we delight in
a "vision, revelation, spectacle, tableau." For example: the
ocean liner in the night, the preening peacock in the snow, the
white cow in the fog, where "frozen in ecstatic abeyance, in
the ravishment of the vision--in the delight of the eye--is the
motion of the world."

1494 Bory, Jean-Louis. "La grotte aux trésors de Federico le
Grand," Le Nouvel Observateur, May 7, 1974, 78-79.
        A careful, very useful explication of the film. Amarcord
is "a mysterious 'Open Sesame' mixing love and memory in a
murmur. We but whisper 'Amarcord' and there is opened for
us a treasure grotto where we are swept away by this incredible Ali Baba of film poetry who is Federico the Great." Gradisca's marriage at the end of the film symbolizes the end of
adolescence and of life "more dreamed than lived."

1495 Bregstein, P. "Amarcord accoord van amore, amaro, en ricordo: liefde, bitterheid, herinnering," Skoop, 10 (May, 1974),
32-36.

1496 "Briefs on the Arts," New York Times, December 26, 1974, 53.
      Amarcord is named best foreign film by the National Board of Review of Motion Pictures.

1497 Broderick, P. D. C. Gazette, 5 (November, 1974), 20.

1498 Canby, Vincent. "Critics Choice: The Eleven Best Films of 1974," New York Times, January 5, 1975.
      Amarcord is one of the "eleven best." Gives a brief description of the film.

1499 _____. "Fellini Again at the Top of His Form," New York Times, 124 (September 29, 1974), Section II, 1+.
      Amarcord is "a haunting, funny, beautiful work that makes most other recent movies ... look as drab as winter fields without snow." Describes many episodes, and concludes that Fellini has a talent "to communicate a sense of wonder, which has the effect of making us all feel much younger than we have any right to."

1500 _____. "Funny, Marvelous Fellini Amarcord," New York Times, September 20, 1974, 32.
      A long favorable review. Compares the town in Amarcord to the town in Vitelloni. But now there is something "magical" about the town and the people who live there. It is "a film of exhilarating beauty."

1501 _____. "Looking at the Thirties Through Rose-Colored Glasses," New York Times, December 8, 1974, Section II, 15.
      Article about the plethora of films which deal with the '30s -- the vivid colors and the art deco sets. Amarcord is the best because of its romantic, dream-like quality.

1502 Castell, D. Films Illustrated, 4 (November, 1974), 88.

1503 Cavell, Marcia. "Bergman's Misgivings, Fellini's Memories," New Leader, 57 (October 28, 1974), 23.
      Two-thirds of the review are on Scenes from a Marriage, one-third is on Amarcord. The memories are in a form "so explicitly mythical it becomes our past too." The "rhythm" of the film is "paced to the seasons, and its drama is simply the daily events of village life." But though there are "good moments," these do not "add up to a film. I get tired of Fellini's love of caricature, dear whores and wriggling bottoms, clowns and clowning."

1504 Cinéaste, 6, n. 4, 52.
      Brief notations when the film was released. "Well worth seeing."

1505 Cinema Nuovo, 22 (July-August, 1973), 272.

1506 Cocks, Jay. "Fellini Remembers," Time, 104 (October 7,
      1974), 7+.
            The film represents "some of the finest work Fellini has
      ever done--which means that it stands with the best that any-
      one in films has ever achieved." There is a strong political
      subcurrent, but the film never becomes preoccupied with poli-
      tics. In the film, fascism is portrayed as "a crack-brained
      aberration that allowed for some moments of ritual absurdity
      even as it brought forth a kind of cagey, half-comic defiance."

1507 Codelli, L. "Nuit et gel (sur Amarcord)," Positif, n. 158
      (April, 1974), 15-17.

1508 Cole, L. "Federico Fellini's Magic in Amarcord," People's
      World, 37 (November 23, 1974), 10.

1509 Coleman, J. "Manine," New Statesman, 88 (September 27,
      1974), 440.
            Mentions that he previously reviewed the novel Amarcord.
      Says that the film adheres closely to the novel--neither of
      which he liked. "This is by no means Fellini at his best, but
      then--for a truly complete film--one still has to go back as
      far as I vitelloni for that."

1510 Crist, Judith. New York, 7 (October 7, 1974), 96.
            A short piece on Fellini, his films, and especially Amar-
      cord. "Fellini's year--from the bonfire of celebration of
      Spring to the return of the seed puffs after the snows--is from
      the lives of us all. And that is his art."

1511 _____. New York, 8 (December 30, 1974), 84.
            Amarcord is number one on her list of the ten best films
      of 1974.

1512 Cristaldi, Franco. Catholic Film Newsletter, 39 (October 30,
      1974), 88.

1513 Davies, Russell. "Italian Milk Wood," Observer (London),
      September 29, 1974, 29.
            Fellini's final scene in Amarcord "suggests that he is
      still stuck in his own groove for better or worse." Fears that
      it is for the worse--until he "moves out of the village of mem-
      ory ... towards some sort of urban renewal."

1514 Delain, Michel. "Cannes: de Fellini à Mahler," L'Express,
      May 13, 1974, 44-49.
            Very illuminating comparison between Fellini's films in
      general, and Amarcord in particular, and Fellini's essay La
      Mia Rimini (see 115 and 123) from which he says this film
      "is born." He lists a number of parallels between photos in
      La Mia Rimini and scenes in Fellini's films. The article in-
      cludes a 1934 photo of Fellini and his brother Riccardo in black-

shirt uniforms of the time. Amarcord is another continuation of Fellini's "eternal return" to Rimini, where he frees himself from his "reminiscences" as from an illness.

1515 Dent, James F. "Fellini Scores Again," Charleston Gazette (West Virginia), February 2, 1975.
Gives long description of many of the episodes. Claims that Amarcord "does not have a central, cohesive plot. It is, instead, a series of vignettes connected only because they happen in the same town and involve essentially the same persons." Since Fellini is fascinated by faces, the faces in Amarcord are "memorable." The film is "hauntingly beautiful" and "unreal."

1516 Desjardins, V. Cinématographe, n. 8, June/July, 1974, 2-3.

1517 Dias, A. Celuloide, 17 (July, 1974), 15-16.

1518 Drexler, Rosalyn. Vogue, 164 (November, 1974), 110.
Just when you've decided to take movies for granted something like Amarcord comes along and "transports" you to and through a different world--a higher level--"the level of Art." Amarcord "celebrates life: the never-ending circle of life that cannot be broken. And it is mythic: the effigy of a witch who represents winter (age is cold, old, and must make way for springtime, youth, and hope) is cindered in a huge bonfire." One is full of joy and love after seeing this film.

1519 Dutourd, Jean. "Amarcord ou l'amer plaisir d'avoir cinquante ans," Paris-Match, June 15, 1974, 9.
Charming, as well as illuminating, remarks. He is a man of Fellini's generation, in his fifties, when one's memories are sufficiently deformed to serve for the subject matter of a work of art and when "one is mature enough in talent to make them live again." One's youth is when "one didn't have toothaches, or rheumatism, or smoker's cough, or grey hair, or bags under the eyes, or cholesterol in the blood. Pretty women were inaccessible, and so one dreamt of them--which is perhaps better than possessing them." He finds Fellini's film full of charm and poetry, "imbued with a mocking tenderness that never disappoints, that is just what one uses to tell stories about one's youth."

1520 Eder, K. "P teshestvie v spomena," Kinoizkustvo, 29 (July, 1974), 74-76.

1521 Elley, D. Films and Filming, 20 (September, 1974), 40-42.

1522 Escobar, R. Cineforum, n. 131 (April, 1974), 269-282.

1523 L'Espresso, December 23, 1973.

1524 Etudes, 341 (July, 1974), 133-137.

1525 Farber, Stephen. "Amarcord and Lacombe Lucien: Illumina-
      tions of Things Past," New York Times, November 3, 1974,
      Section II.
            A long article, but only one-third of it deals with Amar-
      cord. Lacombe, Lucien is discussed along with Amarcord
      since they make good "companion pieces" because of their si-
      milar themes. Lacombe, Lucien is "naturalistic" and Amar-
      cord is "dreamlike" yet they both "... probe the guilt of or-
      dinary people whose passive acquiescence gave the dictators
      their real power." Discusses the beauty and nostalgia of Am-
      arcord, but claims that the fascist element is not permitted
      to be forgotten. "Fellini involves us in his meditation on the
      past, and forces us to recognize our own complicity."

1526 "Fellini's Amarcord Nabs Lion's Share of Nastri d'Argento,"
      Variety, June 26, 1974, 31.

1527 "Fellini's Arrival," New Yorker, 50 (October 7, 1974), 33-35.
            With Fellini, Giulietta, and publicity crew driving in from
      Kennedy airport to Manhattan. Suggests what Fellini goes
      through when having to publicize his films. "I am the author
      of the picture, not a salesman.... But I am asked to help,
      so I try to help." Of seeing That's Entertainment: "It's an
      American Amarcord. It's cruel. It shows how stupid we were
      in those days."

1528 Films and Filming, 20 (June, 1974), 37-41.

1529 Finetti, U. Cinema Nuovo, 23 (January/February, 1974), 57-
      59.

1530 Forristal, D. Furrow, 26 (March, 1975), 172.

1531 Giannetti, Louis D. "Amarcord: The Impure Art of Federico
      Fellini," Western Humanities Review, 30 (Spring, 1976), 153-
      162.
            The film is "impure" in the sense that good films must
      mirror the contradictory nature of reality, the kind of film
      that Guido said he wanted to make in $8\frac{1}{2}$. Considers Amarcord
      probably Fellini's greatest work since $8\frac{1}{2}$. The key motifs are
      those depicting escape and romantic longing. The count's pea-
      cock is part of this motif. Teo's madness (when he cries, "I
      want a woman") "seems to consist primarily of his proclaiming
      publicly what everyone else is dreaming privately." The film's
      title is a "linguistic fusion" of amo (I love) and amare (bitter)
      with mi ricordo (I remember).

1532 Gili, J. A. Ecran, n. 25 (May, 1974), 61-63.

1533 Gilliatt, Penelope. "Of Dreaming and Mayhem, (Amarcord;
      Scenes from a Marriage)," New Yorker, 50 (September 23,
      1974), 95-98.
          The film is "anecdotal yet all of a piece, comic but stir-
      ringly saddening. "

1534 Grandjean, P. Travelling (Switzerland), n. 42 (May/June,
      1974), 44-47.

1535 Green, Benny. Punch, 267 (October 2, 1974), 546.

1536 "Gross, Vulgar Lenny Opens Westlake Beside Fine Amarcord,"
      Journal Star (Peoria, Illinois), March 2, 1975.
          "Fellini has offered a series of old photographs from for-
      ty years ago, breathed life into the people and given them a
      kind of universal immortality. They are sinners and saints,
      fools and heroes, capable of love, grandeur and the most in-
      credible venality. "

1537 Guiguet, J. C. Revue du Cinéma/Image et Son, n. 288/289
      (October, 1974), 8-9.

1538 Hatch, R. Nation, 219 (October 12, 1974), 350.
          "I seem to be a minority of one, and am therefore pru-
      dent enough to acknowledge that I may be wrong, but I cannot
      look on Amarcord as anything but further evidence that Feder-
      ico Fellini runs a lively risk of becoming the cinema's most
      eminent bore. " Asks what has happened to the Federico Fel-
      lini of La strada, Sceicco bianco, Cabiria, and Dolce vita.

1539 Hayman, Ed. "Fellini's Amarcord Could Be the Italian Amer-
      ican Graffiti," Flint Journal (Michigan), February 23, 1975.
          Amarcord is "a symphony, combining marvelous perform-
      ances, a lusty script by Fellini and Tonino Guerra, the grace-
      ful and often stunning cinematography of Giuseppe Rotunno and
      the rich variations of Nino Rota's delicate musical theme. "
      The film is put together "like one of grandmother's imprecise
      but mouthwatering recipes--a pinch of this, a dash of that, a
      smidgen here, a handful there, stir a few times, just enough
      but not too much. "

1540 Hermann, R. Movietone News, n. 39 (February, 1975), 34-35.

1541 Hirsch, Foster. Film Quarterly, 24 (Fall, 1975), 50-52.
          Fellini's "thinnest performance. " The film lacks "the
      joyous high spirits and sense of release" of Fellini's chief
      works. The point of view is "shifting" and "confused. " There
      is no "unifying presence. " He asks "from whose perspective"
      are we seeing the events. The main family are "simply stage
      Italians. " When the mother dies, "the pathos is unearned. "
      The film is "flavorless," the town "never really comes alive. "
      The finale lacks "the sense of communion or the joyous reso-
      lution or the formal beauty" that has marked every one of Fel-
      lini's previous endings.

1542 Hjort, Ø. "Fellini foer Rubicon: Amarcord," Kosmorama,
      20 (April, 1974), 172-175.

1543 Hogner, Steve. "Amarcord Blends Old, New, Borrowed,
      Blue," American-Statesman (Austin, Texas), March 1, 1975.
            An exceptionally sensitive and illuminating review. Fel-
      lini's "most accessible film in twenty years" and nothing less
      than his "definitive masterpiece." Captures "the flow and fla-
      vor of the times when women swooned over Gary Cooper and
      young men swooned over women." The film is tied together
      with a "bond of beginnings and endings. For every beginning,
      there is an ending." The film is "a tale of lost virginity."

1544 Independent Film Journal, 74 (October 30, 1974), 5-6.

1545 Jung, F. Jugend Film Fernsehen, 18 (1974), n. 2, 92-93.

1546 Kauffmann, Stanley. New Republic, 135 (September 28, 1974),
      22+.
            "Fellini, the most honest and lovable faker who ever made
      a film, presents here a beautiful carnival show of the sacred
      things in his life." Like other artists, Fellini has faced mat-
      ters that have been "haunting" him all his life and has devoted
      a whole film to them. Amarcord is "lovely." Praises Rug-
      giero Mastroianni's editing--because he ends each episode with
      a slow fade-out to "imply the curves of conclusion and conti-
      nuity."

1547 Keyser, L. J. "Three Faces of Evil: Fascism in Recent
      Movies," Journal of Popular Film, 4 (1975), n. 1, 21-31.
            Amarcord is much more "complex" than a simple remem-
      brance since no one remembers like Fellini. It is "a quite
      personal and idiosyncratic vision of social history." Fascism
      is understood only through the "little-noticed occurrences of
      day-to-day existence." This is what Fellini shows us in Am-
      arcord. "The very emotional, and seemingly harmless, at-
      tachments and taboos Fellini so lovingly delineates grew into
      a mass movement, a fanatical movement where inflamed emo-
      tion replaced reason." Urges us not to neglect the "obvious
      charms" of the film because fascism is not all there is to Am-
      arcord.

1548 Kissel, Howard. Women's Wear Daily, September 19, 1974,
      12.
            "Amarcord is one of Fellini's richest, funniest, warmest
      films."

1549 Larsson, M. "Fellini och den gamla Kaerleken," Chaplin, 16
      (1974), n. 2, 65.

1550 Leirens, J. "Amarcord le dernier Fellini," Amis du Film et
      de la Télévision (Belgium), n. 215, April, 1974, 18-19.

1551 Levy, D. Télécine, n. 190 (July/August, 1974), 24-25.

1552 Loynd, Ray. "Fellini's Rich Tapestry," Los Angeles Herald
      Examiner," April 10, 1975.
             Amarcord just won the Oscar for the best foreign film.
      And "it is difficult to imagine a more worthy choice." "While
      the film is a memoir, it is a recollection expanded by the ad-
      ult who not only remembers how it was to be fourteen or fif-
      teen in a provincial town but who filters his memory through
      the knowledge he has today. The result is the erasure of nos-
      talgia and a heightened sense of fantasy."

1553 McElfresh, Tom. "Amarcord: A Film You'll Remember,"
      Cincinnati Enquirer, January 1, 1975.
             Amarcord is a "fantastically good film." It has "no co-
      hesion of plot" but "leaps" by way of a "submerged line of re-
      collection"; and when it has finished "spinning its web," you
      find that it is "overflowing" with detail.

1554 Le Maclean, 15 (February, 1975), 4, 8.

1555 Mass Media Ministries, 11 (November 25, 1974), 15.

1556 MD Medical News Magazine, 18 (December, 1974), 126.

1557 Messaggero, December 19, 1973.

1558 Mihailescu, M. "Clovnii viitorului," Cinema (Bucharest), 11
      (August, 1973), 28-29.
             Report of a visit to the set of Amarcord.

1559 Millar, Gavin. Listener, 92 (October 3, 1974), 441.
             "Fellini's films have the distinctive mark of fine camera-
      men, but beyond that and beyond their predictable idiosyncra-
      cies, they are beautifully organized pieces of movement."

1560 Miller, E. Seventeen, 33 (December, 1974), 35.

1561 Minton, L. McCalls, 102 (December, 1974), 42.

1562 Le Monde Hebdomadaire, May 9, 1974, 13.
             Fellini opens the 27th Cannes Film Festival with Amar-
      cord.

1563 Murray, James P. New York Amsterdam News, November 2,
      1974.

1564 New York Post, April 9, 1975, 5.

1565 New York Times, January 27, 1975, 18.
             Amarcord wins the New York Film Critics Circle award
      for best film.

1566   New York Times, April 9, 1975, 28.
       Amarcord wins Oscar for best foreign film.

1567   Nowell-Smith, Geoffrey.   "Italy Sotto Voce," Sight and Sound,
       37 (Summer, 1968), 146-147.
              On the artistic effect of and the economic reasons for
       dubbing (post-synchronization) of films made in Italy.   Genesis
       of the article was a bitter manifesto against post-synchroniza-
       tion signed by a number of Italian directors including Antonioni,
       Bellocchio, Bertolucci, Lattuada, Pasolini and Pontecorvo, but
       not by Fellini.   The manifesto considered that dubbing "consis-
       tently compromises the expressive values of the film."

1568   "OD'ed on Movies," Dallas Morning News, February 3, 1975.
              Amarcord is not a "cerebral movie."   Anybody looking
       for a "message or even a plot is apt to come away confused."
       Fellini is concerned more with "painting images," images that
       "dazzle and awaken the sense."   The film is a "gusty celebra-
       tion of life."

1569   Ortmayer, Roger.   Film Information, 5 (November, 1974), 2.

1570   Oster, Jerry.   "Fellini's Amarcord Peopled by Freaks," New
       York Daily News, September 20, 1974.
              Describes some of the more spectacular episodes in Am-
       arcord.   The film hasn't a plot, but the main structural de-
       vices are the changing of the seasons, growing old and dying,
       growing older and growing up, abandoning dreams for more
       practical reality.   Claims that the episodes do not connect in
       any way.   And if a connection does exist, it is in Fellini's
       mind.   The film could have been "more rigorous in its narra-
       tive, less private in its jokes."

1571   Pechter, William S.   "Four Europeans," Commentary, 59
       (January, 1975), 84.
              Likes the Fellini up to Giulietta, but after that his films
       seem to be "garish, rotund, and overblown."   Fellini's later
       work is a "shameless cannibalization and grotesque parody of
       the earlier."   Pechter absolutely hates Amarcord.   Says,
       "Probably, one couldn't exactly say one had seen everything in
       Amarcord before, despite the numerous echoes in it of Felli-
       ni's early work (though Nino Rota's Fellini-movie music has
       certainly come to sound like a broken record), but the film
       does strike me as the sort of thing Fellini can spin out by the
       yard, endlessly, which probably amounts to the same thing...."

1572   Playboy, 21 (December, 1974), 48.
              "Italy's phenomenal Federico Fellini makes movies the
       way Picasso painted pictures or, better yet, the way the great-
       est poets reduce a universal human truth to one glistening
       phrase."   Deals briefly with the politics in Amarcord but says
       that the film is not about politics but about life.

1573 Prouse, Derek. "Fellini the Exorcist," Times (London), September 29, 1974, 38.
Compares and contrasts Amarcord with Vitelloni. Is happy that Amarcord is more "mellow" than his later films. Says that Fellini has declared that he makes films to "exorcise his obsessions" and hopes that Fellini has exorcised--for good--"the adolescent idea of male urination as a surefire source of mirth," since there are three such instances in Amarcord.

1574 Racine, R. Bob. Mass Media, 11 (November 25, 1974), 7.

1575 "Reaction to Kazin and Simon," New York Times, January 26, 1975, Section II, 19.
Two letters, one anti-Simon's review and one pro-Simon. One letter says, "The saddest thing about John Simon's review of Amarcord is that Simon has seen humanity and found it ugly."

1576 Reed, Rex. "Fellini's Amarcord Warmed-Over Spaghetti," New York Daily News, September 27, 1974, 89.
Fellini just "re-plows the same tired old terrain."

1577 Reilly, C. P. Films in Review, 25 (November, 1974), 566.

1578 Rinaldi, Angelo. "Fellini: pèlerinage aux sources avec Amarcord," L'Express, February 25, 1974, 42-43.
Sensitive, lovely reaction to the film. Fellini, who has "forgotten nothing." The film is the "artist's workshop; all his tools are there, his easel and palette, his sketches, his finished pictures, his fantasies and his obsessions." Here especially is that feeling of his of sin before the mysteries of the flesh that makes Fellini "without question the foremost Catholic director of our time." How the wedding by the sea, at the end, appears to Rinaldi: "where an old musician, a Virgil of the accordian, leads Fellini, as the poet of Antiquity accompanies Dante, his hand on his shoulder."

1579 Ripp, J. Parents, 49 (November, 1974), 16.

1580 Robinson, David. Times (London), September 27, 1974, 10.
"It is life seen as variety show, with act following act. A lot of the turns and tricks are as fresh and brilliant as ever." Says that Amarcord is the center section of a trilogy, with Clowns being part one and Roma part three. Doesn't like Amarcord much and calls the ending a "stock Fellini ending." The autobiography has reached the stage of "perilous diffusion and self-indulgence."

1581 Roos, James. "Amarcord Fine Remembrance," Miami Herald, January 18, 1975.
"Calls it a memory mosaic by a master, with the understanding that the artist may remember a lot more than ever

happened. " "The whole thing is awash in life and color and
music borrowed from everywhere that flows and splashes and
dances. "

1582   Rosenbaum, J. Monthly Film Bulletin, 41 (September, 1974),
       195.

1583   St. Anthony Messenger, 82 (February, 1975), 8.

1584   Sarris, Andrew. Village Voice, 19 (May 23, 1974), 93.
          Fellini and René Clair were both honored at the Cannes
       Film Festival. The festival opened with Amarcord. The film
       is "Felliniesque to a fault, so much so, in fact, that Fellini
       can be charged by his detractors with having become his own
       most slavish imitator. " Claims that Fellini's appeal to the
       eye has "far surpassed" his appeal to the mind or to the heart.

1585   _____. "Federico to a Fare-Thee-Well," Village Voice, 19
       (September 19, 1974), 83-84.
          Mostly a discussion of Fellini and Fellini's most recent
       films--and in particular, Amarcord. Says, "...Amarcord
       seems to mark a continuation of Fellini's third and least stimu-
       lating 'period,' a period of ostentatious introspection. " "My
       biggest problem with Amarcord is that I can't really tell how
       much of it is supposed to be personally autobiographical and
       how much officially historical. " "Furthermore, the gallantry
       of his grotesques seems merely tedious in 1974, and the
       pseudo-sensual spectacle of his monstrously fat women seems
       as dated as the tradition of the circus clowns. "

1586   Sibler, I. Guardian, 27 (February 26, 1975), 18.

1587   Simon, John. Esquire, 82 (December, 1974), 20+.
          Fellini is "a former giant of the cinema" who lives on to
       make "some of the world's worst films. " "The most contempt-
       ible film of the new season. " It is "episodic and disjointed. "
       The events of the film "lack the charge that would make them
       coalesce; there is no human or historical insight. " Fellini
       just cannot "mold" the material into a "unified whole" as he
       did in Vitelloni. For example, the Uncle Teo episode does
       not bear on the other characters or on what happens in the
       rest of the film. There is no point to the Sheik/Peanut Vendor
       episode at the Grand Hotel, nor to Gradisca and the Prince.
       The Rex episode "is no wise integrated into the rest of the
       film. " The "final insult" is that in Amarcord, Fellini's atti-
       tude toward mankind is one of "self-serving smugness and gen-
       eral indifference. " In the early Fellini films, mankind was
       encompassed by Fellini's love: "No one was too stupid or frail,
       too guileful or beastly to forfeit Fellini's comprehending
       care.... It was a sadly, tenderly, all-pervasive compassion. "
       To Simon, the tone of Amarcord is precisely the opposite.

1588 _____ "The Tragic Deterioration of Fellini's Genius," New
York Times, November 24, 1974, Section II, 17+.
Written presumably after his Esquire review (see 1587)
and after he has looked over his notes on Fellini (since he
quotes from several old articles by other writers on Fellini).
In short, written not in the heat and haste of a quick review
but in the cool, contemplative atmosphere of a careful critical
appraisal. He reviews Fellini's career since The Miracle
(Simon doesn't like any Fellini film after Cabiria, and he's
not that sure about that one. He excoriates all of Fellini's
work since Cabiria; e. g. , he finds the finale of 8½ "one of the
most dishonest endings in the history of cinema. ") The "worst
thing" about Amarcord is "that the chief joke is human ugli-
ness. " All the characters in the film that Simon personally
finds ugly, he considers that Fellini finds ugly and is cruelly
making fun of. "The joke is always on humanity.... Where
is compassion?" In Simon's view, Fellini's heart has hardened toward all Fellini's fellow human beings.

1589 Sterritt, David. "Cannes Openers--a New Fellini, an Old René
Clair, a British Bomb," Christian Science Monitor, May 23,
1974, 5.
Amarcord is "an expressionistic journey down this unique
artist's own bizarre brand of memory lane. " Amarcord is a
"mental journey" by Titta who is "both defined and trapped"
by the small town in which he lives. Fellini's memories "float
across the screen in a typical Fellini mixture of fact and fantasy, dream and actuality, past wish and present circum-
stance. "

1590 Tablet, 228 (October 5, 1974), 966.

1591 Tassone, A. Revue du Cinéma/Image et Son, n. 284, May,
1974, 90-93.
The film, "classic and filtered in its style," is "the least
autobiographical" of Fellini's films despite the apparent paradox
of its title. Fellini has found once more "the fresh and en-
chanting simplicity of his early works. " Amarcord has a "new
serenity," like a wine that has been decanted. The "hero" of
Amarcord is no longer the subject that is doing the remember-
ing but what is being remembered: the people of Romagna.
(Tonino Guerra told Tassone that the province hasn't changed
in thirty years.) The society described in the film is the
product of "the repression and the rhetoric" of fascism. Why
then, ask the Left critics, hasn't Fellini decisively indicated
how repelled he is? Tassone answers, "But a poet doesn't
spit in the plate he's eaten from. For good or bad, millions
of Italians have grown up in this obscure placenta, and Fellini's
instinctive repulsion is tempered by a certain nostalgia, not
for the way the world was then, but for his childhood, 'which
is no more. '" The key to the film is the closing dance of the
Clowns. It is "not by chance" that the same music serves as
the leitmotif in Amarcord. "Life is a circus, life is a dream.
Let us take each other by the hand and live it in joy. "

1592 _____. "Entretien avec Tonino Guerra," Image et Son, n. 279, December, 1973, 67-82.

1593 Taylor, John Russell. Sight and Sound, 43 (1974), n. 4, 244-245.
Fellini "playing it cool, toning down the extravagances, trying, heaven help us, to make a tasteful film.... But who really wants a tasteful, restrained Fellini?" "It is as though there is something slightly faded and tired about the whole film, some indefinable lack of vitality which leaves it all looking a bit dusty and distant." He tries hard to like the film, but just can't, and he is sad about it.

1594 Il Tempo, December 20, 1973.

1595 Tournes, A. Jeune Cinéma, n. 80, July/August, 1974, 7-9.

1596 Turroni, G. Filmcritica, 25 (May, 1974), 201-202.

1597 L'Unità, December 19, 1973.

1598 Variety, October 2, 1974.

1599 Variety, February 12, 1975, 72.

1600 Vincent, Mal. "Amarcord Surprisingly Dull," Virginian-Pilot (Norfolk).
Likes Fellini and is "surprised" to find the eagerly await-ed Amarcord "dull." The film lacks "the wit that has been so much a part of the Fellini trademark." If we compare Amar-cord to Fellini's other films, we can come to but one conclu-sion--the "master" is "slipping." "Personally, I can see little in this film that warrants the kudos it has been given."

1601 Walsh, Moira. "Holiday Nostalgia and Fantasy," America, 131 (December 21, 1974), 411.
"Alas, though the picture represents a notable improve-ment over his last few ventures, I found the mixture very much as before--brilliance in form, marred by self-indulgence and only partially concealing a deficiency in substance and view-point."

1602 Weiler, A. H. "Film Critics Cite Amarcord and Fellini," New York Times, December 31, 1974, 12.
Fellini's Amarcord was cited as best film and Fellini as best director in the fortieth poll of the New York Film Critics Circle.

1603 _____. "What Next, Federico?" New York Times.
Now that Roma is "triumphantly" in New York, Fellini plans his new movie, Il Borgo. Fellini's producer says that Il Borgo is "vaguely like Sherwood Anderson's Winesburg, Ohio

or, better still, like Fellini's own I vitelloni. Set in a small
town some thirty years ago, it deals with a family and their
friends, day by day, through an entire year. " Il Borgo was
the original title for Amarcord.

1604 Werb. Variety, January 16, 1974, 18.
         Instead of "lensing" a nostalgic look at the past and re-
capturing the "happy simplicity of existence," Fellini did "just
the opposite. "

1605 Winsten, Archer. "Fellini's Amarcord at Plaza," New York
      Post, September 20, 1974, 36.
         Amarcord is a "distinctly minor Fellini picture that you
can enjoy.... "

1606 Zimmerman, Paul D. "Growing Up Fellini," Newsweek, 84
      (September 30, 1974), 106-107.
         Gives a little prologue to Fellini's "new style" that start-
ed with $8\frac{1}{2}$. Amarcord is "the fully realized incarnation of
Fellini's quest for a form flexible and capacious enough to
contain his teeming imagination. " "... it is a contemporary
comédie humaine whose range is the scope of human life itself. In many ways, it represents a summation of all his
work. " "Amarcord is the most beautiful movie Fellini has
ever made and a landmark in the history of film. "

Casanova

1607 Bachmann, Gideon. "Federico Fellini's Casanova," Take One,
      5 (March, 1977), 11-13.
         Says that the key to the film can be gleaned from some
lines that were cut. Someone says to Casanova, "You do not
know women and you do not know yourself. You do not pursue
women; you flee them. Loving that many means that what you
are seeking is probably a man. " Bachmann says that "once
we accept Fellini's own identification in the nightmare he has
conceived for Casanova, we can begin to read the film quite
simply. " The film is not about the 18th-century Casanova but
about the 20th-century one, "the veteran from Cinecittà. "

1608 Boyum, Joy Gould. "Casanova as a Dull Blade," Wall Street
      Journal, February 28, 1977.
         Fellini's "deflating conception of Casanova as 'meaningless
universality' and Casanova's world as 'nothing' have led him
into the aesthetic trap of making a film whose characters are
devoid of personality, whose action is dull and mechanical,
and whose atmosphere is washed of all reality and historical
detail. "

1609 Canby, Vincent. "Fellini's Casanova Is New Revel," New York
      Times, February 12, 1977.

1610 Carroll, Kathleen. "A Puppet on a Fling," New York Daily
      News, February 12, 1977.
            Like its title character the film is eventually victimized
      by its own excesses. The "overwhelming sumptuousness" be-
      comes "as coldly distancing and emotionally unfulfilling as a
      pantomime." Sutherland is Fellini's puppet and must play a
      "sad-eyed Pierrot whose life is a continuous fresh show."

1611 Chemasi, Antonio. "Fellini's Casanova--The Final Nights,"
      Film (U.S.), September, 1976, 8-16.
            The final week of shooting. Fellini characterizes Casa-
      nova's life as "a life that has in fact been lived under ice."
      Sutherland, asked what sort of character Fellini was asking
      him to play, says he doesn't know. Chemasi says that the
      huge head rising from the water was variously symbolic to
      Fellini: the goddess of Venice, the goddess of the Mediter-
      ranean Venus herself--all suggesting love, creativity, fecundi-
      ty. Lots of on-the-set business and chit-chat. Article in-
      cludes twelve good stills from the film.

1612 Crist, Judith. "Fellini without Feeling," Saturday Review,
      February 19, 1977.

1613 "De Laurentiis Cancels Casanova," Variety, July 24, 1974, 3.
            Dino De Laurentiis claims he couldn't give Casanova "the
      attention it deserved."

1614 Delain, Michel. "Un doublage signé Chéreau," L'Express, n.
      1337 (February 21-27, 1977), 13.

1615 "Fellini Abandons Casanova Project," Variety, 277 (January
      22, 1975), 42.

1616 "Fellini's Casanova," Parade, September 26, 1976, 6.
            Tells what Sutherland went through for his part as Casa-
      nova. Fellini sees Casanova as "a nothing, a coward, a mon-
      ster I despise." As in all other Fellini films, Fellini is the
      "true star."

1617 "A Fog for Fellini," People, April 26, 1976, 85.
            Fellini back at work on Casanova after a few "set-backs."

1618 Forestier, François. "Casanova--Fellini: le grand men-
      songe," L'Express, n. 1337 (February 21-27, 1977), 10-11.

1619 "From Coward to Casanova," New York Post Magazine, July
      8, 1975, 7.
            William Marchant is off to Rome where he wants to write
      a diary of the filming of Casanova.

1620 Goldstein, Richard. "A Little Night Music for Fellini," Vil-
      lage Voice, 19 (October 3, 1974), 87.
            Retells the evening at a party in New York for Fellini.
      Fellini and Giulietta put in a brief appearance.

1621 Hatch, Robert. Nation 224 (February 26, 1977), 252-253.
     "It is strange--Fellini fails here with a much lesser book
as he failed with the superb Satyricon. He seizes upon everything in it that is sordid and unclean; he overlooks the vivacity
and insight that makes it worth consideration." Likes the
chandelier sequence and found the "Bruegel-like roadshow" unforgettable.

1622 Janos, L. "New Fellini: Venice on Ice," Time, 107 (May
     17, 1976), 75-77.
     On the set during shooting. Says Fellini is comparing
Casanova to a typical, modern Italian and quotes him, "He is
all shop front, a public figure striking attitudes ... in short,
a braggart fascist." Says that Fellini hated Casanova's book:
"No nature, animals, children, trees. The stronzo [turd]
roamed the whole world of Europe, and it is as if he never
moved from his bed." Fellini chose Sutherland for the lead
because he was "completely alien" to the conventional idea of
Casanova as a dark Italian. Sutherland reflects Fellini's thinking about "estrangement" in connection with the hero. Janos
calls the final dance across the ice between Casanova and the
doll played by Leda Lojodice "a final pirouette to the game of
life."

1623 Kael, Pauline. New Yorker, February 28, 1977, 92.
     Really copped-out on reviewing Casanova. She went to
see the film all "primed," but left after one hour. Says,
"Fellini gives great interviews; he has turned into the Italian
Orson Welles. He talks such a remarkable movie that maybe
he doesn't need to make it. He has become the work of art."

1624 Laporte, Catherine. "Sutherland sous le maquillage," L'Ex-
     press, n. 1337 (February 21-27, 1977), 12.

1625 "Launch Casanova in Italy in Best Way to Escape Censors,"
     Variety, December 15, 1976, 42.

1626 "A Negative Theft," Washington Post, August 28, 1975, Section
     B, 1.
     Some of the footage of Casanova is stolen. Fellini calls
the theft "a mad act."

1627 New York Post, December 14, 1976.
     Fellini has reportedly sued an Italian magazine for libel.
It seems that the magazine reported that Fellini had "lost his
head" over a young actress in his new film, Casanova.

1628 New York Times, August 28, 1975, 28.
     Portions of Fellini's film, Casanova, have been stolen
and may be held for ransom.

1629 New York Times, September 5, 1975, 13.
     Sandy Allen (7 feet 5 inches tall) will play the role of a
gladiator giantess in Casanova.

1630 Owen, Michael. "It's Take Two for Casanova Film," Evening
      Standard, April 8, 1976, 5.
            Fellini is back at work on Casanova after a three-month
      break when the money ran out.

1631 People, August 11, 1975.
            Photo showing how Sutherland is made into Casanova.

1632 "People," Time, September 8, 1975.

1633 "People in the News," New York Post, December 24, 1975,
      29.

1634 "Pix Pessimism Out of Style in Italy; Casanova Helps It Bump
      Slump," Variety, 279 (May 14, 1975), 5+.

1635 Playboy, 21 (March, 1974), 26.

1636 Playboy, December, 1976, 127-131.
            A group of stills, mostly nudes, of scenes for the most
      part not in the film. Shows Casanova with giant-breasted
      Chesty Morgan, who was to play Barbarina. Fellini is quoted
      as saying he signed the contract for the film before he had
      read the Memoirs: "When I did, I was immediately overcome
      with a sense of giddiness ... with the mortifying impression
      that I'd made a false move." He says, "There is nothing in
      the Memoirs. Only dust raining down upon you." Fellini is
      said to portray Casanova as "something of an erotic robot,
      devoid of emotion, untouched by the people he touches."

1637 Porterfield, Christopher. "Waxwork Narcissus," Time, 109
      (February 21, 1977), 70.

1638 Rich, Frank. "Fellini's Casanova Falls Flat," New York
      Post, February 12, 1977, 17+.
            Amarcord, which Rich liked, was really an "aberration."
      Casanova takes us right back to where Fellini had been before:
      We get the Satyricon Fellini at his absolute worst. The film
      is "meanspirited, egomaniacal, flatulent, mindless, and gross."
      It is also an "unconscionable bore." The point of the film:
      "that Casanova was a mechanical hedonist whom even sex could
      not bring to life." Asks, "Has there ever been this much ug-
      liness on screen, Fellini's movies included?" There is no
      irony in the film and nothing to suggest that the "stones" Fel-
      lini is throwing at Casanova "are ricocheting into his own
      glass house."

1639 Sarris, Andrew. "Fellini's Casanova: A Failure in Communi-
      cation," Village Voice, February 28, 1977, 39.
            True to form, Sarris here talks more about Sarris than
      about the film. He "grossly underrated" 8½ when it first came
      out, but he still thinks it is "formally messy" and that its

"anti-intellectualism" is "wildly demagogic." He still prefers Bunny Lake to Giulietta. And Casanova? It is "a joyless, sexless, often pointless caricature." Fellini's "very precisely visualized fear and loathing of femaleness in the universe through a symbolic rendering of vaginal labyrinths now seems too parochial a response to the turbulent shifting of relationships between men and women." He thinks there should have been some showmanship in the film, like the striptease in Dolce vita.

1640 Schwartzman, Paul. "Fellini's Unlovable Casanova," New York Times Magazine, February 6, 1977, 22+.
        On the set during the shooting of the film. The colossal woman's head coming out of the Venice lagoon had its origin in a dream of Fellini's. The film opened in Italy to longer box-office lines than King Kong. Fellini says that the film tells about Casanova and his "non-existent life." Schwartzman categorizes Fellini, at least as shooting began, as "volubly" detesting his hero. But after the three-month pause (when Fellini was having trouble with his producers) and as Casanova became older, the figure was made more sympathetic, more noble. "The old man's refusal to accept approaching death became an affirmation of life.... Casanova's stumbling, painful fight assumed an element of tragedy." The frozen Grand Canal of the final scene is a symbol of "Casanova's icy incapacity to love" despite his many affairs. What we have in the movie is "Casanova as modern man: self-preoccupied, yet alienated from himself; plunging into experience, yet alienated from others ... redeeming himself, if at all, through his writing, his art."

1641 Simon, John. "Casanova: Dead Film in a Dead Language," New York, 10 (February 21, 1977), 57-59.

1642 Time, October 20, 1975, 59.
        Photo of the real Casanova and Donald Sutherland made up like Casanova.

1643 Wall Street Journal, August 28, 1975, 20.

1644 Wilson, Earl. "A Casanova with Character," New York Post, May 12, 1975, 22.

1645 Withers, Kay. "On Casanova Set," Miami Herald, November 2, 1975.
        Some details on the stealing of the negatives of the first three weeks of shooting and listing some of the scenes involved. The rest, and most, of the article is an on-the-set description of Fellini at work with Sutherland and Sandy Allen. Allen said she didn't know from one scene to the next what she was to do. Sutherland of Fellini: "He's very clear, and very precise. He describes very carefully a flower then says, 'Get it in and make the petals move.'"

1646   Wolf, William. Cue, 46 (February 5-18, 1977), 35.
       "For two hours and thirty-five minutes he dazzles, as-
       saults, and entertains us with his stunningly creative version
       of Casanova's legendary amatory exploits. " Loves Sutherland
       as Casanova; casting him as Casanova was a "brilliant idea. "
       Rota's score is "outstanding. "

1647   ____ . Cue, 46 (March 19-April 1, 1977), 10.
       Carli Buchanan had a small part in the film. She re-
       counts her "moment of glory. " An ex-college teacher, she
       flew to Rome at her own expense, called up Fellini, and was
       given a part. She played the princess who volunteers her ser-
       vices to Casanova in a sex-act contest, but whom he rejects.

H. AUDIO-VISUAL MATERIAL

Cassette

1648 Schuth, H. Wayne. $8\frac{1}{2}$. Classic Film Lecture Series. De-
land, Fla. : Everett/Edwards.
Cassette. 30 minutes. Critical commentary and expla-
nation of theme and technique.

Documentary

1649 The World of Federico Fellini.
A documentary mentioned in L'Avant-Scène, October, 1972.
We've not been able either to confirm or trace this.

35mm Slides

1650 Album-Diapositives Federico Fellini. Paris: L'Avant-Scène.
120 35mm color slides, with descriptions, from Fellini's
films from Sceicco bianco through Satyricon. We believe that
they are directly from the films and not stills. Listed (1977)
as being available in the United States from New York Zoetrope,
31 East 12th St. , New York, N.Y. 10003.

1651 Reviewed: Braucourt, Guy. "Fellini en 120 Diapositives:
du chevalet à la fresque," L'Avant-Scène, n. 129, October, 1972, 69-70.
Although "just" a short review of this album of slides,
this is one of the most illuminating articles on Fellini
around. Fellini's films, he says, are like paintings that
can pass the test, full of opportunities and dangers, of
the slide collection. Fellini uses "the great white screen-
wall of our collective unconscious" to paint a strange,
disturbing, phantom world: our own. There are three
periods: (1) From Sceicco bianco to Cabiria, the "easel"
period, where shadows of the everyday world keep being
worn away by the bright light of the dream. Here, "the
pessimistic painter that Fellini is," doesn't feel the need
to "separate from reality what he has himself seen or ex-
perienced. " (2) From Dolce vita to Giulietta, the "etching" period: the blacks get harsher and the whites more
garish in order to capture a universe still realistic but

265

that is getting set to plunge into the abysses of an interior vision. " It is no longer the idealist dream that projects itself on to the outline of the world of the everyday,
but "another world of delirium, which, like some monstrous iceberg, begins to loom up and crack the surface
of the rational. " Giulietta is confronted by "black phan-
toms, " despite the fact that the film is in color.   (3)
From Toby Dammit to Satyricon: this "fresco" period,
where color and the fantastic shoot out huge flames; the
soft light on the face of the young girl of Dolce vita,
whom Marcello likened to an angel, gives way to the violent light that "flashes on the little girl of Toby Dammit
the flames of hell. " The Fellini light has become the
light of someone having visions.   The slides, by freezing
the movement and gestures, still work "in a strange Fellinian sense": they evoke the spectral grandeur of "a
parade of the damned. " The Fellini dynamic, with its
funeral splendors, "tends ineluctably toward death. " This
movement, "which is that of life itself," the slides suc-
ceed in capturing.

1652   Reviewed: Ciment, Michel.   Positif, n. 131, October,
              1971, 78-79.

APPENDICES

A. HOW TO RENT 16MM PRINTS OF FELLINI'S FILMS

Information on 16mm film rental availability is chancy and dates quickly. One distributor drops a film, another picks one up. Some films are suddenly, swiftly, and mysteriously withdrawn from circulation. The information listed below has been compiled from 1976 catalogs. (We've included only rental sources in the United States. For sources in other countries consult the latest annual International Film Guide, ed. Peter Cowie, London: Tantivy Press.)
Full names and addresses of the rental sources follow the list of films.

Films on Which Fellini Collaborated

1945 - Open City (Roma città aperta). Budget, Kit Parker.

1946 - Paisan (Paisà). Audio Brandon.

1947 - Without Pity (Senza pietà). Audio Brandon.

1948 - The Miracle (Il miracolo). Audio Brandon.

1950 - The Path of Hope (Il cammino della speranza). Audio Brandon.

Films That Fellini Directed

1950 - Variety Lights (Luci del varietà). Audio Brandon.

1952 - The White Sheik (Lo sceicco bianco). Audio Brandon.

1953 - I vitelloni. Corinth Films.

1953 - Love in the City (Un' agenzia matrimoniale, episode in Amore in città). Audio Brandon.

1954 - La strada. Janus.

1955 - Il bidone. Audio Brandon.

1957 - Nights of Cabiria (Le notti di Cabiria). Audio Brandon.

1959 - La dolce vita. Audio Brandon.

1962 - Boccaccio '70 (contains Le tentazioni del dottor Antonio).
       Avco Embassy.

1962 - 8½. Audio Brandon.

1965 - Juliet of the Spirits (Giulietta degli spiriti). Audio Brandon.

1966 - Spirits of the Dead (Toby Dammit, episode in Tre passi nel
       delirio). Budget, Modern Sound, United Films, West-
       coast, Wholesome.

1968 - Fellini: A Director's Notebook (Fellini: Block-notes di un
       regista). Boston University, Films Incorporated, Indiana
       University, University of Arizona, University of Califor-
       nia. (Probably available for sale from National Broad-
       casting Company--Television.)

1969 - Satyricon. United Artists/16.

1970 - The Clowns (I clowns). Films Incorporated.

1972 - Roma. United Artists/16.

1973 - Amarcord. Films Incorporated.

Film Documentaries on Fellini

1964 - (On Giulietta degli spiriti). Fellini: The Director as Crea-
       tor. Films for the Humanities. (Also available for pur-
       chase, in 16mm film form and videocassette.)

1969 - (On Satyricon. See 177). Ciao, Federico! Audio Brandon,
       University of California.

Addresses of Rental Sources Listed Above (January, 1977)

Audio Brandon Films, 34 MacQuesten Parkway South, Mount Vernon,
    New York 10550.

Avco Embassy Pictures, 750 Third Avenue, New York, New York
    10017.

Boston University Film Library, 756 Commonwealth Avenue, Massa-
    chusetts 02215.

Budget Films, 4590 Santa Monica Boulevard, Los Angeles, California
    90029.

Corinth Films, 410 East 62 Street, New York, New York 10021.

Films for the Humanities, P.O. Box 2053, Princeton, New Jersey 08540.

Films Incorporated, 144 Wilmette Avenue, Wilmette, Illinois 60091.

Indiana University Audio-Visual Center, Bloomington, Indiana 47401.

Janus Films, 745 Fifth Avenue, New York, New York 10022.

Kit Parker Films, Carmel Valley, California 93924.

Modern Sound Pictures, 1402 Howard Street, Omaha, Nebraska 68102.

United Artists/16, 729 Seventh Avenue, New York, New York 10019.

United Films, 1425 South Main, Tulsa, Oklahoma 74119.

University of Arizona Film Library, Tucson, Arizona 85721.

University of California Extension Media Center, Berkeley, California 94720.

Westcoast Films, 25 Lusk Street, San Francisco, California 94107.

Wholesome Film Center, 20 Melrose Street, Boston, Massachusetts 02116.

B. ADAPTATIONS MADE FROM FELLINI'S FILMS

Of La strada:

La Strada. Musical stageplay. Adapted by Charles Peck.
Music by Lionel Bart. Opened in New York c. December 14, 1969.

Of Le notti di Cabiria:

Sweet Charity. Musical stageplay. Book by Neil Simon, music by Cy Coleman, lyrics by Dorothy Fields. Conceived, staged,
and choreographed by Bob Fosse. Starring Gwen Verdon. Opened
in New York in January, 1966. Ran for 4608 performances. Original Broadway cast album, Columbia KOL 6500. , album cover notes
by C. Burr: "As Charity, the basic character remains the same
but translated to the American and turned on. In a sense, her body
is still for hire; she works in a dance palace. But the basic innocence and inexplicable purity are still there; Charity would much
rather give away for love what others might sell. "

Sweet Charity. The 1969 film version of the stage adaptation.
Starring Shirley MacLaine as Charity, with John McMartin, Chita
Rivera, Paula Kelly, Stubby Kaye, Ricardo Montalban, Sammy Davis,
Jr. Original soundtrack album, Decca DL 71502.

C. NAMES FOR FELLINI'S FILMS IN SIX LANGUAGES

		ITALIAN	ENGLISH	FRENCH
1.	1950	Luci del varietà	Variety Lights	Feux du music-hall
2.	1952	Lo sceicco bianco	The White Sheik	Le sheikh blanc / Courrier du coeur
3.	1953	I vitelloni	I Vitelloni / The Spivs / The Young and the Passionate	Les vitelloni / Les inutiles
4.	1953	Un' agenzia matrimoniale (episode in Amore in città)	A Matrimonial Agency / Love Cheerfully Arranged (episode in Love in the City)	Agence matrimoniale (episode in L'Amour à la ville)
5.	1954	La strada	La Strada	La strada / Le grand chemin
6.	1955	Il bidone	Il Bidone / The Swindle / The Swindlers	Il bidone
7.	1957	Le notti di Cabiria	Nights of Cabiria	Les nuits de Cabiria
8.	1959	La dolce vita	La Dolce Vita / The Sweet Life	La douceur de vivre
9.	1962	Le tentazioni del dottor Antonio (episode in Boccaccio '70)	The Temptations of Doctor Antonio (episode in Boccaccio '70)	La tentation du Docteur Antoine (episode in Boccaccio '70)
10.	1963	$8\frac{1}{2}$ / Otto e mezzo	$8\frac{1}{2}$	$8\frac{1}{2}$ / Huit et demi
11.	1965	Giulietta degli spiriti	Juliet of the Spirits	Juliette des êsprits
12.	1968	Toby Dammit (episode in Tre passi nel delirio)	Toby Dammit / Never Bet Your Head on the Devil (episode in Spirits of the Dead)	Toby Dammit / Il ne faut jamais parier sa tête avec le diable (episode in Histoires extraordinaires)
13.	1968	Fellini: Block-Notes di un regista	Fellini: A Director's Notebook	?
14.	1969	Satyricon / Fellini Satyricon	Satyricon / Fellini's Satyricon	Satyricon / Fellini-Satyricon
15.	1970	I clowns	The Clowns	Les clowns
16.	1972	Roma / Fellini Roma	Roma / Fellini's Roma	Roma / Fellini-Roma
17.	1973	Amarcord	Amarcord	Amarcord
18.	1976	Casanova / Fellini Casanova	Casanova / Fellini's Casanova	Casanova / Fellini-Casanova

		G E R M A N	R U S S I A N	P O L I S H
1.	1950	Lichter des Varietés	Ogni var'ete	Swiatła Variété
2.	1952	Der weisse Scheich / Die bittere Liebe	Bely sheykh	Biały Szejk
3.	1953	Die Müssiggänger	Vitelloni / Mamen'kiny synki	Wałkonie
4.	1953	Ein Heiratsvermittlungsbüro / Eine Agentur für Heiratsvermittlung (episode in Liebe in der Stadt)	Brachnaya kontora (episode in Lybov' v gorode)	Biuro Matymonialne
5.	1954	Das Lied der Strasse	Doroga	La Strada
6.	1955	Der Schwindler	Moshenniki	Niebielski Ptak
7.	1957	Die Nächte der Cabiria	Nochi Kabirii	Noce Cabirii
8.	1959	Das süsse Leben	Sladkaya zhizn'	Słodkie Życie
9.	1962	Die Versuchungen des Dottor Antonio (episode in Boccaccio '70)	Iskushenie doktora Antonio (episode in Boccaccio '70)	Kuszenie Doktora Antoniego (episode in Boccaccio '70)
10.	1963	8½ / Acht und halb	8½ / Vosem' s polovinoy	8½ / Osiem i Pół
11.	1965	Julia und die Geister	Dzhul'etta i dukhi	Giuletta i Duchy
12.	1968	Toby Dammit (episode in Histoires extraordinaires)	Tobi Dammit (episode in Tri shaga v oblakakh)	Toby Dammit
13.	1968	?	Zapisnaya knizhka rezhissera	O Natatniku Rezysera
14.	1969	Satyricon	Satirikon / Satirikon Fellini	Satyricon
15.	1970	Die Clowns	Klouny	Klowni
16.	1972	Roma	Roma / Rim	Roma / Rim
17.	1973	Amarcord	Amarkord	Amarcord
18.	1976	Casanova	Kazanova	Casanova